4/26/11
#28.00

'In this second edition, Lauret offers a fuller, richer, more compelling, updated text that showcases the impressive range and depth of her investigations into Walker scholarship.' – **Loretta Woodard, *Marygrove College, USA***

Alice Walker, Pulitzer Prize-winning author of *The Color Purple*, is one of America's major and most prolific writers. She is also among its most controversial. How has Walker's work developed over the last forty years? Why has it often provoked extreme reactions? Does Walker's cultural, political and spiritual activism enhance or distort her fiction? Where does she belong in the evolving tradition of African American literature?

Alice Walker, second edition:

- examines the full range of Walker's prose writings: her novels, short stories, essays, activist writings, speeches and memoirs
- has been thoroughly revised in light of the latest scholarship and critical developments
- brings coverage of Walker's work right up to date with a new chapter on *Now is the Time to Open Your Heart* (2004) and discussion of her recent non-fictional writing, including *Overcoming Speechlessness* (2010)
- traces Walker's lineage back to nineteenth-century visionary black women preachers and activists
- assesses Walker's prose *oeuvre* both in terms of its literary and its activist merits and shortcomings.

Ideal for students and scholars alike, this established text remains an essential guide to the work of a key US author as it explains her unique place in contemporary American letters.

Maria Lauret is Reader in American Studies at the University of Sussex, UK, where she teaches American literature. Her previous publications include *Liberating Literature: Feminist Fiction in America* and *Beginning Ethnic American Literatures*.

Also by Maria Lauret

Liberating Literature: Feminist Fiction in America (London and New York: Routledge 1994)

with Helena Grice, Candida Hepworth, Martin Padget, *Beginning Ethnic American Literatures* (Manchester and New York: Manchester University Press 2001)

Alice Walker

Second Edition

Maria Lauret

palgrave
macmillan

© Maria Lauret 2000, 2011

First edition published 2000
Second edition published 2011 by
PALGRAVE MACMILLAN

Palgrave Macmillan in the UK is an imprint of Macmillan Publishers Limited, registered in England, company number 785998, of Houndmills, Basingstoke, Hampshire RG21 6XS.

Palgrave Macmillan in the US is a division of St Martin's Press LLC, 175 Fifth Avenue, New York, NY 10010.

Palgrave Macmillan is the global academic imprint of the above companies and has companies and representatives throughout the world.

Palgrave® and Macmillan® are registered trademarks in the United States, the United Kingdom, Europe and other countries.

ISBN 978–0–230–57588–2   hardback
ISBN 978–0–230–57589–9   paperback

This book is printed on paper suitable for recycling and made from fully managed and sustained forest sources. Logging, pulping and manufacturing processes are expected to conform to the environmental regulations of the country of origin.

A catalogue record for this book is available from the British Library.

A catalog record for this book is available from the Library of Congress.

10   9   8   7   6   5   4   3   2   1
20   19 18 17 16 15 14 13 12 11

Printed in China

Para mi amor

Paul Roth
1951–2005

Contents

Acknowledgements

Thanks are due to Sonya Barker and Felicity Noble at Palgrave Macmillan for their persistence and patience, and to my colleagues and friends Peter Nicholls and Peter Boxall for reading and commenting on drafts of the first edition. Among my family and friends, professional and personal, who offered places of safety in my year of living dangerously, I want to thank especially Rosemary Bardelle-Carrier, Sue Dare and Graham Dawson, Richard Follett, Emmanuel Käs, Else-Marie Lauret and Chris de Mol, Jac Matthews, Jan Mathew, Susan Brown Roth and Alejandro Roth, Carole and Pascale Sweeney, and Yola de Lusenet and Kees Versteegh.

This second edition was written in memory of Vivien Hart, feminist colleague and friend; David Nicholls, whose perennial question 'What are you writing now, my dear?' could only be answered belatedly; Enrique Roth, who offered the light of a father's smile; and my husband, Paul Roth, to whom this book is dedicated in love, sorrow, and gratitude.

M. R.- L.

PERMISSIONS

Fragments of Chapter 4 were previously published in '"I've Got a Right to Sing the Blues": Alice Walker's Aesthetic', in Richard H. King and Helen Taylor (eds), *Dixie Debates: Perspectives on Southern Cultures* (London: Pluto Press, 1996), pp. 51–66, and I thank Wiley-Blackwell for permission to reproduce fragments from 'Alice Walker', in David Seed (ed.), *A Companion to Twentieth Century United States Fiction* (Oxford: Wiley-Blackwell, 2010), pp. 489–96.

Foreword to the Second Edition: *Alice Walker* Ten Years Later

Alice Walker is a prolific writer, and it is therefore no surprise that ten years after the first edition of this book appeared a second proved necessary to keep up with Walker's new work and with criticism published since the turn of the century. The past ten years have also seen an enormous increase in scholarly resources available on the World Wide Web, from which my research has benefitted and which it is now possible to share. In addition, Evelyn C. White's authorised biography of Alice Walker, published in 2004, has enabled me to provide a fuller context for Walker's work and thought. As a result, this second edition is much expanded and significantly revised to cover Walker's literary production to date as well as critical and biographical commentary and analysis of her fiction and essays.

In detail this means that Chapters 1 and 8 have been rewritten to cover the new collections of essays and memoirs, *The Way Forward Is with a Broken Heart* (2000), *Sent by Earth* (2001), *We Are the Ones We Have Been Waiting For* (2007), and *Overcoming Speechlessness* (2010). Chapters 2 through 6 have been updated and revised to take account of new scholarship, including biographical sources and interviews. Chapter 7 has been extended and offers the first sustained critical engagement with *By the Light of My Father's Smile* (1998) and *Now Is the Time to Open Your Heart* (2004), novels that hitherto have received hardly any serious attention. With the further addition of new critical approaches such as queer theory and masculinity studies, this second edition of *Alice Walker* brings the reader right up to date not only with Walker's literary *oeuvre* and its reception but also with her activism and the controversies it has generated over the four decades of her career.

Maria Roth-Lauret, 2010

1

Alice Walker's Life and Work: An Introduction

> You ask about 'preoccupations'. I am preoccupied with the spiritual survival, the survival *whole* of my people. But beyond that, I am committed to exploring the oppressions, the insanities, the loyalties, and the triumphs of black women. ... For me, black women are the most fascinating creations in the world.[1]

Anyone interested in Alice Walker's work could do much worse than turn to her essays and interviews as a first port of call, since they seem to be the 'ships at a distance that have every reader's wish on board', in Zora Neale Hurston's words. Walker's non-fictional prose harbours a treasure trove of source materials, from the auto-biographical to the political and from the literary to the anecdotal, with everything but the kitchen sink – no, that too – in between. The quotation above, from an interview with John O'Brien in 1973, is as good a summary as any that can be given of her writerly concerns in a few lines. Here are the ironic scare-quotes around 'preoccupa-tions', signalling Walker's *commitment* to black women rather than a mere personal interest in them. Here too is the 'spiritual survival, the survival *whole* of my people' which is so often quoted, and so rarely analysed. Spiritual survival equals wholeness, in this phrase, and it is a hallmark of Walker's work *as* a black woman's writing that the spiritual dimension is always foregrounded, not so much *against* a materialist or more obviously 'political' stance, but as necessary and integral to it. This is why, in *We Are the Ones We Have Been Waiting For: Inner Light in a Time of Darkness* (2007) Walker concludes each chapter with a meditation. Written and published during the George W. Bush years and with the threat of climate change looming ever larger, she characterises this collection of memoirs and essays as 'a companion for a specific time, which I consider probably ... the most dangerous, frightening, unstable time that the earth has

1

known and that human beings have ever known'.[2] Her concern for the survival of humanity as a whole throws a different light on the phrase 'My people' in the extract above: though referring principally to black people, she sides with anyone who has suffered and survived with this spiritual dimension intact. The interview with John O'Brien continues:

> Next to them, I place the old people – male and female – who persist in their beauty in spite of everything. How do they do this, knowing what they do? Having lived what they have lived? It is a mystery, and so it lures me into their lives. My grandfather, at eighty-five, never been out of Georgia, looks at me with the glad eyes of a three year old. The pressures on his life have been unspeakable. How can he look at me in this way?[3]

Childlike glee in the eyes of an old man, and suffering that has not destroyed beauty: these are key themes in all of Walker's work, and the question of what makes that possible is explored over and over again. Often, as here, it is done autobiographically, with a personal memory that becomes the starting point for an argument, a poem, a story, or a novel. What might otherwise be abstract notions or wishful thinking are brought into the realm of the possible and the actual when the author puts her own life experiences into the frame and invites the reader to do the same. This may be why, as Cheryl Wall observes, 'Few late twentieth-century essayists have been more widely read than Walker', and why, in Wall's judgement, the essay form is where Walker has done her best work:

> ... few critics have commented on the lucidity of Walker's prose, the richness of her humor and irony, and the power of her passion in these pieces. [...] The form of the essay, which strives to produce the effect of the spontaneous, the tentative, and the open-ended, lends itself to exploring the complex and contentious issues that Walker addresses. She invites readers to puzzle the issues out with her and welcomes them to share those epiphanies she achieves.[4]

Yet, distinctive as this autobiographical voice is in the non-fictional prose, and effective as it is once its didactic ramifications become clear, Walker is not unique in drawing upon her own experience in her essays. Other black women writers, such as June Jordan and

Audre Lorde, have addressed political issues of race, class, sexuality, and feminism in the personal voice of recollection and reflection too.[5] After all, the essay form by its very nature is 'indefinable', an 'anti-genre', 'an effort to approximate, to approach (like the original meaning of essay (*essai*) itself): to approach and explore and "attempt"' an act of writing that is neither pure argument nor mere observation, as Ruth-Ellen Boetcher Joeres and Elizabeth Mittman point out.[6] The essay sits between short story and academic article and although it seeks to persuade, it never makes quite explicit what the reader is to be persuaded *of*. Besides use of the personal voice, Joeres and Mittman give as further characteristics of the essay the pursuit of subversive and speculative thought, meandering (rather than linear) movement, and the fact that many essays are either akin to or originate in diary-entries, letters, and speeches. Walker's essays have all these features, as do Jordan's and Lorde's, and those written by that other well-known and well-read woman essayist, Virginia Woolf, of whom more later.

It is thus not the form or the voice of Walker's non-fictional prose that is particularly unusual, but rather the way in which it relates to her fiction: as explication and sometimes defence, but more often as an early articulation of issues and themes that are subsequently dramatised and concretised in the novels. Where Woolf's essays function as a relatively separate sphere, distinct from her novels, in Walker's work fiction, poetry, and essays are integral to each other and to her stature as a writer whose activism consists primarily *in* the act of writing and in writing across different forms. In this chapter therefore we shall use the essays as a way into Walker's life, times, and work, but primarily into her *writing life*. What does Walker's non-fictional prose have to tell us about significant figures, experiences, and life-changes that have inspired or shaped the work in some way, and what does it reveal about factors that have hampered the writing? Why do Zora Neale Hurston and the Civil Rights movement have such an important place in the early essays, and why are later ones more preoccupied with New Age thinking, world politics, and the critical reception of her work? What, in short, does Walker feel has enabled or inhibited her writing? And should we take her word for it?

In his pathbreaking essay 'The Death of the Author', Roland Barthes set out the dangers of biographical interpretation, of reading literature through the writer's life. Barthes argued that such an approach reduces the many possible meanings of texts – which are, after all, multi-interpretable linguistic artefacts – to an author's life-events, and thus does not treat the work as art, but as self-revelation. Literary texts for Barthes, as for me, have lives of their own, and should not be so delimited.[7] Since this is a book about Walker as a novelist, the following chapters will discuss her fiction in its own right; that is with only occasional reference to the author's views as expressed in her essays and interviews. But because keeping this author out is not easy, this first chapter addresses the *problem* as well as the didactic effectiveness of Walker's essayistic autobiographical voice and the experiential authority it invokes. In Walker's case it is quite clear that the author is *not* dead: she makes herself heard as a commentator on her own work in *In Search of Our Mothers' Gardens* (1983) and *Living by the Word* (1988) and increasingly loudly and intrusively so in *Anything We Love Can Be Saved* (1997), *The Same River Twice* (1996), and *We Are the Ones We Have Been Waiting For*. And so, since this author's voice insists on being heard and cannot be stifled, the best we can do in trying to maintain a critical distance is to give Walker's autobiographical voice due attention by putting it back in its place as *text*, as a self-representational *strategy* rather than self-evident truth. As Candice M. Jenkins writes apropos of *The Same River Twice*, a book entirely devoted to the controversy around *The Color Purple*: 'Walker's writerly body is subject to *interpretation* in the same way that the narrative body of her fiction is'.[8] Laurie McMillan adds to this that

> [her] particular style of performance involves the use of story narratives [*sic*] that emphasize the highly constructed and textually mediated qualities of her self-representation. Readers are thus encouraged to interpret Walker's writing on multiple levels – not only as personal testimony but also as literary criticism and allegory – effectively bringing the personal voice into criticism without falling into traps of essentialism.[9]

Bearing all this in mind, I want to begin with a biographical sketch that is largely extracted from the essays and interviews, and is therefore told in Walker's own words, as it were. This will serve a double purpose: one, to convey the salient facts in the development of this particular writing life and, two, to show how the author's construction of that life is part of a self-fashioning that serves her literary–political concerns and tries to direct the reception of her work. All life-writing works with selection (of salient life events) and construction (of the persona whose life is being narrated) and I shall draw in addition on two biographical sources that bring Walker's self-representation further into focus: Evelyn White's authorised biography *Alice Walker: A Life* (2004) and Rebecca Walker's memoir *Black, White, and Jewish: Autobiography of a Shifting Self* (2001). Throughout this chapter I shall be interested not in the person that is Alice Walker, but in the *writing* person, the author and artist, who writes about her own creative practice and that of two important literary foremothers: Zora Neale Hurston and Virginia Woolf. Comparing Walker's self-representation in essays and interviews with biographical sources will fill out some gaps in her self-narration. More importantly, it will bring into sharper focus the way this author fashions an 'Alice Walker' persona through the use of her autobiographical voice, and highlight the kind of authority that persona then assumes for a reader or a critic like you, or me.

LIFE/WRITING AND THE WRITING LIFE FROM THE 1940s TO THE 1980s

Alice Walker was born in 1944, the youngest of eight children in a family of poor, black sharecroppers. In her birthplace of Eatonton, Georgia, biographer Evelyn White explains, the law 'allocated $1.43 for the schooling of a black child, compared to $10.23 for a white one', which prompted Walker's parents to help build a school for the education of local children like their own.[10] This was an early example of community activism in Walker's life. She remembers how '[the school] was immediately burned to the ground by white landowners', but also that the black community's response was to build another one in defiance of implacable white hatred and violence.[11] Her childhood, lived in poverty in the rural South, is remembered with ambivalence in an early essay, 'The Black Writer and the Southern Experience'. On one hand she feels that, as a black Southern writer, she has inherited a sense of community and solidarity that comes out of shared poverty and enables interdependence without shame, so long as it is not internalised as a feeling of worthlessness or imposed from the outside through 'deliberate humiliation'.[12] On the other hand, Walker notes that Southern black life is not something to be romanticised, dominated as it was by hard work in the fields, poor housing, and the greed and ruthlessness of white employers who worked her parents nearly to death. Southern black writers thus have a legacy of love and hate to draw on, she concludes, but also an 'enormous richness and beauty'.[13] Besides, as Walker has explained in interview, the possibility of another, better life was held out to her by her independent, sexy, and sassy aunts who came visiting from the North, and of whom she refused to believe that they earned their living by cleaning other (read: white) people's houses.[14] These aunts inspired in part the portrayal of Shug in *The Color Purple*, but they are also recognisable in *The Third Life of Grange Copeland*, where they lead Brownfield to dream of a better life in the North, as we shall see in Chapter 2.

Walker's early years then provided her with a mixed Southern heritage; as she writes in her memoir 'Childhood', the farming and gardening that she still does have their origin in the poverty of the South, but they also exemplify its richness.[15] Other parts of this Southern heritage are stories of the Depression passed on by her mother, one of which became the source for the short story 'The Revenge of Hannah Kemhuff'. In her little-known children's writing, Walker in many ways takes on her mother's role as a storyteller and preserver of the cultural heritage of the black South.[16] Unlike the closeness she experienced with her mother, however, the relationship with her father and brothers appears to have been much more distant and negative, marked as it was by sexism and violence. In the early essays it appears that the domestic abuse she exposes in her fiction had its parallels at home, but the negative portrayal of male family members shifts to a more conciliatory tone in the later essays (from *Anything We Love Can be Saved* onwards) and fiction (such as *By the Light of My Father's Smile*). 'Beauty: When the Other Dancer Is the Self' is a crucial early essay on male violence, because here Walker describes the traumatic event that formed her as a writer and activist:

> It was great fun being cute. But then, one day, it ended.

> I am eight years old and a tomboy. [...] Then my parents decide to buy my brothers guns. [...] Because I am a girl, I do not get a gun. Instantly I am relegated to the position of Indian. [...] One day ... holding my bow and arrow and looking out towards the fields, I feel an incredible blow in my right eye. I look down just in time to see my brother lower his gun.[17]

Recounted in various essays and interviews, the shooting changed Walker from being everybody's (and her own) darling into a victim marked by a disfiguring scar. Only when her daughter Rebecca, years later, sees the scar tissue as a 'world' in her mother's eye is the victim redefined as a survivor, and blindness turned into vision: it enables Walker to interpret the trauma of being blinded by her brother's gun as a 'patriarchal wound' like that of women who have undergone genital mutilation.[18] Later termed a 'sexual blinding', female genital mutilation becomes the central theme of *Possessing the Secret of Joy* and *Warrior Marks*, in which Walker tells African women that 'Your wound itself can be your guide', meaning: suffering can be transformed into activism and resistance to patriarchy, as we shall see in Chapter 6.[19] But the wound also gives birth to writing. As Walker explains, the blinding makes her feel like an outcast, but it also causes her to grow up fast and to study the relationships she sees around her, through observation and reading, but also through writing poems.[20]

The loss of childhood innocence means that this prematurely 'old' girl now feels more at home and at ease in the life of the mind than she does in her family and in her own body. In 1961 she makes her escape from the rural South to Spelman College in Atlanta, an institution not dissimilar to Saxon College in *Meridian*. Walker has described how she soon began to find Spelman's social and intellectual environment stifling, especially by comparison with the relative freedom of Sarah Lawrence College in Westchester, New York, to where she moves two years later.[21] The world now begins to open up, literally when she travels to Africa in 1964, and intellectually too. At Sarah Lawrence she is taught by the poet Muriel Rukeyser, who encourages her writing and passes her poems on to Langston Hughes, who will be instrumental in the publication of the first collection of poems, *Once*, in 1968.[22] Walker's literary debut is the result of another traumatic event: while at Sarah Lawrence she finds herself involuntarily pregnant, and the emotional scar of an illegal abortion gives rise to the same creative impulse as being shot in the eye by her brother had done. As she tells John O'Brien: 'That week I wrote without stopping ... almost all of the poems in *Once*'.[23]

By the mid-1960s Walker is already involved in the Civil Rights Movement, another experience crucial to her development as a writer. *In Search of Our Mothers' Gardens* has several essays on Civil Rights, and in particular on Dr Martin Luther King Jr, who first appears in her life on the TV news, and makes a big impression: 'Because of the Movement, ... because of "black and white together" ... because of the beatings, the arrests, the hell of battle during the past years, I have fought harder for my life and for a chance to be myself'.[24]

In this last line from 'The Civil Rights Movement: What Good Was It?' Walker's allegiance to the movement's Christian, non-violent, and redemptive philosophy still shows. It is an ethos of which she will retain the pacifism and the notion of suffering-as-healing, minus the Christianity she comes to reject: a shift that begins to be charted in *Meridian*, is more fully explained in *The Color Purple*, and finds its full articulation in the opening essay of *Anything We Love Can Be Saved*:

> What a burden to think one is conceived in sin rather than in pleasure; that one is born into evil rather than into joy. In my work [...] I create characters [...] who explore what it would feel like not to feel imprisoned by the hatred of women, the love of violence, and the destructiveness of greed taught to human beings as the 'religion' by which they must guide their lives.[25]

Walker is involved in Civil Rights campaigns from 1965 until 1968; she canvasses for voter-registration in her native Georgia, and is employed by Headstart in Mississippi to teach black history to adults for SNCC, the Student Non-violent Co-Ordinating Committee. Teaching, which for Walker is a form of activism, turns out to be hard work not least because the white bias of Bible stories – such as that of the curse of Ham, used to justify racism – has been internalised by Southern black people.[26] But despite this insight into the pernicious ideological effects of (white) Christianity, non-violence and the Civil Right's Movement's belief that segregation can only be overcome by 'black and white together' nevertheless remain Walker's creed.[27] In 1967 she marries the Jewish Civil Rights lawyer Mel Leventhal, and their life together in Jackson, Mississippi, at a time when interracial marriage is still illegal, is both strengthened by the comradeship of being involved in the same cause and marred by the prejudice of others, black and white alike.[28] In 'Breaking Chains and Encouraging Life', an essay written in 1980, Walker recalls that her literary work in the sixties was often dismissed by black reviewers because of her interracial marriage. Often her critics were themselves married to white women, or they admired the work of writers who were (Richard Wright, Jean Toomer, Langston Hughes, James Baldwin, LeRoi Jones) and so, Walker concludes, the 'traitorous union' in itself could not have been the problem, but rather the fact that she, as a black woman, had had the temerity to do the same as they.[29] This inter-racial marriage moreover, embattled as it was, becomes an interracial family with the birth of Rebecca Leventhal Walker in 1969, 'miraculous' in Walker's words, both because Rebecca helps her father evade the draft for Vietnam and because she arrives three days after the completion of *The Third Life of Grange Copeland* (where the birth of Ruth – named after Walker's sister – is described as 'miraculous' too).[30]

Perhaps because of motherhood, perhaps because of burn-out and the Civil Rights Movement's loss of momentum after Dr King's death, Walker's activism shifts round about this time to the North and to teaching and writing rather than campaigning in the South. As an academic at the upper-class and largely white Wellesley (women's) College in New England she designs a course on black women's writing – 'the first one I think, ever' – that includes such authors as Zora Neale Hurston, Nella Larsen, Frances Ellen Watkins Harper, Ann Petry, and Paule Marshall.[31] She finds that in this privileged environment the consciousness-raising of students, but primarily of faculty, is badly needed. In '*One* Child of One's Own', the essay in which these years are remembered, Walker writes famously of *The Female Imagination* by Patricia Meyer Spacks, an early work of feminist criticism that doesn't see fit to discuss any black women writers at all. She asks, rhetorically, why not and answers that, to Spacks, 'the' female imagination is evidently white. Spacks' defence, that she cannot write about black women because she isn't one, is countered by Walker with devastating logic: 'Spacks never lived in nineteenth-century Yorkshire, so why theorize about the Brontës?'[32] This passage offers the most succinct critique of identity politics in the classroom you could wish for, and one that still applies whenever the notion of experience is invoked as an excuse for ignorance – or indeed guilt. However mixed Walker's feelings about herself as a teacher may have been, it is clear from this and other examples in her early essays that her didactic sense was sharply honed and, when applied in her literary work, extremely effective.

As well as teaching black women's writing, Walker also founded around this time, together with her friend June Jordan, a black women writers' group called the Sisterhood. According to Walker's biographer, the group 'gathered, informally, to socialize, share their creative work, and debate the political issues of the day', and its members included Toni Morrison, playwright Ntozake Shange, and food writer Verta Mae Grosvenor.[33] Frustration may nevertheless have induced Walker to shift her attention from academic teaching to full-time writing. From the mid-1960s on she had been receiving awards and fellowships that enabled her periodically to find the solitude necessary for sustained creative work, and these become more frequent in the 1970s and 1980s, allowing her to devote herself fully to her art. A Radcliffe Institute Fellowship for example enables her to write *In Love and Trouble* and *Meridian*, and she obtains Guggenheim and National Endowment for the Arts Fellowships in 1979 to work on *The Color Purple*, which wins her both the Pulitzer Prize and the National Book Award in 1983. *The Color Purple* is a turning point in Walker's career in more ways than one. For the writing of it, she moves to California in 1977, taking up dual residence in San Francisco and in the countryside around Mendocino. The latter, she explains in 'Writing *The Color Purple*', was necessary because her characters demanded to get out of the city and into an environment as close to their native Georgia as possible, 'only it was more beautiful and the local swimming hole was not segregated', she adds archly.[34] In an interview with the British journalist Duncan Campbell in 2001, the move is explained slightly differently: 'It was what she saw as the cynicism of the East Coast that led her to settling in California', Campbell observes, to which Walker adds:

> I felt in Georgia and on the east coast generally very squeezed. [...] I feel a greater fluidity here. People are much more willing to accept that nothing is permanent, everything is changeable so there is freedom and I do need to live where I can be free.[35]

That desire to be free led to the end of marital life too; a year before moving to California, Walker and Mel Leventhal had divorced, and she now set up home with the writer and editor Robert Allen, and – alternately every two years – with her daughter Rebecca. Walker's volatile relationship with Rebecca post-divorce is one of those wayward biographical facts that is hardly addressed in the essays, but we glean from White's biography and Rebecca's memoir *Black, White, and Jewish: Autobiography of a Shifting Self* that the custody arrangements gave rise to much pain and resentment on both sides.[36]

CELEBRITY AND CONTROVERSY: AFTER *THE COLOR PURPLE*

By the 1980s, and permanently settled in California, big changes are afoot in Walker's life and writing. Publication of *The Color*

Purple brings popular acclaim as well as controversy, and launches Walker as a bestselling author. It brings her into contact with Steven Spielberg and Quincy Jones, who make the film of *The Color Purple*, and into conflict with Oakland schools and – later – black community groups, who object to the novel and the film because of their depiction of lesbianism, sexual violence, and domestic abuse.[37] In the essay 'In the Closet of the Soul' Walker gives a measured riposte to such criticism:

> A book and movie that urged us to look at the oppression of women and children by men (and, to a lesser degree, by women) became the opportunity by which black men drew attention to themselves – not in an effort to rid themselves of the desire or the tendency to oppress women and children, but, instead, to claim that inasmuch as a 'negative' picture of them was presented to the world, they were, in fact, the ones *being* oppressed.[38]

The Same River Twice (1996) continues this defence of *The Color Purple* in great detail and at great length: it is a book entirely devoted to the making of the film, the critical controversy, correspondence with Spielberg and Jones, letters and articles of support from friends, and so on. The perceived necessity for such a volume testifies to the importance of *The Color Purple* as a catalyst for (African) American cultural debate, but it also heralds the appearance of a new theme in Walker's non-fictional writing. The autobiographical voice, represented in the essays as that of a self-styled recluse in the northern California foothills, is still concerned with making social or political arguments, but it becomes more self-reflexive and more interested in new age thinking, which is then often enlisted in coming to terms with the trials and tribulations of being a literary celebrity. Walker's voice – in the words of one interviewer – now comes to resemble that of 'an American mystic', visionary, but at times also verging on the defensive (see Chapter 8).[39] What develops in *Living by the Word* (1988) and especially *Anything We Love Can Be Saved* (1997), *The Way Forward Is With a Broken Heart* (2000), and *We Are the Ones We Have Been Waiting For* is a lifestyle politics or a *spiritual* activism that she communicates through reporting on journeys actual and of the mind in her essays and memoirs. Drawing on the creative and spiritual wisdom of peoples all over the globe, from the Swa of the Amazon basin to the Maori of Australia and the Hopi of the United States, Walker shares her insights with her readers in the conviction that such wisdom is a precious resource. So precious that it runs the risk of being lost if it is not passed on – in her fiction, but also in afterwords and reading lists appended to the novels and essay collections. Some of the most enlightening essays concern Native American culture and history, stemming from right where she is, in Northern California. Walker's identification with the cause of Native Americans as victims of European conquest and violence is of long standing, as the childhood memory of her blinding in which she positioned herself as an 'Indian' – naively, but in retrospect significantly – shows. But children's play is not the only cultural script in which Indians and African American girls are destined to lose. Historically, slavery and miscegenation bound African and Native Americans together too:

> We have been slaves *here* and we have been slaves *there*. The white great-grandfathers abused and sold us *here* and our black great-grandfathers abused and sold us *there*. [...] We are the mestizos of North America. We are black, yes, but we are 'white', too, and we are red. To attempt to function as only one, when you are really two or three, leads, I believe, to psychic illness: 'white' people have shown us the madness of that. (Imagine the psychic liberation of white people if they understood that probably no one on the planet is genetically 'white').[40]

In this essay, 'In the Closet of the Soul' (1986) Walker characteristically brings her Cherokee grandmother into the historical picture as well as her great-great-grandfather, a white slave-owner. Such a view of racial and cultural hybridity links her to Zora Neale Hurston, who had very similar ideas, but it also earned her the opprobrium of black nationalists for whom such a rejection of racial/cultural purity is anathema. None of this has deflected Walker from the path of writing-as-spiritual-healing, however, guided by a philosophy that combines elements of Native and African American 'folk' belief with ecology, Buddhism, and, of course, womanism and bisexuality (or 'homospirituality'). 'Paganism' is what she calls this philosophy, and we find an early articulation of it in the same interview with John O'Brien that opened this chapter:

> If there is one thing African-Americans have retained of their African heritage, it is probably animism: a belief that makes it possible to view all creation as living, as being inhabited by spirit.

This belief encourages knowledge perceived intuitively. It does not surprise me, personally, that scientists are now discovering that trees, plants, flowers have feelings ... emotions, that they shrink when yelled at; that they faint when an evil person is about to hurt them.[41]

This was 1973. In a speech delivered more than twenty years later, very similar ideas are advanced as the result of a personal spiritual quest: '"Pagan" means "of the land, country dweller, peasant", all of which my family was. It also means a person whose primary relationship is with Nature and the Earth [cf. Native Americans]'.[42] Paganism, which regards nature as a goddess and the mother of all life, enables Walker not only to connect her family history with African and Native American thinking, but it also unites her womanist interest in ancient goddess worship with the theory of creativity, gender, and childhood trauma that she finds articulated in the work of Carl Jung and that of Jungian analysts such as Alice Miller.[43] Both *The Temple of My Familiar*, in which Miss Lissie is its high priestess, and *Possessing the Secret of Joy* preach this hybrid and syncretic philosophy on virtually every page, as do the later novels *By the Light of My Father's Smile* (1999) and *Now Is the Time to Open Your Heart* (2004). We only have to look at the almost interchangeable titles of Walker's prose collections since the mid 1990s (*The Way Forward Is With a Broken Heart* (2000) *We Are the Ones We Have Been Waiting For: Inner Light in a Time of Darkness, The Same River Twice: Honoring the Difficult* (1996), and *Anything We Love Can Be Saved: A Writer's Activism* (1997)) to know where their author is coming from – intellectually, politically, and spiritually. These collections also bring us up to date with Walker's life/writing, documenting as they do her domestic life, including various relationships with men and women, deaths of family members, illness and depression, political campaigns past and present (see Chapter 8), travels in body and spirit, and reflections on the writing life itself. And the *writing* life is where, for Walker, the focus remains: when comparing what autobiographical disclosures she gives in her essays and memoirs with the way her life is represented by her biographer and her daughter, it becomes abundantly clear that Walker's essayistic voice creates a deceptively open, but (perhaps necessarily) one-sided self-portrait. Particularly when it comes to matters of the heart she is mercifully discreet and unfailingly generous in her writing, largely, I surmise, because it aims to teach rather than to reveal, confess, or disclose her private life for the sake of it. In her sometimes brutal honesty about the pain of love, relationships, and the controversy that celebrity brings, however, Walker can seem defensive too. Despite her stated awareness of 'being human and therefore limited and imperfect', the author's persona as represented in the life/writing from the late 1990s onwards is increasingly that of a visionary and an 'elder' who, in her wisdom, explicates her own work and brooks no contradiction.[44]

What, then, can a critic do? At the end of this book, we shall look in more detail at Walker's reception, her responses to it, and the kinds of problem her self-portrayal creates for the reader and critic who, although interested in and beguiled by Walker's work, nevertheless does not want to read it *only* on the author's own terms. For now, having charted Walker's self-fashioning as victim/survivor, activist/teacher, writer/healer, and finally visionary/elder through the non-fictional prose, I want to turn the spotlight on two figures who have been instrumental in shaping some of Walker's best known and most important ideas and themes. Zora Neale Hurston and Virginia Woolf enable an understanding of Walker's oeuvre above and beyond what influence she herself has acknowledged. They give us a useful insight into the factors that have helped and hindered Walker's own writing, as we shall see, and they have helped her forge her two most influential theories: that of womanism, a term and a philosophy which have gained ground as a corrective to (white) feminism, and that of black women's creativity as grounded in 'her mother's garden', the domestic sphere of everyday life, rather than in high art and literature.

WALKER AND HURSTON, OR HOW TO SAFEGUARD A LITERARY LEGACY

We are a people. A people do no throw their geniuses away

And if they are thrown away, it is our duty *as artists and as witnesses for the future* to collect them again for the sake of our children, and, if necessary, bone by bone.[45]

This familiar quotation from 'Zora Neale Hurston: A Cautionary Tale and a Partisan View' is generally used to shore up Walker's claim to have rediscovered Zora Neale Hurston in the early 1970s, while doing research on her short story about voodoo, 'The Revenge of Hannah Kemhuff'. In the essay that follows it, 'Looking for Zora',

Walker further recounts her attempt at recovering Hurston almost literally 'bone by bone' by visiting her burial place and marking it with a headstone, proclaiming Hurston 'a genius of the South'. In 1979, before publishing both these essays in *In Search of Our Mothers' Gardens*, Walker had enacted another kind of re(dis)covery by publishing a Zora Neale Hurston reader titled *I Love Myself When I am Laughing ... and Then Again When I Am Looking Mean and Impressive*.[46] Walker's celebration of Hurston, however, is not without anxiety, as Diane Sadoff notes. We can read this anxiety in the extract above, which brings various uncomfortable questions in its train. Will Walker's *own* work survive, or who is going to recollect it? Why was Zora's literary legacy lost for so long, and who is to say that the culture's disrespect for black women's writing in her day will not result in oblivion for the work of Walker's generation too? Sadoff's answer is that Walker *needed* a literary foremother to validate her own writerly identity, that she 'virtually invents Hurston before she defines herself as indebted to Hurston's example'.[47] *That* 'Anything We Love Can Be Saved' is Walker's own, much later rationalisation for the anxiety of loss, as if in saving Zora Neale Hurston's legacy for posterity, like a dutiful daughter should, she was also safeguarding her own. Hurston then is not only a role model and ancestor, but also a legitimating presence for Walker in the African American literary tradition. Her biographer Evelyn White puts it thus in an interview: 'I think Zora's work affirmed choices Alice had made in turning her attention to blacks in the South – meaning, her people.'[48] In search of her mother's garden, Walker not only discovers the creativity of the woman who gave birth to her, she also *fails* to find Zora's grave in the overgrown piece of land where it is supposed to be. The recollection, then, is by necessity a matter of conjecture or indeed (re-)invention. As Kadiatu Kanneh has said,

> Black cultures of resistance as well as Black self-recognitions are not always, or ever, *simply* inherited. Black/feminist identities, in order to gain a valid political voice, have repeatedly and contextually to reinvent themselves in dialogue and conflict with racism.[49]

In Walker's fear of loss it is not just racism that causes the loss and forgetting, but also sexism and the failure of oppressed people, at times, to honour their own. Kanneh's idea of a constructed, rather than simply inherited or found, matrilineage applies to Walker and Hurston in more ways than one. Walker is a daughter, who cherishes Hurston's legacy, but she is also Hurston's mother in (re-)discovering the work and making sure it finds its way (back) into the world, with much less risk of it being lost again.

Many have written about the similarities between Hurston and Walker, and Lillie P. Howard has even devoted a whole book to this literary coupling. Yet it does seem that in this endeavour most critics simply follow Walker's lead rather than interrogate what her invest-ment in Hurston actually might be.[50] If we chart the similarities first: they consist in a joint commitment to Southern folk culture and more especially the black vernacular; in the self-emancipation of black women like Hurston's Janie Crawford in *Their Eyes Were Watching God* and Walker's Celie in *The Color Purple*; in the struggle, also, for a farmer's daughter like Walker and the granddaughter of a slave like Hurston to live by the word as self-respecting and respected black women intellectuals and writers. Similarities in the work – especially the parallels between *Their Eyes Were Watching God* and *The Color Purple* – are traced by critic after critic in article after article, and rightly placed in the African American tradition of signifying, where one writer revises or talks back to another's work. Yet few dare to ask with Henry Louis Gates, Jr in 'Color Me Zora', where Hurston's pres-ence in Walker's fiction is to be found other than in *The Color Purple*. As Michael Cooke observes, the two have interests in common but 'Walker operates on a different pitch and scale'.[51] That difference in tone is identified by Walker herself in an interview with Sharon Wilson, in which she contrasts Hurston's lightheartedness and opti-mism with her own thematics of black women's suffering and strug-gle. Again with the exception of *The Color Purple*, Walker is earnest and serious where Hurston's prose is notoriously slippery and *slant* and plays tricks on its readers.[52] The question of Walker's interest in or, rather, identification with Hurston is then only partially answered with a need for self-legitimation. Many of the parallels and shared interests cited are of Walker's own and conscious making – such as giving Celie the autonomous voice that Janie lacks in *Their Eyes Were Watching God*, where her vernacular speech is framed by the narra-tor's standard English. Others are of her choosing: Hurston's focus on black women is only evident in that one novel and much less prominent in her other texts; Hurston was a political conservative and cultural separatist, whereas Walker is the opposite, and so on.

Yet it seems clear that folk culture and the black vernacular are what Walker values in Hurston and what she needs from her. Trudier Harris's comparison of some of Hurston and Walker's short stories enables us to think about Walker's migration from the South and the distance she has travelled from family and cultural roots, a distance that her work constantly seeks to undo. Harris argues that Hurston and Walker do not occupy the same position when it comes to African American folk culture: '[it] is the difference between intimate knowledge of the culture as usually possessed by the insider, and acquaintance with the culture as usually possessed by those who are to some extent outside'.[53] Harris's point is that Walker uses Hurston to get back to her Southern roots, with varying degrees of success. In stories such as 'To Hell with Dying' it works, but in 'The Revenge of Hannah Kemhuff' and 'Strong Horse Tea' it does not in Harris's view, because in those two stories Walker in effect discredits rootworking and conjuring. As mentioned earlier, Walker relates how 'The Revenge of Hannah Kemhuff' originated in a story told by her mother about an incident that happened to *her* mother during the Depression. Walker then went to research rootworking and found *Mules and Men*, Hurston's anthropological work on voodoo (from which the story quotes a curse collected by Hurston in the course of her research).[54] What this genealogy of the story shows is Walker's need to verify and to legitimise her mother's discourse with reference to scholarly work. The delight Walker expresses in finding *Mules and Men* ('this perfect book') in a library is in large part due to the fact that Hurston's scholarship can indeed confirm the 'truth' of her mother's private and domestic snippet of history.

Something similar goes on in the story 'Everyday Use', in which an educated daughter returns to the South to claim her mother's quilts as art, thereby legitimating and valorizing domestic labour, except in this story the narrator is clearly critical of such high-cultural validation (and appropriation) of an indigenous and *useful* folk practice.[55] The argument in 'Everyday Use' and the implication of the essay where Walker relates her excitement in discovering Hurston's legitimising book, are therefore at odds with each other. Still, it may well be that the recognition of Hurston as a kindred spirit enabled Walker to bridge the distance between her (by then) educated middle-class Northern existence and the life of hard rural labour that was her parents' lot in the South. This desire for a 'cultural return' to the South is not unique, nor is it only a personal preoccupation on Walker's part. Jean Toomer's *Cane*, a book of imagist prose, poetry, and a play that Walker greatly admired, was, after all, the product of a trip to the South in search of – what Toomer assumed was – a dying folk culture too. In addition, Walker shares the experience of migration to the North with many African Americans in the twentieth century and with many of her generation, who left the South for reasons of education and employment and have felt ambivalent about their Southern roots too.

In a 1984 interview Walker stated in so many words that the vernacular of *The Color Purple* represents another means of recovering Southern black culture:

> This was the way my grandparents spoke, this is the way my mother speaks today, and I want to capture that. Especially for my daughter, who has a very different kind of upbringing and who doesn't get to Georgia very often. I want her to know when she grows up what her grandparents, her great-grandparents, sounded like, because the sound is so amazingly alive.[56]

Celie's vernacular letters also link Walker's mother's and grandmother's speech with Hurston's achievement in *Their Eyes Were Watching God* for, as Walker explains in another interview, '[Zora] saw poetry where other writers saw merely failure to cope with English'.[57] Hurston, in short, binds together the private world of Walker's family history and the public one of anthropology and the literary tradition. The discovery of her work makes it possible for Walker to shift her activism from Civil Rights to teaching and writing without losing touch with Southern culture, at a time when she is geographically and in terms of class and education removed from it. But this is not the only tie that binds. Even more importantly Hurston's example enables Walker to articulate her critique of race and gender relations in the feminist post-Civil Rights era and to theorise it in the concept of womanism, to which we now turn our attention.

WALKER AND HURSTON'S WOMANISM

Walker's definition of womanism at the beginning of *In Search of Our Mothers' Gardens* presents less a political analysis of black women's oppression, let alone a programme to end it, than a depiction of a positive role model:

> **Womanist 1**. From *womanish*. (Opp. of 'girlish' i.e. frivolous, irresponsible, not serious.) A black feminist or feminist of color.

[...] Usually referring to outrageous, audacious, courageous or *willful* behavior. Wanting to know more and in greater depth than is considered 'good' for one. [...] Responsible. In charge. *Serious*.

This first set of epithets for the womanist woman does three things: it invokes the black folk speech ('womanish') that Zora Neale Hurston liberated from its degraded status as defective English; it posits a model of black femininity that Hurston's lifestyle and demeanour embodied perfectly ('outrageous, audacious') – and which is in many ways antithetical to Walker's own; and it implicitly contrasts this black femininity with white feminism. In the bracketed reference to 'girlishness' Walker appeals to a notion prevalent in black feminism of the 1970s that white women's sense of their own oppression was like the cry of a spoilt child. Echoing Sojourner Truth, they felt that middle-class white women might protest against feminine passivity and agitate for their rights to paid employment and reproductive freedom, but that they should not be left in blissful ignorance of the active, hard-working lives that most American women (black and working class) led out of sheer necessity. In *Meridian* such a view of white women as wide-eyed and unserious is articulated by the protagonist herself:

Who would dream, in her home town, of kissing a white girl? Who would want to? What were they good for? What did they do? [...] One never heard of them *doing* anything that was interesting. [...] On the other hand, black women were always imitating Harriet Tubman – escaping to become something unheard of. Outrageous.[58]

In the second section of Walker's definition of womanism this critique of 1970s white feminism continues:

2. *Also*: A woman who loves other women, sexually and/or non-sexually. Appreciates and prefers women's culture, women's emotional flexibility ... and women's strength. Sometimes loves individual men, sexually and/or non-sexually. Committed to survival whole of entire people, male *and* female. Not a separatist, except periodically, for health. Traditionally universalist [= aware of the fact that] 'the colored race is like a flower garden, with every color flower represented'. Traditionally capable [= leading slaves to escape to Canada].

The last line obviously echoes Meridian's admiration for Harriet Tubman, famous conductor on the Underground Railway, and the ones leading up to it draw both on Hurston's notion of African Americans' diversity and on white radical feminism's valorisation of woman-bonding and women's culture. But in its refusal of separatism – which can apply to racial and lesbian separatism – it revises both. Hurston is reputed to have been against the desegregation of schools in the 1950s, believing that black children did better when educated apart from whites, like her own upbringing in the all-black town of Eatonville, Florida. Feminist separatists of the 1970s believed that heterosexuality and feminism were incompatible, because to love men meant to 'sleep with the enemy'. Walker's definition refuses such separatism as an ideology, but still leaves the door open for temporary autonomous organisation or – significantly – for the validity of Hurston's view as a strategic choice based upon experience. Significant also is Walker's emphasis on the 'traditionally' universalist and the 'traditionally' capable, which again can be read as targeting the naivety of white women's self-styled 'revolutionary' demand to be released from patriarchal bondage. Black women have always been 'revolutionaries', and black women have a long history of struggle against oppression. They have also always been aware of diversity within a common cause, and this is a lesson white women have yet to learn, Walker implies. The womanist is committed to both her gender and her race on preferential and historical grounds rather than those of biology, and she values the culture that history has given her:

> 3. Loves music. Loves dance. Loves the moon. *Loves* the Spirit. ... Loves struggle. Loves the Folk. Loves herself. *Regardless.*

Pleasure and sensuality are foregrounded here; womanism is articulated as a political identity that is integrated into everyday life, non-elitist, and positive/active rather than determined by victim-status. Again Zora, who loved the Folk, the Spirit and herself, serves as a model. Walker ends her definition with a clinching of her polemic with white feminists:

> 4. Womanist is to feminist as purple to lavender.[59]

Tuzyline Jita Allan, who has given the concept of womanism more theoretical attention than any other feminist critic, sees this last line in Walker's definition as divisive. 'Walker sets up (black) womanism and (white) feminism in a binary opposition from which the former emerges a privileged, original term and the latter a devalued, pale replica', she argues.[60] I don't think this is quite right; there is another, more inclusive way of reading this line. American lesbian feminists took lavender as their colour in the 1970s, well before *The Color Purple* and *In Search of Our Mothers' Gardens*. Walker intensifies this colour, deepens and darkens it by mixing it with black; in this way she not so much rejects white feminism as absorbs it into her project and *radicalises* it. Allan's charge that womanism is an essentialist notion, because it pertains to 'black feminists and feminists of color' and thus excludes white women, may seem valid at first but is not, if we read womanism as subsuming (white) feminism in this way.[61] Within the larger scheme of the essays in *In Search of Our Mothers' Gardens* and of the later novels, in which Walker frequently revises white feminism for her own purposes, there is much more scope for feminist/womanist integration than it might at first appear. And this makes sense, not only because of Walker's allegiance to the Civil Rights ethos of 'black and white together', but also because her brand of spiritual universalism embraces all who are aware of their hybrid natures – including white women.

What we see, then, is that Walker needed Zora Neale Hurston as a literary foremother and as a reconnection with the South and the black vernacular, but also to formulate womanism as a radicalisation of (white) feminist analysis and aspiration. Such an analysis had been formulated by the Women's Liberation Movement of the late 1960s and '70s, for example in Kate Millett's bestseller *Sexual Politics* (1970), published in the same year as Toni Cade's *The Black Woman: An Anthology*. Although the latter was clearly a feminist text, it was not nearly as well known as Millett's controversial book, and the term 'feminism' was in the early 1970s still largely associated with white, middle class, educated women. Walker contributed the short story 'Diary of an African Nun' to Cade's anthology, but she never mentions Millett's *Sexual Politics*. Judging from the essays in *In Search of Our Mothers' Gardens*, therefore (some of which were originally written for the feminist magazine *Ms*), it seems that her critique of white feminism was primarily conducted as a *literary* campaign to create a cultural space for, and to advance, African American women's writing. For that purpose Walker revised and signified on the work of another literary foremother, much less recognised in Walker criticism than Hurston, but no less enabling: Virginia Woolf.

WALKER AND WOOLF: IN SEARCH OF OUR MOTHERS' GARDENS, AND AN INTER-RACIAL TRADITION

Walker mentions Woolf on two occasions: first in the essay 'Saving the Life That Is Your Own: the Importance of Models in the Artist's Life', among other writers who have served her as models, but adding that Woolf 'saved so many of us'; and second in *The Same River Twice*. There, she explains that Olivia in *The Color Purple* was named for the Olivia of Woolf's famous closet-lesbian line 'Chloe liked Olivia' in *A Room of One's Own*, 'a book that made me happy to be a writer, and bolstered and brightened my consciousness about the role other women, often silenced or even long dead, can have in changing the world'.[62] And if that is not enough to establish Woolf as a literary foremother, in *A Room of One's Own* we also find a passage that may well have directly inspired *In Search of Our Mothers' Gardens*:

> they [women] had no tradition behind them, or one so short and partial that it was of little help. For we think back through our mothers if we are women. It is useless to go to the great men writers for help, however much one may go to them for pleasure.[63]

'Thinking back through our mothers' to find literary predecessors was difficult for both Walker and Woolf, but Woolf at least could find a more or less continuous line of women writers in the European tradition from medieval times onwards. When Walker thinks back through *her* Southern black mother and her Native American grandmother, she finds a long and continuous line of non-writers, illiterate women burdened with domestic and wage-labour, to whom the world of literature was either unknown or barely conceivable. How was black women's creativity kept alive, when for centuries literacy itself was a punishable crime for black people, Walker asks pertinently.[64] Other than Phillis Wheatley, the household slave who in 1773 had her *Poems* published (anonymously!) in London, and a handful of other black women writers – Hurston among them – Walker had no examples from which to draw and was left to her own devices. But that dismal fact, ironically, led her to a different theory of creativity altogether: in her critical revision of *A Room of One's Own*, Walker finds that artists of daily life and everyday use (quiltmakers, weavers, cooks, African hut-painters, gardeners, and last but not least storytellers) were the Shakespeare's sisters of the African American tradition, and a rich tradition it is too. Extrapolating from Woolf's statement that the ubiquitous 'Anon', author of so many poems, was often cover for a woman's name, Walker concludes that her mothers and grandmothers handed on the creative spark, also anonymously, through their domestic production and their example.[65] Woolf's legacy as a foremother who handed on the creative spark then evokes, like Walker's Southern heritage, feelings of ambivalence: on the one hand, Walker's use of *A Room of One's Own* makes visible the class and racial limitations of Woolf's argument and exposes white feminism's universalist assumption that all women share the concerns of the educated white middle class as fallacious. On the other hand, Woolf also makes it possible for Walker to go in search of her mother's garden and to formulate her theory of black women's creativity, which – as we have seen – comes to inform her womanist theory.

Walker's most literal reference to Woolf occurs in the title of her essay on motherhood, white feminism, and the tradition of women's writing '*One* Child of One's Own: a Meaningful Digression within the Work(s)'. Here she examines not only her own initial ambivalence about motherhood (in the thought that her writing would not be compatible with having children) but also the assumption *of women writers themselves* that motherhood and writing cannot go together. She cites, for example, Tillie Olsen's bald statement that most women writers of the past were childless, to which she silently adds: 'and *white*'.[66] Walker addresses in this essay not just *literal*, but also *literary* motherhood. Can white women writers serve as role models for black women writers like herself? Significantly the essay opens with a tribute to the poet Muriel Rukeyser, who sponsored Walker's work from the beginning, when she was still a student at Sarah Lawrence. Rukeyser, it seems, *can* and does serve as such a model because of her interest in – what Walker consistently refers to as – 'The Child', a sentiment that chimes, of course, with the centrality of the child in Walker's own work.[67] '*One* Child of One's Own' ends, however, on a slightly different note, with a poem in the form of an admonishment to herself, that begins: 'Dear Alice/Virginia Woolf had madness', and moves via 'Zora Hurston (ah!) had no money/and poor health' to 'You have Rebecca – who is/much more delightful/and less distracting/than any of the calamities/above'.[68] What the poem and the essay seem to argue is that Walker, as a black woman writer *and* as a mother, is so much better off than her white *and* black literary foremothers. Adopting the musing, and sometimes amusing style of Woolf's *A Room of One's Own* Walker wonders not about the fate of Shakespeare's sister but ponders, instead, the position of 'our mother', who raises a child and writes.

Since Walker draws on Woolf and Hurston for both insights, as a daughter thinking back through her female line of ancestry, but also in a way as a mother with a wider perspective and a different experience who wants to protect and correct that ancestry, the question arises whether Walker sees herself as part of an interracial tradition of women's writing across difference. She answers that question herself, in 'Saving the Life That Is Your Own': 'black writers and white writers seem to me to be writing one immense story – the same story, for the most part – with different parts of this immense story coming from a multitude of different perspectives'.[69] The relative silence that surrounds the Walker/Woolf nexus in feminist criticism might suggest otherwise; to date, the domains of Woolf criticism and of African American criticism have remained largely segregated. Tuzyline Jita Allan, who reads *Mrs Dalloway* and other white women's texts by Walker's womanist lights to productive critical effect, is an exception to what seems to be an unwritten rule: that white women write of Woolf, at great length and in great quantity, while black feminist critics focus their attention overwhelmingly on African American literature. Writing itself, however, as Walker acknowledges in the quotation above, does not work in this way, nor can it afford to. Reading does not work in this way either. Recent debates about canon formation recognise – however fraught they may otherwise be – that a segregated canon is unsatisfactory. Walker herself has explained that she needed to read Hurston *and* Flannery O'Connor, Nella Larsen *and* Carson McCullers, Jean Toomer *and* William Faulkner to even begin to feel well educated at all, as Cheryl A. Wall also notes in her study of *In Search of Our Mothers' Gardens*.[70]

In a perfect world, such interracial inclusivity would all be well and good, but in an unequal one it may not be. If we are not to read Walker's work purely in terms of 'the' African American tradition, as is usually done, but put it in dialogue with writers like Woolf, there is a danger that we are implicitly positing an indebtedness and a hierarchy of value that is misplaced. Once more, Walker herself is the chief consciousness-raiser of this phenomenon: '[T]his is what has happened to black culture all these years: We produce and produce and create and create and it finds its way into mainstream culture ten years later, white people assuming they are the source of it.'[71] The 'immense story' that black and white writers are evidently piecing together like a quilt, Walker points out here, may be a collective and colourful story 'coming from a multitude of different perspectives', but it does not get written in any idealised setting of sisterly equality and collaboration. In the context of literary institutions such as prizes, educational establishments, canon formations, and the publishing industry, writers and artists compete for recognition and, indeed, ownership of ideas and creative practices. In thinking about Woolf as one of Alice Walker's ancestors or foremothers, the 'assumption that whites are at the source of it' would seem to be reproduced. Or maybe not, not necessarily so. It may be that what parts of the 'immense story' already exist, and are legible as 'mainstream', are therefore also available for revision, appropriation, and unexpected identifications on the part of their readers. Walker's work lends itself – some might say all too easily – to interracial reading; the black and white feminist criticism her work has generated testifies to this. Conversely, it is likely that young black women like Walker read *A Room of One's Own* or *Three Guineas* at Spelman or Sarah Lawrence in the 1960s, before the flowering of black women's writing as we know it today had come into being. They may indeed have felt alienated by it, but they may equally well have 'recognised' Spelman in Woolf's depiction of Newnham and Girton, and they may have cheered Woolf's pacifist stance in the light of the Civil Rights movement and protests against the Vietnam War, less on the grounds of gender per se than on those of race.

Woolf's polemical work, in other words, is productive for African American writers like Alice Walker, while at the same time our engagement with Walker illuminates Woolf, highlighting gaps in gender analysis as well as the racist assumptions embedded in the latter's critique of empire and colonialism. When writing of 'the' woman as outsider to all the institutions of Englishness for example, Woolf impersonates the 'educated man's daughter' to interrogate patriarchal and patriotic ideology:

> 'Our country', she will say, 'throughout the greater part of its history has treated me as a slave; it has denied me education or a share in its possessions. 'Our' country still ceases to be mine if I marry a foreigner. [...] 'For', the outsider will say, 'in fact, as a woman, I have no country. As a woman I want no country. As a woman my country is the whole world.'[72]

When reading Woolf with Walker, through Walker's eyes, the word 'slave' stands out here and cannot just be passed over as a familiar metaphor for the position of 'women' in patriarchy. Second, we note that Woolf's feminist internationalism is as nicely inclusive as Walker's 'immense story' being written by black and white together, but also that it obscures differential relations of power in the same way. Woolf's intended solidarity with women all over the world sounds hollow in light of what we know about non-metaphorical, real slavery, and about the difficulties of forging a global cross-cultural sisterhood. And we know this principally through the efforts of an Alice Walker, a Toni Morrison, or the African American and post-colonial critics of more recent vintage whose internationalism is of a different, more complex and nuanced, kind.[73] Walker revises Woolf very consciously when she writes:

> Of the need for internationalism, alignment with non-Americans, non-Europeans and non-chauvinists and against male suprema-cists or white supremacists wherever they exist on the globe, with an appreciation of all white American feminists who know more of nonwhite women's herstory than 'And Ain't I a Woman' by Sojourner Truth.[74]

Race *and* gender are inscribed here in a more sophisticated global alliance than Woolf proposed, because of Walker's rejection, in the last phrase, of a rigid identity politics. Her 'appreciation' of white women's self-education about cultural difference echoes Woolf's insistence on women's self-education about gender and literary ancestry, and it invalidates the charge of womanist essentialism in the process.

Tuzyline Allan remarks on 'a closeness in the sensibilities of Walker and Woolf', and the picture that emerges of them is that they are, in fact, remarkably similar writers, more similar than Walker and Hurston.[75] Both feel at home in different forms and are able to parody and stretch those forms in the service of race- and gender-critique (*Orlando*; *The Color Purple*); both use the essay form subversively, employing a storytelling technique that draws us unsuspecting readers in, turns our heads and by such distrac-tion gets us to exactly the place where Woolf and Walker want to have us. Both also examine the interplay of individual and social histories through the crucible of one family living, and being lived by, those histories (for example *The Years*, *The Third Life of Grange Copeland*, and *The Color Purple* again). Putting Woolf and Walker in dialogue with each other suggests different readings of both. It also highlights differences in the use of the autobiographical persona, as Allan once more makes clear when she contrasts Woolf's modernist impersonal and 'disinterested' voice with Walker's apparent self-revelation.[76] Toni Morrison writes, with regard to such interracial comparative reading, that:

> We are not, in fact, 'other'. We are choices. And to read imaginative literature by and about us is to choose to examine centers of the self and to have the opportunity to compare these centers with the 'raceless' one with which we are, all of us, most familiar.[77]

Morrison's first 'we', of course, refers to African American writers. Reading Woolf with Walker and Hurston along parallel lines defamiliarises the 'we' and 'us' of a white feminism that can no longer assume itself to be the implied reader of 'women's' writing. Conversely, reading Walker with Woolf shows how 'books continue each other' in a literary tradition that is neither entirely male and Eurocentric nor exclusively female or African American. Walker and Woolf and Morrison and Hurston create cultural spaces where few or none have gone before, and juxtaposing them opens up a culture's difference in the very act of ostensibly closing it. Hurston and Woolf's work then, we can safely conclude, has been productive for Walker's literary career, even if their lives and premature deaths have also generated anxiety and have prompted Walker to reflect on conditions conducive to, and destructive of, creative practice. We shall revisit that theme, and the related question of criticism, in Chapter 8. For now, it will be clear that there are comparisons to be made *and* differences to be articulated; the relationships between black women writers and white, as between sisters, or daughters and mothers, are problematic and difficult – and all the more worthwhile for that. They are one place where different patches of the 'immense story' are stitched together, and in the chapters that follow we shall examine, closely, the work of Walker's hand as it has developed over the past forty years.

2

The Third Life of Grange Copeland (1970)

It is always tempting to read an established writer's first novel either as the founding text of a coherent *oeuvre*, or as a youthful experiment in which the older writer's powers can perhaps be glimpsed, but are not as yet fully realised. By 1970, when her first novel *The Third Life of Grange Copeland* came out, Alice Walker was twenty-six years old and already a published poet and short story writer.[1] Her first reviewers therefore were able to read the novel on its – and their – own terms, unhindered by the benefit of hindsight, but also unprejudiced by the writer's youth and gender.[2] Some forty years later it is not so easy to read *The Third Life of Grange Copeland* in this fresh and open-minded way. This is partly because of its apparently radical difference in form from such later works as *The Color Purple* or *Possessing the Secret of Joy*, but in part it is also because Walker's critique of African American gender relations is now so familiar that its erstwhile novelty and daring are easily obscured by the mists of time. Yet it is useful to remind ourselves of 'the risks that many African American women writers took during the period of black nationalism', especially 'when writing about intimate violence', in Amanda Davis' words.[3] Davis reads Walker's novel in the context of an African American activism that had its cultural corollary in the Black Arts Movement, whose aim was 'to garner support for the works of black artists and [to develop] a black aesthetic that stressed racial stability and solidarity'.[4] As we shall see, black nationalism has a prominent place in Grange Copeland's third life, but there is a long road to travel before we get there. The reader who comes to *The Third Life of Grange Copeland* after, say, *The Color Purple*, will be surprised by this novel's ostensible realism, its conventionality, its subject matter too – because here men take centre stage, with women characters in a subordinate role. And yet the subordination of the women and the violence and brutality of the men, though shocking still, are already known to us from Walker's later work. As we

28

become familiar with the world of Grange Copeland, the awareness that we are reading backwards in Walker's development becomes more acute, and Grange comes to look like an earlier version of Mr___ in *The Color Purple*, Ruth reminds us of a younger Meridian, and maybe in Celie's memorable first few letters we now hear an echo of Margaret and Mem's despondency. Reading *The Third Life of Grange Copeland* today and not in the early 1970s, we almost inevitably attribute its problems to Walker's youth and inexperience, at the same time as we also 'recognise' it as a blueprint for the later work. But this practice of 'reading back' is not all there is to Walker's first novel, for – as noted above – *The Third Life of Grange Copeland* is also an original and in some ways polemical fictional intervention in African American cultural and political debate of the early 1970s, particularly around black nationalism. Part of that intervention is Walker's engagement with the canon of African American literature before the rise of black women's writing, such as Richard Wright's *Native Son* and Ralph Ellison's *Invisible Man*, as we shall see. Part of it is also Walker's stringent critique of African American masculinity, which is represented in Brownfield Copeland's degradation on the one hand and Grange Copeland's redemption in his third life on the other. But before we move on to detailed discussion of how *The Third Life of Grange Copeland* positions itself in the heated cultural and political issues of its day, it is useful to examine the novel first for its form and subject matter. What, then, does it have to say?

A barebones account of the plot might read something like this: *The Third Life of Grange Copeland* is a family saga spanning three generations, set between 1920 and the mid-1960s. It tells the story of Grange Copeland's three lives: the first as an exploited sharecropper in the American South, the second in New York, where he works as an itinerant labourer, and the third, again set in the South, in which he develops a close relationship with his granddaughter Ruth, whom he raises and educates. In taking on this parental role Grange breaks the cycle of domestic violence and emotional abuse that has ruled his previous two lives and those of his first wife Margaret, their son Brownfield, and Brownfield's wife Mem.

This is, indeed, only the skeleton narrative; a more fleshed-out summary would inevitably engage in some interpretation. After all, every repetition of a plot is not just a condensation but also a reconstruction of it, and in this chapter that reconstruction centres on the themes of mobility, domestic violence, and transformation of African American masculinity. To prepare the ground for that analysis we should address some of the novel's formal problems, its critical revision of the Oedipal story, and its relation to some key texts in the African American literary tradition that are similarly concerned with black masculinity and social and/or geographical mobility.

AN 'APPRENTICE NOVEL': PATRIARCHAL PLOT AND FEMINIST PERSPECTIVE

Brownfield stood close to his mother in the yard, not taking his eyes off the receding automobile [...] a new 1920 Buick, long and high and shiny green with great popping headlights like the eyes of a frog. Inside the car it was all blue, with seats that were fuzzy and soft. Slender silver handles opened the doors and rolled the astonishingly clear windows up and down. As it bumped over the road its canvas top was scratched by low elm branches. Brownfield was embarrassed about the bad road and the damage it did to his uncle's car. (3–4)

This is how *The Third Life of Grange Copeland* begins: with a visit from Uncle Silas and his wife and children from Philadelphia, whose wealth (exemplified by their lavishly described car) contrasts starkly with the Copelands' abject poverty. For young Brownfield, the Northern relatives represent the hope of a better future, a hope that is never to materialise in his own life. Poverty and racism take their toll on the Copeland family, which is racked by violence of both a physical and psychological kind. As Brownfield grows up, his father Grange absconds to the North in search of freedom, and abandons his family in the process. Brownfield's mother, Margaret, kills herself after long years of abuse by Grange and her white employers. Brownfield himself wants to follow his father to the North, but stops at Josie, Grange's former mistress, with whom he lives for a while as a kept man, at the Dew Drop Inn. His marriage to Josie's niece Mem, a schoolteacher, provides a brief interlude of happiness and economic advancement, but bad housing, insecure jobs, and too many children soon get the better of them, as does Brownfield's masculine pride, which leads him to abuse and even-tually to kill Mem. Brownfield goes to prison for the murder, and we lose sight of him as the spotlight moves back to Grange, who has now returned from the North. We never see directly what has happened to him there, since his second life in New York is told only in retrospect, but on his return to the South Grange marries Josie, in part to gain access to her material assets tied up in the Dew Drop Inn. With Mem dead and Brownfield in prison, Grange takes on the role of substitute parent for their daughter Ruth, who is left alone and effectively orphaned. A strong bond develops between Ruth and her grandfather, which distances Grange from Josie and further alienates Ruth from Brownfield, and Grange and Ruth live happily together until Brownfield is released from prison to claim his daughter. After a court case in which Brownfield is awarded custody of Ruth against her will, Grange kills Brownfield and then is himself killed by the police. At the end of the novel, some forty years after the Philadelphia relatives drive away from the Copelands' house in their Buick, another car appears at Grange's farm, but this time the visitors are Civil Rights workers organising for voter registration. They seem to offer hope of a different kind of better life than that of mere material advancement; committed to non-violence, the Civil Rights workers hold out the promise of social and political change. Neither Brownfield nor Grange live to see the era of Civil Rights for African Americans however, and Ruth is left, alone of the Copelands but with the Civil Rights workers, to fend and fight for herself and the future.

It is significant that the novel starts and ends with cars, because – as so often in American literature – it is the car that represents mobility in the literal and metaphorical sense. The new 1920 Buick, coupled with later images of consumer goods that Mem selects from the Sears Roebuck catalogue (and which she either cannot have or cannot hold on to) signals modernity and economic advancement, both of which are crucial to Walker's argument regarding African American emancipation in this novel. More importantly, perhaps, the car connotes mobility not just to a different region or mode of production, but to a new era in African American Southern history: a shift from the rural existence and exploitative economic relations of slavery and sharecropping to industrialisation and urban migration. It is significant that the first car, with the Philadelphia cousins, recedes from, whereas the Civil Rights car arrives at, the Copelands' compound. The fate of the Northern relatives later in the narrative illustrates, after all, that economic and geographical mobility are not all they are cracked up to be: Uncle Silas gets killed in a robbery, and Margaret concludes that 'All the time coming down here in they fancy cars and makin' out like *we* so out of fashion – I bet the Norse is just as much a mess as down here' (17). As Grange also discovers in New York (cathartically, in his confrontation with the pregnant white woman who refuses his help), neither the North nor urban wage-labour deliver the promise of release from physical, economic, and psychological bondage, because Northern whites as well as Southern black people still live with the legacy of slavery in their hearts and minds. Only with the arrival of the Civil Rights movement, Walker implies, do African Americans have the chance to emancipate themselves from such bondage and to enter modernity on their own terms. Yet the road to such enlightenment is every bit as bumpy as the one that damages Uncle Silas's car. Familial violence forces the characters in *The Third Life of Grange Copeland* to recognise and work through their history of bondage, which has internal (psychological) as well as external (economic) manifestations. Walker's portrayal of Brownfield, who seems to be the conduit – victim as well as perpetrator – of such violence is particularly illustrative in this regard, as we shall see later on. His development is sharply contrasted with that of Grange and raises the question of what *kind* of historical and personal change can offer a way out of the chains of violence that dominate the narrative. As Klaus Ennslen observes, Grange and Brownfield embody 'diametrically opposed options for the black man under white supremacy', but whether the way out of their dilemma lies simply in individual responsibility, as Ennslen believes, or a combination of collective action, material security and individual growth, as I think, depends on our reading of the text's ambiguities.[5]

The Third Life of Grange Copeland is centrally concerned with a rewriting of the interrelationship of (public) history with the (private) family. The novel can almost be read as a political argument on a dialectical model of thesis (the historically determined *stasis* of racial oppression and violence in the South) antithesis (modernity and migration) and synthesis (return to the South and advancement through education and political action). Such a dialectical model may well look too abstract, too neat and too dry for a novel that is messy and bloody as well as contradictory and confused. But it may be that its very contradictions and problems come out of Walker's desire to transcend the ravages of history in a fusion of personal and political change. This desire for transcendence leads to a kind of idealist overreach which does not quite work in the realist terms that the text seems to set up for itself. *The Third Life of Grange Copeland* is, in many ways, incoherent: the chronology reveals itself only in fits and starts and apparently haphazardly; there are many gaps and silences in the plot development as well as conflicting character portrayals; and the narrative logic is quite difficult to reconstruct. Critics have interpreted this awkwardness of form in various ways. Kate Cochran, for example, sees Grange, Brownfield and Ruth as 'more instruments of Walker's narrative than multi-dimensional characters. That is to say, Grange's heroic and benevolent characterization mid-book in his third life bears little relation to his earlier presentation as a silent, brutal farmer'.[6] And in his book *Race, Gender and Desire* Elliott Butler-Evans presents a useful structural analysis that highlights the unevenness of narrative development in *The Third Life of Grange Copeland*. He explains what another critic, Hortense Spillers, may have meant by calling it 'an apprentice novel':[7]

> The early stages ... are clearly focused on the dehumanizing aspects of racial and economic oppression. The novel then proceeds to focus on victims other than Black males [e.g. Margaret and Mem, Daphne and Ornette]. And the characterizations of Grange and Brownfield, two men marked by exaggerated qualities of good and evil, become signs of opposing ideological positions, with the narrator clearly on the side of Grange.[8]

This black-and-white representation of Grange and Brownfield serves all too obviously to illustrate a polemical point that Walker wants to make about good and bad black masculinities. Yet there are ambivalences and inconsistencies in the characters of the women too. As Butler-Evans notes, Josie is now good, now evil, sometimes held up as a victim who deserves our sympathy and then again vilified in the narrative discourse because of her vindictive alliance with Brownfield. Her daughter Lorene is an even more extreme example of overdetermined characterisation. She is introduced as some kind of witch or monster:

> She was cursed with the beginnings of a thick mustache and beard. Her hard, malevolent eyes were a yellowish flash in her dark hairy face. She was sinewy as a man. Only her odor and breasts were female. She reeked of a fishy, oniony smell. 'Yep', said Josie ... 'that's the pride of her mama's heart.' Lorene turned and hissed something vile, her tongue showing through her lips like a snake's. (34–5)

Not only is this passage poorly written, it is also not at all clear what motivates such nastiness in the representation of a Southern black woman. It might be that we get to see Lorene from Brownfield's point of view, but that impression is belied by Josie's comment, which comes from an impersonal narrator. The scene exemplifies a problem with narrative perspective: ostensibly this is a linear and chronological novel, with an omniscient narrator at the helm, but it is – as we see here – also the work of a writer who is not yet entirely in control of her material. Walker herself said in an interview with John O'Brien that she prefers short literary forms (like the Japanese haiku, which 'express mystery, evoke beauty and pleasure, paint a picture') to more discursive forms that dissect or analyse.[9] Short forms (poem, essay, short story, or episodic novel) are undoubtedly Walker's forte, and it is as if in *The Third Life of Grange Copeland* she was attempting a conventional form that simply did not suit her – even if this one, too, is composed of eleven parts and forty-eight short chapters. The main problem throughout lies with a narrator who is both too directive and unstable; omniscient, but not consistent in maintaining a transcendent perspective because it sometimes merges with the characters' own. Brownfield's portrayal in particular suffers from this oscillation between inside (character) perspective and outside (narratorial) judgement. In this passage, for example:

> His crushed pride, his battered ego, made him drag Mem away from schoolteaching. Her knowledge reflected badly on a husband who could scarcely read and write. It was his great ignorance that sent her into white homes as a domestic, his need to bring her down to his level! [...] His rage could and did blame everything, *everything* on her. And she accepted all his burdens along with her own and dealt with them from her own greater heart and greater knowledge. He did not begrudge her the greater heart, but he could not forgive her the greater knowledge. It put her closer, in power, to *them* than he could ever be. (55)

The first sentence seems to emanate from the omniscient narrator, but presumably the second reflects Brownfield's own opinion – we know of Brownfield's deprived childhood and lack of education by this stage. But in the third sentence it is not at all clear whether Brownfield judges *himself* and feels guilty, or whether the narrator judges him. The same goes for the rest of this extract: in *whose* view does Mem have 'greater heart and greater knowledge'? Is the whole passage meant to demonstrate Brownfield's awareness of his mistreatment of Mem and his motivation for it (envy – she has more power than he has, so she is more like *them*, white people) or is it, on the contrary, an explanation of something Brownfield does *not* know and refuses to see, which earns him the narrator's moral condemnation? Klaus Ensslen puts a positive gloss on such confusion by explaining it as a 'mobile' narrative perspective, but he concedes 'the veiled dominance of authorial control over distribution of action' because 'Alice Walker manages to exert considerable influence on the normative level on her fictional characters and on their reception by the reader'.[10] In his analysis of the novel's narrative discourse and what he calls its 'feminist ideologeme' W. Lawrence Hogue puts it slightly differently: '[The] strategy of using characters to articulate certain ideological forms causes internal dissonance within the text and contradictions in character development', but really he is making the same point.[11] Didactic writing often works in this way, and so in itself that level of control need not be a problem, so long as it is exercised consistently. Because it isn't – as Ensslen shows in some detail – it remains unclear how we are to judge Josie, for example, or Brownfield. Grange, by the novel's end, is obviously the moral centre, but he has not always been so, and his transformation from absent father and violent husband to kindly grandfather is rather sudden. Significantly, there is only one character in whom we can consistently invest our trust: Ruth, because only she remains sheltered from and untainted by violence – and its counterpart, victimization – throughout.

Relevant here is the publication date of this first novel, not just because of Walker's youth but also because of the ways in which the text draws on – then current – competing ideologies of race and gender relations. The year 1970 indicates a historical stage in African American political thought when feminist, black nationalist, and Civil Rights discourses were at war with one another, and we see the traces of this war in *The Third Life of Grange Copeland*. In *Black Women Novelists and the Nationalist Aesthetic* Madhu Dubey understands Walker's womanism (see Chapter 1) as the integration of black nationalism and feminism, and her attention to both race and gender enables her to foreground the specificity of African Americanisms in Walker's writing (such as Ruth's description as a 'womanish gal'). But although Dubey is right to identify feminist and black nationalist strands in this novel, she misunderstands quite how these discourses work – or rather, fail to work, that is: fail to integrate. Dubey argues that various aspects of the novel contradict each other or are in conflict with nationalist ideology, such as the ending in which the West African ideal of the 'wholistic personality' is collapsed – as she sees it – into an individualist liberal humanist stance, and she regards this as an ideological cop-out.[12] But Dubey seems to assume that Grange's nationalist outlook, combined with the novel's feminist critique of violence against women, is validated by the narrative. This is not the case: the ending quite clearly shows that Grange's separatist leanings are misguided and have no future – this is why he has to die. Black nationalism and feminism do not womanism make; at this point in her writing career Walker's theory of womanism is not yet developed, and so instead of a coherent analysis we see a working-through of disparate political positions in the novel that do not as yet merge into a new fusion. The contradiction between the representations of Brownfield and the young Grange on one hand, and the older Grange on the other, sets a victimised black masculinity against one that is politically emancipated (indeed, by black nationalism) and has come into agency through the acceptance *in addition* of personal responsibility. But this contradiction is not just the effect of a fluctuating narrative perspective; it also shadows an ideological shift on the cusp of 1960s (Civil Rights and black nationalist) and 1970s (feminist and womanist) discursive formations. Diffuse narrative technique and the filtering through of conflicting extra-literary discourses thus produce inconsistent characterisation and ideological confusion in *The Third Life of Grange Copeland*. Here, a feminist perspective on 'patriarchy's plot' against women comes up against racism's hold on the economic and psychological agency of black men. Rather than see this conflict simply as a flaw, however, it is more interesting to regard it as a sign of the times, evidence of live debate about African American gender relations both in the wider world and in the aesthetic development of a writer for whom healing the rift between the African American man and woman was to become a major priority.

AFRICAN AMERICAN MASCULINITY AND THE BLACK FAMILY

It is not difficult to see, in the light of Walker's later work and her reputation as a womanist writer, why some critics have focused their attention on the representation of women in the novel. W. Lawrence Hogue, for example, sees in Walker's portrayal of Mem and Margaret as passive victims a desire to solicit 'a sympathetic response from the reader because the reader always identifies with the helpless victim'.[13] He argues that *The Third Life of Grange Copeland* is a feminist novel designed to counter existing stereotypes of domineering black women with new images recognising their oppression. Undoubtedly Walker's women fit the mould of later victims, like the young Celie in *The Color Purple*, or the mutilated Tashi before she recovers her traumatic memory in *Possessing the Secret of Joy*, but Celie and Tashi become survivors in a way that Margaret and Mem cannot.

At the beginning of this Chapter I summarised *The Third Life of Grange Copeland* in the terms set by its title, that is: as being about Grange Copeland. I did this in spite of Walker's own description of the novel as only *ostensibly* about Brownfield and Grange, '[but] it is the women and how they are treated that colors everything'.[14] Walker said this in an interview in 1973 and, while it may be true that what happens to the women 'colors everything', it may also be true that here Walker colours her own development as a writer, to give it a more womanist hue. This womanist overlay can easily obscure Walker's concern with the crucial role of African American men in personal and political change, which also becomes a recurrent theme in her later work. *The Third Life of Grange Copeland* as a text that is not just ostensibly, but indeed about a man and his son brings to mind Truman in *Meridian*, Albert in *The Color Purple*, and Suwelo in *The Temple of My Familiar* for example. Grange Copeland's transformation and self-healing demonstrate the necessity and ability of black men to change the course of history, starting with the most intimate history of all: that of the black family in the American South. In this way the novel rebuts from the outset the kind of criticism that takes Walker to task for her negative portrayal of black men. Reading this first novel for Grange and Brownfield and Ruth, rather than solely for Margaret and Mem, thus prepares the way for reading Walker's work with a sense of continuity in its portrayal of the transformative potential of African American men as well as women. When Grange takes on the 'women's work' of raising Ruth, when he takes on the task of educating her in African American folklore and history and the ways of a racist world, and finally when he shoots Brownfield, he earns by degrees the wisdom, love, and manhood he had been searching for all his life. 'You want to be with your *real* daddy, don't you, Ruth?', the judge asks her in the trial that will decide whether

her future lies with Grange or with Brownfield's guardianship, but Ruth's answer is an unequivocal 'No Sir' (244). Ruth knows, even if she does not articulate it, that *real* fatherhood has little to do with material provision, and even less with biology. A real father does the work – of caring, of guiding and of loving. Mothering and fathering go together in Grange Copeland's development, as Madhu Dubey points out, and in that limited but important sense his self-education foreshadows Walker's later womanism.[15]

Reasons why Walker should be so concerned about the plight of the black man and woman as to devote a whole historical novel to it can be found, as we have already seen, in the historical moment of its publication as well as in the author's incipient, but not yet developed, womanist agenda. The construction of African American gender relations as pathological does not, however, originate in Walker's work or in that of her black and feminist contemporaries like Ntozake Shange (*for colored girls/when the rainbow is not enuf*) or Gayl Jones (*Corregidora*) or Toni Morrison (*The Bluest Eye*), but has a much longer history that deserves a brief discussion of its own before we return to Walker's treatment of black masculinity and domestic violence. Ultimately – as Marlon B. Ross puts it – 'the African race has been constructed as a failure to meet civilized gender norms from the start'.[16] To assume that this failure is somehow *intrinsically* racial (African or African American) is, of course, to confuse the historical condition of enslavement with a biological trait or propensity. As is well known, the 'failure to meet civilized gender norms' dates back to slavery times, when it was impossible for male and female slaves to constitute and sustain stable relationships and families, subject as they were to the absolute rule and abuse of their masters. With Reconstruction and the subsequent movement for racial uplift came the aspiration to (on the part of the black middle class) and the imposition of (on the part of white society) such 'civilized' (read: white, bourgeois, heterosexual) gender norms and the creation of stable families on a white patriarchal model. A black man, in other words, could only be a 'real man' (and no longer be infantilised as the 'boy' of white racism) if he could provide for his family, pass on property, and protect his wife and children. As a result, virtually all movements for African American emancipation until the advent of black feminism have conflated the fate of the race as a whole with the social status of African American men: black *men* were enfranchised at the end of the Civil War, black *men* were the torchbearers of Marcus Garvey's United Negro Improvement Association, and black *men* overwhelmingly represented the successes of the Civil Rights movement and the revolutionary fervour of the Black Panthers. In all these movements, the claim to full manhood stood for the claim to equality with whites. Conversely, however, contemporary society's moral panic about the decline of family life as a result of rising divorce rates is fueled by the image of a pathologised African American family model. Tied up with the undermining or loss of the traditional role of the father, contemporary views of 'the' family in crisis condense the nightmare scenario of patriarchal decline particularly in the figure of the absent, or failing, *black* father (and the single, head-of-household, *black* mother). David Marriott puts it thus:

> 'What is wrong with black fathers?' 'What is wrong with black men?': these questions loom over postwar American culture, part of a more pervasive anxiety about the decline of paternal authority, the so-called 'crisis of masculinity' in contemporary cultural life.[17]

The 'crisis of masculinity' is thus personified in the presumed perpetual failure of black masculinity. However, if we examine how black masculinity is constructed in mainstream America, how it compares to the impossible standard of a (hetero-)normative 'real man', then it becomes clear that the (re-)construction of African American masculinity cannot be a mere matter of 'doing the right thing' or making different individual choices. As Delgado and Stefancic write:

> The stereotype of the ideal man is forceful, militaristic, hypercompetitive, risk-taking, not particularly interested in culture and the arts, protective of his woman, heedless of nature, and so on. [...] Men of color are constructed as criminal, violent, lascivious, irresponsible, and not particularly smart.[18]

It seems that the contemporary stereotype of black masculinity still owes a good deal to the one plantation-owners habitually espoused to legitimise slavery and, later, segregation.

These contemporary and historical constructions of black masculinity, however, are similar but not the *same*. It is worth bearing in mind here that mainstream definitions of black versus white (or normative) masculinity vary over time. In *The Third Life of Grange Copeland* we still see, in the sharecropping South, hangovers from slavery in that both Grange and Brownfield are emasculated in the presence of the white men who, in some way or other, control them and their labour. Yet today's popular culture is saturated with images of hypermasculine black men who set an enviable standard of masculinity for white boys the world over. How to explain this shift from degraded or inadequate to superior and envied masculinity? Paul Gilroy puts it thus: 'An amplified and exaggerated masculinity has become the boastful centerpiece of a culture of *compensation* that self-consciously salves the misery of the disempowered and the subordinated'[19] (my emphasis). Gilroy refers here to black culture heroes like rap stars and athletes, and the kind of super-masculinity they project, one that belongs largely to young black men without familial attachment. For the purpose of our analysis of *The Third Life of Grange Copeland*, it is helpful to make a distinction between African American masculinity per se and black fatherhood. With Brownfield, the issue seems to be that he has not had a real and present father in Grange; consequently he cannot be a real and present father to his own children either. David Marriott shows how John Edgar Wideman addresses this generational passing on of 'bad father' models, and how it relates to masculinity, in his novel *Fatheralong*: 'the lost fathers cannot claim their sons, speak to them about growing up, until the fathers claim their own manhood'.[20] For Grange, this claiming of his manhood can only happen once he has fled the South and has lived his second life in New York. Even so, and again, true fatherhood cannot be taken up simply as a gesture of individual will because, as Wideman also observes, 'Arrayed against the possibility of conversation between fathers and sons is the country they inhabit, everywhere proclaiming the inadequacy of black fathers, their lack of manhood in almost every sense the term's understood here in America'.[21] Given the weight of racist discourse (and history and practice) militating against new and more positive and productive constructions of black masculinity and fatherhood, how then is it possible to bring about change? The editors of *Representing Black Men* give one possible answer: 'By eschewing the discourse of the *real* black man', they write, because

... the reconstruction of the true black man [is] among the defining obsessions of contemporary racial discourse. Most often labeled as nationalist and recuperations [sic] of patriarchy, these racial discourses join [...] with a conservative cultural agenda to redefine the problem of race as a problem of skewed family structures and gender roles.[22]

Alternatives to the discourse of 'the real black man' are to be found, if anywhere, in black women's writing like that of Alice Walker, Ntozake Shange, Toni Morrison, or a host of other black feminist authors and theorists. We have thus come full circle: far from *creating* the 'problem' of black masculinity and pathological gender-relations, black feminism is part of its (dis-)solution, which is why much of the theoretical and cultural work on African American masculinity has taken its cue from African American women's writing, as Marcellus Blount argues:[23]

> Now that black female artists and critics have assumed their rightful status as the most compelling voices of Afro-American culture, one of our present goals must be the engendering of black men within the context of gender ideologies that encourage a range of possibilities for male selfhood. In this sense, black feminism may provide real alternatives for black men as we define our notions of black masculinity. By exploring the possibilities of feminism, we can revise our sense of what it means to be men.[24]

Note the emphasis here on a *'range* of possibilities for male selfhood', rather than insistence on any single definition of a 'real' black man; particular constructions of black masculinity have repercussions, not just for gender-relations, but for the survival ('and survival *whole'*, as Walker would say) of the African American family and community itself.

The black family became a particularly hotly debated issue in the 1960s, with the publication of the government-commissioned Moynihan report titled *The Negro Family: The Case for National Action* in 1965, that is: before black nationalism and black feminism formulated their positions on African American gender roles. Given the long and convoluted history of racial discourse on African American gender outlined above, we can now see how the Moynihan report fitted in with, rather than stood out from, a tradition of thinking about the black family in terms of pathology and abnormality. Marlon B. Ross notes, once more, how the fate of not only the African American family, but of the nation as a whole is tied up with black masculinity:

> Moynihan's report casts Black men paradoxically as both overly masculine (they indulge their desire for women too much and out of proper bounds) and not masculine enough (they fail to enact

the patriarchal role of breadwinner and family enforcer), both too present and too absent as *American men*[25] (original emphasis).

Ross is writing in 1998, but contemporary reactions to the Moynihan report were no less critical and astute. Joyce Ladner explains in her 1971 classic *Tomorrow's Tomorrow* how Moynihan's argument 'that the black family had reached a stage of breakdown because of the high percentage of female households' was used both by some black men and by white society to serve racist and sexist interests. On the one hand, Ladner argues, the report fell into line with fear of a black matriarchy and legitimised the theory, already circulating among black men, that 'Black men [had] been psychologically castrated because of the strong role Black women played in the home and community'.[26] On the other hand that same argument assumed, and in fact shored up, a patriarchal white model of the nuclear family in which men *should* dominate women. Ladner shows convincingly that Moynihan's thesis was damaging to both black men and black women, because it insinuated that the men failed to look after their families, without either questioning the model of the white nuclear family or taking into account the (un-)employment statistics for black men. In exaggerating black women's strength and stressing the failure of the black man as provider and *paterfamilias*, white society drove a wedge between men and women, which, in time-honoured tradition, usefully deflected the issue of racism and attributed the 'problem' of black family breakdown to 'deviant' gender roles within the black community. Ladner cites Robert Staples' famous article 'The Myth of the Black Matriarchy', published in *The Black Scholar* in 1970, to make this point, but many similar arguments and refutations of that myth on behalf of the black woman can be found in Toni Cade's pathbreaking anthology *The Black Woman* of the same year. Both texts further illustrate how much of a live debate the issue of the black family had generated by the turn of the decade.[27]

It is, then, not at all surprising that Walker chose to tell a 'deviant' family saga in *The Third Life of Grange Copeland*, foregrounding the black woman's double jeopardy as victim of racism and sexism rather than as dominatrix of black men. She adds a further dimension to the family debate in her exploration of the fate of children in poor and violent families, and again this is a theme she would return to in her later work. Walker explains in the interview with John O'Brien that, in first draft, *The Third Life of Grange Copeland* was to be a novel about a Civil Rights lawyer (Ruth) in confrontation with her drunken father (Brownfield). But Walker felt that a novel set in the present would be too superficial, and that instead she should look at 'how it happens that the hatred a child can have for a parent becomes inflexible'.[28] It seems that, in the interview, Walker means Ruth when she speaks of the child, but of course in the finished novel Brownfield also develops an inflexible hatred of his parent – and one that takes up rather more narrative space. Brownfield is the crucial link in the chain of familial violence that unwinds in *The Third Life of Grange Copeland*, and my analysis therefore focuses, to begin with, on him. Two scenes stand out that typify his deprivation. The first is his daydream, as a fifteen-year-old boy, of ideal family life. The second is an image of his actual existence, abandoned as a small child on the steps of the sharecropper's shack while his parents are out at work in the fields. These two scenes are at the heart of what Walker has to say – really in all her work – about what is necessary for 'the survival *whole* of my people', and we will look at them from a psychoanalytic perspective because they are most productively read in that way. To see how Walker draws on Freud and revises him we should begin with the old man himself.[29]

BROWNFIELD'S DAYDREAM: OEDIPUS AND A FAMILY ROMANCE

'The liberation of an individual, as he grows up, from the authority of his parents is one of the most necessary though one of the most painful results brought about by the course of his development'.[30] This is how Sigmund Freud begins his famous essay 'Family Romances', in which he explains how small children imagine a better life for themselves in daydreams once they have discovered that their parents are neither as powerful nor as fully available to them as they would like them to be. In such daydreams, writes Freud, 'both his parents are replaced by others of better birth'.[31] The child's wish for a position of absolute privilege within the family is first figured in class terms. Later a sexual dimension is added, which expresses the child's curiosity about – in particular – his mother's sexuality and places her in sexual liaisons with other men. In this scenario, the father is displaced by these other lovers and the child's siblings, fantasised as the product of the mother's secret liaisons, are consequently bastardised and made illegitimate. The fantasy thus takes revenge upon both the father and the younger siblings in order to secure the child's privileged access to the mother's affections.[32] For Freud, the family romance is a quite normal fantasy and one that is likely to resurface in adult life in dreams, without harmfully affecting the adult's 'normal state' of having liberated him- or herself from the authority of the parents. 'On the other hand', writes Freud, 'there is a class of neurotics whose condition is recognizably determined by their having failed in this task'.[33] We can take Brownfield Copeland to be a fictional example of such failure. This is Brownfield's family romance:

> He saw himself grown-up, twenty-one or so, arriving home at sunset in the snow. […] he pulled up to his house, a stately mansion with cherry-red brick chimneys and matching brick porch and steps, in a long chauffeur-driven car. The chauffeur glided out of the car first and opened the back door, where Brownfield sat puffing on a cigar. Then the chauffeur vanished around the back of the house, where his wife waited for him on the kitchen steps. She was the beloved and very respected cook and had been with the house and the chauffeur and Brownfield's family for many years. Brownfield's wife and children – two children, a girl and a boy – waited anxiously for him just inside the door in the foyer. They jumped all over him, showering him with kisses. While he told his wife of the big deals he'd pushed through that day she fixed him a mint julep. After a splendid dinner, presided over by the cook, dressed in black uniform and white starched cap, he and his wife, their arms around each other, tucked the children in bed and spent the rest of the evening discussing her day (which she had spent walking in the garden), and making love.
>
> There was one thing that was odd about the daydream. The face of Brownfield's wife and that of the cook constantly interchanged. So that his wife was first black and glistening from cooking and then white and powdery to his touch; his dreaming self could not make up its mind. His children's faces were never in focus. (17–18)

Brownfield's fantasy, five years after the visit from his Northern cousins in their new 1920 Buick, bears a striking similarity to Freud's scenario. He imagines himself arriving home in the snow (the North) in a large, chauffeur-driven car. Cigar smoke, successful business deals, a manor house, a black cook and a white wife, as well as two adorable children, are all props for the Hollywood movie that plays in his head. The *mise en scène*, however, is more problematic; Brownfield's daydream, which clearly is also a masturbatory fantasy, ends in sexual intercourse, but whether he makes love with the cook or the wife is unclear, just as the faces of his children are out of focus. Why should this be? The dream, conceived as a film in black and white, holds him – 'at times it possessed him' (18) – yet it dissolves into shades of grey at the point of narrative climax: sexual union with the cook (the black woman, his mother) is as unimaginable and forbidden as the wife (the white woman, the film star) is unattainable and prohibited as a sexual object. We could say that, in classic Freudian terms, the incest taboo and castration anxiety make their appearance here and account for Brownfield's inability to direct his home movie to its satisfying conclusion, but we are dealing with more than mere infantile fantasy. In his daydream, after all, Brownfield significantly desires two women simultaneously, one black and one white, one of a higher and one of a lower class. Castration anxiety in relation to the cook, the image of his mother, would be quite enough to dissolve her image, but such dissolution is exacerbated in his sexual desire for a white woman; in the South of the early twentieth century, black men were being lynched for less. As late as 1955 Emmett Till, then fourteen years old, was killed by white men for whistling at a white woman. The Emmett Till case is notorious, but it is only one of many instances when the pretext for lynching was a black man's (assumed) desire for a white woman.[34] It is understandable, then, that even in fantasy Brownfield cannot picture the colour of his wife's face nor those of his children, blurred as they are by the twin taboos of incestuous desire and miscegenation.

And there are other kinds of blurring going on too. Brownfield pictures himself not as a privileged child but as an adored father and husband, who receives as an adult what he has never had as a child. At the same time, it is as if he is also fantasising his own conception and childhood, in an ideal world regulated by wealthy *and loving* parents. In real life, conception and parentage are more problematic. Brownfield does not know who fathered Star, for example, the odd-coloured baby brother/sister whom he is supposed to look after but for whom he feels no kinship, let alone affection. Star is the illegitimate offspring of Margaret's liaison with a white man, and this baby elicits Brownfield's hostility at worst, and indifference at best, attitudes he later replicates with his own children. Freud's remedy of revenge against the father by fantasising other lovers for the mother is no mere fantasy here but a reality ensnared in the convoluted sexual politics of Southern race relations. In the daydream, furthermore, the revenge on father (the chauffeur) and mother fails because Brownfield cannot resolve his conflicting desires to, on the one hand, match his real mother's interracial betrayal by his own marriage to a white woman, and on the other displace his father through a sexual liaison with the cook. For Brownfield, as for the reader, it is impossible to put him in the frame of his own primal scene, and if it is true that we cannot achieve what we cannot imagine, then this may be why he is destined to repeat the script of failure in sexual and parental relations for life.

This same sense of inevitable failure pervades the social mobility element of the fantasy too, for the bitter irony of Brownfield's American daydream is immediately and painfully obvious. Here we are reminded of an earlier vivid scene involving Brownfield as a small child, left alone in the yard while his parents are out to work:

> When he was four he was covered with sores. Tetter sores covered his head, eating out his hair in patches the size of quarters. Tomato sores covered his legs up to the knee – when the tomatoes in his mother's garden were ripe he ate nothing but tomatoes all day long – and pus ran from boils that burst under his armpits. (7)

However many critics have read *The Third Life, of Grange Copeland* as a womanist text that is *really* about the victimisation of Margaret and Mem, somehow the image of Brownfield sucking on a sugar-tit while the flies buzz around his face haunts the novel. His ultimate fate – debased and deserved as it is by the time Grange comes to shoot him like a rabid dog – returns to, or perhaps remains sealed in, this early moment of abuse and neglect. As Robert Butler writes, Brownfield 'is gradually victimized by a uniquely Southern system of segregation and sharecropping which infects his life. He eventually becomes exactly what his social environment wants him to be – an extension of its most pathological impulses'.[35]

Contrast the image of Brownfield on the porch steps with the Swiss psychoanalyst Alice Miller's depiction of a small child's needs in her book *Banished Knowledge*: 'A baby requires the certainty that he will be protected in every situation, that his arrival is desired, that his cries are heard', and if this doesn't happen what results is 'an interference with his ability to feel, to be aware, and to remember', no less.[36] Miller has made it her life's work to criticise and reconstruct Western child-rearing practices which, in their emphasis on harnessing the child's needs to society's (and parents') desire for discipline and order, inflict – as she sees it – an habitual form of violence on children. It is clear that the family into which Brownfield Copeland is born falls far, far short of Miller's ideal. This is in large part due to the Copelands' sharecropping existence, which demands the labour of all family members around the clock; Brownfield himself is sent into the fields at the age of six. Proper parenting, in other words, is a luxury the Copelands cannot afford. Because Brownfield never experiences it, he grows up with precisely that inability 'to feel, to be aware, and to remember' that Alice Miller talks about, and this turns him into a cruel husband and father by the time Mem, Daphne, Ornette, and Ruth come along. External causes of poverty and exploitation are thus transmuted into internal causes of aggression and (self-)hatred, and in this way Brownfield's daydream and his early abandonment present a case study, not so much of individual pathology, but of *institutionalised and systemic* violence and abuse. These scenes memorably work on the reader to reveal the impossibility, the inconceivability of the 'successful' (by white, middle-class standards) black family in the South before the Civil Rights era.[37] Brownfield's fantasy is a white fantasy, then, not just a fantasy of being white but a fantasy generated by a white world. It takes over his life, insofar as he is destined to live out his Oedipal fixation on the father, here figured as both a literal father (Grange) and the white father/authority figure/personification of the law in Southern race relations (Captain Davis, J. L., and Judge Harry).[38]

In *Black Skin, White Masks* Frantz Fanon writes that Oedipal neurosis is not the universal phenomenon that white psychoanalysts have made it out to be, but that neuroses are generated by the particular cultural situation in which a person finds him- or herself, notably that of a black person in a white world.[39] Again, Brownfield's plight illustrates this. He is possessed throughout his fictional life by the twin desires of hurting or destroying his father and seeking his mother – even after her death. He does not find her in other women, whom he therefore wants to destroy: instead of mother he finds Josie, his father's erstwhile lover and later wife; instead of mother he finds Josie's niece Mem, whom he kills. This particular Oedipus, then, persists in his revenge fantasy, replacing Grange as a figure of failed authority with various incarnations of the father 'of better birth', that is: the white men Mr Shipley, Captain Davis, Mr J. L., and later Judge Harry. This revenge fails, however, for two good reasons, and this is where Walker critically revises Freud's not-so-universal scenario. First of all it fails because Brownfield's Oedipal battle is not the war, and the ultimate cause of his misery lies not in his relationship with his parents, but in the wider social environment in which he grows up, which is in turn the product of Southern history, and particularly of slavery. Unlike Grange, Brownfield does not have the psychological and historical understanding to confront that legacy within himself; unlike Ruth and the Civil Rights workers he also lacks the political tools to even conceive of taking it on in the outside world. Second, Brownfield fails to resolve his Oedipal fixation because Grange – paradoxically – is not a father to him except in the most narrow biological sense. Even when Brownfield is still very little Grange 'cannot bear to touch him with his hand'; neither then nor later will Grange recognise him, or speak to him, let alone function as a figure of manly identification for Brownfield (21). Recognition is something that Brownfield yearns for, and – not having had it from his father – he mistakenly seeks patronage from Judge Harry towards the end of the novel, invoking the fact that they knew each other as children (222). The absence of father as role model is paralleled by the fact that Brownfield grows up without any male examples of respect for his mother, and thus for women in general. This is what he observes about Grange and Margaret's marriage, when he is ten years old: 'He thought his mother was like their dog in some ways. She didn't have a thing to say that did not in some way show submission to his father' (5). Clearly Brownfield here articulates a feminist insight on Walker's behalf; his perception of his mother's subordinate position implies a critique of the idea that the redemption of black masculinity should lie in some version of black patriarchal authority – as proposed by black nationalism and by the Moynihan Report of the 1960s, as we have seen. Instead, Walker shows how the domination of black women by black men within the family is part of the problem, not the solution, because it is merely a link in a longer chain of mastery and subordination. This becomes clear when Brownfield witnesses for the first time his father's submission to 'the man who drove the truck', the white man, Mr Shipley:

'Say "Yessir" to Mr Shipley', […]
    Brownfield, trembling, said 'Yessir', filled with terror of this man who could, by his presence alone, turn his father into something that might as well have been a pebble or a post or a piece of dirt. (9)

Black children in a racist society such as that of the American South between the wars do not grow up with an archetypally strong image of father as patriarch, and are only too aware of the power of class and race in holding them back from the American aspirations that the dominant culture at the same time bombards them with. We are drawn back once more to Fanon, who counterposes the Oedipal myth with what he calls the Negro myth: that of racial inferiority. Fanon writes: 'The Negro is unaware of it as long as his existence is limited to his own environment; but the first encounter with a white man oppresses him with the whole weight of his blackness'.[40] This is what happens to Brownfield when he first meets Shipley. Racism cannot be reduced to class relations: the power of white people to hire and fire, to humiliate and hurt, to violate black women and vitiate the lives of black men, and act as judge and jury to the violence that results, is specific to the Jim Crow South in which *The Third Life of Grange Copeland* is set. Racism and poverty, or more specifically the inequities of the sharecropping system, ring-fence Brownfield Copeland's one life and all the people who figure in it, except for Ruth.

Brownfield's Oedipal trajectory then runs along different lines from that of the classic Freudian account. Psychoanalysis (here Oedipus and the family romance) does not reveal 'the truth' about Brownfield's condition, but it provides useful grounds for comparison between types of cultural stories by which we understand ourselves and the world, including the world of fiction. In reading Brownfield's daydream as a case history, I am not analysing *him*, let alone his author, but the psychic script of cultural violence that Walker presents. Linda Ruth Williams puts it succinctly: 'It is not that the analysand makes up the stories of [his] early life but that the stories have *made up* [him]. The subject is a creation *of* the story' (original emphasis).[41] In *The Third Life of Grange Copeland* we can see what the culture does to a child when the only available stories make him up in such a way that he can have no place in them. The question then remains whether it is true that a person's fate, a culture's development, is *determined* by stories generated to keep the powerful in power, and the others out. The text's answer in the end is clearly 'no', but it would be useful to trace how it gets there. The striking contrast between the early part of the novel, in which the reader's sympathy for Brownfield is engaged in no uncertain terms, and his later development, which is one of increasing depravity and violence, is relevant here. It would be wrong simply to put Brownfield's pathology down to his social position as a black man in white society – clearly the novel has something much more complex to say about him than that. Conversely, it would be wrong to attribute his violence and suffering solely to arrested development, or to his unsuccessful negotiation of his Oedipal relationship with Grange. Both the psychoanalytic and the political explanations for Brownfield's fate, which the text on one hand invites, are deterministic narratives of subject formation that it ultimately *refuses*. They explain why Brownfield is as he is, but they are not – for the novel – excuses. Instead, Walker makes a Utopian jump to Grange, and creates an epistemological break in the narrative of Brownfield's victimisation which moves from pity to condemnation, after which individual responsibility and social change are posited as the only hope for personal and political change. Because this hope is personified in Grange and Ruth, we have to turn back to the question of how personal and public histories intersect, and look at the way in which Grange Copeland's three lives unfold in parallel with slavery, modernity and the Civil Rights era.

THE THREE LIVES OF GRANGE COPELAND: FROM SLAVERY AND SHARECROPPING TO BLACK NATIONALISM AND CIVIL RIGHTS

In *No Crystal Stair: Visions of Race and Sex in Black Women's Fiction*, Gloria Wade-Gayles describes Alice Walker's first novel as 'a southern work of art', not only because of its setting in America's deep South, but also because of the insularity and violence of its black characters.[42] While the story of Grange Copeland's first and second lives takes place some sixty years after emancipation (roughly between 1920 and 1940), it is clear that slavery casts its shadow long and wide into the twentieth century, both psychologically and in economic terms. This narrative, in effect, re-enacts at an individual level what slavery and reconstruction represent in collective history. When, at four years old, Ruth Copeland says to her father: 'you nothing but a sonnabit', she speaks the truth about Brownfield in a way that perhaps only she, in her childlike innocence, can (108). Because *as* a 'sonnabit' Brownfield is named, not as the son-of-a-bitch of contemporary parlance, but as the son of the bit that slaves were forced to wear, the slave who is Grange in his first life.

In this first life, narrated in only twenty pages of the novel, the sharecropper Grange Copeland is to all intents and purposes still enslaved by the white man, Shipley, who keeps him from being able to provide for his wife and family and robs him of his dignity. In sharecropping, the farmworker is paid for his labour in kind: he gets a predetermined share of the crop at the end of the growing season. However, if the crop fails or its market price drops, he may not be able to pay his debt to the landowner for his keep and the materials needed to farm the land, and so he will have to work even harder the next season. In this cycle of debt and dependency, the landowner, as Richard Godden explains, 'exerts an absolute authority over the labourer', just like the master does over his slave.[43] References to slavery are frequent and explicit in the early part of the novel. For example, after Grange has run away, Brownfield sees Shipley turning up at Margaret's funeral, hoping to 'catch Grange' like any slave-owner would in order to recover his property. But such figurations of slavery go further than just labour relations. Just as Shipley seems to own his father, young Brownfield assumes that Grange, in turn, owns his mother (22). Unable to understand his family's poverty by comparison with the wealth of his Northern cousins, he fantasises that 'Maybe he [Grange] had tried to sell her and she wouldn't be sold – which could be why they were still poor and in debt and would die that way' (11).

Brownfield's childlike mind both understands and misunderstands his parents' marriage as another incarnation of the relationship between slave and master. He has certainly caught on to Shipley's command not just of Grange's labour, but also of Margaret's sexual services, and he 'knows' about the money that she could make from white men as a prostitute. Unlike Grange, who in leaving his wife and children at least liberates himself, Brownfield internalises the violence done to him, exchanging one white master for another, and retaining his view of women (and children) as property to be acquired and dispensed with as it suits him. He repeats the sins of his father both with Josie and with Mem, on whom he is economically and emotionally dependent without wanting to recognise it. Brownfield's world never gets bigger than the porch steps: even after his marriage to Mem, when their circumstances improve and he has gained, through *her* efforts, literacy, decent housing and employment in the city, he persists in his definition of manhood as the power to dominate and enslave women. And Brownfield goes to court to get Ruth back, 'not because he wanted her, but because he didn't want Grange to have her' (227). It is then Brownfield who lives out, in effect, the first life of Grange Copeland after Grange has abandoned it. His *need* for the white men to recognise him keeps him firmly bound within the master/slave dialectic, Hegel's terms for understanding the psychic machinations of power and subordination to it.

In the 1987 'Afterword' to the novel Alice Walker states that she wants the reader to see the connection between the oppression of black women and children on one hand, and the oppression of African Americans as a people on the other.[44] This political insight is personified in Brownfield as a slave, living Grange's first life. Yet the overall message of the novel is a different one and marks the contrast between Brownfield, the bad father, and Grange, the absent one, because the latter mends his ways while the former cannot. In his second life Grange comes into contact with different stories and different histories that lead him to a new conception of himself, the race, and American society as a whole. Brownfield never gets the benefit of his father's re-education, which is also a personal *reconstruction*, but Ruth does, and it is she who gives Grange his third life, in which he has to learn still more.

As the title of the novel indicates, this third life matters most, because only then does Grange come into his own, gaining a real presence in the text. Before that, Brownfield dominates the textual space of his first life and Mem that of his second. It is she who, like Grange, tries to move out of the condition of virtual slavery into a modernity that is figured as migration to the city, waged labour, and improved material circumstances. Having moved her family to a house in the city in a bid to save them herself if Brownfield cannot, Mem wants to turn Brownfield's dream of a car, a house, and a devoted wife and children into reality. Enthralled by the Sears Roebuck catalogue, Mem dreams of shiny indoor toilets and a 'deep white bathtub with greenish blue water' (80–1). Her legitimate aspirations for decent housing and material comfort then chart the historical transition from an agricultural economy to consumer capitalism in the South of the 1920s and '30s, but even this modest American dream does not last very long. With the changing economic fortunes of Brownfield's family, Walker makes the point that modernity and progress are not necessarily the same thing; the Copelands' initial upward mobility proves fragile due to fluctuations in the labour market of which they are the first casualties. Brownfield, who cannot abide Mem's determination to take advantage of the economic opportunities that the city affords her as an educated black woman, sabotages their advancement and decides that they should go back to the country. 'Moving to Mr J. L.'s place' means, in effect, moving back to sharecropping and slavery, to an earlier stage of economic development. Mem does not take this regression lying down and, in a scene reminiscent of Janie's 'cussing out' of Joe Starks in Zora Neale Hurston's novel *Their Eyes Were Watching God*, she turns the gun on Brownfield. But, as Amanda Davis points out, 'Through Brownfield's continuous threats ("You say one more word, just one more little goddamn peep and I'll cut your goddam throat") Mem's voice, like her body, is subject to constant regulation'.[45] Unable to pull the trigger, she eventually succumbs to Brownfield's ploy to subjugate her. Upward mobility for Mem, unlike Janie, cannot be sustained in a sex/class/race system that assigns black women the role of 'mule of the world', to use Zora Neale Hurston's words. Mem's period of 'reconstruction' in the city is thus short-lived; defeated, she burns her books, and with them her dreams.

Grange Copeland's sojourn in the North ends similarly in a return to the rural South, but for different reasons and with a different outcome. For him, migration is an education in the discourses of resistance to racism but also a confrontation with its entrenchment in the *de facto* segregation of the North. Like the brief period of Reconstruction after the Civil War, Grange's flight to New York does not deliver what it promised. 'He had come North expecting those streets paved with that gold', but the only way he can make a living is as a hustler, selling bootleg whisky, drugs, and black women to white men (144). Grange Copeland gains the political insight in New York that there is no such thing as the Promised Land.[46] After he has 'murdered' the white woman in the park by letting her drown, he experiences a change in himself that leads him to hate white people. This change is articulated in terms highly reminiscent of two classics of African American literature, Richard Wright's *Native Son* and Ralph Elison's *Invisible Man*. In the latter, the nameless protagonist feels himself to be invisible in Harlem just as Grange Copeland does: 'The North put him in solitary confinement where he had to manufacture his own hostile stares in order to see himself. For why were they pretending he was not there?' (145). And like Bigger Thomas in *Native Son*, he feels that murder liberates him: 'He believed that, against his will, he had stumbled on the necessary act that black men must commit to regain, or to manufacture their manhood, their self-respect. They must kill their oppressors' (153).

As a result of this realisation, Grange then starts to preach his gospel of hate on the streets of Harlem and adopts a separatist philosophy that in part echoes the ideas of another major figure in African

American history, Marcus Garvey. Like Garvey, Grange concludes that the only promised land was the 'forty acres and a mule' of Reconstruction which should have enabled former slaves to become economically independent. But his calling white people 'blue-eyed devils' chimes with Malcolm X's black nationalist rhetoric of the 1960s too, and in many ways Grange's separatist philosophy and his hatred of whites evoke the image of the Black Panthers, who with their militant appearance probably posed the strongest challenge to white constructions of African American masculinity.

Unlike Garvey and Malcolm X, however, who advocated emigration to Africa or the formation of a black nation within the US, Grange returns to the segregated South. With the money he has earned and robbed in New York (and from Josie) he buys a farm and land to realise his dream of self-sufficiency; the fence he builds with Ruth's help functions metaphorically and literally to create an all-black domestic space in which he can raise Ruth and teach her black folklore and history.[47] Ruth's education is, in other words, a lesson in black nationalism, instilling kinship with Africans and other non-white peoples of the world – just as Garvey in the 1920s and Malcolm X in the 1960s preached that African Americans should educate themselves, rather than rely on a formal education that had no place for them. As Ruth realises, however, in liberating himself from his first life as a slave, Grange in his second life has become imprisoned in his righteous hatred of whites. As Kate Cochran astutely observes, 'Oftentimes what Grange thinks he is teaching Ruth contrasts with what Ruth learns'.[48] True freedom, for Ruth, comes about through the non-violence and forgiveness brought to their doorstep by the Civil Rights workers, whom Grange grudgingly learns to admire but cannot bring himself to join.

Grange Copeland's second life in New York and Mem's brief sojourn as a city dweller connect with a wider historical narrative insofar as they are representations of the Great Migration, the African American mass exodus from the South to the industrialised North after the First World War. As precarious moves into modernity, they break the insularity of rural existence that Gloria Wade-Gayles identified as typically Southern, but unlike the official version of history, progress – like storytelling – is not linear for Walker but a movement of back and forth and around. *The Third Life of Grange Copeland* is an historical novel in this didactic and transformational sense. As Melissa Walker has noted, it does not follow a rigid chronology of twentieth-century African American history – from post-Reconstruction Jim Crow via two world wars and the Depression through to Civil Rights – although the timespan of the novel suggests that. For her, this deviation from chronological order and lack of realist detail in *The Third Life of Grange Copeland* are critical shortcomings:

> In all but the final scenes of the novel, characters show no aware-ness that they might be affected by or affect history. Not one fights in World War I, participates in the Garvey movement, or loses property during the Depression. [...] For the first two-thirds of the novel, the characters have no public existence: no birth cer-tificates, no draft cards, no bank accounts.[49]

The accuracy of this criticism is debatable: Garvey is not explic-itly mentioned but the ideas are there, as we have seen, and the Copelands do not have any property to lose in the Depression. But, quite apart from this and the question of whether we have to care about characters' birth certificates, Alice Walker's view of history is rather more complex than Melissa Walker assumes it to be. Her conception of fiction, exemplified in this novel as in the later ones, is as a re-vision, reinterpretation, restructuring of official historiog-raphy. The Copelands' insularity, the fact that they know little of the issues that affected African Americans in the United States at large, let alone of world affairs during this period, is in my view best read as an aspect of this revision. Newspapers, in this novel, poignantly cover the walls of a draughty house or line the shoes of a murdered woman; the Copelands' ignorance of the wider world reflects their overall impoverishment and a psychic reality bent only on material survival. Mem exemplifies this. An educated woman and a teacher, Mem nonetheless relinquishes her vocation and burns her books when Brownfield decides to 'move back'; in the world of slavery on 'Mr J. L.'s place' she will have no use for them. More importantly, perhaps, the Copelands' isolation is also a deliberate abstraction from realist detail that enables Walker to zoom in on intra-familial dynamics. In this way, she shows that the oppressed, who do not get to write history, therefore remain invisible to it and in effect live out-side it (just as women for centuries were 'hidden from history' too). The purpose of Grange Copeland's third life is, then, to fulfil the promise of Reconstruction of a century before, and to reintegrate the public and private narratives of African American progress. That fulfilment necessitates a move back to the South and to the past, which has to be confronted before it can be redeemed. Again, we are reminded here of an African American classic: Jean Toomer's *Cane*, which, in the final section titled 'Kabnis', dramatises a similar necessity for the protagonist to return to the South in order to confront his history. Kabnis fails to do so, whereas Grange Copeland succeeds; just as Walker revises Richard Wright's existential stance on black manhood, so also does she revise Toomer's despondent image of a vanishing South whose history is too painful for a modern man to work through and then rise above.

By the time Grange returns from the North and begins his third life, the characters who hitherto have taken centre stage recede into the background. To Grange, Brownfield is already dead because he is determined to continue on his path of (self-)hatred and destruction, whereas Mem, having given up her dreams and surrendered her 'educated' speech, is dead to herself even before Brownfield murders her. The second half of the novel is then almost completely taken up with Ruth's education and the rehabilitation of Grange that it brings in its train. Walker's didacticism is here writ large, because the reader learns, along with Ruth, the lessons in African American history, folklore and the arts of everyday use (such as dancing and winemaking) that Grange chooses to teach her and that bring her into conflict with the official history she learns at school.

When Ruth is born the old man exclaims: ' "Lawd knows the *whole* business is something of a miraculous event. Out of all kinds of shit comes something clean, soft and sweet smellin" ', (71). From the beginning, Grange takes an interest in this child in a way he had never cared for his own, a bitter irony not lost on Brownfield: ' "If you think it so *sweet smellin'*, you *take* it," said Brownfield, seeing his baby with entirely different, unenchanted and closely economic eyes' (71). For Brownfield, Ruth represents yet another burden on a family already racked by the poverty he is unable to alleviate. And while the men fight over Ruth's crib, Mem lies silent, with the wind howling through the window, 'moving the newspapers under the bed' (71). Ruth's birth in poverty and strife nevertheless proves auspicious. Before Grange Copeland says it in so many words, this birth has been described, a few pages before, as 'miraculous' already, for Ruth 'had popped out by herself, without the help of any (wo)man's hand' (67). In the rest of the narrative, Ruth's independent existence, which remains innocent and ignorant of most, if not all, of the family's history of violence and oppression, enables Grange's transformation into a loving parent and guardian. Sheltered from the 'closely economic eyes' of the white world, which has claimed Brownfield's soul and Grange's first and second lives, Ruth grows up to be a woman who is equipped to oppose depression and destruction within and without. As Peter Erickson points out, the relationship between Ruth and Grange is a 'mutually redemptive' one, reminiscent of Walker's short story 'A Sudden Trip Home in the Spring', which is also about a young woman and her love for her grandfather.[50] Ruth's upbringing by the transformed Grange Copeland is completed when, in the final pages, she can teach *him* a lesson in political philosophy: '"If you fight", she said, placing soft black fingers on Grange's arm, "if you fight with all you got, you don't have to *be* bitter"' (242). In *Possessing the Secret of Joy* this same insight is expressed in even stronger terms: resistance is the secret of joy. Without it, oppression leads to the kind of bitter resignation and depravity Brownfield is reduced to, or to depression and suicide, as in Margaret's case. Resignation (compliance with the white order/Brownfield), resentment (black separatism/Grange) and resistance (Civil Rights/Ruth) are the three positions the characters are forced to take up when confronted with the 'changing same' of white racism in the American South. Mem briefly experiences the joy of resistance when she stands up to Brownfield, but Mem, like Margaret before her, is finally beaten down by her husband's hatred of himself and their family. The gun she had wielded against him is in the end turned on her to disastrous effect: violence, for women as for men, in the end begets more violence, and cannot produce liberation. The novel is dedicated to Walker's mother, who 'made a way out of no way' and the miraculous event of something good and whole being born out of all kinds of 'shit' is paradigmatic for all of Walker's work. In this, as well as many other ways, *The Third Life of Grange Copeland* prepares the ground for the later novels, essays, and short stories. The 'shit' of family history, domestic violence, poverty, and economic oppression which somehow gives birth to Ruth is parallelled by the 'shit' of Southern history, in which slavery and Jim Crow segregation give way to the Civil Rights Movement, apparently out of nowhere.

Is a 'miracle' good enough to explain such a major historical shift? Here the connection between domestic and collective African American histories is more muted, although it is possible to draw parallels between the personal transformation, the reconstruction Grange achieves after he returns from the North, and the development of the Civil Rights movement in the South. In this sense

I think *The Third Life of Grange Copeland* can, at a stretch, be read as a *Bildungsroman* about Grange, not Ruth as Madhu Dubey sees it. There is little support in the novel for Dubey's argument that '*The Third Life* unquestioningly employs the *Bildungsroman* to map Ruth's movement towards maturity, a linear process that culminates in Ruth's enlistment into the regimes of heterosexuality and reproduction', if only because Ruth never gets that far in her fictional life.[51] Yet Grange's development does evidence something of a critical rewrite of what it means to grow up into responsible adulthood. Raising Ruth is for Grange also an act of love, and a process of atonement, a way of making a 'no count' life count, and count for two, and so despite his separatist leanings his third life has a redemptive quality that is certainly akin to the spirit of the Civil Rights movement. Sandi Russell echoes this view of Grange and Ruth's relationship as one that redeems the past. She reads the novel as a story of 'regeneration' in which the African American family stands for the 'global family', and the relationship between men and women is conceived as the 'basis for the transformation of society' with self-love as a necessary – but not sufficient – condition.[52]

But in the end even Grange, 'the beautiful old man', as Alice Walker calls him in her 'Afterword', cannot save himself from his violent past. In killing Brownfield Grange commits a necessary act of murder in order to seal Ruth's fate, that is to free her from the vicious cycle of familial violence. Grange's own death becomes a sacrifice to Ruth as the embodiment of a healing and non-violent future. With Brownfield and Grange, resignation and resentment are buried, and with the arrival of the Civil Rights workers active resistance is born.

The Third Life of Grange Copeland then is a realist novel, but not in Melissa Walker's narrow, empirical sense of faithfully depicting the way it was for African Americans in the South during the first six decades of the twentieth century. What we have instead is a fissured text that explores the development of the African American family *from within* as an alternative, domestic history to be read against the historiography of African American public life. 'In Europe as in every country characterized as civilized or civilizing', wrote Frantz Fanon, 'the family is a miniature of the nation'.[53] Walker's Copelands can, as such, be read not only as a microcosmic representation of the history of African Americans but of America as a whole, and it is, then, a history of violence and oppression that is passed down a chain of racial, class, and gender supremacies from which education and the entry into modernity can provide only a partial release. Ultimately that history can be redeemed by the 'miracle' of individual transcendence and collective action, but also – and crucially – *by writing*. As we have seen, Walker's narrative draws on and revises several other narratives of the (African American) family and the formation of (black) subjecthood, notably that of masculinity. The Copeland saga, as an alternative domestic history, is at odds with official historiography, the Moynihan report, the Oedipal story, and also with fictional representations of black male emancipation in Richard Wright's *Native Son*, Jean Toomer's *Cane*, and Ralph Ellison's *Invisible Man*. It revises Lorraine Hansberry's fantasy script of black social mobility in *A Raisin in the Sun*. Whatever its technical flaws, Walker's first novel is less simple and straightforward than it might at first appear, and in its ambition to 'talk back' to the tradition *The Third Life of Grange Copeland* sets the agenda for Walker's later work. *Meridian*, the second novel, takes up the Civil Rights theme where it was left with Ruth; Mem and Margaret are revived and rehabilitated in the figure of Celie in *The Color Purple*; and Grange Copeland's history teaching is echoed in Suwelo, who – like Grange – also learns a spiritual lesson in *The Temple of My Familiar*. The theme of child abuse, furthermore, is treated with a different inflection and in a different cultural setting in *Possessing the Secret of Joy*, which takes clitoridectomy as its subject. Fragmented and episodic storytelling, likewise, remains a hallmark of Walker's fiction and becomes a strength in the broken-up form of *Meridian* and the epistolary organisation of *The Color Purple*, rather than the structural weakness it is in *The Third Life of Grange Copeland*. Personal transformation, finally, is at the heart of every Alice Walker novel, and in that sense Grange Copeland's third life is only the first of many reincarnations to come.

3
Meridian (1976)

As if to take up where *The Third Life of Grange Copeland* left off, with Ruth on the threshold of a new life with the Civil Rights movement, Walker's second novel is all about a young African American woman's activism in the deep South of the 1960s. It revisits the question Alice Walker asked in her earlier essay 'The Civil Rights Movement: What Good Was It?' by exploring the case of the eponymous Meridian, whose life as a young, black, unhappily married woman with a baby in a small Southern town, is turned upside down by the arrival of voter-registration activists, and then transformed beyond recognition.[1] Among those activists is Truman who, with the charm of his conviction that political change is necessary and possible, draws Meridian into the movement. She leaves her husband and gives up her child, distances herself from her devout Christian mother, and dedicates her life to activism. As a result of her involvement with Civil Rights she is given the opportunity to go to Saxon College in Atlanta on a scholarship provided by wealthy white Northern sympathisers, and takes it. She finds the college environment, designed to make young black women into ladies 'chaste and pure as the driven snow', stifling and hypocritical, however (89).[2] An unwanted pregnancy that ends in abortion clinches her decision to return to the Civil Rights movement and the real world of Southern race relations.

When Truman deserts Meridian for a white Northern woman, Lynne, sexual politics and the integrationist ethos of the Civil Rights movement come into conflict with each other. Meridian is baffled by Truman's choice of a white woman for his new lover, but continues to work in the South. Meanwhile Truman, and also Meridian's college friend Anne-Marion, abandon non-violent activism and become militant black nationalists in New York – at least in theory. Truman's interracial union with Lynne does not square easily with his newfound nationalism, and eventually he and Lynne return to the South and separate after the murder of their daughter Camara. Other deaths in the movement take their toll on Meridian, too: she loses weight, her hair falls out and she is prone to fainting spells, especially after protest actions in which she finds herself increasingly alone. Anne-Marion tells her that she is carrying on a form of action that has long since become outdated: 'Meridian ... like the idea of suffering itself, you have become obsolete', she proclaims (124). Battle fatigue and increasing isolation force Meridian to reconsider what she is doing; in answer to Anne-Marion's (nationalist) question whether she will 'kill for the revolution', she now concludes that perhaps killing is permissible in self defence. At the same time, Meridian also has to reconsider her relationships with Truman and Lynne, both of whom turn to her for help and guidance after their separation and the loss of their child. Through witnessing the sexual humiliations Lynne is forced to undergo at the hands of battle-scarred black men, who take their anger out on her, Meridian becomes aware of sexual as well as racial oppression, and this enables her to be more sympathetic to Lynne. Truman, meanwhile, realises the error of his black nationalist and sexist ways and takes up Meridian's place in grassroots community work at the end of the novel.

What good the Civil Rights movement did, then, is represented here as a matter of personal as well as political transformation; the movement exposed rifts between black and white and between men and women, which only an integration of its commitment to non-violence with a feminist analysis of sexual politics – *when really lived through* – could heal. Put like this, it is clear that Walker in this novel retraces the steps that led real-life female Civil Rights activists to feminism, and that she affirms the movement's integrationist stance despite – or perhaps because of – the problems that interracial activism entailed.[3]

The experience of reading *Meridian*, however, is very different from the linear trajectory that I have just sketched out and that, in many ways, does violence to the novel's aesthetic achievement. Leigh Anne Duck designates *Meridian* an 'experimental novel ... inconsistent with the literature of social movements'.[4] This is an interesting observation because African American and 'ethnic' writing are rarely seen as 'experimental', not because they do not exemplify innovative formal features, but rather because critics tend to read them for social, political, and historical content, while paying little attention to form. Yet *Meridian*'s broken up, episodic, fragmented, and fragment*ing* form cannot be ignored. What, then, is that reading experience like, and what does Walker achieve by putting the reader through the hoops and loops of its complicated narrative structure?

In 1984 the writer and critic David Bradley published a long article about Walker in *New York Times Magazine,* in which he stated that
he had been 'terribly disappointed with "Meridian"':

> In this I was, to all appearances, alone. 'Meridian' had been
> touted by *Newsweek* as 'ruthless and tender', by *Ms.* as 'a classic
> novel of both feminism and the civil rights movement', and by
> The *New York Times Book Review* as 'a fine, taut novel that ... goes
> down like clear water.' But to me it seemed far more elliptical and
> episodic (three parts, 34 chapters) than her first novel, without
> having that novel's warmth and simplicity. The title character,
> an itinerant civil-rights worker, seems less pacifist than passive
> [*sic*].[5]

It was inevitable that critics like Bradley would draw comparisons
between *The Third Life of Grange Copeland* and *Meridian* and find
either the one or the other wanting, since they appear to be so different. In contrast with the first novel, *Meridian's* broken-up form
makes for a startling and – apparently – deliberately disorienting
reading experience, and this obviously irritated Bradley. That he
found the main character 'passive' – which, after all, is a strange
thing for a political activist to be – is also understandable, since the
portrayal of Meridian is closer to that of a martyr or a saint than to
the media images we have of 1960s Civil Rights workers, tirelessly
on the march or getting beaten up in sit-ins and bus boycotts. Yet
Bradley overlooked the continuities and similarities between the
two novels, which reveal themselves only on a closer reading. In
Meridian Walker shows, to begin with, a continuing engagement
with African American history from the inside, in the novel's exploration of a black woman's experience in the Civil Rights movement
'on the ground', that is: at the grassroots and beyond reach of the
media spotlights. This engagement with history goes deeper than
Meridian's personal development through the 1960s and 1970s,
because the narrative keeps dipping into other layers of history
through the interspersed stories of slavery, and the even earlier
presence of Native Americans in Mississippi. In this view of the
very recent and very distant past *Meridian* both takes up where *The
Third Life of Grange Copeland* left off and tells the latter's pre-history
in the mutilations and miscegenations of African American people
from the fifteenth to nineteenth centuries. Similar to *The Third Life of
Grange Copeland* also, *Meridian* has a tripartite structure that moves

from the South ('Meridian') to New York ('Truman Held') and back again ('Ending'); like Grange Copeland, Lynne, Meridian, and Truman discover that the scars of their time together in the South cannot heal until the original trauma is confronted by returning there. Part of that healing process is an integration of what we can recognise as feminist and black Civil Rights positions, an integration brought about by a Meridian who lives out Ruth Copeland's philosophy of resistance without resentment. More clearly than in the previous novel, Walker is concerned in *Meridian* to work through her relationship to (white) feminism and, as David Bradley also notes, this often takes the form of awkward dialogues in which opposing ideas are voiced by different characters and argued out. Whereas in *The Third Life of Grange Copeland* white people hardly ever get to speak – however importantly they figure as forces of oppression in the background – in *Meridian* the presence of Lynne forces Truman and Meridian to examine and re-examine their political positions in dialogue and through conflict with her. Walker's critique of black nationalism, already present in *The Third Life of Grange Copeland* and in short stories like 'Roselily' and 'Everyday Use', continues here, and Truman's art in painting black women as 'magnificent giants, breeding forth the warriors of the new universe' is satirised, if not ridiculed, through Lynne's weary eyes (170). Lynne herself, in turn, changes from a naive idealist who romanticises black people and the South into a kindred spirit who, after relinquishing her white, middle-class privilege, experiences the cost of resistance and comes to a more realistic appraisal of black people's human flaws as well as her own. Integration, as a political goal of the Civil Rights movement, does not simply mean love and forgiveness, let alone a one-way adaptation to white standards of behaviour and achievement in *Meridian*, but is tentatively posited as a process of struggle and suffering for 'black and white together' and for men and women together. The personal and political are thus intimately bound up with each other.

If *Meridian* is understood like this, Bradley's critique of it can be countered in two ways: what he calls Meridian's 'passivity' can conversely be seen as a mode of action, in the sense that she acts as a catalyst for those around her; she leads by example rather than exhortation or authority. And the question of whether *Meridian* is a novel at all, implicitly posed by Bradley, can be answered positively, for the realist story of Meridian and Truman and Lynne is *meaningfully* interrupted by myths, anecdotes, parables, and asides that have a bearing upon the protagonists' gradual self-enlightenment about their place in history.

In contrast with *The Third Life of Grange Copeland*, Walker's mastery of the short form is allowed to shine here in a way that it could not before. Walker explained in an interview with Claudia Tate that she wanted *Meridian* to be like a crazy quilt, similar to the collages that the African American painter Romare Bearden made, or like the patterning of Jean Toomer's *Cane*, which is made up of portraits of Southern women, poems, worksongs, sketches, and a play.[6] Walker's comment on the quilt metaphor is illuminating:

> You know, there's a lot of difference between a crazy quilt and a patchwork quilt. [...] A crazy quilt ... only *looks* crazy. It is not 'patched'; it is planned. A patchwork quilt would perhaps be a good metaphor for capitalism; a crazy quilt is a metaphor for socialism. A crazy quilt story is one that can jump back and forth in time, work on many different levels, and one that can include myth. It is generally much more evocative of metaphor and symbolism than a novel that is chronological in structure, or one devoted, more or less, to rigorous realism, as is *The Third Life of Grange Copeland*.[7]

Meridian certainly is evocative and, like the crazy quilt and Meridian herself, '*looks* crazy' but is, in fact, purposeful. Yet the plan is by no means obvious, and my attempt here to draw out a covert pattern from the overt craziness and a politics of form from the apparent formlessness, is only one of many possibilities. In 'Art, Action and the Ancestors: Alice Walker's *Meridian* in Its Context', Christine Hall makes a link between the reader 'as the active maker of meanings' and 'Meridian's own search for an interpretation which will make sense in and of her life'.[8] *Meridian*'s 'craziness' is, as Walker and Hall both indicate, self-consciously polysemous and every reader, in every reading of the text, will have to do his or her own work in stitching a meaning together out of disparate bits. I begin my handiwork with Anne-Marion's question whether 'killing for the revolution' is justified, a question that will lead us, first of all, into a Southern black church and to the ganglands of LA, unexpected as this may seem. It is because the question of revolutionary killing frames the novel's political and spiritual concerns that I want to use it as a kind of vignette for contemporary times as much as the 1960s, when the Black Panthers first voiced it.

GANGSTAS AND ANGELS: AFRICAN AMERICAN MUSIC AND POLITICS IN THE 1960S AND TODAY

The setting is New York, some time in the mid-1960s, and a group of political activists are engaged in a planning and consciousness-raising meeting. Meridian's friend, Anne-Marion, has pledged her commitment to the revolution by stating that she is prepared to kill for it, but Meridian is as usual engaged in remembrance of things past:

> Meridian was holding on to something the others had let go. [...] what none of them seemed to understand was that she felt herself to be, not holding on to something from the past, but *held* by something in the past: by the memory of old black men in the South who, caught by surprise in the eye of a camera, never shifted their position but looked directly back; by the sight of young girls singing in a country choir, their hair shining with brushings and grease, their voices the voices of angels. [...] If they committed murder – and to her even revolutionary murder was murder – *what would the music be like*? (15) (original emphasis)

Several critics cite this passage, highlighting the importance of music as a motif in the novel and stressing its resonance with African American cultural tradition, of which music is arguably the major form.[9] No one has taken the question of what the music of revolutionary murder would be like as more than merely rhetorical however, and yet reading *Meridian* some thirty or forty years later we know what that music sounds like because it exists: in gangsta rap, the music of the urban ghettoes of New York, Los Angeles, or Chicago's South Side. This is a music that, in bell hooks' words, glorifies 'sexist, misogynist, patriarchal ways of thinking and behaving' and it is successful because, not in spite of these characteristics.[10] As early as 1988, Maya Angelou characterised rap in general as 'unpoetic', merely 'the cheapest way out of saying something about the street', and she laid the blame for this 'literary laziness' at the door of established black (nationalist) writers of the 1960s who 'told any Black person that if you're Black you can write poetry'.[11] In the debate around gangsta rap, therefore, more is at stake than just misogyny or violence; there is also a division – exemplified here – between black high and popular culture that articulates political differences. If we are to understand Walker's project in *Meridian*, then I think the question 'what would the music be like?'

deserves to be addressed because it presupposes, after all, a diagnostic connection between cultural expression and the health of the body politic that is akin to hooks' and Angelou's views on black popular music.

Meridian is *held* by the past in a specific personal and in a very general sense, because she is the product not just of her parents' upbringing, but also of America's colonising history.[12] Throughout the novel, the question of violence in its multifarious forms is explored in her individual past and in the history of the nation. The issue of killing for the revolution thus brings a host of others in its train, all connected to the theme of violence and the question of whether ends justify means. Slavery and the conquest of Native American lands – both, according to the history books, essential to the historical identity of the South and of the US as a whole – are recalled in the novel as part of a repetitive cycle of violence, supposedly justified in official historiography by the revolutionary project of nation building. Rape, harassment, reproductive control, and enforced childbearing are also constituted in the novel as forms of violence, legitimised in various political discourses (including white feminism and black nationalism) as mere means towards greater, liberatory, and revolutionary ends. Meridian's abortion and subsequent sterilisation, for example, bring on an acute psychological crisis that has everything to do with Meridian's awareness that her mother and previous generations of African American women 'had not lived in an age of choice' (123). The demand for reproductive control, in white feminism seen as a means to achieve women's liberation, is not enough of a justification for Meridian, who is mindful of white women's historical role in 'controlling' the reproduction of black women. Neither is Tommy Odds' rape of Lynne justified, in her view, by the black man's need to liberate himself from white oppression by taking revenge upon white women. In both cases, *Meridian* poses no either/or solution but a series of questions that contextualise political and ethical dilemmas in concrete circumstances, aware of historical difference but also of the destructive force that *any* kind of violence exerts – on perpetrators and victims alike. Anne-Marion's question to Meridian, whether she is prepared to 'kill for the revolution', is therefore not rhetorical, but a question that is already determined, or perhaps overdetermined, by American history (killing Indians for the revolution) and more particularly that of African American women (who could or could not keep their babies, depending on the nation's needs).

Meridian, like Walker's previous novel, engages in the working-through of such big historical and ethical questions about ends and means, but unlike the occasionally intrusive narrator in *The Third Life of Grange Copeland* this novel lacks a narrative voice telling us what to think, even if Meridian herself is obviously invested with a moral authority that is hard to refuse. John F. Callahan relates this structural and political openness of *Meridian* to Walker's refusal to be a traditional storyteller: 'Walker', he says, 'like Meridian, invites "the rest of them" (and us) to participate in a generation's unfinished personal and political work'.[13] Attuned to the sounds of her age, of the Civil Rights movement and the more distant past, Meridian finds her own voice only after her journey of self-exploration is completed, in which actions (and her body) speak louder than words. Then she vows to mop up the blood behind the 'real' revolutionaries, but also to

... come forward and sing from memory songs they will need once more to hear. For it is the song of the people, transformed by the experience of each generation, that holds them together and if any part of it is lost the people suffer and are without soul. (205–6)

These songs 'from memory' are not just the famous Civil Rights songs such as 'We Shall Overcome' and 'This Little Light of Mine', but also the older spirituals that date back to slavery. Meridian's music, the music of the choir-girls and the black church, is gospel music. The black Southern church has always drawn upon slavery in its interpretations of biblical teaching, and gospel music reflects that legacy still. One of Howell Raines's informants in *My Soul is Rested*, an oral history of the Civil Rights movement, describes the black church as a brand of Christianity that

... has always seen God as being identified with the downcast and the suffering. Jesus' first text he used when he preached his first sermon was taken from Isaiah, which is 'The Lord has anointed me to preach the gospel to the poor, to deliver the oppressed, to free the captive ...'[14]

This Christianity is a far cry from Meridian's mother's authoritarian (and 'whitified') faith, typified by her statement that 'All He asks is that we acknowledge him as our Master' (16). God as 'our Master' has, of course, deliberate overtones of slavery, and the notion of having any kind of duty to any kind of master is challenged by the end of *Meridian* and rejected altogether in *The Color Purple*. Unlike the 'white' church music that accompanies this authoritarian Christianity, gospel music is not a form of high culture designed to inspire fear and awe in the presence of God, but a mode of creating the Beloved Community by means of active participation. And unlike the blues, the 'devil's music' that is so central to *The Color Purple*, gospel is not merely *of* this world but *for* this world: it is not so much, or not only, a matter of ends (salvation, freedom) but equally of means: creating a community of spirit. The Civil Rights activist and womanist musician Bernice Johnson Reagon remembers how Fannie Lou Hamer, fellow activist and songleader in the movement during the 1960s, could transform a mass meeting into a 'community of singing'.[15] For Hamer, for Reagon and for the Civil Rights movement as a whole, communal singing had a ritualistic and redeeming function, creating a sense of strength, resolve and resistance all at once. James Farmer recounts, for example, how communal singing became a mode of resistance in prison, when Civil Rights workers would drive their jailers to distraction with their freedom songs.[16] And Reagon explains:

> There is something I feel when sound runs through my body. I cannot sing without experiencing a change in my mood, a change in the way I feel. In the African-American culture, that is a major function of singing. [...] the aim is to be sure that whatever shape you were in before you started to produce this sound is transformed when the singing is over.[17]

But times have changed, and the singing *is* over. *Meridian's* rhetorical question – *what would the music be like?* – is answered today in a way that could not have been anticipated in the 1960s and 1970s. Perhaps it is significant that rap is not sung but spoken, that it is not the 'flight of doves' Meridian and Bernice Johnson Reagon hear in choir song, but the rhythmically punctuated rat-tat-tat of gunshots. Anne-Marion's infatuation with armed resistance, when she tries to get Meridian to pledge that she will 'kill for the revolution', is of a piece with the Black Panther thinking of the late 1960s, which has since fed into gangsta rap. Andrew Ross notes that 'just as the Black Panthers made theatrical appearances with guns in public, rap's romance with the gangsta has consciously tested the official taboo against images of armed black men (with the exception of black policemen)'.[18] For Meridian, however, there is no theatricality in that image. She considers, instead, its revolutionary reality: 'Would they ever be face to face with the enemy, guns drawn? Perhaps. Perhaps not. [...] the point was, she could not think lightly of shedding blood. And the question of killing did not impress her as rhetorical at all' (15). Both questions, then – the one about music and the one about killing – are serious, and both are explored rather than directly answered in the novel.

Re-entering a church after a long period of renunciation of Christianity and all it stands for, Meridian witnesses a memorial service for a 'martyred son' of the (armed) black struggle of the late 1960s. She finds that the church has changed; faced with the dead man's father, who is distraught and almost speechless with grief, the preacher gives a brief political sermon. Short on words, long on silent mourning, this service is one in which Meridian can feel free to contemplate the question of killing for the revolution once again. The stained-glass window of musician B. B. King, 'With Sword', sums up how the music has changed: it is electrified, infused with a righteous anger that enables her to believe, at last, that 'yes, indeed she *would* kill, before she allowed anyone to murder his son again' (204). The New Testament overtones of this last sentence, 'before she would allow anyone to murder his [God's] son [Jesus] again', are obvious, but there is a difference too, for this is a *real* father, no religious abstraction, and a *real* son who died 'for his talk alone (as far as his father knew, or believed, or wanted to know)', at the hands of the state (201). At this moment of enlightenment, then, Meridian realises that the question of killing for the revolution cannot always, unconditionally, be refused, if the effect of such refusal is that people *get* killed for what they believe. Unconditional non-violence is as much an abstraction as 'the revolution' or recognising 'God as your Master'; instead, Meridian concludes that 'the contemplation of murder required incredible delicacy as it required incredible spiritual work, and *the historical background and present setting must be right*' (205; my emphasis).

On the face of it, rap music that draws on the 1960s rhetoric of 'killing for the revolution' does not meet these conditions. Spiritual work, never mind historical background, seems diametrically opposed to the glorification of the 'killing for sport' that Brent Staples identifies in gangsta rap; bell hooks in turn criticises Staples for failing to take 'white supremacist capitalist patriarchy' into account when considering the popularity of rap music among young *white* men.[19] Then again, rapper (since turned actor) Ice Cube explains the 'present setting' in an interview with hooks:

> Killin' has become away of life. Very little talkin', a lot of shootin'. And, I mean, that really has a big effect on us, you know. Television [...] Now they can show an actual murder on TV, you know what I'm sayin'? [...] And it's like, it wasn't even shocking. It's a thin line between reality and the fake movie stuff.[20]

We can still wonder what would have happened, what the present setting would look like, if non-violence had carried the day in 1960s African American activism. But the reasons why it didn't are good historical reasons, as Ice Cube is well aware, because black non-violence was met with every conceivable kind of violent resistance to change on the part of American society at large, from the outright murder of political leaders and grassroots organisers to subversion of Civil Rights organisations as well as the intimidation, humiliation, and ridicule of individuals. Gangsta rap and gang warfare are partly the legacy of white intransigence in the 1960s: rap articulates, in the idiom of the African American oral tradition, all-American values of masculine dignity (see Chapter 2) and the right to bear arms, while rival gangs act out those values in a (mostly intra-racial) 'killing for sport'.[21] Since the logical end of such killing is self-destruction, it is clear that in gangsta culture means have overtaken ends. *Meridian*, by contrast, explores the other side of that 1960s legacy, that of non-violence: what would it be like if, as in the singing of gospel music, means and ends evolved together? 'The present you are constructing should be the future you want', the playwright Ola says in *The Temple of My Familiar* (see Chapter 5).[22] We see the same philosophy of prefigurative action dramatised in *Meridian*, but before we get to it we must look at the way in which the novel constructs the history that in turn produces such a present and future.

HISTORICAL BACKGROUND AND PRESENT SETTING

Meridian is often described as a Civil Rights novel, but if it is that, it is surely in a class of its own. Unlike Thulani Davis' *1959*, which tells in realist terms of the campaigns for school desegregation and voter registration in the mid- to late 1950s, and unlike the assessment of the aftermath of the Civil Rights movement in Toni Cade Bambara's *The Salt Eaters, Meridian* is perhaps less a novel *about* the Civil Rights era than *of* it, in the sense that it embodies and explores the long term costs and benefits of non-violent direct action.[23] Roberta Hendrickson agrees, and discusses 'the connection between Walker's experience in the Movement and the novel'. Although aware that 'Walker is concerned with history, not autobiography, in *Meridian*', Hendrickson does draw attention to the way Walker can examine the Civil Rights movement from the inside, as a psychological as well as a political experience, because of her own Mississippi years working in voter registration (see Chapter 1).[24] *Meridian*'s 'present setting', at the very end of the novel when Truman takes Meridian's place, is some time in the 1970s, long after Civil Rights as a movement has ceased to be a viable force of significant legal, political, and social change in the American South. Its 'historical background' is, however, much more fragmented and difficult to identify; as noted above, this background embraces American history right back to the conquest and settlement of Native lands, before the Civil War and even before the American Revolution. This treatment of 'deep history' is perhaps best understood as a series of layers superimposed upon one another, such as an archaeologist might systematically uncover in the course of excavation, as Alan Nadel puts it.[25] *Meridian*'s father's interest in Native Americans, the serpent-shaped burial mound, and *Meridian*'s great-grandmother Feather Mae's mystical experiences are all part of the deepest, most ancient layer. The next contains Crispus Attucks, the first martyr to the American Revolution. Truman makes a sculpture of him out of a sense of kinship with this black man who was killed for his allegiance to a revolutionary ideal. Another layer is formed by three women: the slave Louvinie, the liberator of slaves Harriet Tubman, and the preacher and former slave Sojourner Truth, in their own way sisters and resisters like Meridian. And just as Meridian's grassroots work follows in the footsteps of these foremothers, so too is Crispus Attucks's martyrdom echoed in the Civil Rights movement, because the town of Meridian in Mississippi was the birthplace of James Chaney, a black man killed in 1965 along with fellow white Civil Rights workers Andrew Goodman and Michael Schwerner.[26] By now we have reached the present, where yet more political martyrs are buried. John F. Kennedy and Dr Martin Luther King Jr's funerals are represented in the novel, and there is one untitled chapter that – like a headstone – simply bears the names of selected dead from black and post-colonial struggles of the 1960s. The well-known names of Malcolm X, Medgar Evers, Che Guevara, and Patrice Lumumba, among other male leaders, are listed there alongside the lesser-known names of the four black girls who died in the bombing of a Birmingham church, and a white woman who was killed while driving Civil Rights workers home from a political meeting. This catalogue of names, along with the Native American references and remembrances of slavery and the American Revolution, serves to show how the period that has become known as the 'swinging sixties' is in fact riddled with dead bodies, willing and unwilling martyrs to revolutions of various kinds.

Historical background, then, is not so much background as deep space and time that *foregrounds* the cost in human lives of the African American social and political struggle. In a very interesting alternative reading of Meridian (the character)'s historical layers, Leigh Anne Duck argues that

> Walker's narrative suggests the temporality of psychoanalytic treatment [...] events such as the denunciations of her mother and the pain of her abortion and sterilization do not recede into the past or into the even flow of time. Instead, they are felt, inconsistently, as monads in the present: condensations of experience, understanding and feeling.[27]

Drawing on this insight we might then say that *Meridian*'s present setting is suffused not just with her own traumatic past but also with history in various ways: actual in the sense that it makes reference to real historical events whose legacy lives on in the present, discursive in that it borrows from African American women's texts and speeches which likewise echo down the centuries and decades, and spiritual in its use of myth and religious symbolism. We shall look at each of these in turn.

Insofar as we get a potted history of the Civil Rights movement in *Meridian*, that history is confined to events and campaigns in Mississippi from the early to mid-1960s. In *This Little Light of Mine: The Life of Fannie Lou Hamer* we find many parallels with Meridian's efforts at voter registration as represented in the chapters titled 'Travels' and 'Treasure'. Hamer's biography shows that such work as going from door to door trying to persuade people to register to vote was not just laborious but often frustrating. Would-be voters had good reason to fear repercussions from their white employers and neighbours: many who persevered in trying to exercise their constitutional rights lost their jobs, their homes or their welfare cheques. For Fannie Lou Hamer, who herself had been evicted from the plantation where she worked and lived, and who had been beaten and thrown into jail for her activism, personal experience fuelled political fervour:

> [I]f registering to vote means becoming a first class citizen and changing the structure of our state's Government, then I am determined to get every Negro in the state of Mississippi registered. By doing this, we can get the things we've always been denied the rights to. I can say this, we need a change in Mississippi; I'm sick of being hungry, naked, and looking at my children and so many other children crying for bread.[28]

The kind of intimidation Hamer faced as a prospective voter was also extended to the Civil Rights organisers who worked in interracial groups, as the movement demanded. In the summer of 1964 white student volunteers came from the North to help with voter registration because their presence, it was believed, would attract more media attention to the struggle for black Civil Rights. Dave Dennis gives a chilling analysis of the strategic motivation for Freedom Summer, as the summer of 1964 was called: the necessity for white martyrs. He explains that 'the death of a white college student would bring on more attention to what was going on than for a black college student getting it. That's cold, but that was also in another sense speaking the language of this country'.[29]

Freedom Summer is the setting in which Truman meets Lynne, and their subsequent relationship dramatises some of the problems around sexual politics to which the presence of white people, but of white women in particular, gave rise within the Student Non-violent Coordinating Committee (SNCC). It was dangerous, for example, for black and white students to ride in the same car together late at night after the day's work was over, because such interracial fraternising might provoke white racists to violence. More dangerous still were interracial relationships, because the spectre of integration leading to intermarriage and miscegenation ('mongrelization of the races', in the words of white supremacists) aroused a deeply ingrained fear and rage in Southern whites.[30] Because *Meridian* highlights the role of black women in the movement (rather than that of the male leaders with whom we are so familiar), it is less concerned with the danger white supremacists posed to interracial couples than with the pain and loss such relationships entailed for black women activists. Black women felt they were being cast aside by black men in favour of a white ideal of femininity, sanctioned by the culture at large, from which they were by definition excluded and which they themselves did not even want, as *Meridian* makes clear: 'Who would dream, in her home town, of kissing a white girl? Who would want to? What were they good for?' (105). White women, however unwittingly, were thus a divisive presence in the Civil Rights movement because of what they represented as cultural icons, not just in relation to black women, but also to black men. Lynching is invoked in what is said about Lynne's problematic status in the movement: 'To them [black men] she was a route to Death, pure and simple. They felt her power over them in their bones; their mothers had feared her even before they were born', but of course Lynne's forbiddenness as a white woman who at the same time is involved in liberation struggle makes her all the more desirable (135). As Mary Aickin Rothschild explains in an article on the role of white women volunteers in Freedom Summer, for women such as Lynne there was no correct option: refusing black men's advances would be construed as racist, whereas

> The [white] woman who simply accepted the advances [of black men] and 'slept around' faced grave consequences [...] In most cases she was written off as an ineffective worker, and she often became the focal point for a great deal of bitterness for the black women on the project. Additionally, her behaviour was seen as scandalous by many within the black community and this pro-foundly inhibited community organizing, one of the main goals of the projects.[31]

It was because of such – and other – problems around white students' presence that by the mid 1960s whites were no longer welcome in SNCC. A position paper put it thus in 1966:

> [T]he form of white participation, as practised in the past, is now obsolete. Some of the reasons are as follows:
> The inability of whites to relate to the cultural aspects of Black society; attitudes that whites, consciously or unconsciously, bring to Black communities about themselves (western superiority) and about Black people (paternalism); [...] insensitivity of both Black

and white workers towards the hostility of the Black community on the issue of interracial 'relationships' (sex).[32]

Clearly, interracial sex was not simply a personal, but a deeply political issue in the Civil Rights movement, well before Women's Liberation invented the term 'sexual politics'. It is a political/personal issue in *Meridian* too. Truman agonises over his relationship with Lynne after the shooting of his comrade Tommy Odds, who later rapes Lynne as an act of vengeance on white society. Pia Thielmann observes quite rightly that in addressing the extremely vexed issue of black-on-white rape, 'What [Walker] appears to do is not to show a black brute, but to make visible the interlocked patterns of misconceptions about black and white sexuality, misconceptions that have existed for hundreds of years and have been perpetuated by society'.[33] For Truman, love transcends colour but not in any naive, absolute, romantic sense. There is always history to be reckoned with:

> By being white Lynne was guilty of whiteness. [...] Then the question was, is it possible to be guilty of a color? Of course black people for years were 'guilty' of being black. Slavery was punishment for their 'crime'. But even if he abandoned this search for Lynne's guilt, because it ended, logically enough, in racism ... he could not ... keep from thinking Lynne was, in fact, guilty. The thing was to find out how (131).

Truman shows in this passage that he is not the hopelessly unreconstructed male that Meridian sometimes takes him to be, but that he is learning to ask the kinds of questions she incessantly poses to herself. Even so, he never quite finds an answer other than that of Lynne's historic guilt by association, and his reconciliation with Lynne towards the end of the novel can therefore only ever be a partial, non-sexual one. His relationship with Meridian, likewise, cannot be resurrected after all that has happened, but here the role of history is rather different. For, as Meridian realises when she is dragged off to jail by the white sheriff, their relationship was not a matter of love, it was 'that they were at a time and place in History that forced the trivial to fall away – and they were absolutely together' (80).

Even more than interracial relationships and co-operation, the question of the uses and abuses of violence was a bone of contention in the Civil Rights movement. In Joanne Grant's documentary collection *Black Protest* the debate over violence can be traced through numerous speeches, articles, and position statements, from Howard Zinn's 'The Limits of Non-Violence' of 1965, expressing acute frustration at the ineffectiveness of non-violent direct action in the face of white intransigence in the South, through to James Forman's 1969 'Black Manifesto', which argued that time was running out and liberation could only be gained by any means necessary. Forman predicted a 'revolution, which will be an armed confrontation and long years of sustained guerilla warfare inside this country'.[34] Obviously, this is the view that Anne-Marion subscribes to, and that causes Meridian such moral anguish. We can see then that *Meridian*'s ostensibly moral or philosophical questions were not at all abstract but actually very real, day-to-day dilemmas in the experience of working for black Civil Rights in the 1950s and 1960s. Equally concrete and central to that experience was the phenomenon of burnout, or battle fatigue (as one of the chapters in *Meridian* is titled). In the interview with Claudia Tate, Walker herself expresses frustration at some critics' view of Meridian's 'illness' (the paralysis, the catatonic states, the hair loss) as somehow exotic or symbolic, when in fact Civil Rights workers were under such enormous strain most of the time that many did suffer these physical symptoms.[35] Anne Moody, for example, writes in her autobiography of Civil Rights activism *Coming of Age in Mississippi*: 'It had gotten to the point where my weight was going down to nothing. I was just skin and bones. My nerves were torn to shreds and I was losing my hair'.[36] Dave Dennis, whom Moody knew in Mississippi, tells of a Civil Rights worker in his early twenties who had heart trouble – it turns out that this man, because of constant fear and danger, had the heart function of a 70-year-old. Dennis speaks of voter registration in Mississippi as a war experience, in which you did not know, when setting out campaigning in the morning, whether you would see your fellow workers alive at the end of the day.[37] And Lawrence Guyot, another voter-registration veteran of Mississippi, describes how he suffered periodic paralysis on the left side of his body as a result of exhaustion and permanent anxiety.[38] Yet despite such extensive documentation of battle fatigue in the Civil Rights movement of the early 1960s, and despite what Walker herself thinks of it, the representation of Meridian's 'illness' in the novel amounts to more than mere realistic portrayal of activists' health problems. Her symptoms do have symbolic and spiritual resonances in the novel, and are indeed reminiscent of the mystic's ecstasy, which connects her with a long line of African American ancestors, as we shall see.[39]

'DEEP HISTORY': BLACK FOREMOTHERS AND NATIVE AMERICAN ANCESTORS

Representations of the Civil Rights movement in this 'crazy quilt' that is the novel, accrue meanings beyond those of their literal and historical referents because of the myths, anecdotes, and (very) short stories that are stitched across the main pattern and radiant centre of Meridian's life narrative. Some of these cross-stitchings hark back to the words, visions, and ideas of African American women who, like Meridian, took part in political struggles of the past. One such is Amy-Jacques Garvey, the wife of Marcus Garvey, the leader of the United Negro Improvement Association (UNIA), at the beginning of the twentieth century. In a 1925 editorial in *Negro World* titled 'Women as Leaders', Amy-Jacques Garvey wrote: 'The doll-baby type of woman is a thing of the past, and the wide-awake woman is forging ahead prepared for all emergencies, and ready to answer any call, *even if it be to face the cannons on the battlefield*' (my emphasis).[40] Compare this with *Meridian*'s opening chapter, in which we see Meridian leading a group of black children to view a mummified 'doll baby' white woman with long, red hair; in order to gain access to the show she puts herself in front of a white tank and 'stares it down'. Later this military reference is extended when Meridian is 'thrilled ... to think she belonged to the people who produced Harriet Tubman, the only American woman who'd led troops in battle' (106). Unlike Amy-Jacques Garvey, whose name is never mentioned in the novel, Harriet Tubman repeatedly figures as a role model for Meridian, since she led slaves to freedom in the North – singing particular songs by way of a password or, if all was not well, warning. Just so does Meridian, in her own way, lead the poor and the young to demand their freedom – whether that means seeing a plastic circus attraction ('The Last Return') or registering to vote ('Travels'), or reminding the town's mayor of his responsibilities by presenting the body of a drowned black child at the town hall ('Questions'). There are other resonances, from other texts and other black women leaders as well, and together they form a chain of association that leads us ever further into 'deep history'. Anne Moody describes in her autobiography a conversion experience that is remarkably like the one Meridian has when she returns to the black church. Moody writes:

> As I walked in, Reverend Cox was leading the adults in 'Oh Freedom'. It was so moving that I forgot about the ministers and joined in the singing. [...] When I listened to the older Negroes sing, I knew it was the idea of heaven that kept them going. [...] But listening to the teenagers, I got an entirely different feeling. They felt that the power to change things was in themselves.[41]

It is entirely possible that Moody and Garvey were sources for Walker, just as Greil Marcus notes that the final chapter in Camus' *The Rebel*, which is about the question of justifiable killing and is titled 'Thoughts at the Meridian', is also a silent reference in the novel. The same is true, of course, of Jean Toomer's poem 'The Blue Meridian', with its call for the poets to 'spiritualise America'.[42] But whether they are conscious influences or not does not really matter; the thing is that *Meridian* works as a novel both of Civil Rights *and* of black feminism through such literary and historical resonances, and particularly through such associative links with African American women leaders.

Of these, the major one is Sojourner Truth, who is cast as Meridian's spiritual and political foremother. The Sojourner is a tree on the Saxon College campus that has grown on the spot where the slave Louvinie's tongue was buried, after it was cut out by her slave-master to stop her telling murderous tales to his children. When the students want to bury the Wild Child, a homeless girl who is killed by a car, on Saxon ground and the college authorities refuse them permission to do so, they destroy the tree in riotous protest. The Sojourner, also known as the Music Tree, does, however, rise Phoenix-like from its own ashes when it grows new branches at the end of the novel. This coincides with the re-growth of Meridian's hair; both are simultaneous marks of regeneration and projection outwards, into the world. There is a hidden pun in Walker's use of Sojourner in this way, because Sojourner Truth was not born with that name: her slave name was Isabella Baumfree, and the German word *Baum* means 'tree'. Truth explained why she changed her name when she embarked on her mission to preach the gospel across America:

> When I left the house of bondage [slavery] I left everything behind. I wa'n't goin' to keep nothin' of Egypt on me, an' so I went to the

Lord an' asked him to give me a new name. And the Lord gave me
Sojourner because I was to travel up an' down the land showin'
the people their sins an' bein' a sign unto them. Afterward I told
the Lord I wanted another name 'cause everybody else had two
names; and the Lord gave me Truth, because I was to declare the
truth to the people.[43]

In 'A Name is Sometimes an Ancestor Saying Hi, I'm with You'
Walker furthermore invokes Sojourner Truth's name by analogy
with her own: 'Sojourner ("Walker" – in the sense of traveler,
journeyer, wanderer) Truth (which "Alice" means in Old Greek) is
also my name', she claims.[44] Parallels with Meridian, her travelling
and 'declaring the truth' and showing Truman and Lynne – well,
perhaps not their sins, but certainly their misconceptions – are
evident. And like Meridian, Sojourner Truth refused white models
of femininity also, because the nineteenth century cult of True
Womanhood did not and could not include her as a black woman,
a slave, and a worker in the cottonfields. In asking, famously, 'Ain't
I a Woman?' Truth insisted on the dignity and strength of black
femininity and motherhood, a dignity and strength earned through
suffering, the forced loss of her children, and hard physical labour.
Her speeches in support of the abolition of slavery and for women's
rights, combined with her spiritual work as an itinerant preacher
and mystic, make her in Alice Walker's terms the first womanist,
according to the definition of that term in *In Search of Our Mothers'
Gardens* (see Chapters 1 and 8). Sojourner Truth was illiterate, but
she did have a voice; it is as if in *Meridian* and in this definition
of womanism Walker put in writing what her foremother a century before had been putting into speech – and practice. And the
chain of association going back to 'deep history' does not stop here,
because the Sojourner is in turn connected with the sacred tree, of
which Black Elk speaks in the dedication to *Meridian*: 'the nation's
hoop is broken and scattered. There is no center any longer, and
the sacred tree is dead' (n. p.). Unlike Black Elk's view of the Native
American past, which is irrevocably lost and can only be mourned,
the Sojourner – the African American past – does not die. Instead,
in using this quotation from Black Elk's famous book and in making
Native Americans part of Meridian's own history and geographical
space, Walker regenerates a Native American spiritual legacy along
with that of black Christianity. This intermingling of cultural and
racial histories has again a basis in the historical record, and again

its meanings radiate outwards and take on symbolic and mythical significance as well. The historian Jack Forbes draws attention to the oft-forgotten fact that the first slaves in America were Native Americans, and that Native American/black African intermixture was very common in the colonial period, thus creating a mixed race of what he calls 'Red–Black peoples'.[45] In *Meridian* Walker seems to begin a re-examination of the binary divide between black and Native, and this project continues in *The Temple of My Familiar*. The chapters 'Indians and Ecstasy' and 'Gold', interspersed in the narrative of Meridian's early life, are therefore not merely of exotic or factual interest, but integral to the novel's theme of the ravages of history. Black Elk speaks of 'the butchered women and children lying heaped and scattered all along the crooked gulch as plain as when I saw them with eyes still young' (n.p.) and *Meridian* mourns these mothers and children along with Fast Mary, Louvinie, Sojourner Truth, James Chaney, Lynne and Truman's daughter Camara, and the little black boy who drowned in a 'swimming hole' as a result of segregation. Mothers and dead children are, therefore, yet another recurrent motif that can help us discover a pattern in *Meridian*'s crazy quilt.

MOTHERS AS MARTYRS: THE POLITICS OF RACE, REPRODUCTION, AND BLACK LEADERSHIP

In a speech before the Convention of the American Equal Rights Association in New York in 1867, Sojourner Truth addressed her audience on the issue of black women's rights: 'if colored men get their rights, and not colored women theirs, you see the colored men will be masters over the women, and it will be just as bad as before'.[46] Truth's statement can be read as an early articulation of womanism, combining race consciousness and pride with a feminist awareness that refuses to exempt African American men from the responsibility of granting equality and respect to black women. Sojourner Truth significantly invokes in that speech her authority as a mother as well: 'I want you to consider on that [the question of women's rights], chil'n. I call you chil'n; you are somebody's chil'n, and I am old enough to be mother of all that is here'.[47] It is this legacy of heroic and all-encompassing motherhood, embodied by a woman who bore thirteen children and saw them sold off into slavery, and who then made herself into a spiritual and political 'mother of the race', that haunts Meridian. Unworthy of this legacy, because she cannot love her son Rundi/Eddie Jr and has an abortion when she becomes pregnant by Truman, Meridian lives out a heretic's existence as regards the duties of the black mother. As Christine Hall notes, in fact the theme is already announced in the first chapter, when the mummified white woman Marilene O'Shay is described as 'Devoted Mother Gone Wrong'. Not only did she go wrong as a mother, but also as wife and obedient daughter – just like Meridian, who cannot live by her mother's rules and fails to meet the domestic standard of wifehood that Eddie Sr demands of her.[48] But this does not mean that Meridian's political activity and spiritual soul-searching are merely induced by guilt at this early dereliction of duty, as Martha McGowan seems to think, or that her interest in the question of when killing is justified 'is due to her view of herself as a mother, a creator rather than a destroyer of life', as Barbara Christian puts it.[49] Susan Willis has argued that it is ironic that Meridian as 'mother' in this sense ends up with rather a lot of dead children on her hands; in my view she can therefore at best be seen as *preserver* and defender of life (her son's, the Wild Child's) and as chief mourner and protester against the low price white society sets on black children.[50] That protest is, however, attenuated by an awareness of the damage done to children by mothers who never wanted to have them in the first place, but who are resigned to 'duty' – such as her own mother, Mrs Hill. The question of motherhood, then, is not so clear-cut as some critics make it out to be, and this is because *Meridian* is grappling with conflicting models and discourses of femininity and of the politics of reproduction at the same time, models that do not fall simply into a black–white dichotomy. For example, Christine Hall is right to note that Meridian and the doll-woman Marilene O'Shay have something in common in failing – or perhaps refusing, which is different – to live up to an oppressive ideal of female submission. On the other hand, neither the white ideal of feminine beauty and domesticity, nor the African American model of the heroic, self-sacrificing mother who also works outside the home *and* has a role to play in the collective welfare of the community, are viable images for a modern black woman like Meridian. As so often, Meridian's position is awkward, if not impossible: she is caught both ways, because she cannot conform to either standard and has no black feminist discourse available to her to articulate the dilemma – the novel as a whole has to do that for her, and for us as its readers.

Again we need to look at 'historical background and present setting' to put this in context. The Women's Liberation movement of the 1970s called for the right to abortion and women's bodily self-determination, and mounted a strenuous critique of the nuclear family and of heterosexuality itself as oppressive institutions for women. But African American women's necessary and historic alliance with black men and extended kinship and community networks were ignored in this analysis. The history of black women's enforced childbearing *and* sterilisation was temporarily forgotten until black women theorists like Angela Davis and bell hooks resurrected it in their work, revealing the supposedly universal demand for 'women's' reproductive rights to be confined largely to the needs of *white* women.[51] In *Meridian*, then, we see the issue of reproductive rights dramatised in what seem to be (but are not) contradictory ways; there is neither the celebration of family and community that some black feminists invoke against the white feminist 'attack' upon the family, nor do we find a defence of women's reproductive rights in the universal abstract. Meridian decides to give her child away and she has an abortion, but the reasons are neither selfless (as Sethe's murder of Beloved is, in Toni Morrison's novel of that name) nor selfish.[52] Having 'stolen' her mother's life, as Mrs Hill never fails to remind her, Meridian can barely hold on to her own right to existence, let alone reproduce it. Getting Eddie Jr/Rundi adopted and the pregnancy terminated are thus responsible acts, but they are not merely a matter of claiming women's 'liberation'. For Meridian lives in history, is *held by* something in the past that she cannot simply shed but has to come to terms with. That something is the legacy of Sojourner Truth, Harriet Tubman, Ida B. Wells, and other black women leaders and 'mothers of the race', who literally or symbolically looked after their own.

In an article on the dilemmas of black female leadership, Rhetaugh Graves Dumas writes of the crushing weight such symbolic investment in the African American woman as mother imposes upon black women professionals and activists:

Bad mothers who are white seem to be more easily tolerated than bad mothers who are black; bad mothers who are black and female border on the intolerable. Indeed the rich imagery invoked by black women comes as close to the Great Mother as one might imagine. When the black woman leader fails to give people what they believe they need, she is believed to be deliberately depriving and rejecting, and therefore, hostile and potentially destructive.[53]

The woman leader as Great Mother then is always in danger of becoming a martyr to her cause, and is expected to put not just her skills and experience and insight, but also 'her *person* at the disposal of those around her'.[54] Again, this statement resonates strongly with Meridian, who lets ideas penetrate her and whose body is like an archaeological site on which the various traumatic layers of the past become visible. In the Civil Rights movement, women leaders like Fannie Lou Hamer, Ella Baker, and Ruby Doris Smith Robinson conformed to this all-encompassing 'mother of all that is here' kind of role, but it took its toll upon their health and sometimes significantly shortened their lives.[54]

Like the question of killing for the revolution, the question of refusing to be a mother is tied up with moral and political integrity and potential martyrdom. Meridian realises that her reproductive decisions are decisions about terminating life, even in self-defence, and therefore they also need 'spiritual work'. Not because of guilt, however, but because if mothering is one kind of responsibility for the passing on of culture and racial pride, then political organising and consciousness-raising can be another. Martyrdom, which can be connected with guilt, has to be rejected too since it is a form of self-destruction. 'The only new thing now', says Meridian, 'would be the refusal of Christ to accept crucifixion. King ... should have refused. Malcolm, too, should have refused. All those characters in all those novels that require death to end the book should refuse. All saints should walk away' (150–1). And this is indeed what she does – walk away, leaving Truman and Lynne to get on with their own processes of enlightenment, after she has shown them how, by her example.

Meridian is neither a martyr nor a leader, if by leadership we mean qualities manifested by the likes of Dr Martin Luther King Jr and Malcolm X, men who had a strong public presence, were in charge of an organisation, and gained a media prominence that ultimately led to their violent deaths. Perhaps it is more accurate to liken her to the kind of *organiser* that Ella Baker was, democratic to a fault and absolutely committed to grassroots work rather than speechmaking and media attention. 'Strong people don't need strong leaders', Baker said famously, meaning they need organisers and motivators.[55] This model of female leadership, often combined with that of the mother, which Meridian refuses, was widespread among black women Civil

Rights workers. For many of these women, political activism naturally arose out of their role in the church – not as ministers, but as ministering angels, organisers of church events, visitors of the sick and dying, 'community mothers'. Lawrence Guyot asserts that 'It's no secret that young people and women led organizationally' in the SNCC.[56] But this organisational 'leading' was often not as high-profile as the work of the ministers in other Civil Rights organisations such as the Southern Christian Leadership Conference (SCLC, led by Dr Martin Luther King Jr) or the Congress for Racial Equality (CORE) or the National Association for the Advancement of Colored People (NAACP). It was often slow, laborious, frustrating toil, demanding a lot of personal as well as political discipline. Guyot describes voter-registration campaigns as collaborative work, in which means and ends often blurred:

> You don't alter the basic format that you walk into. Let's say you is riding past a picnic, and people are cuttin' watermelons. You don't immediately go and say, 'Stop the watermelon cuttin', and let's talk about voter-registration.' You cut some watermelons, or you help somebody else serve 'em. [...] The SNCC organizers were no saints. We asked discretion. We were never able to enforce it.[57]

Guyot's oblique approach to political campaigning, via practical help with whatever poor people need, is represented in *Meridian* in the seemingly anecdotal stories at the end, 'Travels' and 'Treasure', and in Meridian's early organising experiences with Lynne, who does not as yet understand the South and must learn Guyot's 'discretion'. Where *Meridian* espouses non-violence against the call for armed warfare and foregrounds female over male leadership in the Civil Rights movement, it also favours grassroots organising and co-operation with the people over imposition of a party line or any other form of authoritarianism. And this anti-authoritarianism is, I would suggest, applicable to the way we interpret the form of *Meridian* too: like Guyot's fieldworker (and Civil Rights organisers were not called that for nothing), the reader cannot alter 'the basic format you walk into' but has to collaborate with the novel's characters, feel her way around the lie of the land before getting to the heart of the matter and pass critical judgment. Like the Civil Rights worker, then, the reader must exercise discipline and discretion in not drawing premature conclusions, making partial meanings or giving up before the collaborative work, working *with* this Southern text, is done. Until we can appreciate Walker's use of spirituality as a 'fourth dimension' to complement her feminism, socialism, and antiracism, that work will not be completed. Only then will we be able to see how Meridian, as a secular saint, takes up where Sojourner Truth left oft and how *Meridian*, as a novel, rewrites the Civil Rights movement as a personal/political transformation and a spiritual legacy for the decades to come.

'HITTING THEM WITH SOMETHING THEY DON'T UNDERSTAND': THE POLITICS OF SPIRITUALITY

In a 1989 speech that was clearly directed against the New Right's attack on abortion legislation in America, Alice Walker invoked the history of Native American genocide, of forced breeding and sexual abuse of women slaves, of compulsory sterilisations and abortions for women of colour, of environmental pollution, and of the lack of adequate support services for poor black children and their mothers, as crimes that white men have perpetrated against black women. In order to defend abortion as an act of mercy, or even of self-defence, 'I will recall all those who died', Walker said, 'of broken hearts and broken spirits under the insults of segregation'. The upshot of her argument was that, until these crimes have been redeemed, and the white man can agree 'to sit quietly for a century or so, and meditate on this', he has no right to speak to the black woman about the right to life.[58] In this speech, as in *Meridian*, Walker performed an ideological tightrope act, typical of her incisive and insightful style of interrogating political dogma. By simultaneously mourning the lost children of the race and yet defending women's right to make their own reproductive decisions, her argument flew in the face of both black nationalist 'race suicide' prophets and white religious fundamentalists. It is important to realise that Walker's defence of abortion was *not* articulated as a matter of individual self-determination, but as a recognition of the difficulty of a black woman's position in a racist, capitalist, and profoundly self-destructive society that does not value children. This society, Walker argued in a spiritualist and environmentalist vein, preaches a 'right to life' at the same time that it in fact commits murder of every kind on living things, without thinking, every day of the week, in its defence spending, its advocacy of welfare cuts, its participation in war, and its refusal to protect the environment.

It is this political analysis and this kind of historical perspective that Walker, in *Meridian*, brings to other feminist issues such as rape and sexual harassment.[59] The Tommy Odds–Lynne episode about interracial rape again highlights the difficulty of Meridian's position as an activist for whom abstract questions (is rape as an act of the black man's revenge on white society ever justifiable? Can black and white women unite as victims of sexual violence no matter who perpetrates it?) always have to be examined in their 'present setting and historical background'. But the interracial rape shows more than that; it is also a key issue in the relationship between Truman and Lynne, and Lynne and Meridian, a kind of microcosm of personal/ political tensions that Walker had previously explored in the short story 'Advancing Luna – and Ida B. Wells'. Lynne's guilty feelings as a white woman prevent her from valuing her bodily integrity enough to name the event as rape, and Truman's confusion about 'whether one can be guilty of a color', noted earlier, is never quite resolved.

Meridian's position as confidante of both is that she cannot take sides, since as a black woman she is – yet again – obliterated from a binary structure in which *'All the Men Are Black*, [and] *All the Women Are White'*, as the title of a seminal book on black women's studies has it. In that title, however, the follow-up is *'But Some of Us Are Brave'*, and Meridian's refusal of binary thinking and living leads her to persevere in her emotional courage to neither reject Truman nor Lynne, to develop her racial solidarity, *and* to open herself up to Lynne's friendship.[60] Torn by the demands that both Truman and Lynne make upon her, demands that in political terms would translate as comrade-in-arms and feminist sister respectively, Meridian is for most of the novel drawn into a *ménage à trois* because the three of them have something to work out together. Neither Truman nor Lynne can quite do without her, as indeed neither can Meridian's erstwhile friend, Anne-Marion; Anne-Marion keeps writing her letters even though the communication is one-sided. In the end, the threesome experience a transformation and enlightenment of a personal/political nature. For Truman and Lynne this entails a shedding of borrowed languages, revolutionary posturing and misconceived ideas.

Christine Hall astutely notes a contrast between Meridian, who is rooted, like the Sojourner, in the South on one hand, and 'Truman, with his spoken French, his African prince performance and his Che Guevara outfit, [who] represents an example of cultural expressions which are not rooted in the community' on the other.[61] Such root-lessness and theatricality are also characteristic of Lynne, who often speaks in borrowed idioms and voices, whether they be those of black street-talk or Hollywood. On the occasion when she confronts Truman in his flat in New York and finds 'a tiny blond girl in a tiny, tiny slip that was so sheer she had time to notice ... that the girl's pubic hair was as blonde as the hair on her head' there, she mimics the Southern speech of *Gone with the Wind*: '"Don't shut up Sugah", she said, "Talk. I wants to hear Miz Scarlet talk"' (172–3). After the death of her and Truman's daughter Camara, who is yet another variation on the theme of murdered children, Lynne learns (in 'Two Women' and 'Lynne') to relinquish her idealisation of black people and her identification as a Northern white woman. Her rootlessness, after she has lost husband, child, and home, leads her back to the South and back to Meridian. In jokey conversation with the latter Lynne admits, finally, that 'Black folks aren't so special' and that her marriage to Truman taught her that the time for white women to jump – or be pushed – off their pedestals had come – in her case that had happened, after all, a long time before, when she started working for black Civil Rights (185).

Truman, similarly, is affected by the way Meridian lives authenti-cally in a way that he cannot, and learns from her. '"Your ambiva-lence will always be deplored by people who consider themselves revolutionists, and your unorthodox behavior will cause traditional-ists to gnash their teeth", said Truman who was not, himself, con-cerned about either group. To him, they were practically imaginary' (227). The fact that they have become 'practically imaginary' shows his progress in shedding convention and worry about conforming to revolutionary styles. With the final poem, in which Meridian forgives him his trespasses, he falls to the floor in a re-enactment of Meridian's fainting spells, puts on her cap and gets into her sleep-ing bag. Truman at that point takes on her mission of making the abstract concrete, working through questions of means and ends, and learning to live with ambivalence.

Walker's essay 'The Civil Rights Movement: What Good Was It?' cites an old lady, a 'legendary freedom fighter in her small town in the Delta' who, to the question of whether the movement was dead, replied: '"if it's dead, it shore ain't ready to lay down!"'[62] This essay was written nine years before *Meridian* was published, but the spirit of that black woman's reply has remained with Walker in her subsequent writing career. The theme of changes in personal lives because of the movement, and of 'a debt we owe to those blameless hostages to the future, our children' has likewise persisted, notably in *Meridian* but also in poems, essays, and the later novels.[63]

I called *Meridian* earlier in this chapter a novel not so much *about* the Civil Rights movement, but *of* it, and by that I meant that its significance lies primarily in Walker's literary use of Civil Rights values and strategies. This needs some explanation, but we can take as an example the model of the crazy quilt. The quilt, which requires piecing together by the reader, can be likened to the Civil Rights movement's goal of integration, a joining of 'black and white together' or, as Walker would probably have it, a joining of peoples of all colours within the fabric of society, but with distinct patterns, identities, and histories still visible and yet harmoniously combined. Skill and artistry lie in the joining process, which in *Meridian*'s case is the attempt to dissolve traditional ways of thinking in binary oppositions: black/white, male/female, leader/follower, realist/ mythical, political/spiritual, sick/healthy, and so forth. These pairs are progressively taken apart by the stitching-in of certain other elements that figure in the novel, such as the Indian motif (which breaks up the black/white dichotomy), Meridian's 'queer' androgy-nous appearance and role (challenging gender stereotypes), and her community leadership (dissolves the distinction of leader/led). The crazy quilt is not so crazy after all, just as Meridian is not, in fact, either a 'weird gal' or 'God'. Neither, indeed, is she 'sick'; through letting conflict play havoc with her body and by following its course she is, instead, in the process of healing herself. Concepts and prac-tices like Beloved Community and non-violent resistance intervene in the opposition between the political (socialism) and spiritual (Christianity), by ridding the latter of its institutional hierarchy (the Church) and focus on the hereafter, while shedding the former's instrumentalism ('killing for the revolution') and giving its mate-rialism and collectivism a moral grounding. The historical suffer-ing of non-white peoples, of women, and of children provides that moral grounding in a recognition that change cannot be brought about by 'doing unto them as they have done to you', because that would only reverse the binary rather than challenge its destructive logic. Or, as one Civil Rights activist put it in typically less pious and more tactically astute terms: 'We knew that probably the most powerful weapon that people literally have no defense for is love, kindness. That is, whip the enemy with something that he doesn't understand'.[64]

The pattern I am tracing then, in this crazy quilt, is Walker's strategy of 'whipping the enemy with something that he doesn't understand', and the novel's form is as much a part of that deliberate strategy as are its enigmatic heroine and her peculiar story. Meridian and *Meridian* embody this ideal in which means and ends are merged – at enormous physical and psychological cost and artistic as well as didactic gain. For reading *Meridian* is, in many ways, a political and personal education, and whatever good the Civil Rights movement did or did not do – and this will look different today from the way it did in 1976 or in 1967 – this novel *of* Civil Rights is a powerful reminder of the movement's imaginative and philosophical legacy. Fannie Lou Hamer puts the question of killing for the revolution in perspective for the last time: 'You can kill a man, but you can't kill ideas. 'Cause that idea's going to be transferred from one generation 'til after a while, if it's not too late for all of us, we'll be free'.[65]

4
The Color Purple (1982)

In 1970, two women – one white, one black – get together to collect money for a headstone to mark the grave of Bessie Smith, blues singer extraordinaire, who had died in 1937. One of them, Juanita Green, attends the unveiling of the stone, but the other stays away so as not to detract attention from the commemoration of 'the Empress of the blues'. That absent woman is Janis Joplin.[1]

In 1973, Alice Walker flies to Eatonton, the birthplace of Zora Neale Hurston, African American writer and anthropologist extraordinaire, to meet a white woman named Charlotte Hunt. Together they want to find Hurston's grave and put a headstone on it with the inscription 'a genius of the South'. Although they do not succeed in finding the exact location of the grave, they have the headstone placed in the middle of a circle as a monument to Hurston. Alice Walker later relates this event in 'Looking for Zora', a monument in essay form which occupies a central place in Walker's *oeuvre*.[2]

Yet the most striking monument to Hurston is Walker's third and best known novel *The Color Purple*, which creates literature out of an abused black girl's letters to God, written in the African American vernacular of black Southern speech, the only language she – Celie – has. American literature has been interested in representing the speech of the people at least since Mark Twain, but not the speech of black people, much less black women, unless as an object of ridicule or comedy. In Walker's hands that speech, long regarded as backward and degraded, becomes a vibrant literary language that gives voice to a girl, a woman, a people, and a subject hitherto not regarded as worthy of, or fit for, writing – let alone literary writing. This voice did not come out of nowhere. In Celie's speech, we hear an echo of Janie Crawford, Hurston's protagonist in *Their Eyes Were Watching God* (1937), a novel Walker brought back to the reading public's attention after decades of neglect. A dramatisation of womanism as a practice of self-determination and speaking back to power in everyday life, *The Color Purple* is the story of a young black woman who is abused and routinely humiliated by her (step)father and husband. She is barely *seen* at all by those around her: 'He laugh. Who you think you is? he say. You can't curse nobody. Look at you. You black, you pore, you ugly, you a woman. Goddam, he say, you nothing at all' (176). But Celie survives, and more than that: she triumphs. She takes her husband's lover Shug for her own, and makes common cause with feisty, audacious Sophia and other women of her extended family. Celie even manages to transform her husband Albert from a wife-beating brute who insists on being called Mr___ into a caring, supportive companion. The link between Celie and Shug on one hand, and Walker and Hurston and Bessie Smith on the other, is made explicit when about halfway through *The Color Purple* Celie and Shug start looking for the grave of Celie's parents. They find 'nothing but weeds' and in the end they decide to stick a horseshoe in the ground by way of a marker. It is at this point that Shug tells Celie 'Us each other's peoples now' and kisses her, thus declaring their kinship and sisterhood and creating a new familial bond in place of the one that is irrevocably lost (156).[3]

It may be that Janis and Juanita, Alice and Charlotte, and Celie and Shug were simply honouring their ancestors: singers commemorate a singer, writers a writer, daughters their parents. But – like Sethe in Toni Morrison's *Beloved* – they may also have been engaging in an act of redemption for those who had been loved or celebrated in life, but died in ignominy. According to African American folk belief, people who 'die bad' will haunt the living until their spirits are appeased and their bodies laid properly to rest. Bessie Smith died prematurely in a car accident, Zora Neale Hurston from poverty and illness, and Celie's parents through acts of violence. In belatedly honouring them, the daughters performed their filial duty in appeasing the spirits of their ancestors, and paid their artistic debts to those whom posterity had denied recognition and respect. As Felipe Smith puts it: '[Walker's] effort at textual resuscitation of Zora Neale Hurston is redemptive in the sense that [she] attempts to reverse the catastrophic effects of poverty, isolation, and critical neglect'.[4] Shug's vow of commitment to Celie, then, is a crucial moment in this narrative because it seals a bond that stretches across generations and affirms a common ancestry. In addition, Shug's words and her kiss define a new sense of family that does not depend on blood relations but on chosen relation*ships* of love, sex, and solidarity. This transformation applies to virtually all the characters in *The Color Purple*. Candice Jenkins argues that '*The Color Purple* … engages in a project of "queering" the black family, reshaping it in unconventional ways that divests its black male members of a good deal of power, thereby reconfiguring the very meaning of kinship'.[5] 'Queer' is a key word for *The Color Purple* not only because Celie and Shug become lovers, but more so because Walker turns the whole structure of the patriarchal family inside out and thereby 'queers' it to open up possibilities for love and community that were hitherto unheard and undreamt of. Walker's third novel, first published in 1982, thus marks the graves of Bessie Smith and Zora Neale Hurston, obliquely through the many 'buried' references to their work, but more significantly so in the novel's tribute to the spirit of women's blues and African American English, which Zora Neale Hurston celebrated in her writing and Bessie Smith personified in her performances and recordings. As a writer of black speech, Celie shows her indebtedness to Zora, while Shug, the singer, embodies Bessie Smith's legacy. But more of queer theory, the blues, and vernacular foremothers later. In order to see the multifarious ties that bind Bessie Smith and Zora Neale Hurston to the characters of *The Color Purple*, we need to look first at the whole network of textual relations that makes up the fabric of the novel. *The Color Purple* is more like a shapely garment made of finely textured cloth than the patchwork crazy quilt that is *Meridian*, as we saw in the previous chapter. Where *Meridian* advertises its formal artifice, *The Color Purple* dresses its shocking contents in something like the 'folkspants' that Celie sews: they are custom made, yet 'one size fits all'. Perhaps it is because of the ironic contrast between Celie's innocent voice and what that voice tells us that critics have found so much to say about *The Color Purple* and yet have contradicted each other so frequently. Here is how Celie begins her story:

> Dear God,
> I am fourteen years old. [...] [He] [j]ust say You gonna do what your mammy wouldn't. First he put his thing up against my hip and sort of wiggle it around. Then he grab hold my titties. Then he push his thing inside my pussy. When that hurt, I cry. He start to choke me, saying You better shut up and git used to it (3).

Celie's language is simple, matter of fact, and brutal in that simplicity. One size does, indeed, fit all, but the question is what *specifically* individual readers see in a novel of abuse, rape, incest, battery, and exploitation. What is the appeal of this text? How is it that *The Color Purple* has become – with Toni Morrison's *Beloved* – *the* teaching novel of choice in the emergent canon of African American women's writing? And what do Zora, Bessie, the blues, and womanism have to do with it?

READING THE CRITICS: THE SUBSTANCE OF FORM

Few novels of so relatively recent a vintage as *The Color Purple* have generated as much critical activity. Scores of articles have been written about it, every critical anthology of feminist literary scholarship contains multiple references to it, and the release of Steven Spielberg's film in 1985 yielded a whole new crop of journalistic and academic responses, as well as protest marches and public debates.[6] We can get a taste of the vehemence of this controversy from *Banned*, Alice Walker's small volume on the short stories that have found disfavour with school boards and parents in the US, which includes a section on the furore around *The Color Purple* (see also Chapter 8). We encounter again the familiar theme of objections to Walker's representation of black men:

> ... because so few films are produced with black themes, [*The Color Purple*] becomes the only statement on black men. 'Purple' points us away from the fact that Nelson Mandela, Martin Luther King and Malcolm X overcame the system's psychological warfare and produced healthy, non-incestuous, non-brutalizing relationships with women. Their women never needed a 'Shug'. Furthermore, most of us will be men in spite of white men and women who only publish books by black women or homosexual black men with degrading themes or passive attitudes – and then make them into movies of 'the Black experience'.[7]

Homophobia is writ large here, as is the assertion of a 'healthy' black masculinity that regards women as possessions (*'their* women') and rules through heteronormativity. But the novel as well as the film drew critical fire and condemnation: the Souderton Area School District, another contributor to the debate, did not need so many words to voice its outrage. It simply declared that Walker's novel was 'inappropriate reading for tenth graders because it is "smut"'.[8] *The Color Purple* then seemed a most unlikely text to be adopted by the mainstream, given the controversial nature of its political and sexual content. Did it achieve canonical status because of such controversy or in spite of it? Alan Sinfield takes the latter view in arguing that Celie's story seemed to promote 'a privatised, essentialist humanism' that made it all too easily co-optable into a liberal ethos.[9] Sinfield's response was perhaps indicative of *The Color Purple*'s generally much less controversial reception in Europe than in the United States, where sex and religion are always rather charged subjects. Then again, it is equally possible that the legitimisation of Walker's third novel by educational establishments and the critical industry was due to a genuine shift in teaching and publishing practices in Europe as well as in the US. This shift came about as a result of what has come to be known in America as the 'culture wars' of the 1980s and 90s, when critics and educators engaged in raging debates about what should be read, valued, and therefore taught in a rapidly changing multiracial and multicultural society.[10] *The Color Purple* made it possible for that debate to be staged in the classroom, not just because it elicited controversy around the issue of what would be suitable reading for tenth graders, but more importantly because it invited such questions as: what constitutes literary language, who writes it, what kinds of texts have been allowed historically to count as literature, and why. Very likely Celie's story presented itself as one that could be taught and studied and written about because it was *already* being read widely. This is bell hooks' view: 'Unlike most novels by any writer it is read across class, race, gender and cultural boundaries. It is truly a popular work – a book of the people – a work that has many different meanings for many different readers.'[11]

A thumbnail sketch of the plot of *The Color Purple* gives us some clue to its popularity. A poor, uneducated and 'ugly' African American girl in the American South is transformed from a fourteen-year-old rape victim and incest survivor into a successful lesbian businesswoman in her forties, a property owner and 'mother' of an extended family clan who gather around her to live in peace and harmony for ever after. The familiar script of rags to riches, combined with sexual and emotional fulfillment, is instantly recognisable to us from popular fiction, and therefore may account for some of *The Color Purple*'s success. But the intricacies of Celie's progress – and, more importantly, the way her story is told – belie the ostensible formulaic simplicity of this narrative. As befits any romantic or, for that matter, feminist heroine, Celie has to go through many trials and tribulations to gain her final victory, but her trials are not of the sort we usually find in fiction. Neither is her victory of her own individualist making – as the tradition of Harlequin romances or popular women's fiction would demand. After having been repeatedly raped by her father, Celie's children are taken away from her, her mother dies, and she is married off – effectively sold – to an older man, Mr___, who beats and humiliates her. She also loses the one friend and confidante she had in her sister Nettie, who emigrates to Africa to work as a missionary. Her new friend Sofia ends up in prison after a confrontation with white racists, and Celie is left to look after her husband's children as well as his mistress Shug, who at first treats her like a doormat. As we have seen, the change in Celie's fortunes comes when she and Shug make common cause with each other against the exploitation – sexual and otherwise – of women by men, and fall in love. Even then, Celie's sorrows are not over because she loses Shug to a younger man and finds out that the letters she has been sending to her sister never arrived. Conversely, Nettie's letters to her turn out to have been confiscated and hidden by Mr___ for years. When Celie finally does get to read them, she discovers that her children are safe with Nettie and the missionary couple with whom she has been working in Africa, and that the man who raped Celie is in fact not their real father. When the rapist/stepfather dies, Celie inherits the estate of her biological father, a property owner who had been lynched by white people. Her real father's money then enables her to start a sewing business, 'Folkspants Unlimited', which rapidly becomes successful. In the meantime Nettie and Celie's children, Adam and Olivia, prepare to return to America, but their voyage home coincides with a war in Europe and they are presumed dead after their ship is reported sunk near Gibraltar. As luck would have it, however, the State Department has made a mistake and at the end of the novel Celie and her sister, her children, Shug and Sofia, as well as Mr___ celebrate a family reunion on the Fourth of July, America's day of liberation from colonial rule and obviously also Celie's day of liberation from all the forces that have oppressed her.

This story, even when told as neutrally as I can tell it, is full of holes, unlikelihoods, and strange coincidences, and any literal-minded reader would be left with lots of questions. Why do Celie's letters return unopened? How can an abused woman reconcile herself with the husband who treated her like dirt, and come to love his mistress? Why has no one ever told Celie about her real parents? How likely is it, really, that a black woman is allowed a successful business venture (making unisex trousers, of all things) if we are also asked to accept that her father was lynched for just such an enterprising spirit? And isn't it a little too convenient that an inheritance should arrive just as our heroine needs it to make her happiness complete? All these are questions that would arise in the mind of anyone who is looking for more than merely a sob-story that turns out well in the end, a reader who wants a mode of telling it which will make it coherent, or someone who is looking for role models in this womanist fable. After all, the epigraph to the novel is Stevie Wonder's 'show me how to do like you/show me how to do it', and seems to invite such an inspirational reading. None of those wishes is on first reading fulfilled. There is a lot of vagueness too, about time and place and the historical details of the relation between Africa and America. Why does Nettie go to 'Africa', rather than to a specific country or region of that vast continent? Did the tribe she works among, the Olinka, really exist? Why is the novel not set in a recognisable real time frame (for example, the first forty-five years or so of the twentieth century) and in a real place, but are both collapsed into some fantasy space and history?

Clearly, to a more imaginative and less literal-minded reader such concerns are beside the point. To try to read *The Color Purple* in the terms of what we usually understand by realism is futile, because we simply are not given enough information in the text to make the story remotely 'convincing'. Such vaguenesses, coincidences, and inconsistencies derive from the style and form of *The Color Purple*, rather than simply its plot. As in *Meridian*, formal features demand attention, because it is they that make *The Color Purple* into an exceptional literary achievement, rather than just a formulaic production providing all the thrills and frills of popular fiction. In terms of style, for example, we note even upon first reading that Nettie's letters in standard English are in sharp and stilted contrast to Celie's African American vernacular, which looks like transcribed speech. The style is therefore uneven, or rather modulated with internal differences of tone and pitch. It is also often 'unashamedly sentimental' in Robyn Warhol's words (especially at the end) and in places didactic, as when Nettie writes about conditions and customs in Africa in order to teach Celie (and us) something she (and we) need to know of the world beyond the American South.[12] Rather than assume that this is a matter of simple inconsistency or sloppy writing ('telling, not showing'), we might more usefully ask how these modulations function not just within the text but also outside it, as markers of particular forms of social discourse that are of relevance to the *reader's* present rather than Celie's historical reality. Second, we may wonder why *The Color Purple* is written as an exchange of letters. This form

seems to draw upon the early history of the novel, that of the epistolary novel of the eighteenth century, as many critics have noted, and
yet its content is at odds with a time frame of two centuries ago.[13]
This anachronistic use of the epistolary form has made *The Color
Purple* a veritable goldmine for critics to exercise their wits upon. In
order to read it well, that is: with attention to form as well as content,
we therefore have to clear up the question of how epistolary discourse functions here and what other genres Walker has woven into
her fabric. Genre conventions, after all, determine *how* we read, *what*
we can expect, and *why* a text is organised in the way it is. It may be
that the mixture of generic strands we find in *The Color Purple* has
tripped readers up- and this has affected the professionals no less
than the amateurs, as we shall see in a brief survey of the various
possibilities suggested in the critical literature to date.

Most critics regard *The Color Purple* as an historical novel of some
sort, because it is set in a time that is clearly not the present, but is only
in a generalised way the past. This past we cannot pin down very
accurately except by using historical markers, such as the appearance
of automobiles and mention of a global war. Because *The Color Purple*
does not seem to care too much about historical facticity, Lauren
Berlant argues that it offers a critical rewrite of the historical novel.
As such it is not concerned with the public history of war and conquest, but with domestic strife and victory: a women's version of the
historical novel, in other words.[14] Darryl Pinckney situates its historical setting in the inter-war period of the twentieth century, but adds
that '[T]he novel, ... with its flat characters, sudden revelations, and
moral tags, has a doggedly nineteenth century quality'.[15] Pinckney,
like Berlant, thus notes that there is something strange about *The
Color Purple*, but puts this down to accident –Walker's inadequacy
as a writer – rather than design. Others, like bell hooks and Melissa
Walker, focus on the realism we can expect in an historical novel – and
find it wanting. In hooks' case this leads to an uncharacteristically
crude and literal reading, in which she complains that the portrayal
of lesbianism as socially unproblematic ('Homophobia does not exist
in the novel') is not only unrealistic, but also politically suspect.[16] For
Melissa Walker the fact that *The Color Purple* 'does not contain a single
date' seems to be a problem. She is troubled by the foregrounding
of the domestic sphere that Berlant also noted, because in Melissa
Walker's view this focus on home and family implies that public history in the novel is 'something that happens to white people', whereas
black people seem to live only in the private domain and are thus

effectively placed outside of history.[17] Priscilla Leder rebuts this argument quite effectively: 'Walker's novel provides little of the minute,
realistic period detail that characterizes most historical novels. She
aims not to re-create the period but to help today's readers, especially
black women readers, come to terms with contemporary issues'.[18] In
Leder's view then, *The Color Purple* draws on the nineteenth century
domestic or sentimental genre of women's writing, but really this is a
contemporary novel in period costume.

A host of other, not primarily literary, critics have also got in on the
act of writing about *The Color Purple*. Psychological readings tend to
use Celie's story to illustrate the development of individual selfhood,
and a number of women theologians have looked at its reconception
of the biblical Father as an immanent deity, an idea that fits in with
post-1960s feminist theology.[19] Apart from Berlant's astute insight into
Walker's use of the historical novel, these kinds of realist or instrumental readings do not yield anything very productive. They tend to
flatten the text and rewrite it into something more coherent and rather
less provocative and radical than it is if we take its contradictions and
confusions more seriously. This is not to say that these critics simply
get it wrong – their observations are by and large accurate in their own
terms – but they do not dig deep enough into the novel's metafictional
layers and textual strategies. By that I mean that *The Color Purple*, like
Meridian, has an embedded critical dimension to it that comments on
the (white) Western literary tradition itself. Critics who do recognise
the significance of Walker's use of the epistolary form are therefore
able to interpret, for example, the politics of language in the contrast
between Celie's and Nettie's letters to better effect, as we shall see.

Aware of this critical dimension of the text, Wendy Wall for example
notes how the miscommunication between Celie and Nettie explodes
any easy notion of community and mutual understanding between
black sisters. This miscommunication, says Wall, has wider repercussions because it also applies to the reader in 'call[ing] attention to the
inherent problems within the processes of reading, writing and interpretation'.[20] The sisters' difficulty in connecting through writing over
time and between two continents should make us more conscious
of what we ourselves are doing as readers trying to connect with a
different time, place, and culture; there will be more on reading *The
Color Purple* across cultural difference later on in this chapter.

Many other critics foreground the theme of orality and literacy in
The Color Purple and note how Walker emancipates not only Celie,
but more importantly the African American vernacular by making

Celie's voice *as transliterated speech* the privileged discourse.[21] Frequent reference is made to Zora Neale Hurston's *Their Eyes Were Watching God*, which, as mentioned above, also uses the black vernacular to spectacular literary effect, but without allowing its protagonist Janie to tell her own story in the first person from beginning to end. In that sense, critics note, *The Color Purple* completes a feminist project that was already begun by Hurston.[22] And wherever orality and literacy are highlighted, silence figures too – as a trope that traditionally has been associated with the sexually abused woman. This adds a further layer of signification to Celie's troubled discourse and allies her with Marguerite in Maya Angelou's *I Know Why the Caged Bird Sings*, who is silent for several years after she has been raped by her stepfather: women writers write what abused girls cannot speak.[23] Christine Froula, in a psychoanalytic reading, sees Celie's letters as a breaking of the patriarchal taboo on women speaking out about abuse and she relates Celie's and Squeak's voices to that of Ovid's Philomela, who in the *Metamorphoses* turns into a nightingale after she has been raped. Surprising as this classical contextualisation may seem, it strikes a chord given the recurring motif of (blues) singing in *The Color Purple*, but also, as Martha Cutter notes, because Celie's eventual victory 'gives Philomela a voice' and thus revises this ancient myth of female victimhood.[24] Froula also argues that it is by no means imperative to see *The Color Purple* as a realist text. If we read it as *part of* (as well as a reflection on) the Western canonical tradition and do not confine its ancestry to women's writing or African American fiction – which up until recently had been largely excluded from that tradition – then we would do better to regard it as an epic or classical romance. Molly Hite presents an illuminating analysis of Walker's novel according to the conventions of Shakespearean romance, with Celie as a pastoral character who epitomises innocence and with powerful male figures of evil who are redeemed at the end. Most valuable in Hite's reading is her recognition of *The Color Purple*'s comic impetus, which, she says, 'is so powerful that it absorbs questions of probability and motivation' (e.g. realism).[25] Priscilla Walton is of the same view, but argues it differently: as an inversion of the conventions of the comedy of manners, which after all provides 'a critique of social limitations'.[26] Few others have noted the many ways in which *The Color Purple* does not take itself quite seriously, when it plays – especially towards the end – with the conventions of the epistolary novel and the *Bildungsroman* in such a way as to make these forms look slightly ridiculous; and surely this is the point. Celie's progress is, after all, no more the product of coincidence, remarkable reversals of fortune, and miraculous feats of sudden reformation of character than is, to name a favourite novel of Alice Walker's and mine, *Jane Eyre*, as Elizabeth Fifer usefully observes.[27] One way of naming this comic, or rather satirical, tendency is to say, as Linda Abbandonato does, that *The Color Purple* transgresses the genre of epistolary writing by invoking the tradition of Samuel Richardson's *Clarissa* – another novel of female sexual danger and abuse – and then turning it inside out.[28] Walton goes as far as to call it

> ... an intellectual comedy in that it is a comedy of ideas: it drama-tizes possibilities and completes itself in a vision of an ideal world – a world which is matriarchal, a parody of the boy-gets-girl endings of most comedies and fairy tales. This world is also an ideal one which is in direct opposition to the rigidly closed society that is in evidence in the opening pages of *The Color Purple*.[29]

Another way of understanding the anarchic and metafictional impulses of *The Color Purple* is to read it as a 'pastiche' (meaning: an uncritical mimicry of an earlier text, unlike 'parody', which is a negative, satirical aping of conventions) of Zora Neale Hurston, as Henry Louis Gates suggests, or to put it in the context of postmodern fragmentation, as Wendy Wall does.[30] For our purposes, however, terms like 'pastiche' or 'postmodern fragmentation' are too general in that they deny or ignore the 'race-d' nature of Walker's project in this novel. It would be more accurate to say that *The Color Purple* on one hand 'signifies on' the early history of the novel, the novel of letters as written by Richardson, but also by Fanny Burney and other white women. On the other hand, it pays homage to Hurston and other writers and singers of the black vernacular – and these are queer bedfellows indeed. What does it mean to characterise Walker's novel as the hybrid, 'queer' offspring of the epistolary tra-dition and that of African American vernacular culture, especially the blues? And what do we gain by reading it this way?

SIGNIFYING AND QUEERING: *THE COLOR PURPLE* AS METAFICTIONAL CRITIQUE

'Signifying' is one of those features of African American cultural practice that in recent years have been identified as distinctive in theoretical and critical discourse on black women's writing. As defined in Henry Louis Gates Jr's *The Signifying Monkey*, the *locus classicus* of the term as a theoretical concept, 'signifying' can take many different forms, but basically it comes down to two types of linguistic strategy. It can be a way of covert, indirect communication between members of a group who understand its particular code, and it can be a form of playing tricks on someone outside the group by a devious use of words. In its folktale manifestations the practice usually serves to show how the weak can outwit the powerful, for example how a monkey can beat the lion – the king of the jungle, after all – and this in turn can be read as an allegory of how a slave can get one up on his or her master.[31] 'Signifying', according to Gates, has two crucial features: one is its indirect address, and the other its metaphorical nature and its facility with revision of formal conventions.[32] To 'signify on' a text (or a person) is to talk negatively about it, often in hyperbole and with either a light touch (in jest) or a heavier, more serious didactic intention.[33] Misrecognition of a signifying practice can lead to serious mistakes in literary criticism as much as in the folktales. For example, Marjorie Pryse writes in her introduction to *Conjuring: Black Women, Fiction and Literary Tradition* that

> [w]ithout formal education, Celie can't know what Walker does, that the earliest novels in English were also epistolary. Therefore, Celie is not writing an 'epistolary novel'. She has simply found the form in which both to express and share her deepest feeling, which is love for other black women and men like Albert who accept her newly discovered autonomy.[34]

Of course, Pryse is *literally* right in saying that Celie is not knowingly writing an epistolary novel, but this is neither here nor there, because the point is that *Walker* knows what it means to write in that generic convention. In adopting it on Celie's behalf, Walker 'signifies on' the earliest novels in English, in which white women's suffering in trying to protect their most precious commodity – their chastity – motivates plot and form. On reading *The Color Purple* against this background, we see how such suffering pales somewhat in significance when compared with Celie's lot and that of numerous black women over the last three centuries who were used and abused by their masters. This process of 'signifying' in the novel is both heavy and light. It is heavy, in that it teaches us as readers about dominant assumptions regarding what is great literature and what is not: *Clarissa*'s and *Jane Eyre*'s legitimacy as canonical novels about (and by) 'our' literary foremothers is taken for granted, whereas Celie's has to be established through a catalogue of suffering and Walker's heavily accented alternating use of standard and non-standard (African, American) English in the epistolary exchange. But it is also light, because some of the familiar motifs of the eighteenth century epistolary and nineteenth century domestic or sentimental novel (absent mothers, lost and found relatives on different continents, surprise inheritances, and initially recalcitrant lovers) are rewritten in *The Color Purple* to tragi-comic effect. And this is done so obliquely that we cannot even say that this or that feature is clearly comic, whereas another is tragic: both elements criss-cross each other with the tragic dominating at the beginning and the comic at the end. The picture of Celie and Albert sewing together on the porch, for example, can make us laugh because it seems so contrived. Yet there are times when men take on women's work (as when everyone gathers round to nurse the sick Henrietta), and *vice versa*, that are quite moving and offer a utopian vision of a future in which gender roles, as such, no longer exist.

Or maybe not so utopian, as in this famous passage when Celie and Albert exchange lessons learned, and Walker's didacticism is evident:

> You know Shug will fight, he say. Just like Sofia. She bound to live her life and be herself no matter what.
>   Mr___ think all this is stuff men do. But Harpo not like this, I tell him. You not like this. What Shug got is womanly it seem like to me. Specially since she and Sofia the ones got it (228).

This bit of dialogue, which is about women who behave like men and men who have feminine qualities, works at a literal level, because it sums up what we already know through having observed Shug and Sofia's and Mr___ and Harpo's behaviour. But as a signifying passage this dialogue also rewrites the early epistolary novel's script of rigidly fixed gender roles and compulsory heterosexuality, and it makes of Celie at least as worthy a literary victim/heroine as Clarissa or Jane Eyre. What is more, in *The Color Purple* no female rivals need to be killed off in order to establish Celie's moral superiority, and the love triangle of wife, mistress, and husband is resolved in, first, a lesbian relationship between the wife and the mistress that bypasses Mr___ and only later, once he – the villain – has redeemed himself, in respect and harmony between all three of them.

Another take on understanding what Walker does in *The Color Purple* with her revision of gender roles and her re-creation of family and kinship outside of patriarchal structures can be found in recent queer theory. Philip Brian Harper et al. explain the potential force of queer critique in its ability to traverse and creatively transform conceptual boundaries, as 'a way of reconceiving not just the sexual, but the social in general'; E. Patrick Johnson revises Walker's definition of womanism to coin the word 'quare' for 'odd or slightly off-kilter; from the African American vernacular for *queer*'.[35] The issue here is thus not, or not only, that Celie and Shug engage in a sexual relationship with each other, but rather that a queer/quare reading of *The Color Purple* makes visible the extent to which the conceptual boundaries of the African American family and of heteronormative gender roles are here creatively transformed. Candice M. Jenkins makes this quareing of conventions and queering of roles a little more concrete still, with reference to what she rather cumbersomely calls 'the salvific wish':

> The salvific wish is best understood as an aspiration, most often but not only middle class and female, to save or rescue the black community from white racist accusations of sexual and domestic pathology, through the embrace of conventional bourgeois propriety. [...] [I]nsistence that women in particular suppress their own desires (sexual or otherwise) and surrender to patriarchal control is a part of what might be called rules or tenets of the salvific wish.[36]

Jenkins then shows how Shug Avery as a 'cultural infidel' flouts all those rules of respectable behaviour for black women in the first half of the twentieth century, and how Walker in *The Color Purple* 'demands an entirely new way of defining and understanding gender and male-female interaction, one which begins with men being men *in spite of* patriarchal power, not because of it'.[37] What I earlier described as Walker's utopian vision of how gender roles should be changed or even abolished may thus more precisely be characterized as a *queer* vision, one that upsets and unsettles all conventional categories of identity, sexuality, gender, and race.[38] We have here an instantiation of what Siobhan Somerville argues in *Queering the Color Line*: 'Compulsory heterosexuality has been not simply parallel to discourses of racial segregation but integral to its logic; to disrupt naturalized constructions of racial difference involves simultaneously unsettling one's relationship to normative constructions of gender and sexuality as well'.[39] When Eleonor Jane, the white mayor's daughter, comes to work for Sofia as her maid, 'naturalised constructions of racial difference' are disrupted since the 'normal' state of affairs would demand that Sofia work for her (as she does for her parents earlier on in the novel). We already know about Sofia's 'masculine' qualities: she prefers fixing a roof over domestic work and is physically stronger than her husband, Harpo. Now Sofia is also placed in the position of a 'master', so in her case both the racial hierarchy and that of her gender and class position are reversed. Not only the 'normal', 'white' order is disturbed, however. As we saw in previous chapters, black nationalism demanded that African American men be supermasculine in order to count as 'real men' in a white supremacist world, where they had been habitually addressed as 'boys'. In *The Color Purple*, however, Harpo is a gentle man with feminine qualities, and Mr___, under Celie's and Shug's tutelage, relinquishes his patriarchal power, such as it is, and the novel valorizes both men rather than representing them as effeminate or weak.

By now it will be possible for us to see that critics who read *The Color Purple* in predominantly realist terms fall victim to the signifying monkey's trickery, while those who get the metafictional and queer message will derive more learning, more insight and inspiration, and more fun from the novel. But we have not quite exhausted all the ways in which Walker signifies on other genres, nor have we solved the contentious issue of whether and how Celie's domestic and private story fits onto a larger historical canvas. To begin with the latter: Linda Selzer's article 'Race and Domesticity in *The Color Purple*' can help us, because in line with my use of the notions of kinship and family as re-visions of gender – and sexual relations, Selzer sees kinship as functioning 'as a carefully elaborated trope for race relations', not only between black and white but as significantly between and within the races in Africa as compared to America.[40] Focusing predominantly on Nettie's letters, which only come to light about half way through the novel, Selzer shows how there *is* a larger historical frame present in *The Color Purple*, only it is not one that the uneducated Celie can interpret. But we, as knowing and informed readers, can. From Nettie's letters we deduce the context of British imperialism and colonialism in Africa, for example, and in the Olinka creation myth ('white people is black people's children' (231)) we can divine the theory of monogenesis (meaning that all of humankind originated from one African mother). Perhaps most important of all, what Selzer calls 'the perverted "kinship" relation' between white children and black 'mammies' on the plantation household model is echoed in Sofia's story, and critiqued as Sofia initially refuses to work for the white mayor and later refuses to love or even care for his grandchild and eventual heir, Eleonor Jane's son Reynolds Stanley. Through Sofia's narrative, then, the history of slavery as an economic institution that was built on black field – but also *domestic* – labour is invoked, and in Squeak's rape by the white warden (her uncle) further evidence is given of how black and white 'blood' relations originate not in recognised familial or kinship bonds but in interracial incest and abuse. Selzer concludes:

> Through its embedded narrative line and carefully elaborated kinship trope for race relations, *The Color Purple* offers a critique of race that explores the possibility of treating all people as 'one mother's children' – while remaining unremittingly sensitive to the distance that often separates even the best of human ideals from real historical conditions.[41]

As for the question of how Walker achieves that critique of race in form as well as in content, we turn, finally, to Calvin Hernton, who regards *The Color Purple* as a twentieth-century slave narrative, in which white exploitation of blacks is replaced by men's exploitation of women.[42] Although Hernton's thinking in terms of exclusive binaries is dated (in his schema race is replaced by gender, as if the two categories do not always already intersect and shape each other) he has a point with regard to the autobiographical slave narrative as the founding genre of African American literature, and therefore a likely candidate for Walker to 'signify on' and use. Houston Baker also notes this in a more theoretical context. In his book *Workings of the Spirit* Baker contends that

> [t]he most forceful, expressive cultural spokespersons of Afro-America have traditionally been those who have first mastered a master discourse – at its most rarefied metalevels as well as at its quotidian performative levels – and then, autobiographically, written themselves and their *own* metalevels palimpsestically on the scroll of such mastery.[43]

This is a complicated way of saying that, if we take the slave narrative as our example, the slave who told his or her own story had to prove first that he or she could write, and write *in the language of the slave master* (that is, standard American English) in order to then be

able to take issue, not just with slavery as an exploitative and dehu-
manising system, but also with the slave master's language and
discourses. When Harriet Jacobs ends *Incidents in the Life of a Slave
Girl* with a direct and wry comment to the reader that this story
does not end, as one might expect in a conventional novel, with
marriage but with a precarious freedom, what she does in effect is
critique a dominant literary genre by showing just what kinds of
race-, gender- and class-specific assumptions underlie it.[44] We can
use Baker's insight, and Jacobs' historical example, to look at *The
Color Purple* as a text that is self-aware in this sense. It both shows
evidence of mastering a master discourse at Baker's metalevel (its
use of the epistolary form) and at his 'quotidian performative' level
(Nettie's stilted, 'white' written style), which is subverted by Celie's
and Shug's vernacular/blues discourse. Hernton's model of the slave
narrative in turn connects neatly with the practice of 'signifying' as
the slave's trope, in Henry Louis Gates's term, because it is through
his stylistic mastery that the slave can critique the master.[45] Part of
this critique in *The Color Purple* is – paradoxically perhaps – Walker's
privileging of speech and other cultural practices (music, needle-
work, sexuality, spirituality) over writing. An often overlooked passage in *The Color Purple* is the one in which Shug tells Celie that she
has fallen in love with a much younger man, Germaine, and that she
wants to go away with him for six months. Celie at this point cannot
speak, and answers Shug with written notes instead:

> All right, say Shug. It [the affair with Germaine] started when you
> was down home. I missed you, Celie. And you know I'm a high
> natured woman.
>   I went and got a piece of paper that I was using for cutting pat-
> terns. I wrote her a note. It said, Shut up (211).

This episode, as much as the first letter to God, makes it clear
that Celie's writing is not in itself an act of liberation or even
self-expression, but rather an escape valve when all else fails. Celie
writes, in other words, when telling is impossible: 'You better not
never tell nobody but God' is how the novel starts, and Celie does not
actually break that taboo until about midway through when she tells
Shug that Mr___ beats her. 'Telling' is thus confined to spoken, human
communication, whereas writing to God is an act of last resort, not
self-empowerment. This seems to me an important distinction
to make, because it crucially defines the difference between the

dominant (white) culture's valorisation of writing as against speech. Writing letters or notes, because they are always addressed to a particular person, is as close to speaking as writing can get, and yet we see in *The Color Purple* how writing can malfunction as a mode of communication. This is because writing in its pure form, as it were, is an abstract activity requiring solitude and stillness, whose end product is removed from the circumstances in which it was done. The more impersonal and abstract, the more prestigious writing is, it seems: in a literate, technologised culture, writing aimed at no one in particular and lacking any personal markers is the most prized (e.g. print in the standard language). Speech, by contrast, is a practice of *interpersonal* communication, a call that is only effective if it elicits a response. And call and response is another characteristic of African American cultural practice, whether it takes the form of shouting in church or the audience's active participation in oral storytelling or its loud appreciation of a jazz performance. Speech is not usually regarded as an art form in the way that writing is, *because* of its communal, evanescent, and interactive nature.[46] Christine Hall observes that in *Meridian* Walker already seemed 'to be undermining the ground of verbal discourse upon which her own work rests', because Meridian frequently cannot speak, so choked up is she with the violence of history that she has taken into herself. Instead, it is Meridian's body which speaks in physical symptoms – as indeed Celie's does, in an understated way, because when her father 'sells' her he informs Mr___ that 'God done fixed her', meaning that she has lost her fertility through sexual trauma and will therefore not burden him with any more children (10). In relation to *The Color Purple* we can revise Hall's statement to say that Walker undermines the ground of *written* discourse upon which her own work rests, and agree that, for Walker, '[I]t is by means of art, whether it is story-telling, performance, the visual arts or music, that history can be transformed', a statement that pointedly refuses to privilege writing over other, non-verbal art forms.[47]

The feminist critical cliché that *The Color Purple* charts Celie's progress through her 'finding a voice' is thus, in this construction, to be taken literally as referring to a speaking voice; the fact that Celie also writes is of only secondary importance in the scheme of cultural difference *and critique* that Walker articulates in the novel. We can see the text's insistence on the power and presence of the speaking and singing voice as polemically engaging with white women's literature, which tends to take *writing* as the mark of liberation from patriarchal oppression, in a tradition that ranges from Anne Bradstreet to Charlotte Perkins Gilman and from Virginia Woolf and Tillie Olsen to Hélène Cixous.[48] Clearly, the assumptions all these feminist and proto-feminist writers made about the availability and validity of literacy over orality are culture- and class-specific. In the exchange of letters between Celie and Nettie, likewise, the salient point is that it is *not* – strictly speaking – an exchange, *not* a correspondence, but a miscommunication, as Tamar Katz shows.[49] Literally so, in that letters aren't received or aren't read until much later, so that the sisters do not actually reconnect until they meet each other again in the flesh. And figuratively there is miscommunication too, in that the two constituents of Celie's and Nettie's hybrid national and cultural identities, Africa and America, do not connect, let alone 'map on to' each other in any easy way. Africa is not the Eden from which slaves were brutally taken away, because slavery, as the novel suggests and the historical record confirms, started in Africa with warring tribes selling their prisoners to each other and later to European slave traders. Therefore, as Graham Connah explains, 'the slave trade has a history in West Africa which goes much further back than the advent of Europeans on the Guinea Coast'.[50] And because patriarchy exists in Africa too, albeit in a different form, Africa can neither be black Americans' homeland nor can America assert its 'civilising' influence over it with any legitimacy: American missionaries are merely trying to replace one patriarchal social system with another, Christian one.

This leaves African American women between a rock and a hard place, through which *The Color Purple* attempts to steer a precarious passage. It is not at all clear that the sisters learn anything much from each other, besides African folk remedies (the yam that is used to heal Henrietta) and the relative nature of cultural difference. But *we* certainly do, as we have seen, by reading over the sisters' shoulders and between the lines of the ironic juxtaposition of African and American perspectives in their letters. Where Nettie writes about Samuel's Christian teaching on the evils of polygamy, for example, it is clear that her own *ménage à trois* with him and Corinne is not that different from indigenous households headed by a man with more than one wife. At the same time, such a polygamous arrangement is also mirrored at Celie's end in family structures that incorporate lovers of both sexes as well as spouses and legitimate and illegitimate children.

'Africa', despite its almost mythical presence in the novel, is not celebrated as some idealised space outside the history of women's oppression, but then neither is America held up as a locus of liberation, in spite of the reference to the Fourth of July at the end. Just as Celie's first letters to God echo Sojourner Truth's statement that when she suffered during slavery, 'none but Jesus heard me', so also does the final chapter of the novel reiterate Frederick Douglass's rhetorical question of the mid nineteenth century: 'What to the slave is the Fourth of July [as long as the American constitution does not grant freedom and equality to all its citizens]?'[51] Harpo's answer is that it is simply a holiday for black people to 'spend the day celebrating each other', and that response signals a continuing disaffection with and alienation from the rituals of American national identity (243). The relation between Africa and America is, then, metaphorised as one of precarious kinship, without antecedence or superiority/inferiority. Instead, the kinship means a sharing of some common ground in cultural memory and cultural practices ('And men sew in Africa too, I say' (230)) but one that is not easily recoverable due to the history of European colonialism in Africa and present Euro-American economic imperialism.

The Color Purple is then at least in part a meta-text that 'signifies on' the (white) history of the epistolary novel and white culture's (including white feminists') valorisation of writing over other cultural practices. It also poses the problematic relationship between two continents, Africa and America, and two cultural traditions (at least) that a hybrid African American identity must negotiate. But it is not Celie who does this in *The Color Purple* so much as Alice Walker, who uses the black tradition of a vernacular art in Celie's story in order to establish an alternative model of cultural production and reception to that of white Western canonicity. That alternative model is writ large, of course, in Celie's black language, but it can also be glimpsed in the recurring motif of the blues. In what follows we shall explore that motif to see what the conventions of the blues can tell us about the way Walker interweaves the African American oral tradition with that of the white-identified epistolary novel.

A RIGHT TO SING THE BLUES: IDENTIFICATION AND DIFFERENCE

When Shug sings her tribute to Celie in Harpo's bar, we know that what she sings is the blues. This is important, because if we ignore the blues in *The Color Purple* there is a danger that we read it as a sad story made good, as if the suffering that has gone before is erased in the airbrushed picture of a happy family, reunited in harmony and wealth at the end. Putting that final idealised snapshot of the extended 'queer' family on the porch aside for the moment, we may return to the question of what pleasure this text gives us as readers. Is it, perhaps, based on a sense of identification with Celie's suffering *as an abused black woman*, a suffering we also find articulated in, say, the blues as sung by Billie Holiday in classics such as 'My Man' or 'Good Morning Heartache' or, pre-eminently, 'I've Got a Right to Sing the Blues'?[52] Is reading *The Color Purple*, in other words, an exercise in masochistic identification?

Robyn Warhol addresses this question head-on and answers with a resounding 'no'. A narratological analysis of Walker's novel as belonging to the epistolary and sentimental tradition quickly reveals, writes Warhol, how the *effect* of reader-identification is produced, namely through a narrative point of view that forces us to see the world primarily through the victim's – Celie's – eyes. Just as importantly, that narrative perspective excludes the point of view of her oppressors, so that 'This careful limiting of the narrative point of view to those who suffer and triumph after tribulation can effect a powerful pull on the sensations of a susceptible, cooperative reader', according to Warhol, 'regardless of the reader's historical orientation to the text. [...] In sentimental novels, moreover, the "good cry" is much more often evoked by scenes of triumph than by scenes of sadness'.[53] Warhol's analysis of how narrative technique produces a particular kind of reader response is useful, because it de-mystifies the appeal of a narrative of suffering by showing us how we are being manipulated into an empathetic position, rather than choosing it for good or ill. On the other hand, Warhol's argument can also be taken to de-value the cognitive or political impact of reading *The Color Purple* by reducing the affect of empathy and catharsis to mere narrative effect. Cora Kaplan's essay 'Keeping the Color in *The Color Purple*' for example addresses important questions about reader identification, across the Atlantic and across the divide of racial difference, and sees such identification as a possible instance of (mis)appropriation of black women's historical experience. Kaplan argues that her white British students' reading of Walker's best-known novel was disturbingly decontextualised in that it regarded Celie's story as simply 'women's writing', *sans* tradition, historical reference, or African American specificity. Keeping the colour in *The Color Purple* would therefore require a pedagogy consisting of a lot of historical and intertextual work to remedy cross-cultural ignorance and to counter the 'indulgence' of a too-easy identification that elides the substantial class and racial differences between white women in the UK at the end of the twentieth century and the Celies and Billies of this world.[54] While Warhol's analysis of narrative technique and Kaplan's contextualisation approach undoubtedly help us to read in a more sophisticated way, they don't do much to recognise and valorise the intensity and importance of readers' initial empathic responses, for such responses are not automatically to be dismissed as naïve and lacking in African American cultural context.[55] It may be, for example, that listening to Billie Holiday has prepared the ground for reading Alice Walker's work. After all, reading *The Color Purple* and getting emotionally involved in it is not unlike listening to Billie sing a song of abuse and lost love. However much we are manipulated into such emotional involvement by narrative or vocal technique, when readers feel they can 'identify with' such songs, or 'relate to' the experiences they seem to name so poignantly, there is something they hear in the blueswoman's voice from so far away and so long ago that deserves to be articulated and acknowledged. Billie singing 'My Man' undoubtedly expresses sentiments of love betrayed ('he isn't true') and of domestic violence ('he beats me too') that many women recognise. It is a large part of the appeal of the blues, as Ray Pratt writes, that

> [I]t speaks to, for, and about unmet needs and represents a catalysation of the desire for a kind of freedom as yet unfulfilled, and perhaps not even fully conceived, yet one that invites participation and experience of its particular *feeling*.[56]

The Color Purple has the same kind of appeal and invites a similar kind of participation in feeling, both of suffering and of delight in the happy ending. Still, cross-race, cross-class identification and a certain masochistic investment (if such it is) in women's suffering are problems for any kind of feminist or womanist analysis of Walker's novel and women's blues. To state such problems is not to resolve them. Who has a right to sing the blues? And who can really read them?

The conjunction of Alice Walker and the blues is, of course, no coincidence. Walker has often credited the great women blues singers (Ma Rainey, Bessie Smith, Mamie Smith) in her work, and the short story collection *You Can't Keep a Good Woman Down* is dedicated to them 'for insisting on the value and beauty of the authentic' as well as deriving its title from a Mamie Smith song ('You Can't Keep a Good Man Down'). In that volume the short story 'Nineteen Fifty-Five' takes as its subject the misappropriation of a black woman's blues song by a white male singer, Traynor, who looks remarkably like Elvis Presley.[57] 'Nineteen Fifty-Five' champions the authenticity and the use value of African American culture. It does this in the same way that 'Everyday Use', Walker's rather better known short story about an old woman whose daughters fight over her quilts, celebrates the black woman's tradition of creative yet useful needle-work. Both forms of quotidian cultural production are recast as art, if purposely not 'Art' in Walker's short stories.[58] In *The Color Purple* these two strands of African American women's artistic legacy come together as Celie, the seamstress, and Shug, the blues singer, join forces in their mutually healing and nurturing relationship. Shug's significance *as* a blues singer is crucial. She is not just the one who enables Celie to discover her 'pleasure button' or the colour purple in the fields, because she happens to be a freer spirit than Celie is; Shug is, to all intents and purposes, a liberated woman and it is her art that enables her to be so. As LeRoi Jones writes: '[T]he entertainment field [was] a glamorous one for Negro women, providing an independence and importance not available in other areas open to them – the church, domestic work, or prostitution.'[59] For women like Shug, blues singing was a ticket out of the oppressed condition of black women's domestic or sexual or industrial wage labour in the inter-war period. To this economic account of the blues as work, Hortense Spillers adds the dimension of blues singing as also a performance of sexual self-confidence, because the singer

> celebrates, chides, embraces, inquires into, controls her woman-hood through the eloquence of form that she both makes use of and brings into being. Black women have learned as much (probably more) that is positive about their sexuality through the practising activity of the singer as they have from the polemicist. Bessie Smith, for instance.[60]

Bessie Smith is indeed a good example, for she (in such songs as 'I'm Wild at That Thing' and 'You've Got to Give Me Some') represents another side of women's blues: a sassy, demanding female sexuality far removed from the victimhood of Billie Holiday's best-known songs.[61] In *The Color Purple*, then, we can see against this background that the cultural significance of Shug's occupation goes beyond its mere narrative importance, because Shug evokes a whole tradition of women's cultural activity and self-assertion. As a blues singer Shug can teach Celie a lesson in sexual autonomy and desire, which is part of Walker's womanist philosophy, for which Shug is the mouthpiece throughout. She also wields the power of economic independence over Albert, which means that he cannot control her as he controls Celie. And it is Shug, not Celie, who explains the novel's title in a passage that moves seamlessly from women's sexual pleasure to what pleases God:

> God love all them feelings. That's some of the best stuff God did. [...]
>   God don't think it dirty? I ast.
>   Naw, she say. God made it. Listen, God love everything you love – and a mess of stuff you don't. But more than anything else God love admiration.
>   You saying God vain? I ast.
>   Naw, she say. Not vain, just wanting to share a good thing. I think it pisses God off you walk by the color purple in a field somewhere and don't notice it. (167)

Although in this famous passage the colour purple has purely positive connotations, Shanyn Fiske notes interestingly that it is also often equated with suffering and pain: 'Sofia's beaten face is described as the color of "eggplant"', and 'Purple is the color of Celie's private parts: the site of her sexual violation'.[62] These two aspects of the meaning of purple – pleasure and violence – fit right in with the united opposites of pain and pleasure that are so often found in blues lyrics. And although Shug teaches Celie many lessons in pleasure and assertiveness, conversely and much more obliquely Celie, the archetypal victim, also educates Shug in the ethics, if not the aesthetics, of everyday use. For everyday use is what Celie is to Mr___, and also to Shug when the women first meet: a doormat, nurse, nanny, and cook combined. Shug has to learn to *see* Celie first, and then to value her dignity and integrity over and above her labour.

In 'Black Eyed Blues Connections' Michele Russell calls women's blues a 'coded language of resistance'.[63] In another essay she adds:

> Blues, first and last, are a familiar, available idiom for black women, even a staple of life. [...] We all know something about

blues. Being about us, life is the only training we get to measure their truth. They talk to us, in our own language. They are the expression of a particular social process by which poor Black women have commented on all the major theoretical, practical, and political questions facing us and have created a mass audience who listens to what we say, *in that form* (my emphasis).[64]

In that form is important, because for a long time the blues was the only form in which black women could expect to be heard by the culture at large. To Russell's list of blues subjects we might add sexuality, including lesbianism, which gives us yet another link into *The Color Purple*. I would call Alice Walker's *Leitmotif* of childhood trauma and physical abuse – something she extends cross-culturally to clitoridectomy in her later novel, *Possessing the Secret of Joy* – characteristic of her blueswoman's aesthetic.[65] Even so, it remains vital to realise that the blues as elegy is always counterbalanced by the blues as transcendence. The leap of faith that occurs so often in the final stanza of blues lyrics, softens or tries to undo the mournful qualities of this music, and in Walker's happy endings we see the same thing. Such transcendence takes the form of celebration of the black community, of the South's beauty and artistry, and of a spiritual belief in social and political change. Most of all, it is achieved in the creative act itself, in the singing of the song or the writing and reading of the text. For, as Ray Pratt reminds us, the blues (and Walker's writing) are not sad, but rather *'a way of laying sadness to rest'* (my emphasis).[66]

So far, I have talked about the blues as musical parallel to the patchwork quilt: both are vernacular art forms, made of everyday suffering but giving comfort in their making/performing. But what happens when the blues is taken out of its improvisatory performance context and is committed to paper, frozen and *framed* in a literary form – as Walker/Celie does in *The Color Purple?* In an essay on teaching Walker's novel, June Jordan describes her astonishment at black students' initially negative reaction to Celie's language:

> 'Why she have them talk so funny. It don't sound right.'
> 'You mean the language?'
> Another student lifted his head: 'It don't look right, neither. I couldn't hardly read it.'[67]

This response shows how unrecognisable the black vernacular becomes, even to those who speak it, when it moves out of its familiar setting in the home, the blues song, or the street. Jordan's students do not even *want* to identify or empathise with Celie, because her language elicits feelings of shame and embarrassment: the way she writes/speaks is obviously 'incorrect' by the standards of the literary language to which they are used. Only when Jordan engages her class in translation of the novel's first sentences into standard English do the students find out how difficult that is and how ludicrous the result. 'You better not never tell nobody but God. It'd kill your mammy' becomes 'one should never confide in anybody besides God. Your secrets could prove devastating to your mother'. Through this translation exercise it becomes clear what Walker is doing in writing down Celie's speech: giving black English not just a 'voice' – which *sounds* right – but also a literary legitimacy that *looks* right.[68] And this is where awareness of what Walker does with the epistolary tradition is as important as the recognition of how she uses the blues: the blues discourse functions to 'signify on' standard English and the (white) literary canon, both at once.

IDENTIFICATION AND THE RIGHT TO SING THE BLUES: AUTHENTICITY REVISITED

There is a vaudeville version of the blues classic 'My Man' by Ethel Waters that sounds very different from the painfully plaintive rendering Billie Holiday gives.[69] Using a classical style of singing, with a mock French accent and an exaggerated emphasis on 'mon hoooomme', Waters improvises a whole new song with hardly a trace of the masochistic investment that the lyrics seem to celebrate. Waters' version illustrates vividly women blues singers' capacity for (self-)parody. But also, in this recording, Waters foregrounds the commodification of the blues and its packaging for a white audience – as distinct from the black audiences for whom Bessie Smith's records were made in the 1920s, the so-called race records.[70] It would be mistaken, however, to assume that when Waters sings 'My Man' as crossover music this is automatically a selling-out of the authenticity of the blues. Waters satirises a notion of Frenchness (foreshadowing the pathos of Edith Piaf) and a European vocal tradition that she mimics in the way she uses her voice. Her rendering contains an element of critique, which is doubly ironic in face of the fact that 'My Man' was originally a French song, originally a 'Mon Homme'.[71] Only when Waters says at the end of the song 'It's the same in any language' does she contain that critique by in effect universalising the spirit of the blues, extracting sentiment from song and thereby abstracting it from the Southern blues experience: the blues becomes, precisely, sentiment, a 'song of lost love', the same in any language. In her book *Black Feminist Thought* Patricia Hill Collins explains how an Ethel Waters gave way to, and gave birth to, an Alice Walker:

> Commodification of the blues and its transformation into marketable crossover music has virtually stripped it of its close ties to the African-American oral tradition. Thus the expression of a Black woman's voice in the oral blues tradition is being supplemented and may be supplanted by a growing Black women's voice in a third location, the space created by Black women writers.[72]

As mentioned earlier, Zora Neale Hurston 'framed' African American English in *Their Eyes Were Watching God* and thereby turned it into art; Walker does the same, but in making Celie tell her own story she shows how the art of the oral tradition is also one 'for everyday use'. At the same time, that very act of framing in *The Color Purple* creates a problem for readers, both black and white, because the first-person 'voice' of the letters and the sentimental tradition invites identification with Celie on one hand while on the other her language – which is either un- or all-too familiar – makes the reading experience uncomfortable, at least initially. In June Jordan's teaching experience black American students do not want to identify with Celie's language, whereas in Cora Kaplan's white British students relate to the character's pain and 'forget' about cultural, historical, and linguistic difference after a while. The text thus positions readers differently, and Walker's legitimation of the black vernacular and critique of the epistolary tradition necessitate a self-reflection and distancing that critics and teachers can mediate in order to bring questions of cultural difference and power *as well as* cross-racial empathy into focus. As Paul Gilroy demonstrates in *The Black Atlantic*, authenticity in music – and I would add in writing – is a complex thing:

> The discourse of authenticity has been a notable presence in the mass marketing of successive black folk-cultural forms to white audiences. [...] [I]t is not enough to point out that representing authenticity always involves artifice. This may be true, but it is not helpful when trying to evaluate or compare cultural forms let

alone in trying to make sense of their mutation. More important, this response also misses the opportunity to use music as a model that can break the deadlock between the two unsatisfactory positions that have dominated recent discussion of black cultural politics.[73]

These two unsatisfactory positions are black (cultural) nationalism, which absolutises difference, and a wholesale pluralism that deconstructs the notion of authenticity altogether. Contextualising *The Color Purple* in the history of the blues *and* that of the white European novel helps to identify Walker's epistolary blues discourse *as* a critical, hybrid discourse and focuses the attention on letters as opposed to life, in place of a too-ready identification with Celie's suffering. Even so, readers' experience of having something of themselves articulated in the novel is also valid and need not be delegitimised by this intellectual work.[74] It may well be that (white) students emerge from their study of *The Color Purple* with both a better understanding of racial difference *and* a sense of solidarity/empathy with an experience not their own, but not entirely alien either. And, as June Jordan's essay about teaching *The Color Purple* shows, neither are black students simply suffering from a false 'whitewashed' consciousness if they object to Celie's language. Instead, study of the politics of Walker's signifying use of the vernacular enables awareness of the institutional and social pressures that posit standard English (and what is that?) as the only norm of correctness, adequacy, or creativity.

Who has a right to sing the blues, and who can really read them? The blues, and black women's writing, are now part of the crossover repertoire: crossing over, and crossing back. It is the role of teachers and critics to make readers aware of both movements, and to provide them with the necessary knowledge to track them back and forth. In *In Search of Our Mothers' Gardens* Walker has written of the need for writers and readers to partake of both African American and white literary traditions, and not to be satisfied with a segregated canon (see Chapter 1).[75] For Walker it is essential to recognise that writing and reading do not take place in a vacuum, but are always already informed by a multiplicity of national, racial, and gendered traditions. Paul Gilroy aptly remarks that 'The relationship of the listener to the text is changed by the proliferation of different versions. Which one is the original? How does the memory of one version transform the way in which subsequent versions are heard and understood'?[76] This question is pertinent to our discussion too. For 'versions' read 'readings' or 'interpretations', and it will be clear that I have improvised my blues reading of *The Color Purple* in part from the different versions I have read elsewhere. *The Color Purple* then emerges as a queer cultural hybrid that combines epistolary features with the vernacular of the blues tradition. As we have seen, Walker critiques the history of white women's writing because of its class assumptions and heterosexual matrix, and yet invokes it in her privileging of the domestic sphere and the theme of sexual abuse. She also, as Missy Dehn Kubitschek has shown, takes issue with male writers who have treated such abuse (rape) in literature primarily for its symbolic significance. Even if they do not leave it at that, '[T]he rape victim', writes Kubitschek, 'remains simply a victim' in the male Euro-American tradition, whereas in African American women's writing 'she is a complex woman who has survived the indignity of rape'.[77] Ultimately, *The Color Purple* is a monument not just to Bessie Smith and Zora Neale Hurston, but to the black victims and survivors of sexual abuse who historically have been silenced in white (and in black male) literature, but who have expressed their pain in the black vernacular of the blues. It is also, crucially, a monument in which the black English of the oral tradition is forever set in print. June Jordan explains how important it is that linguistic diversity be affirmed rather than displaced by a spurious notion of standard English:

> Black English is not exactly a linguistic buffalo; as children, most of the thirty-five million Afro-Americans living here depend on this language for our discovery of the world. But then we approach our maturity in a larger social body that will not support our efforts to become anything other than the clones of those who are neither our mothers nor our fathers. We begin to grow up in a house where every true mirror shows us the face of somebody who does not belong there, whose walk and whose talk will never look or sound 'right', because that house was meant to shelter a family that is alien and hostile to us.[78]

In *The Color Purple* Alice Walker shows black and white readers a mirror that reflects them back in a house of fiction where they belong. In a very real way, Celie's bluesy and vernacular letters were indeed written, as critic Valerie Babb observes, 'to undo what writing has done'.[79]

5

The Temple of My Familiar
(1989)

'Last night I dreamed I was showing you my temple', Miss Lissie
said. [...] 'Anyway, my familiar – what you might these days,
unfortunately, call a "pet" – was a small, incredibly beautiful creature that was part bird, for it was feathered, part fish, for it could
swim and had a somewhat fish/bird shape, and part reptile, for it
scooted about like geckoes do, and it was all over the place while I
talked to you. Its movements were graceful and clever, its expression mischievous and full of humor. It was *alive*! You, by the way,
Suwelo, were a white man, apparently, in that life, very polite, very
well-to-do, and seemingly very interested in our ways' (138).[1]

This is how Miss Lissie begins her parable of the temple of my familiar, a parable that explains not just the title of Walker's fourth and most
voluminous novel, but also its message, its narrative strategy, and its
overarching theme. The setting of this scene is near the beginning
of the book, when Suwelo, an African American historian, has come
to Baltimore from San Francisco in order to take care of his recently
deceased uncle's estate. Suwelo is getting acquainted with Uncle
Rafe's close friends, Miss Lissie and Mr Hal. Recognising that Suwelo
is in something of an emotional and spiritual crisis because his marriage as well as his career as a history teacher are obviously in trouble,
the old – and decidedly odd – couple proceed to enlighten him by telling him their personal histories. In Miss Lissie's case, this history is
long and varied, since she can remember former lives stretching back
to a time before humanity even existed. In the passage above she is
remembering a spell as a priestess in – we assume – Africa, where she
is visited by Suwelo in his previous incarnation as a white explorer
'seemingly interested in our ways'. The fact that Suwelo in this story
is a white man is significant, because at this point in the framing narrative of the novel he is likewise still 'a white man' by education and
inclination, trying to save his marriage to Fanny, and unable to teach

history as anything other than what is on record, that is: written in white men's books. What we see in this scene then is a confrontation between African and Western cultures and modes of knowledge, a confrontation that leads to the escape of Miss Lissie's familiar – in both senses of that word. For, in order not be distracted from her conversation with the explorer, the priestess tries to contain the familiar by imprisoning it in ever more drastic ways, until in the end it breaks out of its prison and flies away. The lesson Miss Lissie learns from this is that the urge to curb another's freedom always rebounds on you, or as the epigraph to Part Two of the novel has it: 'Helped are those who learn that the deliberate invocation of suffering is as much a boomerang as the deliberate invocation of joy' (164).

But there is another lesson too: Suwelo's imposition of his male/ white discourse on Miss Lissie causes her familiar – here in the sense of women's ancient wisdom and cultural lore – to escape. As an academic historian, Suwelo is alienated from his African American past; he has lost sight of his African heritage as well as his female side, and this wilful blindness makes for his increasing emotional and intellectual confusion. Miss Lissie's parable of the familiar serves to reconnect him (and us, as readers) with an unrecorded history; it is her personal *memory* that explains the epistemological break caused by colonialism, a break that discredited African tradition and orality and replaced it with Western rationality and written discourse. Therefore, the loss of the familiar is not only lamented because of its beauty or its status as faithful companion or 'pet', nor is the familiar simply a symbol for discredited knowledge; it has multiple associations. In the context of the novel as a whole, the combination of its birdlike, fishlike, and reptilian features makes it into a hybrid creature, much like the human characters whom we get to meet and who are all of mixed ancestry, even if they do not know it yet. As we shall see, part of the narrative's trajectory is the tracing of this ancestry back to a common source, that of humankind's unity with the natural world. When that unity was fractured – first because of men's domination of women, and then again because of colonialism – humans were set adrift, divided from each other along racial and gender lines and divided within themselves, their spirits broken. Suwelo's and Carlotta's lives at the beginning of the novel are broken too, but both recover their wholeness in the course of their search for regeneration. The extent to which others can help them in their quest is signalled by their connection with the natural world. Snakes, fish, lions, and monkeys populate Miss Lissie's memories as

well as her paintings, for example. Zedé and Arveyda are the feathered creatures, both of Indian ancestry. They have the red parrot as
their familiar (146), while Fanny's earliest memory is also of a red
bird (175) – an early indication of her spiritual kinship with Arveyda.
The peacock feathers that Zedé uses to make her capes are echoed
in the name of the great-great-aunt of the white American woman
who rescues her, Eleandra Burnham-Peacock, a cross-cultural trav-
eller like Zedé herself. As the his- 'n' her- stories of these characters
gradually become more intertwined, their identities and distinctive
features begin to merge into one interracial and multicultural family,
a hybrid organism like the familiar. And the familiar can be taken as
a metaphor for the novel's form too, as Bonnie Braendlin observes:

> This hybrid creature offers a clue to Walker's narrative strategy
> in *Temple*, which mixes tones and styles with abandon; at times
> Walker's language is serious and beautifully lyrical, at other times
> comic and clichéd. An unconventional, non-narrative text, the
> novel may be read as pastiche –a juxtaposing of the profound and
> the mundane not intended to 'gel at any junction'.[2]

No doubt Braendlin is right in seeing the familiar as a figuration of
the novel's formal project, but her argument that it can usefully be
read as a pastiche of the *Bildungsroman* and is not intended to 'gel'
is less convincing. For *The Temple of My Familiar* does hold together,
not 'at any junction' but at virtually every point, as will become clear
later in this chapter. Out of its various source materials a unity is
forged that is perhaps best described as conceptual or philosophical
rather than manifesting itself as structural or narrative coherence.
Just as the novel's content fuses history with memory, booklearning
with spirituality, and humanity with the natural world, the familiar's beauty, composed of the talents and traits of various species,
metaphorises and synthesises the multiplicity of stories and characters we find here.

That said, making sense of the plot is a challenge for readers and
critics alike. How do you read something as startlingly experimental as 'a romance of the last 500.000 years', in Walker's own words?[3]
All the usual expectations of a novel have to be suspended, which is
why Lillie P. Howard calls it a 'maddening' book:

> *The Temple* is about everyone and everything. [...] Its movement
> flings one back and forth across millennia. [...] The result is mental

and physical disorientation. [...] The work defies full explanation because it is meant to be experienced, without judgement, rather than explained or rendered anew.[4]

If Howard is right, then the critic's job becomes almost impossible, yet it is important to at least try to find a meaningful way through this epic story across centuries and continents, and to discover what Walker's purpose in deliberately disorienting the reader might be. In what follows I shall suggest three possible approaches, not mutually exclusive, that might give some shape to the ostensible chaos which is *The Temple of My Familiar*. They are, in order of appearance: the increasing influence of Jungian psychology on Walker's writing, to be continued in the next chapter; the family saga as a generic model with a long ancestry in Southern fiction; and the concept of diaspora literature as developed in post-colonial literatures and theories. These three approaches are all centrally concerned with the interplay of history and memory, as my concluding remarks will make clear, so that *The Temple* becomes more familiar through the forging of a hybrid critical method of my own.

JUNG, THE CREATIVE PROCESS, SPIRITUALITY, AND THE CRITICS

At the end *of The Color Purple* Alice Walker thanks 'everybody in this book for coming' and signs off as 'A. W., author and medium'. Walker explains what she meant by that intriguing statement in the essay 'Writing *The Color Purple*'. There she describes how Celie, Shug, and some of the other characters first were trying to contact her by speaking *through* her and then, having forced their author out of New York and San Francisco, came to 'visit' her in the northern California countryside in order to tell their stories. Less than a year after she had started to write it *The Color Purple* was finished and, says Walker, it was as if she had lost everybody she loved at once.[5]

What are we to make of this? Was Alice Walker suffering from delusions? Or did she, on the contrary, express here some ancient African understanding of the spiritual world that conventional, rationalist Western thinking regards as superstition? *Or* is there a third possibility, that she was merely trying to explain the intractable forces that compel an artist to create something she cannot necessarily predict, control, or plan in advance? On the face of it,

Walker's schizophrenic account of characters who talk not only through, but also *at* their author in the process of creation, combines two contradictory notions of what writers do when they write. On one hand, the author constructs and controls the characters like a puppeteer, scattering them across the globe and giving them a hard time only to reunite them, happily ever after, at the end. On the other hand, the medium records what the characters tell her of their own lives, and acts simply as a conduit for their stories and their voices. The medium, in other words, is unable to control the characters' independent existence; she becomes their instrument and mouthpiece. In designating herself 'author and medium' Walker thus is *both* puppet (her string pulled by her characters) and puppeteer: she claims *and* disavows responsibility for the creative process at one and the same time. Perhaps we should not be too quick to assume that this paradox reflects an impossible combination of Western and non-Western conceptions of artistic production. After all, Walker's experience of her characters as real people who talk to her accords with that of many creative writers. Gloria Anzaldúa, the Chicana poet and theorist, describes her writing process in terms very similar to Walker's:

> When I create stories in my head, that is, allow the voices and scenes to be projected in the inner screen of my mind, I 'trance'. I used to think I was going crazy or that I was having hallucinations. But now I realize it is my job, my calling, to traffic in images.[6]

Walker's description of a sense of loss upon finishing the novel is equally commonplace and not at all surprising. If we imagine, first, a writer's seclusion with those voices and scenes for months on end, then it becomes easy to understand what a void is left behind once the process of externalisation in writing is completed. In the context of *The Temple of My Familiar*, Walker's self-designation as 'author and medium' more importantly concords with a Jungian conception of the self in which each of us, whether we acknowledge it or not, is always already two: a conscious and an unconscious being. 'It is by no means a pathological symptom', writes Jung, 'it is a normal fact that can be observed at any time and everywhere. [...] This predicament is a symptom of a general unconsciousness that is the undeniable common inheritance of all mankind'.[7] In his therapeutic practice Jung developed this idea, as Anthony Storr explains, to the extent that he encouraged his patients to personify, or anthropomor-phise, different aspects of their own personality, even to the point of giving them names and having dialogues with them. Jung himself conducted conversations with a figure who appeared in his dreams, and whom he named Philemon. 'The language he uses about such figures suggests that, *as mediums believe*, he thought of them existing in an "imperishable world" and manifesting themselves from time to time through the psyche of an individual', according to Storr (my emphasis).[8] Walker is thus not alone in her delusion, if such it is, that Celie and Shug exist in some other sphere beyond that of what we commonly perceive as reality. But neither do we have to believe that she is uniquely gifted as a medium or blessed with second sight, because of the fact that she does perceive them. Jung believed that all of us have that capacity, if only we would use it, and far from driving us mad it would actually enhance our well-being and make us more sane, because 'Modern man [...] has lost his spiritual values to a positively dangerous degree. His moral and spiritual tradition has disintegrated, and he is now paying the price for this break-up in world-wide disorientation and dissociation'.[9] We can hear the voice of Miss Lissie here, harmonising with Jung's. Alice Walker's signature as 'author and medium', then derives from a Jungian conception, not just of the creative process, but of subjectivity and psychic health itself.[10] In such a conception of psychic health the conscious activity of writing is happily joined with an unconscious receptivity to the spirits, and in *The Temple of My Familiar*, as in *Possessing the Secret of Joy* where he appears in human form, Jung's spirit is pervasive.

It doesn't take much more than a superficial reading of *The Temple of My Familiar* to see that Walker is concerned, here, with the 'world-wide disorientation and dissociation' diagnosed by Jung, and with the rehabilitation of 'superstition' in order to heal humankind and put the world back together again. It is obvious in the journey that Suwelo makes, for example, that rationalism is not the *episteme* of choice in this novel, just as it is clear that his initial conception of a book-learnable, linear history that can be taught and swallowed whole will not hold in Walker's larger scheme of things. Carlotta, who discovers this before Suwelo does, believes that academic knowledge is now obsolete, because '"It's too late to teach people what they need to know by the methods that are used in colleges"' (417). Why should this be so? The implication in *The Temple of My Familiar* as a consciousness-raising novel for the new age is that that new age demands much more than a distanced and disengaged book-learning, and this wider and more 'organic' conception of education has a political dimension too, as Suwelo discovers. The 'American' history he is so disenchanted with is clearly a white and a dominant history, written – as the cliché goes – by the winners. The African writer Ngũgĩ wa Thiong'o argues in his seminal essay 'Decolonising the Mind' along similar lines that the education he received in Kenya, modeled on the British university system, did not empower people but made them feel diminished as Africans: 'Education ... tends to make them feel their inadequacies ... and their inability to do something about the conditions governing their lives. They become more and more alienated from themselves and from their natural and social environment'.[11] The revised model of education Walker presents in *The Temple of My Familiar* is remarkably similar to the one Ngũgĩ puts forward. For both, the oral tradition and the cultural memories embedded in everyday practices such as storytelling, music, and dance are central to the project of educating or re-educating black people, whether they be Africans or African Americans. As far as Walker is concerned, anybody who is willing to question the hegemonic Western tradition that produced slavery and colonialism as well as rationality and scientific progress must subject him- or herself to such a process of re-education (see also Grange Copeland in Chapter 2). And this is what *The Temple of My Familiar* is all about, as Lissie Lyles' epigraph to the novel testifies: 'If they have lied about Me/they have lied about everything'.

It is important to understand that this novel is designed to engage its audience in a project of re-education, because critics, reviewers, and many so-called ordinary readers have not taken kindly to *The Temple of My Familiar*. What they see as Walker's increasingly mystical tendency to foster belief in spirits, to hear voices, and to consort with creatures encountered in former lives, as Miss Lissie does, is in fact a misrecognition of the serious questioning of Western thought that goes on here, or – indeed – indicative of a refusal to engage with it in the first place. It betrays also, of course, an ignorance of the Jungian dimension of Walker's critique, and whatever one may think of its validity, at least it should be noted that the system of thought put forward in *The Temple of My Familiar* has a pedigree and is not just conjured up out of thin air. Still, a brief discussion of the novel's critical reception can give us a good sense of the forces Walker is up against with her re-education project, and may help to elucidate some of the novel's more obscure passages.

In 'A Turning of the Critical Tide?' Carol Iannone is hopeful that with *The Temple of My Familiar* Walker fans will finally see the error of their ways. She notes that reviews have been highly critical of Walker's generalisations, 'smugness', and inaccurate uses of history; that her inability to 'create plot and structure effectively' is now evident for all to see, and that the attraction of ever happier endings is beginning to pale. *The Temple of My Familiar*, Iannone concludes, is 'a sorry sack of silliness' and the sooner we recognise that the better it will be for us and for literature at large.[12] Obviously, from a critic who states first off that she is against the 'infusion of politics into literature' and who dismisses the positive reception of *The Color Purple* as 'literary affirmative action', we cannot expect a serious engagement with Walker's work. Nevertheless it is worth taking note of Iannone's argument, because it is one that better-informed and well-meaning readers have advanced as well. Walker's move to faddish, frivolous San Francisco has done her work no good, some say, and her womanism has lost its roots in Southern blackness and is worshipping a Californian goddess of the good life instead.

Indicative of such a shift from a concern with political and social issues in the earlier novels to the realm of the spiritual in this one, might be Walker's explanation, in *The Temple of My Familiar*, of how the Americas' original inhabitants came to be named 'Indians'. Whereas received wisdom has it that European travellers mistook the native peoples of the Americas for those of India on the next continent along (and thus misnamed them, as colonisers have a habit of doing) Carlotta discovers that 'an Italian explorer considered them, on first take, to be *indios*, "in God"' (19). Carlotta, who here stands in for Walker, borrows this idea from the Native American activist Russell Means, who argues that it is quite acceptable to call Native Americans 'Indians', because it is to see them as people-in-God.[13] On this account Columbus, the Italian explorer, unwittingly got it right, and colonial misprision is redefined as respectful recognition of a superior spirituality: 'Indian' is now not an improper, but a proper name for the native peoples of the Americas. Walker, following Means, thus appropriates the colonised's name and turns it into an honorific. What matters here is not so much whether the received or the new wisdom about how the Indians got their name is historically correct, but the way that each functions as shorthand for a particular conception of the colonial enterprise. In renaming Indians as beings 'in God', the colonial record of conquest and (mis)appropriation of lands and peoples (in which the Indian

'Manhattan' becomes 'New Amsterdam', and then 'New York', for example) is erased. Carlotta's discovery then absolves the colonists of their historical guilt, but it also robs them of their victory, and a negative is turned into a positive.

In the Jungian scheme, such a use of the past in order to serve present needs is known as *zurückphantasieren*, or retrospective fantasy.[14] In his 1929 lecture 'Some Aspects of Modern Psychotherapy' Jung advocates retrospection not so much as a means of 'discovering' childhood trauma to explain the cause of present ills, but as a way of unlocking the collective unconscious: '[the patient] will enter first into the treasure-house of collective ideas and then into creativity. In this way he will discover his identity with the whole of humanity, as it ever was, and ever shall be'.[15] Jung clarifies this in terms reminiscent of cultural relativism in another lecture from 1929, 'The Aims of Psychotherapy', in which he says that it is a mistake for the missionary to pronounce the strange gods of the colonised to be 'mere illusion … as though our so-called reality were not equally full of illusion. In psychic life, as everywhere in our experience, *all things that work are reality*, regardless of the names men choose to bestow on them' (my emphasis).[16] If this is so, then obviously the distinction between use and abuse of historiography, and that between therapeutic and ideological purposes of retrospective fantasy, are easily blurred and highly problematic, for historians and literary scholars alike. The critics of Walker's revisioning of history in *The Temple of My Familiar* thus have a point, as do those who see in it a San Franciscan influence of new age thinking. It is true that in this novel Walker's earlier concern with Southern racism, with poverty and the resulting oppression of women and children by means of domestic violence and emotional abuse, has disappeared and is replaced with an exploration of new modes of consciousness amongst the affluent middle class.

It is no longer the poor Southern family, or the mixed-up, messed-up young black woman who takes centre stage, but the artist him/ herself. Towards the end of the narrative Arveyda, the musician, thinks of himself, Fanny, Carlotta, Suwelo, Carlotta's mother Zedé, and all their children as a 'new age clan' (446). And this is exactly how they appear by that stage: unburdened by material worries they can be a loving, creative, extended family which is diverse in plumage and without a care in the world – other than that of the survival of the Planet. Global, spiritual, and ecological concerns have replaced the local, political, and domestic ones of the earlier novels – although, of course, Walker would equate the two: the local is now the global, ecology is political and the spiritual is – precisely – the domestic and familiar. Again we are reminded here of the end of *The Color Purple*, where Celie addresses her last letter to 'Dear God. Dear stars, dear trees, dear sky, dear peoples. Dear Everything. Dear God' and ends it with the happiness that has given her a new lease of life: 'Matter of fact, I think this is the youngest us ever felt'.[17] This is very much in the spirit of *The Temple of My Familiar*, which also ends in universal bliss and harmony. Walker's critical revision of history and of the Western *episteme* thus entails a vision of personal and communal wholeness along Jungian lines, a microcosmic representation of 'worldwide orientation and association' in which 'superstition' is revalued as knowledge and moral and spiritual traditions are reintegrated in a collective consciousness. Celie, Shug, Tashi, and Olivia all make their reappearance here to live out their new age, which paradoxically – but in a way that Jung would understand – means remembering their old, pre-historic ages as well.

San Francisco understands it too, and this may be why Ursula LeGuin, the critic of the *San Francisco Book Review*, is rather more receptive to Walker's time travel in this novel than is J. M. Coetzee in the *New York Times Book Review*. More than this being simply a matter of the difference between East and West coast sensibilities, it is possible that LeGuin understands the imaginative, magic realist qualities of Walker's work as a feminist science-fiction writer would, and is therefore more inclined to accept what others merely see as the indulgence of an absurd kind of fantasy. Coetzee objects that '[W]hatever new worlds and new histories we invent must carry conviction: they must be possible worlds, possible histories, not untethered fantasies; and they must be born of creative energy, not dreamy fads'.[18] LeGuin on the other hand notes that

> So many women are writing such imaginations now that it is surely a communal undertaking responding to a communal need. Those whose minds are locked in the conservatism of 'growth', and ever 'higher' technology based on unlimited exploitation, see these tribal societies (real and imagined) only as escapist regressions; they cannot understand that women are studying such societies in a radical and subversive effort to think back to before things went wrong.[19]

It is not that Coetzee does not recognise the critical edge Walker gives to her reinvention of history – he does – but more that, as a (white)

African writer of historical fiction, he has difficulty with a notion of history as storytelling, whether that story is told by authoritative white males (in their own image and interest) or by counter-hegemonic black women who remember previous lives (in *their* own image and interest). In this case, the reviewers' own position as creative writers thus clearly forces their evaluation of *The Temple of My Familiar* in opposite directions, and it may be as well to remember the polarising effect that this novel tends to have on readers, depending on their political and epistemological orientations. We shall return to the question of history and storytelling in due course, but first we must look more closely at the narrative itself and its extensive cast of characters. The genre of the family saga might provide us with a more conventional map of reading than the Jungian approach of retrospective fantasy does but, as we shall see, the two are intimately connected.

FAMILIAR STORIES: REWRITING THE FAMILY SAGA

Alice Walker's interest in the family saga was already apparent in *The Third Life of Grange Copeland* and in *The Color Purple*. Both are novels set in the South, and both of them tell the story of a dysfunctional family across generations, a family that is made whole again by the action of enlightened individuals. In *The Family Saga in the South* Robert O. Stephens surveys the long pedigree this genre has in Southern literature. He lists the major conventions of the family saga as follows:

> continuity of the consanguine family through multiple generations; identity established at the time of removal to a new homeland; preservation of the family's special attribute; the lingering influence of patriarchal–matriarchal conflicts; displacement of the inheritance; decline in later generations when compared with the strength or nobility of the earlier; work of a historian–narrator to collect and evaluate evidence of the family past; correlation of family history with public history; puzzlement about actions and motivations of the ancestors; recognition of type scenes; awareness of the significance of talismanic objects, places or actions; and achievement of moments of vision.[20]

This is a fairly full description of what the genre entails – in popular as well as 'literary' writing – and some of the traits Stephens identifies are readily recognisable in Walker's work. And yet, rarely will the white bias of a literary genre (or of the definition of it) be so clear as it is here. Although Stephens does discuss the black family saga in his book as well, it is obvious in the description above that the African American family saga is rather unlikely to have 'displaced inheritances' as a major part of the plot, nor is identity likely to be 'established at the time of removal to a new homeland', with the family mansion serving as the Faulkneresque architectural expression of a dynasty's rise and fall. It follows that Stephens' summary finds its full expression in the plantation saga, and African American family sagas can be but poor and deviant relations of this model. Nevertheless, Stephens' schema for the family saga in the South is useful because it sets us on the trail of Walker's revision of it, first in *The Third Life of Grange Copeland*, where few of the features survive other than in bitterly ironised form ('lingering patriarchal–matriarchal conflicts', for example); then in *The Color Purple* (where there is a 'displaced inheritance' and a historian–narrator who achieves moments of vision); and here in *The Temple of My Familiar*, where all the conventions apply in metaphorised or reversed incarnations. For a start, Walker redefines consanguinity, in the story that brings Carlotta's and Suwelo's respective clans together, as spiritual kinship, but a kinship also of the African American and the Amerindian. And not for the first time: remember Meridian's great-grandmother Feather Mae, and the quotation from Black Elk in *The Color Purple*. Here Ola, Fanny's African father, is writing a play about Elvis as an Indian (213), Corinne's mother turns out to have been a Cherokee (172), and we are encouraged to read William Loren Katz's book *Black Indians* along with Fanny.[21] Walker's theory about American hybridity is expressed, as so often, by Ola in this novel, who explains:

> That in [Elvis] white Americans found a reason to express their longing and appreciation for the repressed Native American and black parts of themselves. Those non-European qualities they have within them and all around them, constantly, but which they have been trained from birth to deny [*sic*] (214).

The message could not be stated more clearly. The second characteristic of the family saga on Stephens's list, identity, is therefore established here not as a unitary thing but as a recognition of hybridity, and that recognition comes about not through settlement, but through migration and return. And if we follow the list further, other revisions of the convention also come into focus: 'decline in later generations' here and elsewhere becomes progress in later generations, and the family's 'special attribute' is, if anything, abuse and conflict – notably 'matriarchal/patriarchal conflict' writ large – which are not to be preserved, but resolved. In *The Third Life of Grange Copeland* the theme was the perpetuation of abuse against women and children, across generations, and how to change it. Grange's migration to the North, the political education he receives there and the love he finds, upon his return, for his granddaughter Ruth are the three factors that enable him to redeem himself, the South, and a future for Ruth. Migration then – here in the shape of the Great Migration, which drew so many Southern blacks in the early part of the twentieth century to the Northern industrial cities – is a key element in this early family saga, but equally important is the trope of return to the homeland of the South. Migration enables enlightenment, but it is the return which makes reconciliation and redemption possible. It is probably no coincidence that, as Hazel Carby points out, this same trope of educational journey and a return that then enables the sharing of insights gained, is also evident in Zora Neale Hurston's *Their Eyes Were Watching God*: 'Janie, as intellectual, has travelled outside of the community and defines herself as "a delegate to de big 'ssociation of life"; her journey is the means by which knowledge can be brought into the community', Carby argues.[22] Something similar occurs in *The Color Purple*, if we can see Nettie's journey to Africa as having a role to play in Celie's education, and Shug's multiple departures and returns as part of her experiences of the wider world, which in turn benefit Celie. She, unlike Grange and Janie, does not have the opportunity to explore that world directly, but Celie's and Nettie's correspondence and Shug's blues singing are not just instrumental in, but actually constitutive of, Celie's own journey from victim to heroine, without her ever having to leave home. *The Color Purple* as a family saga therefore takes the themes of repetitive abuse and migration/return further than *The Third Life of Grange Copeland*. It begins, in the mould of the earlier novel, as a figuration of the break-up of the African American family reminiscent of slavery, with family members bought and sold and gender relations in the black family mimicking those of the master and slave on the plantation. We might also note that *The Color Purple* even has a Middle Passage in reverse, when Nettie travels to Africa as a missionary. This journey severs her, albeit unwittingly, from her sister in America through the intervention of Mr—— in the role of Celie's 'Master' and owner, just as the slaves were cut off from their African families when being brought from Africa to America. The novel ends, however, with an integration of the acculturated 'African' and American branches of this fragmented family, when Nettie returns with Celie's now Africanised children Adam and Olivia, the latter of whom reappears in *The Temple of My Familiar*. Adam's African wife Tashi, moreover, becomes the protagonist of Walker's fifth novel, *Possessing the Secret of Joy*, thus making a trilogy of the adventures of Celie's ever-growing family tree. At the same time, of course, these three novels become a family saga in themselves in that they are books that continue each other in the most literal sense: they form a textual family.

The role of Stephens' narrator–historian is most visible in *The Temple of My Familiar*, although Nettie's efforts to piece her and Celie's histories together *and* to put them in context and connect them with the public history of colonialism and Southern racism deserve mention here as well. In a sense, the role of historian–narrator is duly divided in that novel between the sisters, with Nettie as the historian, writing in a public discourse, and Celie as the vernacular narrator. Narrative perspective in *The Temple of My Familiar*, which is third-person but shifts from section to section, does not allow for the conventional younger family member to try to puzzle out her history by reading diaries, hearing stories and leafing through photo albums. Instead, *The Temple of My Familiar* has multiple historians and narrators, some of whom conform to the genre convention very closely, such as Mary Jane Briden and Suwelo. Others – notably Miss Lissie – act primarily as sources, however, and others still are detectives who intrepidly go out in search of clues and follow them through. Fanny is a good example of the latter, and it is not so very startling, given her postmodern condition of psychic fragmentation and feminist frustration, that her clues lead her eventually to the psychotherapist's consulting room. This, we may say, is a very strange family saga indeed, but then that is Walker's point: our true family cannot be found in the home, but first in familiarisation with the self and then in connection with like-spirited others, and finally with the universe as a whole.

As will be clear from what I have said so far, it is difficult, even impossible, to describe the plot of *The Temple of My Familiar* in anything but the broadest *or* the most detailed terms. This is partly, as Madelyn Jablon argues, because the novel has no centre; it is 'an egalitarian narrative in which no character or point of view is privileged'.[23] As a family saga or, rather, as yet another revision of the conventional family story with its generational continuities and structural linearity, it is the story of how two families come together through multiple migrations of mind and body. Beginning with Zedé and Carlotta's flight from Central America to California, where Carlotta meets and marries Arveyda in San Francisco, the story then moves to Suwelo's recent journey from San Francisco to Baltimore, where he meets Mr Hal and Miss Lissie, the 'elders' who become his guiding spirits in a process of re-education that takes him from straight and rational thinking and historiography into the convoluted (oral) histories of the people of the African diaspora. Suwelo's wife Fanny takes her own journey to Africa for personal growth, and in order to shed her hatred of whites. If we concentrate just on this set of main characters, we see how at the end the two opposing couples (Arveyda and Carlotta, Fanny and Suwelo) cross over and mix into an extended family or tribe, epitomised by Fanny's recognition of Arveyda as her spirit, and Arveyda's of Fanny as his flesh (449).

But a lot of water has to flow under the bridge before they reach that point. Their stories are criss-crossed by others, picked up and dropped in a seemingly haphazard way. *The Temple of My Familiar* is packed with stories and sub-stories; its structure – insofar as one is discernible – resembles nothing so much as a Russian doll-type sequence of embedded narratives. Looked at more closely, it becomes clear that all these mini-stories have something to contribute to the larger frame of Arveyda and Carlotta, Suwelo and Fanny. The story about ancient traditions of worship of the Mexican goddess for example, which Zedé uncovers in Central America when she goes there with Arveyda, is later echoed by Miss Lissie's memory of goddess worship in an African context. When Fanny goes to Africa she, in turn, finds out about the kinship between cults around Medusa, Isis and Athena – yet another group of goddesses who are later replaced by male idols. Every element, however apparently anecdotal, is echoed by another, usually from a different cultural context. Or take the story Arveyda hears in his home town, Terre Haute, from the Jewish greengrocer Mr Isaac. He, having left Palestine for America, one day decides to go back to Israel because he misses hearing the sound of Arabic with which he grew up: 'For Arabs had lived all around him in Palestine, just as colored people lived all around him in Terre Haute' (26). Mr Isaac, then, makes his return and becomes another migrant who learns something on his travels, even if it is something he actually already knew.

Perhaps the best characterisation of *The Temple of My Familiar* is that it is an oral novel, a book of conversations and of storytelling. Adam Sol puts it thus: 'The techniques [Walker] chooses are those used between friends or intimates: oral storytelling, of course, but also letters and journals. [...] and we register disbelief, amazement, or wonder as [the characters] do'.[24] Divided into five parts and dozens of chapters, again we see Walker's preference for the short form, albeit in a novel of epic proportions. But then storytelling is another Southern convention, as the novelist Eudora Welty recalls: '[W]e in the South have grown up being narrators. We have lived in a place ... where storytelling is a way of life. [...] We heard stories told by relatives and friends. A great many of them were family tales'.[25] *The Temple of My Familiar* is a storytelling book not because, in Welty's sense, people are rooted in place and community and therefore exchange familiar tales, but precisely because they *lack* such a sense of place and connection: storytelling is a way to achieve it. In the words of Ikenna Dieke, 'the art of conversation [is] raised to a ritual act of phatic communion', which transcends a simple exchange of views and becomes transformative.[26] The narrative frame therefore surrounds representation of a variety of cultural practices in which people pass on their knowledge and experiences. Little actually 'happens' in it, but what action there is is conveyed through exchanges of stories: Miss Lissie reminisces in person and on audiotape, in letters and in the paintings that she leaves Suwelo. Mary Jane/Ann Briden/Haverstock discovers her great aunt's Victorian diary in a library in England, and we read extracts from that diary. Suwelo sorts through Uncle Rafe's belongings and finds among them Miss Lissie's muddied white high-heeled shoes, a material reminder of her life in the South in the 1950s. Fanny recounts her story and her feelings about being a black woman in America to her psychotherapist – a Chicana woman of mixed ancestry like herself. Arveyda learns from his trip with Zedé; Suwelo learns from Lissie's time travelling, Fanny from her analyst and her African father and sister, and Mary Jane/Ann from her own family history. The formal and thematic revision of the Southern family saga that Walker undertakes in this and previous novels thus neatly fits in with the storytelling tradition of her native South, as it does with the process of re-education that the characters, and we as readers, undergo in engaging with *The Temple of My Familiar*. We might even say that ultimately we are the ones who have to undertake the task of the historian–narrator ourselves in joining up the disparate strands presented in the novel. The family saga, then, is one strand, whereas the theme of hybridity and the African diaspora represent another, as we shall see next.

CONTINENTS LOST AND GAINED: WRITING DIASPORA

Walker's textual family has its members increasingly scattered across the globe. *Possessing the Secret of Joy* is set predominantly in Africa but also in Europe and the United States, and *The Temple of My Familiar* moves backwards and forwards, as the slave trade did, between the United States, Africa, Central America, and Europe. Following on from *The Color Purple*'s final reunion of Celie's and Nettie's families, its main focus is on Africa and the United States, but the cultural formation and 'placement' of African Americans is here made more complex by the tracing of connections with Indians and Europeans as well. Hybridity is key in all these migrations. The trip that Fanny, Olivia's daughter and Celie's granddaughter, takes to Africa may at first seem indicative of a search for her African roots. Fanny writes that, upon meeting her African half-sister Nzingha Anne, she felt she was looking into a mirror that reflected only the African (279). Fanny, it appears, has found some kind of racial essence or truth about herself in her half-sister, but on closer inspection it is not quite as simple as that. For what Fanny discovers is a reconnection with *part* of herself, a part (call it blackness or – more accurately – a different, non-Western and non-oppressive mode of being) that has been denied expression in white-dominated America. What looks like a reflection of an essence is in fact, as the critic Terry Dehay puts it, a revelation of something deeper and rather less narcissistic:

> Fanny's discovery of her African self, and also of the truth of the socio-political nature of Africa, helps her to integrate the separate parts of herself and to reconstruct the nature of her relationship with the culture in which she lives. [...] She confronts her anger with white society by returning to the African country that represents *half* of her cultural heritage, where she learns that her anger is real but that in directing it at white people, she is missing the real target: any society that represses the enemy, regardless of color (my emphasis).[27]

Dehay's final phrase recalls the parable of the imprisoned familiar that escapes, but with a variation: any society that represses anything (including its friends, which it cannot recognise as such) is the enemy. In Africa, after all, Fanny finds that governments and ruling élites oppress minority peoples and suppress dissident opinions – like those of her father, the playwright Ola – in ways that are not so dissimilar from Western societies, and this is what Dehay means by Fanny's discovery of 'the socio-political nature of Africa'. Africa is thus not represented here as the homeland that Fanny as an African American can 'return to' in order to find her 'true self', for her true self is more dynamic and variegated than that. Fanny is a woman of many parts, of which Africa and America are but two. Dehay also draws attention to the fact that Fanny's journey to Africa is one of two journeys to a real or imagined 'home' in this novel. Zedé travels to Central America after she and Arveyda (her son-in-law) have fallen in love. For Zedé, born and bred there,

> [I]t is a true return from exile to the Central American country that was her home and to herself as a member of that cultural reality. Her return and remembering of herself also enables her daughter, Carlotta, to incorporate this remembered identity into her own sense of self as a Latina living in the United States.[28]

Not Zedé's and Fanny's journeys are paralleled here so much as the tasks that both Fanny and Carlotta face as hybrid citizens of the United States, *their* homeland, in integrating the different parts of their parents' histories and cultural heritages. And it is no accident that both Fanny and Carlotta live in San Francisco, where the mix of races and ethnicities is particularly apparent. Early on in the novel Arveyda, the rock star from Indiana, sees himself 'mirrored' in Carlotta's Indian looks. Carlotta in turn feels a kinship with the Hmong people in the Bay area, 'who seemed particularly intense and ancient to her, as they carried their tiny babies on their backs in bright multicolored clothing covered with mirrors, bells, shells and beads' (19). Such bells and shells are Carlotta's instruments towards the end of the novel, when she has reconciled herself with Arveyda and become a musician herself. Fanny, Carlotta, and Arveyda then are all of mixed ancestry, and their enlightenment consists in coming to terms with that fact, not in a negative or resigned way but by learning from the diverse cultures and histories that have gone into their making. In various ways, this is true of all the main characters: either literally or metaphorically, they

are of mixed ancestry and have to learn to integrate – first with themselves, and then also with each other. It is true even of Miss Lissie,
because she – who has lived *and remembers* many previous lives – in
the end also has to face up to the fact that she was a white man in at
least one of them (and one in which s/he kills the familiar, rather than
merely letting it escape). Among the more ordinary mortals Mr Hal
goes through his own process of enlightenment and reconciliation.
He tells Suwelo about his 'blissful' childhood on the islands off the
coast of Baltimore, because there weren't any white people around, yet
in the end he makes friends with Mr Pete, a Southern white 'cracker',
in the nursing home where Hal ends up after Lissie's death.

If we think of migration, re-education and integration as major
themes then, it no longer seems so bewildering (or so bad) that *The
Temple of My Familiar* is a book to get lost in. Eva Lennox Birch says
that '[It] demands a high level of reader sophistication to handle the
diversity of characters, and their interrelationships, as well as shifts
in time and location'.[29] This is true, if you are looking to restore a
conventional narrative order, but that may not be the point. Another
way of understanding the novel is to see that Walker does here what
Toni Morrison said of *Beloved*, that it 'yanked' the reader – through
sheer disorientation and confusion – into the world of the slaves,
or, more particularly, into a similarly disrupted subjectivity to that
of the Africans who experienced the Middle Passage and its subsequent physical and cultural violations.[30] *The Temple of My Familiar*
does not, of course, reproduce the violence of slavery but rather
the complexity and geographical, familial, and cultural confusions
and negotiations of the history of the black diaspora, which Paul
Gilroy has called 'the black Atlantic'. For Gilroy, the paradigm of
absolute cultural difference between black and white, Eurocentric,
and African traditions, is not only worn out by now, but was probably always a misrepresentation of the actuality of interchange and
cultural mixing in the traffic between not two, but at least three
continents: Africa, the Americas, and Europe. Gilroy writes:

> Regardless of their affiliation to the right, left or centre, groups
> have fallen back on the idea of cultural nationalism, on the
> over-integrated conceptions of culture which present immutable,
> ethnic differences as an absolute break in the histories of 'black'
> and 'white' people. Against this choice stands another, more dif-
> ficult option: the theorisation of creolisation, métissage, mestizaje,
> and hybridity.[31]

Gilroy then proceeds to offer just such a theorisation, in an effort to make us think more productively and more accurately about the interconnections, as well as the differences, between Western culture and that of Africa and its diaspora. And he is not the only one whose intellectual energy is, in the context of postmodernity and globalisation, devoted to a reconceptualisation of black/white oppositions and their attendant cultural simplifications. In his seminal work *In My Father's House* the philosopher Kwame Anthony Appiah attempts a similar project, beginning with his own experience of a diasporic family, which it is worth quoting at length:

> This book is dedicated to nine children – a boy born in Botswana, of Norwegian and Anglo-Ghanaian parents; his brothers, born in Norway and in Ghana; their four cousins, three boys in Lagos, born of Nigerian and Anglo-Ghanaian parents, and a girl in Ghana; and two girls, born in New Haven, Connecticut, of an African-American father and a 'white' American mother. These children, my nephews and my godchildren, range in appearance from the color and hair of my father's Asante kinsmen to the Viking ancestors of my Norwegian brother-in-law; they have names from Yorubaland, from Asante, from America, from Norway, from England. And watching them playing together and speaking to each other in their various accents, I, at least, feel a certain hope for the human future.[32]

It is not just the last sentence that echoes Walker's sentiments in *The Temple of My Familiar*, delighting in this rainbow coalition of familial ties. It is also the fact that it would be as complicated to describe the two 'clans' that merge into one in that novel as it is for Appiah to enumerate the members of his family of various ethnic and national descents. Walker's families, deriving from South America, the United States, and Africa, and the rest of her cast of characters, which incorporates Europe as well, are no fanciful anomalies or merely the fruits of wishful multicultural thinking; they exist in the real world in ever-increasing numbers. Nor is it the case that Appiah's diasporic family, or Arveyda's multifarious new age clan, are simply produced by class mobility (Appiah is a member of the Asante royal family in Ghana), educational privilege (which got him to England and later America), or by the cosmopolitanism that success affords. Migration, for poor peoples as well as rich individuals, is a dominant feature of the postmodern world, as is the mixing and matching of races, ethnicities, and cultures that goes along with increasing globalisation of the economy and the media. For this reason alone theorists like Gilroy or Appiah feel impelled to look again at our concepts of racial and cultural difference, and to critique the histories of Western nationalism as well as those of Pan-Africanism and black cultural nationalism in the United States, since these concepts and histories are no longer viable today. This is, however, the only thing they have in common with Walker's project in *The Temple of My Familiar*. For Walker is – as noted earlier – more concerned with spiritual lessons to be learned from diasporic cultures than she is interested in their historical development or theoretical validity. As a novelist rather than a theorist, Walker sees her task as an imaginative project of revaluation and revisioning, in which the word 'vision' is crucial. Wolfgang Karrer writes of Walker's characters that

> they may travel to South America or Africa or even Baltimore, but their true home is their common history, the history of humanity embodied in the goddess Lissie. [...] Walker makes them citizens of a multicultural and interethnnic world where going home means going forward into new relationships.[33]

Karrer's observation about 'home' as the 'history of humanity' and Appiah's hope for a multi-ethnic future remind us of what Alice Walker writes in the essay 'Saving the Life That Is Your Own' about the future of literature, as 'an immense story coming from a multitude of different perspectives' (see Chapter 1).[34] It is possible that Walker meant to explain that black and white writing complement each other, and that together they make up the multicoloured quilt that is 'this immense story' of world literature. But it is also possible to read this statement differently, in the light of Walker's concerns in *The Temple of My Familiar*, where she seems to pack the 'multitude of different perspectives' into one novel, which includes the stories of white Europeans as well as those of Native Americans, African Americans, Jews, Africans, men and women. As we have seen, this is not just a matter of content. Walker draws on a 'white' Southern genre like the family saga, but also on the oral, storytelling traditions of Africa and African America, and on Jungian psychoanalysis. In addition, she alludes to South American magic realism and revises an historical fantasy like Virginia Woolf's *Orlando*.

The various genres and forms Walker uses are, moreover, deployed in their appropriate contexts. Suwelo and Fanny are principally involved in the family saga, while Miss Lissie performs the role of the African *griot* (or village storyteller) and keeper of ancient wisdom. Fittingly, features of magic realism are especially evident at the beginning, in the story of Zedé and Carlotta's lives in an unspecified Central American country:

> Life was so peaceful that Zedé did not realize they were poor. She found this out when her father, a worker on the banana plantation they could also see from their house, became ill. At the same time, by coincidence, the traditional festivals of the village were forbidden. By whom they were forbidden, or 'outlawed' as her father said, Zedé was not sure. The priests, especially, were left with nothing to do. [....] Her father, a small, tired, brownskin man with graying black hair died while she was an earnest scholarship student at the university, far away in the noisy capital. Her mother now made her living selling her incredibly beautiful feather goods to the cold little gringa blonde who had a boutique on the ground floor of an enormous new hotel that sprung up near their village, seemingly overnight. (12)

The style of this passage, with its juxtaposition of rural idyll with approaching modernity and political unrest without concrete reference to a particular time and place, is reminiscent of Latin American fiction. It raises more questions and creates more mystery than it answers, in order to keep us guessing but also to posit an alternative reality and sense of time and place to that offered in the conventional realist novel. Later, Zedé becomes a schoolteacher and ends up in prison, from which she is rescued by Mary Ann Haverstock (who is to become Mary Jane Briden) then still a young American woman with radical inclinations and family money to burn, who brings Carlotta and Zedé to America in her aptly named yacht *Recuerdo* (memory). Such happenings, as well as the narrative of Carlotta's father Jesús and his role in the jungle as keeper of the holy stones, 'something not understood by norte americanos', Zedé says, would not be out of place in an Isabel Allende or Gabriel García Márquez novel (88). The use of magic realism is more obvious as pastiche (as it is when Miss Lissie is described, later on, as having been born without a hymen) than the ways in which Walker draws on Woolf's *Orlando* and Jungian psychoanalysis in *The Temple of My Familiar* (124).

Orlando is now chiefly known as the novel in which Woolf put her androgynous theory of writing into practice, but it is also the artistic biography of a poet who lives from the seventeenth through to the twentieth century. Its opening paragraph is cited at the beginning of Part Four, in which Fanny writes her letters to Suwelo from Africa, where she is discovering her heritage. That heritage includes a family history of women warriors, but Fanny's letters also incorporate her critique of African gender relations, and they tell Suwelo of her father Ola's new play, in which he belatedly atones for his abandonment of his first ('bush') wife. All this makes sense as a counter-narrative to Woolf's historical fantasy, whose beginning reads: 'He – for there could be no doubt of his sex, although the fashion of the time did something to disguise it – was in the act of slicing at the head of a Moor which swung from the rafters' (262). Woolf's often ironic tone with regard to gender and official historiography tends to obscure the colonialist assumptions the novel makes about English identity, right from this first sentence. In *The Temple of My Familiar* Walker creates an historical fantasy with an even broader time span than *Orlando*, in which gender roles become mutable not through a change of body (Orlando undergoes a sex-change) but a change of mind. In Fanny's letters, the empire writes back to *Orlando* to remind us of Africa's history before colonialism and women's role within it – like that of Nzingha, the Angolan warrior-queen. Part of Walker's polemical engagement with *Orlando* is also the fact that the artist takes centre stage here not as a noble (wo-)man poet, but as a creative practitioner for everyday use; Carlotta, for example, becomes a musician and Fanny a playwright, like her father. Zedé's craft with her feathers, Arveyda's music, Ola's plays, and also Fanny's massage skills are shown as all being part of a continuum of creative *work*, involving the body as much as the mind and spirit. M'Sukta, Mr Hal, and Miss Lissie's painting are part of this continuum as well: M'Sukta is a hut painter, not one who is engaged in fine art in the Western sense, yet the painting school Mary Jane establishes in her honour builds on this indigenous tradition in order to foster the development of African art. We might look to Jung again for some background to this kind of creativity. Describing how difficult it is in therapy to reshape the conscious ego of troubled adults who have already found a role in the world (even if they are not happy with it), Jung advocates creative expression as a means of access to the collective unconscious, and therefore of connection with the primeval past and with the universal archetypal images. Of this type of patient he says: 'Fully aware as he is of the social unimportance of his creative activity [...] [it] frees him from morbid dependence, and he thus acquires an inner stability and a new trust in himself'.[35] This

valorisation of creativity as therapy or self-fulfilment characterises
Suwelo and Fanny, Carlotta and Arveyda at the end; they are less artists than craftspeople, and less craftspeople than *amateurs* in the true
sense of that word: people who do what they do for the love of it. It is
tempting to interpret Walker's continuum of artistic production as a
comment on the state of the modern novel, and to read it as a loss of
faith in the importance of writing in the postmodern world. Her forays
into film-making (with Steven Spielberg on *The Color Purple* and with
Pratibha Parmar on *Warrior Marks*) might support such a view, if we
believe that they signal Walker's recognition of the fact that we now
live in a media-dominated, post-literate culture. But no great enthusi-
asm for visual media or the new information technologies is evident
in the novel. The arts and crafts that Walker's characters turn to in *The
Temple of My Familiar* are, if anything, of a pre-modern, more organic
kind: massage rather than video performance, and live percussion
rather than electronic music. The distinction critic Susan Willis makes
between mass and popular culture is useful here. Willis writes:

> [P]opular culture defines a cultural community where the pro-
> ducers of culture are also its consumers. [...] This community of
> production/consumption is cancelled out by mass culture, which
> is synonymous with capitalist culture, and the commodity form,
> whose primary feature is the distinct separation between those
> who control and produce the cultural commodity and those who
> buy it. Mass culture limits participation to consumption.[36]

In Willis' terms, *The Temple of My Familiar* foregrounds the kinds of
cultural practices that belong to popular culture *as a mode of resistance*
to mass culture's incursions into subjectivity and daily life. In the
light of this novel's message that the future for humankind lies in a
reconnection with the earth, the spirit, and most of all with the Other
(first and foremost the Other within ourselves), we might read its
form as an experimental one, which attempts to reconnect literary
representation with more 'organic', collaborative modes of imagin-
ing that reunite the realms of production and consumption. Think,
for example, of the African (American) practice of call and response,
which is often enacted in the conversations that are such a feature of
this novel, or of the *motif* of oral storytelling that similarly requires
a response in the form of questions or expressions of wonder for
its development. Bonnie Braendlin writes of an 'interrogative text',
because here 'style functions ... to urge readers toward disengaged

reflection upon self and society'.[37] And we can come at this formal experimentation from an intertextual angle too. Besides Woolf, the African novelist Bessie Head also plays a part in *The Temple of My Familiar*. Head expressed her faith in the future of writing in her autobiographical essay 'Notes on Novels' thus:

> I have found that the novel form is like a large rag-bag into which one can stuff anything – all of one's philosophical, social and romantic speculations. I have always reserved a special category for myself, as a writer – that of a pioneer blazing a new trail into the future. It would seem as though Africa rises at a point in history when world trends are more hopefully against exploitation, slavery and oppression – all of which has been synonymous with the name, Africa. I have recorded whatever hopeful trend was presented to me in an attempt to shape the future, which I hope will be one of dignity and compassion.[38]

The novel as 'rag-bag' and the writer blazing a new trail into the future accurately describe what Walker in *The Temple of My Familiar* is doing, and it is surely no coincidence that Head relates this new form explicitly to the history and current status of Africa as an exploited continent, and of the African novel as a counteracting force. Ngũgĩ wa Thiong'o, cited earlier, says something very similar in 'The Language of African Fiction': 'Not so long ago the novel, like God, was declared dead [...] What's clear is that something answering to the name "novel" has been showing significant signs of life somewhere in Africa and Latin America. The death of the novel was not therefore one of my problems'.[39] Like Bessie Head, and like Walker, Ngũgĩ expresses here a confidence in the future of the novel that is closely allied to post-colonial and to political writing as a mode of resistance to the Western *episteme* of realism, rationalism, and individualism. The fact that he alludes to the search for new gods in this extract as well is fortuitous, because it enables a further analogy between Walker's choice of experimental form in *The Temple of My Familiar* on one hand, and the search for the goddess on the other.

We should now be able to see how the author/medium, in a novel that tries to write the black diaspora and documents the search for the forgotten goddess, abandons the authority of the author as god and puts the god*dess* (or, in Eva Lennox Birch's words, 'a prophet-ess') in its place.[40] For those who accept the validity in Western culture of binary oppositions such as nature/culture, mind/body, and

male/female, the analogy might run something like this: whereas
the nineteenth century novel was concerned with empire, with the
plight of the bourgeois male, with progress – the latter conceived as
linear and mirrored in the novel's structure – and was narrated from
the perspective of an omniscient author-as-god, the new age novel
has the goddess as 'author' (or perhaps 'medium') and is therefore
its opposite. Like female-centred religions, this novel works along
maternal lines, aligns herself with nature and the body, with Africa
and Central America, and with supposedly female qualities such as
nurturing and healing. It has a cyclical rather than a linear structure, no plot to speak of – for it is not interested in the destination
but in the journey – and its narration is conducted through multiple
and speculative voices rather than just one authoritative one. You do
not have to believe that binary oppositions operate in an essentialist
and unchangeable way to see how they nevertheless function hier-
archically in Western culture, and how Walker's critique of the novel
form and of the role of the author serve to highlight that hierarchy by
upsetting it. The novel as 'rag-bag' is thus a hybrid form that reflects
its concern with diaspora and the hybridity of peoples and cultures;
as a matrilinear text it borrows from Head and Woolf, and Miss
Lissie's multiple lives represent the multiple – and silenced – voices
of black women's history, including that of the ancient goddesses of
Africa and Central America.

REMEMBERING THE GODDESS: CHALLENGING HISTORY THROUGH MEMORY

In *When God Was a Woman*, Merlin Stone writes:

> The theory that most societies were originally matrilineal, matri-
> archal and even polyandrous (one woman with several husbands)
> was the subject of several extensive studies in the late nineteenth
> and early twentieth centuries. [...] They suggested that all soci-
> eties had to pass through a matriarchal stage before becom-
> ing patriarchal and monogamous, which they appear to have
> regarded as a superior stage of civilization.[41]

Stone reminds us here of two things: that the study of ancient
female-centred religion is not some recent invention or a crackpot
radical feminist idea, *and* that scholarship is not necessarily true

and objective knowledge production, but a cultural practice invested with particular ideological interests. In the nineteenth century – the age of scientific racism and of Darwinism, after all – those interests often served the status quo of empire, patriarchy, and of progress through exploitation of the natural world. Clearly, Walker wants to reverse this notion of evolutionary superiority, and she employs the character of Miss Lissie to do so. Miss Lissie is polyandrous (she has two 'husbands', Mr Hal and Uncle Rafe) and she has been a goddess as well as a witch in her times. She describes in a letter to Suwelo how – and why – her life as a witch ended: '... whole families in Africa who worshipped the Goddess were routinely killed, sold into slavery, or converted to Islam at the point of the sword. Yes, ... I was one of those "pagan" heretics they burned at the stake' (222). Miss Lissie writes this letter in invisible ink, emphasising the invisibility of this largely forgotten history. However, her supposed 'memory' of being a witch does not enhance the credibility of this history, because here Lissie is more a narrative device than a character in the conventional, realist sense; LeGuin calls her 'a whole cast of characters by herself'.[42] Even so, Miss Lissie's submerged history of the displacement of the Goddess by patriarchy is not something she, or Walker, has simply made up. A body of scholarship now exists in feminist theology and in archaeology that attests to the widespread existence in prehistory of goddess worship and of the violent means deployed (by Christians, Muslims, and Levites) to eradicate it. Besides, in this extract Miss Lissie interestingly links up racism ('They burned us first – well, we were so visible') with the witch-hunts in Europe, and she describes how Christianity retained some of the ancient goddess worship from Africa, by combining the iconography of the Virgin Mary with that of black African goddesses like the Egyptian Isis or Nut/Neith or Hathor. This has a basis in fact: the Black Madonna is worshipped in places like northern Spain to this day. Finally, she blames Christianity and Islam for eradicating the ancient female-centred religions by force, relating in the process how slavery was not just perpetrated by whites, but was in fact already an indigenous practice of conquest in northern Africa. This is also what Merlin Stone argues: despite patriarchy's victory, 'myths, statues and documentary evidence reveal the continual presence of the Goddess and the survival of the customs and rituals connected to the religion'.[43] Miss Lissie thus in one short paragraph gives a potted version of a highly complex historical process. Archaeologist Martin Bernal, author of *Black Athena*, furthermore underscores the need for a revised understanding of ancient history, because not only will it be necessary 'to rethink the fundamental bases of "Western Civilization" but also to recognize the penetration of racism and "continental chauvinism" into all our historiography, or philosophy of writing history'.[44] This issue leads us back to the beginning of this chapter, to the status of *The Temple of My Familiar* as such a rethinking of Western civilisation as well as a recognition, not only of racism and Eurocentrism, but also of sexism in the writing of history. It also leads us back to Jung's notion of retrospective fantasy, and the material that can be found in ancient civilisations as expression of the collective unconscious and archetypal images.

As we have seen, fact and fantasy are almost inextricable from each other in Walker's novel, and this is one important reason why readers and critics have such trouble with it. On one hand, it may be more productive to go with the flow of narrative association than it is to try and distinguish which is which. On the other hand, some detective work can throw up intriguing possible sources and cross-cultural connections, which would otherwise remain invisible or inexplicable. One particularly haunting story, for example, is that of M'Sukta, the African woman who lives in the Natural History Museum in London, where the aunt of Mary Jane Briden's great aunt, Eleandra Burnham-Peacock, 'discovers' her as a live exhibit. It seems incredible now that an African woman should have been put on display in a European museum, but a South African woman called Saartjie Baartman was paraded around Western Europe in the nineteenth century. Billed as 'the Hottentot Venus', she was exhibited as a natural specimen because of the size of her behind and her genitals.[45] Furthermore, at the beginning of the twentieth century, Ishi, the last of the Californian Yahi Indians, ended up on display in a museum at the behest of the anthropologist Alfred Kroeber.[46] The museum where Ishi 'lived' is now the Phoebe Hearst Museum of Anthropology in Berkeley, not far from Alice Walker's home.[47] And there is more: Phoebe Hearst was a philanthropist, and mother of William Randolph Hearst, who founded the Hearst newspaper empire. In *The Temple of My Familiar* Mary Ann Haverstock strongly resembles Patti Hearst, heiress to the Hearst fortune, who caused a scandal in the mid 1970s by joining an American guerilla warfare group, the Symbionese Liberation Army, after she had been kidnapped by them.[48] The parallels are suggestive: Hearst's and Haverstock's stories both involve captivity by American radicals and a subsequent crossing-over in which they shed their bourgeois aspirations and take up the radicals' cause.[49] M'Sukta and Ishi likewise, of course, are captives confronted by a culture and ideology alien to their own. And so, along this trail of associations and connections, we find another family history (that of the Hearsts) and we discover another literary tradition: that of the captivity narrative, which has a long ancestry in American literature.[50] We also see that Walker weaves an intricate web of hidden references – or rather, allusions – which, once excavated, reveal new layers of significance. We might call this allusive method again (as in Chapter 3) 'deep historiography': a revisioning that combines fact with fantasy, and weaves together the method of the (counter-)historiographer with that of Jungian analysis.

The Temple of My Familiar interrogates official historiography in several ways. The first, and most obvious, is through storytelling as a means of passing on submerged or discredited forms of knowledge. At its most informal, Miss Lissie and Mr Hal do this by reminiscing with Suwelo about their lives on the island off the coast of Baltimore, but then, of course, Miss Lissie's memories take a different turn and become more mythical as she goes further back into her previous lives. At the same time, the ways in which her memories are recorded become increasingly formal: she writes, she uses audiotapes, and her paintings and old photographs become another material source for Suwelo to draw upon in his re-education. Arveyda also uses his art – his music – to communicate what he has learned, and Ola's plays and his meetings with Fanny tell her what she needs to know about her history. Fanny in turn passes this knowledge on to Suwelo in her letters. Mary Ann Haverstock, as a white woman, apparently has no such recourse to a living history. Her great-aunt Eleonora Burnham, whom she visits in a nursing home, is already a relic of the past – a confused old lady and a racist to boot. Like a 'proper' scholarly historian, therefore, Mary Ann is left with the moth-eaten archive of her great-aunt's aunt, Eleandra Burnham-Peacock, only to discover that she, too, has precursors in the Victorian women travellers who went to Africa – and who were culture-crossers like herself.[51] The gaps in Eleandra's diary, as well as Suwelo's refusal to read the (academic) books that Fanny recommends to him, highlight the incompleteness and inaccessibility of the official, written record of what counts as knowledge in the Western world. Suwelo's practice had been that of what Carlotta calls a 'guerilla historian' (418):

> He wanted American history ... to forever be the centre of every one's attention. [....] For he liked the way he could sneak in some

black men's faces later on down the line. [...] But now to have to consider African women writers and Kalahari bushmen! It was too much (203).

Clearly, such revisionist history is no longer satisfactory for Suwelo. His plan, later on, to write an oral history of Miss Lissie and Mr Hal similarly comes to nothing. Just as Fanny decides to abandon books and to 'read trees instead', thereby going back to source as it were, Suwelo takes up carpentry in the end and abandons academe altogether. Both of them accept Miss Lissie's conviction that 'The time of writing is so different from the so much longer time of no writing. The time of living separate from the earth is so much different from the much longer time of living with it' (401–2).[52] The equation of literacy *per se* with separation from the earth is not one that the novel as a whole endorses, however – or else Walker would be rendering her own *métier* obsolete. Alongside the validation of orality there are also passages in the novel that emphasise the value of writing – academic as well as creative – because writing is also a way of preserving memory, and the attentive reader comes away with an extensive bibliography of alternative or 'minority' literature.[53] Yet Lissie's point still stands: storytellers can illuminate parts of experience that historians simply cannot reach, even if such parts are ultimately conjectural and speculative – which is precisely their strength. But this is hardly news. What matters more here is the recognition that what looked to Coetzee like 'mythic fantasy' in *The Temple of My Familiar*, or home-grown new age philosophy at the beginning of this chapter, is actually shared ground between novelists, historians, and post-colonial theorists. In other words: between all those who are interested in the gaps in official historiography and who think that memory and orality might be enlisted in writing new histories; histories this time not written exclusively from the point of view of the winners. Walker writes not simply a counter-history to the dominant one, but a different *kind* of history altogether, one that does not try to suppress or eliminate memory, but actively incorporates it and infuses it with imagination. The historian Howard Zinn has described the dominant account of American history thus:

The treatment of heroes (Columbus) and their victims (the Arawaks) – the quiet acceptance of conquest and murder in the name of progress – is only one aspect of a certain approach to history, in which the past is told from the point of view of governments, conquerors, diplomats, leaders. [...] The pretense is that there really is such a thing as 'the United States', subject to occasional conflicts and quarrels, but fundamentally a community of people with common interests. [...] My viewpoint, in telling the history of the United States, is different: that we must not accept the memory of states as our own. Nations are not communities and never have been.[54]

Zinn's *A People's History of the United States* replaces the history of states with the memory of a diverse people. Walker's *The Temple of My Familiar* rewrites the history of the United States as the memory of the black diaspora, which is always already suffused with that of Europe, South America, and Native America. And, finally, what unites Jungian psychoanalysis with the family saga and diaspora writing, is the desire for an imaginative re-visioning of history, where the familiar can finally be rediscovered and restored to its ancient and multifarious splendour.

6

Possessing the Secret of Joy (1992)

Tashi, the young African woman who appears briefly in *The Color Purple* as Celie's daughter-in-law and Adam's wife, gets a novel of her own in *Possessing the Secret of Joy*. Her story traces individual and cultural motivations for female 'circumcision' in Africa and systematically charts the deleterious effects of that practice upon women, children, and ultimately society as a whole. Told through the multiple voices of Tashi and members of her family, as well as those of the anthropologist Pierre and the psychotherapists Jung/Mzee and Raye, the story begins with Tashi's African childhood and ends with her death. She is executed at the hands of the post-colonial government in her country of birth, for murdering M'Lissa, the woman who 'circumcised' her and her sister Dura, who bled to death after the operation.

In her afterword 'To the Reader', Walker states that this novel is not a sequel to either *The Color Purple* or *The Temple of My Familiar* in the strict sense; she has used poetic licence to deviate from the earlier novels in order to tell Tashi's story as she saw fit, selecting only what she needed to write about 'female genital mutilation' or FGM, as Walker insists on calling it (266).[1] Be that as it may, *Possessing the Secret of Joy* does continue the family saga of Celie's clan insofar as it focuses again on the importance of female sexual pleasure for selfhood, albeit from the opposite angle to *The Color Purple*.[2] The single issue of female 'circumcision' and its consequences for subjectivity is here explored as another aspect of African American diasporic relations, which are figured, again, as family relations. Forced migration to America through centuries of the slave trade, and voluntary migrations back, have shaped the cultural differences that exist between Africa and the United States and made 'the relationship between the African continent and the Americas', in Gay Wilentz's words, 'a profound and complicated one'.[3] But they have also forged, for some African Americans, a particular sense of kinship with Africa and Africans. Hence Walker can write in the same afterword that 'I have created Olinka as *my* village and the Olinkans as one of *my* ancient, ancestral, tribal peoples. Certainly I recognize Tashi as my sister' (my emphasis) (268). Kadiatu Kanneh, one of Walker's many critics on the issue of her invention and appropriation of 'Africa' in *Possessing the Secret of Joy*, points out that in claiming Tashi as her sister, Walker

> insists on a collective female experience, possible through empathy … [which] is proposed to exist within the identical and extra-cultural frame of the sentient female body, through which sexual identities and psychologies are assumed to subsist in a (spiritually) communal space of transparent femininity, beyond the artificial barriers of medical and familial cultures.[4]

Kanneh thus highlights the biological essentialism underlying Walker's protest against female genital mutilation, because it is only by virtue of such essentialism that a cross-cultural sisterly empathy can be invoked. Because the critical debate around Walker's novel and her documentary film, *Warrior Marks*, has homed in on the vexed issue of whether there is such a thing as a 'collective female experience' across cultures and continents, an important question addressed in this chapter is whether and how an African American writer like Walker can intervene in African affairs.

After the happy endings of *The Color Purple* and *The Temple of My Familiar*, it is a shock to be confronted in the third part of Celie's family saga with this harrowing story of Tashi's physical and psychological torture, and a surprise to have it presented in such a taut form. Eva Lennox Birch shows that style and content of *Possessing the Secret of Joy* serve each other well:

> The enormity of the 'cleaning out' of the female genitals … is not left to reader imagination. And yet, although the subject-matter is painful, the manner and style of the narrative is not. This novel is less discursive, more economic and concentrated than any of [Walker's] previous novels, in its focus upon one issue and the consequences it had for a woman and her close family.[5]

It is *because* of the taut form in which Tashi's suffering is represented, that that suffering is readable at all as a call for female solidarity; Walker's argument against FGM is so powerful thanks to the novel's tight and careful orchestration of a debate between American and African *mores*, as we shall see later on. First, we may wonder why Walker chose such a distressing topic for a novel beguilingly titled *Possessing the Secret of Joy*. Is it only because, as Walker herself explains, 'Tashi … refused to leave my mind' through the writing of *The Color Purple* and *The Temple of My Familiar*' (267)? Before we address the novel itself and the controversy it has generated, it may be helpful to trace the history of Walker's preoccupation with female genital mutilation. What we then find is that the spectre of the mutilated, de-sexualised black woman haunts Walker's work long before Tashi comes to embody it.

'ONE CHILD OF ONE'S OWN': WHITE FEMINISM AND THE BLACK WOMAN'S BODY

In her 1979 essay '*One* Child of One's Own' Alice Walker writes about a black woman without a vagina. Describing a visit to the artist Judy Chicago's feminist exhibition *The Dinner Party*, in which the great figures of women's history each had their own dinner plates represented as 'creatively imagined vaginas', Walker notes that the plate representing Sojourner Truth is the only one without a vagina, but with a face painted on it instead.[6] Or rather three faces: one weeping, one screaming, and one smiling, to signify the African woman's oppression, heroism, and 'authentic' joy respectively – the latter as if, Walker writes archly, 'the African woman, pre-American slavery, or even today, had no woes'. She then extends her critique of Judy Chicago's exhibition to white feminism's general lack of imagination when it comes to confronting black women's sexuality: white women cannot imagine black women as women, that is, with vaginas, or perhaps 'if they can, where imagination leads them is too far to go'.[7] As well as a critique of Virginia Woolf's *A Room of One's Own* (as discussed in Chapter 1) the essay is a tribute to the poet Muriel Rukeyser, Walker's teacher and mentor while she was a student at Sarah Lawrence. It opens with a grateful acknowledgement of Rukeyser's life-lesson, which 'brought the fundamentally important, joyous reality of The Child into the classroom'.[8] Rukeyser's affirmation of the centrality of the child – of children, but more crucially of the child within one's self – is for Walker 'political in the deepest sense'.[9]

This insight, and the three clichéd faces of the African woman on the Sojourner Truth plate, form the chrysalis of what was to become

Walker's most overtly political novel to date. For anyone who has read *Possessing the Secret of Joy* the importance of The Child, and the scathing suggestion that white women cannot bear to think of African women's woes, let alone of their sexuality, will have a peculiar resonance. As if in answer to the questions she had raised in '*One* Child of One's Own' about the taboo subject of black women's bodies in white feminism, Walker's imagination leads us to consider the situation of Tashi, whose external genital organs have been removed and who has been deeply traumatised by this event.[10] In confronting the question of female genital mutilation head-on, Walker therefore makes an African woman's woes the subject of *Possessing the Secret of Joy*. Discussing Tashi's plight in these terms, however, immediately brings us up against the problem of a politically charged terminology to describe what Tashi and her sister Dura have undergone.

After her 'initiation' Tashi can no longer experience sexual pleasure and has great difficulty giving birth to Benny, as a result of excision of her clitoris and subsequent infibulation. 'Female circumcision', because of its implied parallel with male circumcision, which does not affect sexual pleasure, thus does not accurately describe what Tashi has gone through, while 'female genital mutilation' or 'FGM' is not specific enough either. It is difficult to solve the problem of terminology without prejudicing the discussion that follows later in the chapter about cultural relativism versus cultural imperialism, and Walker's 'right' to speak out about FGM in Africa. Using one phrase or the other means to take sides in a virulent debate, as Obioma Nnaemeka explains: 'Westerners are quick to appropriate the power to name, while remaining totally oblivious of and/or insensitive to the implications and consequences of the naming. [...] Ultimately, the circumcision debate is about the construction of the African woman as the "Other"'.[11] So far, the term 'female circumcision' has been surrounded by quotation marks to signal its inadequacy, while the phrase 'female genital mutilation' has been used when referring to Walker's work specifically. It might seem a good idea to follow the World Health Organization's terminology and use 'FGM' as a catch-all phrase to describe a number of practices.[12] However, in the debate around the discursive politics of 'FGM', opponents of Walker's stance tend to use the term 'circumcision' to signal their dissent from the universalist values espoused by Walker and the WHO as regards the integrity and health of black women's bodies. African participants in the debate in particular have voiced such dissent.[13] The meanings of these terms thus differ ideologically; anthropologist Christine J. Walley puts it thus: 'existing usages are deeply embedded in the "either/or" perspectives characteristic of discussions of female genital operations, with *circumcision* signaling relativistic tolerance and *mutilation* implying moral outrage'.[14] It seems therefore better to adopt her phrase 'female genital operations' for general usage, and to reserve 'FGM' and 'female circumcision' for the different sides in the debate. That said then, how is Tashi's experience of FGM figured in *Possessing the Secret of Joy*?

Like Queen Nzingha and Ola's 'bush-wife', the warriors who appeared in *The Temple of My Familiar* as reminders of women's active role in African history, and indeed like Sojourner Truth herself in American history, Tashi emerges as a woman/warrior who uses her own suffering to help eliminate that of others. By supplementing *Possessing the Secret of Joy* with a film and an explanatory book that contains the screenplay of the film as well as other documentation about the campaign against FGM, Walker in effect makes the novel part of her crusade against a practice that she calls – significantly in the subtitle of *Warrior Marks* – 'the sexual *blinding* of women'. This is meant quite literally. Not only does Walker use this phrase to highlight the continuum of pain between her own injury and that of women who have undergone FGM, but she also says in the film and writes in both books that the light has gone out of the eyes of mutilated children.[15] At the same time, in this formulation, sexuality is seen as a *sense* akin to seeing: without the ability to experience sexual pleasure a girl/woman loses a way of seeing, of feeling, and of knowing. It is this sexual sense, this sense of wholeness that Walker feels *The Dinner Party* exhibition denied Sojourner Truth, who was a mother as well as a preacher, and a fighter for the freedom of women and slaves. White feminists, she argued, did not understand the complex problems that black women in Africa and America have to deal with; instead, they romanticise Sojourner Truth as a heroic figure of the past who embodied both the strength and the suffering of black women and could serve as a role model for whites. In *Possessing the Secret of Joy* Walker returns to this old ground and denies the (white, Western) reader any such romanticisation of the 'strong black woman' in raising awareness of Tashi's woes, but in doing so the latter is not reduced to a mere victim; instead, she calls for female solidarity at the end in the struggle to eradicate FGM. There are, then, intricate connections to be made between 'One Child of One's Own' and this novel, connections that are as problematic as they are also enlightening, and we shall explore these next.

Tashi is introduced to the reader as a child, crying uncomprehendingly over the death of her sister Dura. When she later decides to be 'circumcised' herself, as an act of allegiance to her tribe, she does so in defiance of colonial rule and missionary teaching, but also because she has forgotten or, rather, repressed that she had witnessed as a very young child her sister's death in consequence of the same initiation rite. The ensuing narrative, in which Tashi eventually kills the old woman M'Lissa who 'circumcised' her sister and herself, is as much an acting out of grief for the loss of her own sexuality as it is one of vengeance for what was done to Dura. Unlike in 'One Child of One's Own', then, the question in *Possessing the Secret of Joy* is not whether white women can bear to think of the black woman's body with a vagina, but whether anyone can bear to imagine this African woman's pain of being effectively without. To think of Tashi as a black woman, traumatised, without sexual organs but with her dignity and agency intact, becomes possible because Walker has made it so through her art. The novel tries to preserve a delicate balance between representing the sexually mutilated woman as a victim on one hand, and as a survivor who decides to act in her own cause on the other. That balance is achieved at the level of plot through Tashi's psychotherapeutic experience, which traces her transformation from madwoman to warrior and, in this sense, the narrative resembles a psychoanalytic case study. In America, Tashi (then known as Evelyn) is prone to fits of murderous rage necessitating psychiatric treatment in a mental hospital, which fails to cure her. Only when she visits the psychoanalyst Carl Jung in Switzerland can she begin to remember her African childhood and access the trauma from which her cure will evolve, and such cultural distance from Africa is posited as necessary for the healing process to be set in train.

Jung's approach enables Tashi to confront the memory of what it was like to be whole, able, and willing to experience sexual pleasure. Through dreamwork and painting she can come to think of herself as a black woman who is *in*complete and whose life has been ruined, rather than as 'Completely woman. Completely African. Completely Olinka', which is how she had rationalised her experience of the initiation ritual before she went into therapy (61). Tashi, in short, is represented as having been in possession of the secret of joy before she lost it. Because she has known sexual pleasure and is encouraged to remember it in the safe environment of the Swiss consulting room, she can also confront the reality of pain and take action, an action that culminates after her death in the emerging resistance movement of other African women against the indigenous tradition of FGM. In positing this collective solution at its end the novel goes beyond the psychoanalytic case study, whose successful conclusion normally consists in the individual's reintegration of self. That happens here too, but Tashi's healing process is only properly completed when other women take up the cause of protest, and it is a completion that paradoxically is achieved at the price of her death.

'*One* Child of One's Own' is ostensibly about racism in the women's movement, about how white women, just like black and white men, cannot conceive of black women as *both* black *and* women, used as they are to appropriating the category of (universal) womanhood for themselves. Nontsasa Nako detects an irony in the critical reception of *Possessing the Secret of Joy* insofar as 'the criticism that Walker levels at Spacks and white feminist scholars, is pretty much the same kind of criticism that has been leveled at her for her novel'.[16] After *Possessing the Secret of Joy* Walker herself is accused by her critics of cultural imperialism, of imposing American cultural norms on Africa, whereas in '*One* Child of One's Own' she had argued that for the true feminist, racism is impossible, and white norms cannot be held to be universal.[17] This does not mean that the true feminist is necessarily black, however, for Walker also berates those African American women who believe they must support black men at any price, and who are blind to the feminist cause as *their own* cause.[18] And this is where FGM comes in: women of colour have important work to do in the rest of the world as well as locally, Walker argues '[*f*]*rom the stopping of clitoridectomy and "female circumcision" in large parts of Arabia and Africa*' to taking action against urban poverty and the blights of the ghetto (my emphasis).[19] It is interesting that this mention of 'female circumcision' (already in ironic quotation marks) should appear in the context of a discussion about writing and motherhood. '*One* Child of One's Own' begins with the question whether writers should have children; just as white feminists can't imagine black women as women, it seems, they also cannot conceive of themselves as both writers and mothers (think of Jane Austen, the Brontës, George Eliot, Virginia Woolf). In the process of exploring the theme of writing and motherhood, the essay also addresses what Walker calls 'female folly': the kind of wisdom handed down from mother to daughter that says that she should have more than one child, and that the pain of childbirth is no excuse not to, because – and here she quotes her own mother – the more pain a mother suffers in childbirth, the more she will love her child.[20] Mrs Walker's counsel that the mother–child bond is enhanced by the experience of pain is echoed in Tashi's initial belief that the pain of 'circumcision' will tie her more closely to her people; true womanhood for both thus equals pain and self-sacrifice. But for Walker, both are examples of female folly perpetuated by cultural sanction, and in this sense also *'One* Child of One's Own' prepares the ground for *Possessing the Secret of Joy*.

As many commentators have noted, white vs. black is not the issue here; in this novel the relationship between black women (mothers and daughters and female elders of the community; African and African American women) and the matter of female folly are quite literally put on trial. Orality as the means by which this folly is transmitted from generation to generation is put on trial too, albeit in a much more understated way that deserves some close analysis.

A CHILD'S BIG LETTERS: ORALITY, LITERACY, AND MU(TILA)TED AFRICAN WOMEN

In Olinka culture mothers tell their daughters that they should comply with tradition, that to be 'bathed' – as the euphemism goes – will make them more valuable to their families, their future husbands, and their people. The African oral tradition, in other words, is not in this case the medium for the passing on of a valuable cultural heritage, but the ideological instrument of torture. Walker here breaks with two tenets of Afrocentric feminist thought at one stroke: first, that the oral tradition is a source of alternative knowledge that is to be revered and, second, that mothers always have their daughters' best interests at heart.[21] The female wisdom that 'circumcision' is a necessary and valuable experience for young girls to go through, Walker implies, is indeed female folly, and it is so for two reasons. The fact that it is passed on orally as part of an ancient tribal tradition lends it a cultural authority against the ideological incursions of the West, but it also means that that authority cannot then be questioned from within African culture, for to question it would be an unpatriotic betrayal of the heritage. Second, because the source of this 'wisdom' *is* oral, no one can cite chapter and verse as to where the custom of female genital operations originated and why. There is no written law or religious tract that can be repealed or reinterpreted; there is only time-honoured tribal heritage passed on by word of mouth. As the theorist Walter Ong explains in *Orality and Literacy*, oral cultures by their very nature tend to be traditionalist and conservative:

> Since in a primary oral culture conceptualized knowledge that is not repeated aloud soon vanishes, oral societies must invest great energy in repeating over and over what has been learned arduously over the ages [...] By storing knowledge outside the mind, writing and, even more, print downgrade the figures of the old wise man and the wise old woman, repeaters of the past, in favour of younger discoverers of something new.[22]

In the court case that culminates in Tashi's death sentence there is no reference to a legal requirement for FGM; instead, the trial revolves around the murder of M'Lissa, with the 'circumciser' as a symbolic figurehead of post-colonial national identity. 'They do not want to hear what their children suffer', Adam observes, 'They've made the telling of suffering itself taboo' (155). It is significant then that Tashi, the mutilated woman, defends herself and the integrity of the female body by countering the traditionalist and nationalist authority of orality *in writing*. Preparing to stand trial for the murder of M'Lissa, Tashi sits down to make a sign of protest:

> Scribbling my big letters as if I were a child. It had occurred to me on the plane that never would I be able to write a book about my life, nor even a pamphlet, but that write *something* I could and would (103).

Her sign says 'If you lie about your own pain, you will be killed by those who will claim you enjoy it' (102). The irony, of course, is that Tashi is killed by those – her countrymen – who cannot abide the fact that she did *not* 'enjoy' it. Tashi may be on trial for murder but she is convicted, equally, for betraying the nationalist cause by protesting and making her pain public. Yet her writing is in a sense also mutilated: she writes like a child would, in big letters, not a novel or an autobiography or a political tract, but just a sign. All the same, her big childlike letters make sure that, unlike the tears she cried when she was little, this time her protest and grief will not be ignored.

Although in narrative terms Tashi's action makes sense, when we consider the wider implications of her childlike writing the issue is less straightforward and rather more contradictory. On the face of it, Walker uses this episode in the novel to highlight African women's agency; Tashi's is the central voice in the novel and through trials, tribulations, and therapy she achieves the kind of agency that enables her to write her own protest. But at the same time, in writing and publishing *Possessing the Secret of Joy*, Walker wields her power as a well known African American novelist to take up Tashi's/ African women's cause, thus implying that they cannot speak for themselves. Is Tashi's childlike writing then a case of arrested development? Is she mutilated and muted as a writer *because* she is a mutilated woman?

From the beginning it is clear that Tashi has a writer's imagination: she is introduced to us as a storyteller on the very first page: 'I did not realize for a long time that I was dead. And that reminds me of a story: there was once a beautiful young panther' (3). But this storytelling habit, it turns out, is perhaps less a saving grace than a mere mode of escape; a form of lying to herself, even. When she is in therapy with Raye, the African American analyst, Tashi makes a connection between her pain and her storytelling:

> I mean, if I find myself way off into an improbable tale, imagining it or telling it, then I can guess something horrible has happened to me and that I can't bear to think about it. Wait a minute, I said, considering it for the first time, do you think this is how storytelling came into being? That the story is only the mask for the truth? (124)

Tashi's creativity is here represented as primarily a defence, or indeed, in psychoanalytic terms, a *symptom* of resistance. A symptom, nevertheless, is a clue for an underlying cause, and although her therapist 'looks sceptical' when Tashi advances this theory of what storytelling is for, we as readers are here invited to consider Walker's agenda for the novel: *this* 'way off improbable tale' is merely a mask of multiple stories told by multiple voices *for the truth*. That truth concerns women in Africa who are mutilated by their mothers, grandmothers, aunts, and elders in the name of female wisdom, cultural tradition, hygiene, marriageability, or all of the above, so *Possessing the Secret of Joy* would have us believe, but it is a truth well hidden and silenced by the taboo surrounding it. Yet

African women writers have addressed FGM in their work too. The Egyptian writer Nawal El Saadawi, for example, gives a harrowing description of her own genital operation and her mother's betrayal in *The Hidden Face of Eve*:

> I did not know what they had cut off from my body, and I did not try to find out. I just wept, and called out to my mother for help. But the worst shock of all was when I looked around and found her standing by my side. Yes, it was her, I could not be mistaken, in flesh and blood, right in the midst of these strangers, talking to them and smiling at them as though they had not participated in slaughtering her daughter just a few moments ago.[23]

Awa Thiam, Efua Dorkenoo, Asma El Dareer, and Waris Dirie have all used their writing, whether based on their own or other African women's experiences, in campaigning against FGM.[24] Ama Ata Aidoo begins her article 'Ghana: To Be a Woman' thus:

> I had sensed vaguely as a child living among adult females that everything which had to do exclusively with being a woman was regarded as dirty. At definite traditional landmarks in a woman's life-cycle, she was regarded literally as untouchable.[25]

Aidoo does not mention genital operations in her essay, but she does describe her trials as an African woman writer who, because of her critique of Ghanaian patriarchy, can expect to be read and respected in the West more than in her own country, as 'an internal wound' and 'a ceaseless emotional hemorrhage'.[26] She therefore makes the same connection in her imagery between writing and the body that Tashi represents and that Walker articulates in 'One Child of One's Own': a woman's sexuality is integral to her art; both are forms of creativity that feed, and feed off, each other. But if African women writers have eloquently expressed this truth in their work as part of their critiques of particular patriarchal cultures and practices, was it really necessary for Walker to mask it in Tashi's story? In the critical debate that *Possessing the Secret of Joy* has provoked this is a very real question. Are sexually mutilated African women like Saadawi also mutilated writers like Tashi? Can African women speak for themselves or does Walker have to do it for them? Obviously these questions pertain to the novelist's – any novelist's – right to write about what she pleases; fiction, after all, should be a space for the creative exploration of where the imagination leads us, even if, or especially if where it leads us is 'too far to go'. And yet the paradox we are presented with in *Possessing the Secret of Joy* makes such a view of fiction as a safe and free space untenable, for on the one hand the novel masquerades as story, while on the other it stakes a claim for truth. It does so not only in the thematic treatment of Tashi's mutilated creativity, but also in its form and authorial frame: in her afterword 'To the Reader', Walker gives statistics and a bibliography on female genital mutilation as practised historically and today. Separated from the narrative by only a blank page – a blank page like the many blank pages that signal the gaps in Tashi's discontinuous narrative – the afterword occupies an ambiguous place in the text as both coda and separate entity. As part of and yet distinct from the fictional discourse, 'To the reader' makes explicit the novel's claim to truth – rather than simply storytelling – and in so doing goes beyond the imperative of imagination to the imperative for education and action. Olakunle George makes a similar observation and notes a similar paradox when she writes that Walker's appended acknowledgements and reading list on FGM brings 'her own text into the web of texts on this practice. In this way, Walker shows that for her the work of fiction is not an escape from the world, but an intense self-immersion in that world'.[27] At the same time, George also notes that the representation of M' Lissa as *both* circumciser and victim of FGM herself complicates 'the binary rhetoric of good and evil'. Thus, she concludes, in the complex representation of M' Lissa *Possessing the Secret of Joy* 'lives a life of its own, beyond the reach of earnest but restrictive authorial claims'.[28]

As in her afterword to *The Color Purple*, Walker explains in 'To the Reader' how *Possessing the Secret of Joy* came to be written: Tashi's image stayed in her mind and seeing the young Kenyan actress who played Tashi in Steven Spielberg's film of *The Color Purple* it was as if that image was personified. The actress's presence reminded her of the fact that female circumcision was still being practised in Kenya and that children were dying from it (267). Tashi, however, is not a Kenyan woman but a fictional Olinkan – a member of an invented African tribe with an invented African language. In *Possessing the Secret of Joy*, therefore, Walker goes much further in her political critique than African women writers like Nawal El Saadawi or Ama Ata Aidoo have done, in that she takes on not a specific practice or culture that she knows from the inside or about which specific data are available concerning female genital operations, but a homogenised 'African' culture and an unspecified, but clearly painful and dangerous form of 'genital mutilation'. As we have seen, Walker adopts the plight of 'the' African woman as her own, and because of this appropriation she has been criticised for making an intervention, as an outsider from the West with a Western feminist agenda, into African internal affairs. All kinds of politically thorny issues come to the fore here, of which the justification for genital operations on women is but one, and possibly not the most important. Obviously Walker herself, by representing Tashi as a mutilated writer and by appending the afterword in which she restates the novel's claim to truth, has provoked this debate for the purpose of educating her readership. We shall return to the FGM controversy at the end of this chapter and then again in Chapter 8, because an in-depth discussion of it requires some more groundwork first. Once we understand how aesthetic qualities are manipulated in the novel so as to give the illusion of a convergence of Tashi's story with 'the truth' about 'African women', we are in a better position to weigh up the arguments that critics have levelled for and against *Possessing the Secret of Joy*.

SECRETS OF JOY: SEXUAL PLEASURE, BLACKNESS, AND RESISTANCE

As well as a revenge narrative, a psychoanalytic case history, and in part an ethnographic fiction on 'African' culture, *Possessing the Secret of Joy* also resembles a detective story. As in so many murder mysteries, the question is not *who* committed the crime but *why*, and this pertains both to the death of a child (Dura) and to the murder of an old woman (M'Lissa). We discover that the crime that has caused both deaths is not premeditated murder, but female genital mutilation; every aspect of the plot in this novel points to that single issue over and over again. Yet the central mystery for the reader, who is told about the evils of FGM fairly early on, lies elsewhere: in the novel's title. What is the secret of joy and who can possess it?

'RESISTANCE is the secret of joy' says the banner the women hold up defiantly at the end, when Tashi is executed, but of course there is more to it than this (264). Women's sexual pleasure and self-possession are also secrets of joy, well-kept secrets in Olinka culture because – unlike Tashi – most women never have the chance to experience them. But if African women who are 'circumcised' at the normal pre-pubertal age cannot possess this secret of joy, why is blackness later on in the novel posited as essential to such possession? Mbati, Tashi's pretend-daughter, reads in a book written by a white colonialist woman that 'Black people are natural ... they possess the secret of joy, which is why they can survive the suffering and humiliation inflicted upon them' (255). This statement comes from Mirella Ricciardi's *African Saga*, where it serves to justify colonial exploitation of black people, who are perceived as the 'happy darkies' of racist stereotype.[29] As in *The Temple of My Familiar* Walker inverts the racist meaning of this quotation and appropriates it for her own uses: her title, and Tashi's story of physical death but spiritual triumph – an 'African saga' of suffering and survival, after all. But it is also an American saga, for it is this pain that, in turn, connects her with her adopted country, as Tashi explains:

> Americans ... rarely resembled each other and yet resembled each other deeply in their hidden histories of fled-from pain. [...] an American looks like a wounded person whose wound is hidden from others, and sometimes from herself. An American looks like me (200).

She says this in response to M'Lissa's question 'What does an American look like?' This searching for the traits of a national identity echoes St John de Crèvecoeur in the eighteenth century, who famously asked in one of his *Letters from an American Farmer*, 'What is an American?' Both Tashi and her French colonial predecessor come up with the answer that Americans are refugees, but whereas for Crèvecoeur finding *refuge* is the operative term, Tashi emphasises the pain that the immigrants have fled *from*. America, in her definition, is not the place of proverbial freedom as compared to Africa, but merely a vantage point of cultural difference from which her originary trauma can be examined. In her answer to M'Lissa, who can only conceive of a racially homogeneous nation-state and who thinks of America as the country of 'ghostly whites', Tashi claims the American part of her identity on the grounds of a shared history of oppression and hybridity. So, although her definition of America may look like the hegemonic land of the brave and the free, Tashi suggests that such freedom is not automatically granted by law and democracy, but is a matter of individual integrity: 'wounded persons' are not free as long as they hide their pain from others, or again – and most of all – from themselves. As in Walker's previous works, it is in the confrontation with and working-through of trauma, which necessitates Tashi's return to Africa, that liberation lies and in liberating herself Tashi can also, by example, free other women.

Through the associative chain that links pain with storytelling, Americanness with 'fled-from pain', and blackness with joy, then joy with resistance and women's sexual pleasure, Walker sets up a virtuous circle in which women's sexuality and black American writing are constituted as acts of resistance – a sexual/textual politics – against a culture that, in M'Lissa's words, produces 'torturers of children' in the service of forging a post-colonial national identity (210). This is a strong message indeed. The detective work required to retrace one woman's trauma leads to an indictment of a whole culture, or even a continent, and it is of course no accident that the 'circumciser' herself is made to speak these words and to incriminate herself, unlikely as this seems, because that way the recognition of the 'crime' of FGM comes not just from outside but also from within 'African' culture. No one can be surprised, least of all Walker herself, that this indictment has provoked virulent criticism. Margaret Kent Bass accuses Walker of 'cultural condescension', not because she disagrees with Walker's call for an end to FGM, but because she objects to the way that call is presented in the novel – as an argument for Western values, as if the West can occupy the moral high ground in teaching Africa how to treat its children. As regards the formal organisation of the novel, Bass points out that

> Walker certainly anticipates the criticism that she *could* receive from many readers of *Possessing the Secret of Joy*, and she includes all arguments against her position and attitude in the narrative. In other words, she uses Tashi to offer arguments for tribal custom and uses the enlightened American, Evelyn, as her own voice in the novel.[30]

Bass is right that Walker dramatises the debate over FGM by structuring the novel as an intricate dance of argument and counter-argument. But she is wrong to assume that Evelyn moves on Walker's behalf – this dance has no such obvious lead performers. Evelyn and Tashi represent a double consciousness – 'two unreconciled strivings; two warring ideals in one dark body', as W. E. B. DuBois famously put it in *The Souls of Black Folk* – but not in the sense that Bass perceives it.[31] The character to whom I have so far referred as Tashi, is named variously as Evelyn, Evelyn-Tashi, Tashi-Evelyn and Tashi-Evelyn-Mrs Johnson respectively, culminating in the unhyphenated Tashi Evelyn Johnson Soul of the final chapter. These different names signal different modes of consciousness, different narrators in an important sense, because some are more trustworthy than others. For example, Evelyn does not at first want to believe the white American Amy Maxwell, who tells her that she has experienced clitoridectomy too, not in Africa but in the United States, because to believe that would destroy her (Evelyn's) idealised image of America (177). Evelyn, therefore, is depicted in this chapter as clearly misguided about America's benevolent attitude to women. By the time she tells M'Lissa that 'an American looks like me', meaning like a 'wounded person', she is less naive about this and is therefore named Evelyn-Tashi, because her African memory now informs her consciousness of American reality (200). Conversely, she becomes Tashi-Evelyn once she knows of the African indigenous tradition of goddess worship and the sacred doll Nyanda, which represents women's sexual pleasure (256). Repossessing that secret of joy gives primacy to her African name, which is now merely supplemented by the American Evelyn. What looks at first like an idiosyncratic sequence of naming, therefore, in fact has a logic to it: the different names suggest that the African and American parts of this woman's identity, posed in opposition to each other at first, gradually integrate to form a harmonious whole in which Tashi evolves into Tashi Evelyn Johnson Soul: an African, American, wife, and mother, spiritually alive at last.

TRIANGULATION: FORM, IMAGE, AND ARGUMENT

The dance of argument and counter-argument that structures *Possessing the Secret of Joy* is enacted through the multiplicity of narrative voices. Everyone – even M'Lissa – gets a voice in this novel, and they all have an angle on Tashi's predicament that in some way serves themselves as much as it benefits her, even the psychoanalyst Mzee. Just as M'Lissa gets to recognise in Tashi her own history of pain and alienation from the child that she used to be and forgot (206), Mzee writes to his niece Lisette that he is finding himself in Tashi and Adam as 'ancient kin' from whom he can learn (81). M'Lissa and Mzee, the Old Woman and the Old Man, form one of various contrasting pairs and threesomes of characters who dance the argument that Walker has choreographed for them. M'lissa has caused Tashi's trauma and Mzee is the one who makes the first advances in curing her, but Raye's support and insight accompany her for the rest of the way. Raye synthesises the opposing qualities of Mzee/Carl Jung, the white analyst, and M'lissa, the African circumciser/witchdoctor, in a way that is similar to Adam and Lisette's son Pierre, represented as a 'blended' person who embodies the America of his father and the Europe of his mother. This dialectical model, in which opposites fuse to form a new, positive hybrid, is also figured geographically in the traffic between Africa, Europe, and America: this, again, is a tale of three continents that ultimately finds its origin in the Atlanticist nexus of the slave trade.

Imagery contributes to this sense of strict formal symmetry. Tashi's habit of escaping in storytelling literalises a familiar expression: she takes off on 'flights of imagination'. Tashi is consistently associated with flying, from the bird in her first story that steals the penny that her mother had given her to buy bread (6), to the crow to which she likens herself when she is in America and watches Adam pack his bags to go to Paris (208), and the dragonfly that she imagines herself to be in the courtroom (149). Most startling of all, of course, is her painting of the cock, which rekindles her memory and initiates her recovery, the cock that – horrifically – gobbles up Dura's genitals after her operation. And obviously the cock is not that distant a cousin of the bird who 'steals the penny', since urination – 'spending a penny' – after her genital operation becomes painful and difficult. Another example of rhyming imagery is found in Pierre who, because he is the offspring of Adam and Lisette's adulterous union, becomes the focus of Tashi's hatred while she is in America. Throughout, her anger and pain are imaged as boulders or rocks; Pierre's name, of course, means 'pebble' or 'little stone', and when he arrives at Adam and Lisette's house in California Tashi pelts him with stones in a fit of uncontrollable rage.

The novel's circular frame is yet another example of formal control. The first and last pages mirror each other, since the tale of the female panther Lara, who embraces death contentedly when she kisses her own reflection in the water and holds it 'all the way to the bottom of the stream' (5) is echoed by Tashi's last words: 'There is a roar as if the world cracked open and I flew inside. I am no more. And satisfied' (264). The panther story looks like an African version of the Greek myth of Narcissus, who is so in love with his own image that he drowns in it. Lara's fate prefigures Tashi's own, but not in every detail. Unlike Narcissus, it is not Lara's vanity that condemns her to death, but the envy of her husband Baba and co-wife Lala, whose fighting over her she cannot endure. For Tashi and Lara, narcissism – their newly found self-love – is a saving grace and polygamy is not condemned in the novel but condoned, if it is practised without jealousy. Since Adam cannot achieve pleasurable sexual relations with his wife because of her mutilation, he cannot, the narrative implies, be blamed for seeking fulfilment elsewhere. As in every Walker novel so far, this triangular relationship between Adam, Tashi, and the French woman Lisette, is central. Brownfield Copeland, Truman Held in *Meridian*, Mr—— in *The Color Purple* and Suwelo in *The Temple of My Familiar* were all involved in *ménages à trois* with two women, and in every case the man was displaced from his position of power once the women forged a relationship of love or friendship with each other. Only in *The Temple of My Familiar* is the relationship between Miss Lissie, Mr Hal, and Uncle Rafe harmonious throughout, perhaps because here a woman is at the centre of the triangle. In the sexual and textual politics of *Possessing the Secret of Joy* such an alliance between the women is impossible, for although Tashi is certainly jealous of Lisette's and Adam's union, it is clear throughout that her rage stems from the trauma of genital mutilation. What Lisette has that Tashi lacks is not Adam's devotion (Tashi does have that), but physical integrity and the ability to experience sexual pleasure – even while giving birth. Petit Pierre, Adam and Lisette's son, 'practically slid into the world' (95) in sharp contrast to Tashi and Adam's son Benny, who is brain-damaged due to the difficult conditions of his birth.

These contrasts between Lisette and Tashi, Pierre and Benny are rendered very starkly and explicitly. Lisette is a white European woman, physically whole, independent and with a feminist bent – the exact opposite of the damaged Tashi. With Benny and Pierre, likewise, not just the manner of their birth is sharply opposed, but also their later development: while Benny suffers from mental retardation which means that his memory is impaired, Pierre trains as an anthropologist at Harvard. He is the one who finally enlightens Tashi and her supporters about a cultural myth that has served since time immemorial to disguise – and justify – the reason why female genital mutilation is considered necessary; as an ethnographic helper he is as instrumental in effecting Tashi's cure as the psychoanalyst Raye is in uncovering her cultural memory. At the heart of this myth about the clitoris, figured as a termite hill, lies the belief that men and women should be clearly distinguished from each other: '[W]hen the clitoris rose ... God thought it looked masculine. Since it was "masculine" for a clitoris to rise, God could be excused for cutting it down' (218). Pierre, the mixed race and bisexual bringer of this news, is the living embodiment of the falsehood of this belief in absolute sexual difference. He epitomises the virtues of hybridity in that he uses his European upbringing by a French feminist, his American education, and his bisexual nature to illuminate his and Tashi's African roots, so as to unmask the brutal patriarchal 'truth' of the oral tradition. Again it may seem that Walker here assumes the authority of Western knowledge over the wisdom (she might call it 'cultural folly') of indigenous cosmology, but again the dance of the argument is more complicated than that: Pierre, the Harvard scholar, does not simply occupy the privileged position of Western enlightenment. The source of his knowledge about the myth of the termite hill is a book by the French anthropologist Marcel Griaule, titled *Conversations with Ogotemmêli*. Ogotemmêli, one of the elders of the Dogon tribe and their self-appointed spokesman, was Griaule's informant during the heyday of French colonialism and its *mission civilatrice*, its civilising mission, which in turn spawned French anthropology. Pierre's detective work to find the original cultural motivation for female genital mutilation thus leads him via his Harvard education in anthropology and a French ethnographic study right back to the source, which is Africa. We now come to another turn in the argument, for just as the American Amy Maxwell's clitoridectomy was 'copied' from the African practice as 'read' by American doctors on the bodies of enslaved, 'circumcised' women, so also is Pierre's knowledge predicated upon a Western reading of African culture. Female oppression on one hand, and the understanding necessary to critique and counteract it on the other, are thus narratively produced by diasporic relations between Africa, Europe, and America. As in *The Temple of My Familiar*, Walker counterposes the criminal diasporic movement of the Middle Passage with the critical, but also potentially liberating movement of return. It is not in America that Tashi finds her freedom or enacts her revenge, but in Africa as *both* the scene of the crime *and* the place of redress. Tashi, the African woman, is liberated in the end with the help of the hybrids Jung/Mzee, Raye, and Pierre, and the triangular relationship between Tashi, Adam, and Lisette represents the triangular dynamic of the African diaspora in both its historically oppressive and its potentially redeeming aspects in the future.

This exposé of structural parallels and formal symmetries demonstrates just how carefully thought out this novel is *as an argument* in which various sides of the question why FGM is practised are explored. Systematically, the reasons *for* that practice are given (resistance to colonialism, hygiene, marriageability, tradition) and dismantled: Tashi's 'initiation' does not make her a better resistance fighter and it alienates her from, rather than binds her to, her people; the operation is dangerous and spreads HIV; Tashi and Adam cannot have proper marital relations; childbirth is well-nigh intolerable for the mother and damages the child. Finally, but by no means least, the vaunted 'tradition' of FGM turns out to originate in a patently patriarchal story of creation which displaced another tradition, that of goddess worship and the valorisation of women's sexual pleasure and bodily integrity, which persists only in the now secret and underground cult of the doll Nyanda.

Convincing as this seems in a highly emotive narrative, there are many problems with it as a novelistic argument. The first may be the question of intended readership: whom does Walker want to convince, and to what end? On the face of it, only the most hard-hearted and stony-faced of readers can come away from *Possessing the Secret of Joy* without being deeply affected by its representation of FGM. Yet to say this is to assume that readers are not already aware of the practice, and that they will automatically share in the novel's condemnation of it because the narrative, through its rhetorical–argumentative strategies, leads them there. It is assuming, in other words, a reader who is not just ignorant of FGM, but also untroubled by the question of cultural difference and the West's historic imperial gaze on Africa. Perhaps most disturbing about this assumption is that such a reader may even believe he or she has gained some knowledge of 'African culture' in the process of reading *Possessing the Secret of Joy*. But this, as a look at Walker's anthropological and psychoanalytic sources will show, is emphatically not the case. Neither our knowledge of how and where female genital operations are carried out in the world (that is: not just in Africa or sporadically in America), nor our knowledge of 'African culture' are advanced by reading this novel. To believe that it is, is to fall for storytelling as truth – it is to escape, as Tashi does, from reality by taking flight in imagination.

STORYTELLING AS ETHNOGRAPHY: WALKER AND THE PREDICAMENT OF 'AFRICAN CULTURE'

In his opening chapter to *The Predicament of Culture: Twentieth Century Ethnography, Literature, and Art* James Clifford makes a strong argument for an historical vision that has hybridity at its centre. 'I argue that identity, considered ethnographically, must always be mixed, relational, and inventive', he writes. 'Intervening in an inter-connected world, one is always, to varying degrees, "inauthentic": caught between cultures, implicated in others'.[32] Walker's intervention in 'African culture' can be read benevolently in the spirit of Clifford's insight that in an increasingly interconnected world we are always already implicated in other cultures and other histories, because they intertwine with our own. In her afterword 'To the Reader' Walker explains why she feels that she has a right to such cultural intervention as *Possessing the Secret of Joy* in effect represents: because of slavery 'I do not know from what part of Africa my African ancestors came, and so I claim the continent' (267–8). The same reasoning underlies her decision to invent an African language and she says, with a Jungian twist, that her invented Olinka words (like 'tsunga' – for circumciser) are 'from an African language I used to know, now tossed up by my unconscious' (267). Any obvious criticism of Walker's inventing a language rather than taking the trouble to learn an existing one, and of inventing an amalgamated continent rather than locating her story in a specific place, culture, and political system, is thus anticipated and averted by the author, who puts her own history of dislocation and dispossession in the frame here. Because her ancestors, who might have come to America with mutilated bodies, were cut off at a stroke from their cultural, historical, and linguistic contexts in Africa, Walker cannot now claim a specific heritage but has to make one up. To question her invented Africa, and to highlight varying degrees of 'female circumcision' in different places, such as Awa Thiam and Nawal El Saadawi have done, is to say that the novel in an important sense dramatises its protest against FGM in a vacuum: it ignores any kind of regional variation and specificity as well as the diversity of meanings with which different versions are invested.[33] Awa Thiam's list of countries where genital operations are carried out on women does not include Kenya, which is the one country mentioned by name, twice, in *Possessing the Secret of Joy*. Jomo Kenyatta, the first president of Kenya, is indicted in the text as one of those leaders who endorsed circumcision during the struggle for independence as a tribal custom to be retained against the influence of Europeanisation (114). And in the afterword Walker mentions Kenya, where in 1982 fourteen chil-dren died from the effects of female genital mutilation (267). We can therefore with reason look at the case of Kenya to see how it compares with Walker's invented 'Africa'.

In Kenyatta's own *Facing Mount Kenya: The Tribal Life of the Gikuyu* some of Walker's contentions are confirmed, such as that it is taboo for men to marry uncircumcised women and that it is feared that if the practice were abolished the whole social fabric would disintegrate. He even admits that one of the reasons why 'circumcision' is considered necessary is to stop girls from masturbating, which is 'considered wrong'.[34] Interestingly, however, he writes of the circumcision of *both* boys and girls, and he insists on the procedure's importance as a mode of initiation into the tribe's laws, customs, and traditions – an educational experience, in other words. Fulminating against the missionaries who in his view have exaggerated the detrimental effects of 'circumcision', in their own 'civilised' image, of course, as a means of fostering Christianity and furthering colonial interests, Kenyatta argues that 'The real anthropological study, therefore, is to show that clitoridectomy, like Jewish circumcision, is a mere bodily mutilation which, however, is regarded as the *conditio sine qua non* of the whole teaching of tribal law, religion and morality'.[35] Note how Kenyatta on one hand does not hesitate to call the procedure 'mutilation', yet on the other defends it on the grounds of cultural integrity – people in the West do not question the civilised nature of Jewish circumcision, he intimates, so why interfere with Africans and call them 'barbaric'? In his detailed account of the initiation rite among the Gikuyu, furthermore, a great deal of attention is paid to the (indigenous) medical care with which the initiates are surrounded, and – likening the circumciser to 'a Harley Street surgeon' – he explains that only the tip of the girl's clitoris is cut off.[36] He also mentions in his Preface that he knows about the procedure as it is performed upon girls because 'the young initiates of both sexes talk freely to each other afterwards'; there is no great secret about it.[37]

Kenyatta is worth citing in such detail not by way of juxtaposing his truth with Walker's fiction – his patriarchal investment is as clear as one might expect from a political leader writing in 1938 – but to highlight the context in which in traditional societies circumcision was practised. John Mbiti, in *African Religions and Philosophy*, also provides such context when he explains how the pain both boys and girls suffer in initiation is meant to prepare them for adulthood, and how the blood that is shed symbolises a rebirth, sometimes accompanied by a new name.[38] Mbiti, who is a Christian, gives many of the same reasons for the practice of clitoridectomy as Kenyatta does and emphasises that in the African world-view generally the

physical and the spiritual are 'but two dimensions of one and the
same universe', even if the manifestations of that union differ in
their particulars in different regions and cultures.[39]

By looking at such African studies of indigenous cultures Walker's
project comes into focus. We now see even more clearly how her
novel counters defences of traditional society, such as those that
Kenyatta and Mbiti put forward, by making Tashi an anomaly and
placing her *outside* her Olinka cultural context. Not 'circumcised'
while she was little (and the country still under colonial rule), she
opts for the initiation voluntarily during and *as part of* the struggle
for independence. In the passage where she explains this decision
to Raye, an explicit parallel is set up between her devotion to Our
Leader (a figure such as Kenyatta or Nelson Mandela) and religious
devotion: Our Leader is frequently likened to Christ, martyrdom
included (108–9). Tashi also intimates that this devotion had an erotic
component, that she could not love Adam because she was in love
'like every Olinka maiden' with Our Leader (114). Cultural nationalism and the Leader's exemplary martyrdom against colonialism
and Christianity (remember Clifford's 'interconnected worlds') thus
'made her do it'. But, equally, the sense of betrayal that Tashi experiences once she has gone through with her genital operation – alone
in the rebels' camp, without the surrounding rituals and honours
normally bestowed on newly initiated girls – parallels, or is mapped
on to, the general betrayal of the people by the post-colonial state.
In other words, Tashi was never a part of the community of women
ready for adulthood that the initiation is supposed to bring into
being, she does not receive any of the benefits and surrounding care
of such a community and ritual, and in that sense also her experience is abnormal. L. Amede Obiora writes that

> Unequivocal empirical documentation of the emotional security
> which prevails among African children seems to argue that had
> Tashi stayed in the confines of her native culture, she might at
> least have found a modicum of affirmation and sanity which
> utterly eluded her in the individualism, narcissism, and racism
> of the West.[40]

To put it bluntly: as a woman she is screwed by her Leader's advocacy
of traditional rites, then screwed over again by the post-independence
government, after the Leader's death, and once more when she is
exposed to the psycho-culture of the West. In this scenario, the

social fabric does not disintegrate because women are not mutilated; it has already disintegrated due to the influence of the missionaries and the in-fighting among the rebels themselves, some of whom are believed to have murdered the Leader. Furthermore, Tashi's contact with Adam and Olivia, the missionaries' children, taints her and isolates her from the community. The way Walker represents Tashi, then, as an outsider from beginning to end, aids her argument but is not representative of the situation of African women today who undergo genital operations, whether voluntarily or not.

Apart from the mention of Kenya and Kenyatta, the only other piece of concrete information we get in *Possessing the Secret of Joy* as regards a particular culture, rather than a generalised and homogenised 'African'/Olinkan one, is the explicit reference to Marcel Griaule's *Conversations with Ogotemmêli* (164). This ethnographic study concerns the Dogon in Mali, whose tribal customs and religious beliefs were observed and documented by a team of French anthropologists in the 1920s and 1930s. Much is made in the novel of the significance of the Dogon creation story and the termite hill, which Pierre interprets in a fashion true to the anthropological tradition. By making various structural analogies between the phallic shape of the termite hill and the tower of Tashi's dream, he arrives at the conclusion that both are clitoral representations of female sexual power. Tashi then discovers that, according to the Dogon myth, 'The dual soul is a danger; a man should be male, and a woman female. Circumcision and excision are ... the remedy' (167). Sexual difference and spiritual difference are thus accomplished, by force, in one stroke of the knife, according to Tashi's reading of Griaule's book, which in turn is Griaule's reading of Ogotemmêli's reading of his own culture. This is presented as ethnographic authority, a final uncovering of the true reason for female circumcision in 'Africa'.[41]

Ethnography however, as James Clifford usefully reminds us, cannot be invested with such authority.[42] Not only is the ethnographic study a textual production like the novel, in which many voices speak, but the ethnographer is also like the literary interpreter, or rather the traditional critic, 'who sees the task at hand as locating the unruly meanings of a text in a single coherent intention'.[43] This is also Tashi's and Pierre's – and by extension Walker's – dubious enterprise: it makes no sense to think of the Dogon creation story as having a 'single coherent intention', nor can one legitimately take the part (the Dogon story) to stand for the whole (as a mythological 'explanation' of female genital mutilation in Africa). Griaule, Clifford points out, did have a native informant in Ogotemmêli but he had no female sources, and the process of gathering his tales and collating them into a cohesive *oeuvre* was a highly complex one. Clifford therefore calls the work of Griaule and his collaborators 'elaborate inventions authored by a variety of subjects, European and African'. He calls them 'inventions' because of the anthropologists' inflated claim that the book was an accurate rendering of the way the Dogon think – or even of the way 'the Negro' thinks, as Griaule was to assert later on in his career.[44] To say that they are inventions, however, Clifford warns, is not to dismiss them, but to 'take them seriously as textual constructions'.[45] The similarity between Griaule's ethnographic text and Walker's novelistic one as both inventions with totalising claims to representing 'African culture', authored – or in the novel's case narrated – by an amalgam of different voices with different cultural interests, will be obvious by now. They should be taken seriously as textual constructions, but not as claims to some ultimate truth. More striking than this less-than-blinding insight, however, is the Jungian resonance in the passage about the 'dual soul' that Tashi reads from Griaule's book. Jung was, after all, convinced of the duality of the human soul, of the *animus* in woman and the *anima* in man, and we know of Walker's interest in Jungian psychology.[46] As in *The Temple of My Familiar*, we have therefore to return to Jung. If *Possessing the Secret of Joy* draws on, but ultimately cannot claim, the authority of an ethnographic text, because it interprets Tashi's body and psyche and via that body misreads, like Griaule did, 'African culture', it might yet be read more successfully as a Jungian case history, which is what we shall turn to next.

THE NOVEL AS CASE HISTORY: JUNG'S FIFTH TAVISTOCK LECTURE

'Negro women', the doctor says into my silence, 'can never be analyzed effectively because they can never bring themselves to blame their mothers.' […] It is quite a new thought. And, surprisingly, sets off a kind of explosion in the soft, dense cotton wool of my mind. But I do not say anything. Those bark-hard, ashen heels trudge before me on the path. […] African women like my mother give harsh meaning to the expression 'furrowed brow' (17–18).

This is the beginning of Tashi's painful process of remembering her childhood. When Jung mentions black women's difficulty in blaming their mothers, the 'explosion' leads her straight to the traumatic memory of walking behind her mother Catherine after Dura's death, the 'furrowed brow' not just an image of her mother's toil and worry, but also associatively linked to the furrow between her legs, and Tashi's own. Carl Jung, in this early chapter, is still referred to as 'the doctor' or even 'this stranger', not yet the 'Old Man' or the honorary African 'Mzee' that he is to become later, as his magic begins to work on Tashi to confront her with her dreams and her archetypal images. And his therapeutic magic does work: Tashi relates her dream of the tower, which is so important as a clue to her repressed sexuality, first to him, and his showing of a documentary film made in Africa sparks off her frenzied painting of the giant cock, which in turn enables her to remember the trauma of actually witnessing Dura's murder. Near the end of her therapy, Jung writes to Lisette that Tashi/Evelyn's case has made him discover a 'truly universal self' through the kinship he feels with her and Adam's suffering:

> They ... are bringing me home to something in myself. I am finding myself in them. A self I have often felt was only halfway at home on the European continent. In my European skin. An ancient self that thirsts for knowledge of the experiences of its ancient kin. [...] A self that is horrified at what was done to Evelyn, but recognizes it as something that is also done to me (81).

This recognition on Jung's part of the other as kin through the therapeutic experience is a clear case of what analysts term countertransference, when the analyst is affected by the emotions of the patient and comes to experience them as part of him- or herself. In his fifth Tavistock lecture of 1935, the subject of which is transference and counter-transference, Jung relates the case of 'an elderly woman of about fifty-eight ... from the United States' who comes to him in Switzerland 'half-crazy' after having been in analysis in America'.[47] He discovers that his approach to analysis, one in which the doctor is not an objective observer but an active participant who shows his own emotions, is so different from the woman's American experience of treatment that it produces the desired therapeutic effect in itself: the mutually affective analytical relationship is what constitutes the healing. If this is reminiscent of the relationship Tashi forges with Jung, there are several other elements in this lecture that link it to *Possessing the Secret of Joy* too. Jung relates in this lecture another case history concerning an American woman 'and I can safely tell you of this case because she is dead', who 'was totally unconscious of herself as a woman; she was just a man's mind with wings underneath'.[48] Jung describes this woman as 'a bird', which in the original German (*ein Vogel*) does not necessarily have a metaphorical connotation, but is suggestive of Tashi's bird-like imagery in the novel. The woman comes to Jung because she is involved in a dysfunctional relationship with a married man. Both, writes Jung, are unconscious of themselves, 'and a woman never becomes conscious of herself as long as she cannot accept the fact of her feelings'. He then relates this woman's lack of self-awareness to the fact that she is American, and he likens the more authentic self, the self she has yet to confront, to Africa:

> We often discover with Americans that they are tremendously unconscious of themselves. Sometimes they suddenly grow aware of themselves, and then you get these interesting stories of decent young girls eloping with Chinamen or with Negroes, because in the American that primitive layer, which with us is a bit difficult, with them is disagreeable, as it is much lower down. It is the same phenomenon as 'going black', or 'going native' in Africa.[49]

Generally speaking Jung's observation is unsurprising, since the idea of Africa as associated with 'the primitive' or the 'lower down' (that is: with sexuality, particularly female sexuality), and of Americans as pragmatic rather than self-reflexive, are favoured stereotypes of Eurocentric thought in the early to mid-twentieth century; Freud, after all, made the same connection in designating female sexuality 'the dark continent'.[50] In the light of Walker's novel, however, the resonance of this passage with Tashi's case is loud and clear, the more so as Jung's lecture then relates how this American woman's cure is effected through analysis of her dreams, culminating in a dramatic climax, 'a sudden explosion'.[51] Tashi, like this woman, has to rediscover and accept the African in herself – however traumatic – before she can become whole. When she first meets Jung, he calls her simply a 'Negro', which angers her because she thinks of herself as an African woman, not a 'Negro', meaning an African American. Yet in his mis-recognition of her Jung in fact turns out to be right, because when she first comes to him she is indeed unconscious of herself, her African self, in the American way. Later on in the Tavistock lecture Jung discusses other themes that we also find in Tashi's case history, such as painting as a diagnostic aid, the distinction between 'active imagination', which provides therapeutic clues (such as Tashi's compulsion to make up stories) and mere wishful fantasy, and the phenomenon of what Jung calls the 'Saviour complex'. The latter is a manifestation, an archetypal image, of the collective unconscious that becomes activated at times of historical change, and refers to the need for people to invest an individual with exalted qualities of leadership.[52] Not only are analysts in danger of having the Saviour complex thrust upon them, but political leaders are as well, and more dangerously so. For Jung, historical events (such as, in the novel, the shift from colonialism to independence, under Our Leader/Saviour) are not brought about by conscious activism but by movements in the collective unconscious.[53] Fanaticism, moreover, whether religious or analytical (or cultural or political, we might add) 'is always a sign of repressed doubt' – just as Tashi's insistence on undergoing her Olinka initiation is motivated by unacknowledged doubt, as her discussion with Olivia makes clear.[54] In the conclusion of this lecture Jung emphasises again that individuals should not look for happiness in events, or circumstances, or saviours outside themselves, but should realise that 'everything depends on whether [the individual] holds the treasure or not. If the *possession of that gold* is realized, then the centre of gravity is *in* the individual and no longer in an object on which he depends' (my emphasis).[55] That 'gold', of course, is the secret of joy that Tashi discovers in herself and in women's resistance at the end of the novel.

It would probably be an exaggeration, and a simplification, to say that *Possessing the Secret of Joy* merely dramatises such psychoanalytic concepts as Jung presents in condensed form in his fifth Tavistock lecture, but the multiple parallels between them are more than just suggestive: they make it possible to read the novel as a case history whose salient features derive from Jungian thought. Yet we do need to note, again, that Walker revises Jung as she revises the anthropological record: Tashi's cure comes about not just through the individual solution of psychoanalytic treatment, but is completed only in collective political action against the mutilation of women. The African American therapist Raye's role is critical in this respect, since it is she who shows Tashi the broader picture of women's oppression in America as well as Africa. Raye disabuses Tashi of the illusion that flight – whether into the imagination, or to America – can relieve the suffering in itself, and Raye makes it possible for Tashi to make cross-cultural connections. Unlike Jung's argument in the lecture, the novel does not construct political action as a mere manifestation of unconscious and unacknowledged motives, but as necessary for individual and collective well-being. With this proviso, we may still conclude that it makes more sense to read *Possessing the Secret of Joy* as a Jungian case history than as an ethnographic text about 'African culture', or even an unambiguously Western feminist protest against female genital mutilation. Walker draws on Jung's African experiences (in Kenya, again) and anthropological interests in order to critique, implicitly, the white bias of classical Freudianism. In addition, however, she uses the transcultural frame of Jungian psychoanalysis to question the romanticised Afrocentrism of black nationalism in the United States, which serves as cultural philosophy to bolster an 'authentic' African American identity.[56] This critical stance vis-à-vis Afrocentric thought is part of the debate that has developed around Walker's intervention on female genital operations in Africa, a debate that is more about discursive power relations than about FGM per se, let alone the literary merits of *Possessing the Secret of Joy*. We shall revisit *Possessing the Secret of Joy* in Chapter 8 as *the* prime example of Walker's activist writing, but I want to close this one with a brief look at the novel's reception, to see just how it divided critical opinion along political lines from the outset.

CULTURAL RELATIVISM VERSUS CULTURAL IMPERIALISM: WHO SPEAKS? WHO LISTENS?

Positive reactions to *Possessing the Secret of Joy* celebrated it as a radical political statement on global sisterhood, and tended to adopt uncritically Walker's humanist agenda and the essentialist analysis of female genital operations that goes along with it. Some critics, like Charles Larson in *The Washington Post Book World*, managed to evade the feminist issue altogether and read the novel as being about the suffering of children, whereas Eva Lennox Birch admired Walker's courage in daring to write about clitoridectomy, not because it is a contentious issue but because of the sheer horror of the procedure.[57] More problematically, other admirers valued the novel because they believed it to be breaking new ground, not aesthetically but in terms of feminist activism. Kimberley Joyce Pollock, for example, said that because of *Possessing the Secret of Joy* 'women are able to speak the unspeakable' and she applauded Walker for showing 'the universality of the act of genital mutilation' by including Amy Maxwell's story. Reviewer Tina McElroy Ansa called the novel a 'stunning beginning' of a much needed political debate.[58] Praise in these terms betrays not just ignorance among Western readers of the practice of female genital operations, but also of the sizeable literature on the subject produced by campaigners in Africa and by women of African descent. As Margaret Bass indicates, African women's resistance against female genital operations has a much longer track record than reading Walker's work would lead us to believe, even if Walker does credit some of that movement's literature in her postscript. Bass charged Walker with sensationalism and 'cultural condescension': 'African women are not creatures enshrouded in helpless, hopeless ignorance and misery – longing for rescue by the West and Alice Walker', she concluded, and 'we' (in the West) should therefore 'leave them [African women] alone'.[59] Bass's call for a hands-off policy where African women's interests are concerned seems hardly satisfactory for those of 'us' who want to have a constructive dialogue between Western and African women's activism, but at least she recognises that an assumed and unproblematic solidarity across cultural difference is unlikely and perhaps undesirable.

'Cultural condescension' is only the mildest term used by critics who are opposed to Walker's novel. 'Cultural imperialism' is more often used, and it is a phrase that, if accurate, makes Walker complicit in the very history of Western exploitation of Africa that she so strongly criticised in *The Temple of My Familiar*.

> 'Female circumcision' has become almost a dangerous trope in Western feminisms for the muting and mutilation of women – physically, sexually and psychologically – and for these women's *need for* Western feminism. Circumcision, clitoridectomy, infibulation become one visible marker of outrageous primitivism, sexism, and *the* Third World woman[60]

writes the critic Kadiatu Kanneh in 'Feminism and the Colonial Body'. Kanneh highlights here the connection between Western feminism's interest in female genital operations and a presumed neocolonial representational dependency of 'the' Third World woman on Western feminists to speak in her behalf.[61] In this analysis, the 'mutilated' African woman becomes the fetishised object of the Western gaze, which is no less imperialist in its effects for all its supposed sisterly empathy. The question we then return to is whether Walker's novel is complicit with, and draws its readers into, an imperialist discourse that homogenises 'the' Third World woman's plight and reduces her to a stereotype of ultimate victimisation once more.

Certainly Gay Wilentz seems to think so, since she argues that 'There is an aspect of voyeurism in Walker's approach; [which] ... puts her in the company of other Western writers before her for whom "Africa" merely represented the exotic or the grotesque'.[62] Wilentz thus accuses Walker of stereotyping, whereas for Angeletta K. M. Gourdine the problem lies with Walker's personal investment:

> Walker excavates Tashi's history and in the process discovers her own connection to Tashi, black woman to black woman. In so doing, Walker categorically castigates African women's histories and possesses their bodies in a bizarre struggle to free her own.[63]

Gourdine's sense that Walker's autobiographical identification with Tashi's 'patriarchal wound' in *Possessing the Secret of Joy* does the novel no good relates to other critics' questioning of the discursive political relations between Western feminism and African women. By putting herself in the frame, as Walker does in the afterword and in *Warrior Marks*, she may – perhaps unwittingly – obscure the image of the African woman and hinder rather than help their cause. For a few years after the publication of *Possessing the Secret of Joy* and *Warrior Marks*, it was as if the campaign against FGM had Walker's name on it, and in the controversy surrounding female genital operations African women's voices tended to get lost. One voice that has rarely been heard in that discussion is that of the woman who values her 'circumcised' body and who sees 'circumcision' itself as part and parcel of her feminism, her right to decide. That voice I found, typically by accident, scribbled in the margins of a library copy of Asma El Dareer's study *Woman, Why Do You Weep? Circumcision and Its Consequence*, where an anonymous woman made it heard. In scribbled annotation after annotation in the margin, amounting to a running commentary on Dareer's text, this woman voiced her dissent.[64] Where Dareer explains the procedure of infibulation in clinical terms that nevertheless do not leave much to imagination, the anonymous woman's voice adds '(= total purity)'. Where Dareer reports that she witnessed a genital operation in which the girl's relatives ululated loudly to drown out the child's cries, the notes in the margin say 'family honor; mothers suffered painful operations but enjoyed the long-term benefits'. And when Dareer describes her meeting with a gynaecologist, who is opposed to the practice and punishes midwives who perform it, this is interpreted in the margin as 'patriarchal authority opposing noble female rites'. Finally, the voice exclaims in exasperation: 'why can't male politicians and medics accept that we *enjoy* circumcision and like the beauty and chastity it gives us?'

This voice, literally marginalised in a library book and metaphorically so in Walker's work, is ignored in the wider debate as well. But however misguided or incomprehensible this woman's experience of female 'circumcision' might seem to an outsider, her voice is worth listening to. If we do not, we cannot possibly understand why the practice is perpetuated, and advocated, *by women themselves*. In *Warrior Marks*, Walker's argument against cultural relativism is that 'torture is not culture'.[65] However, what we can learn from this anonymous and marginalised woman's voice is that one person's torture is – indeed – another's culture. To learn this is not to be flippant about feminist consciousness and political responsibility. It is, rather, to agree with Gina Dent in her thoughtful discussion of Walker's novel in 'Black Pleasure, Black Joy' that

> [T]his 'choice' – between modern, feminist, US-based black culture and traditional African culture – is the paradigm we must learn to unread. [...] It is to begin dismantling our understanding of *the very means by which we are able to know, to decide, and to act* (my emphasis).[66]

7

The Later Fiction: *By the Light of My Father's Smile* (1998) and *Now Is the Time to Open Your Heart* (2004)

Writing about *By the Light of My Father's Smile*, Lovalerie King observes that Walker 'employs recurring motifs of the spiritual journey or questing self, rebirth and transformation, the universality of pain and suffering, and a holistic view of life that brings her idea of connectedness into full relief'.[1] Because this goes for *Now Is the Time to Open Your Heart* as well, the two novels can usefully be discussed together, because they are both distinctively part of Walker's later work. From *The Temple of My Familiar* (1989) onwards, described by herself as a 'wisdom tale', and 'a romance of the last 500.000 years', she begins to develop what we might call a 'spiritual activism' that is communicated through storytelling.[2] Writing about real and invented tribes, whether it is the fictional African Olinka in *The Color Purple*, the Dogon of Mali in *Possessing the Secret of* Joy (1992), the Mundo of Mexico in *By the Light of My Father's Smile* (1998) or the Mahus of Hawai'i in *Now Is the Time to Open Your Heart* (2004), Walker draws on the creative and spiritual insights and practices of peoples all over the world. Her interest in writing about or creating such tribes is not merely ethnographic, however. She wants to tell the stories of the world because she believes the world needs them to survive, and to survive better than it has done hitherto. Storytelling then is a resource, more precious than oil, an invitation to enlightened thinking, acting, and feeling. To spread this gospel, Walker shares her sources of inspiration and creative thought in postscripts to her novels and essay collections, with reading lists of ethnographic and spiritual works for the delight and instruction of her audience. 'I continue to write the stories I believe to be spiritually authentic, creatively true. Stories

that are medicine – sometimes bitter, but also sweet – for myself
and for the tribe', she says, by way of explaining her artistic creed
as it has developed over the four decades of her career.[3] In a novel
such as *Now Is the Time to Open Your Heart*, the literature that results
from that creed reads almost like orature, oral tradition put into
writing, like an elder addressing the tribe in a village council, or
a wise grandmother telling stories to her little ones. Almost like
orature, but not quite: the voice we *read* is no longer the vernacular
voice we *heard* in Celie's letters in *The Color Purple*; it is less pithy,
and more overtly didactic than any of Walker's Southern characters
in the earlier work were allowed to be. All the same, *By the Light of
My Father's Smile* and *Now Is the Time to Open Your Heart* are in many
ways a reprise of that earlier work. A reprise can be a summary or
a culmination, and we find each in the endings of these two novels.
The close of *By the Light of My Father's Smile* is particularly evocative: on the final page, we witness the death of an author and the
burning of her books, as if in anticipation of the ending of Walker's
own life and career.[4] Yet in *Now Is the Time to Open Your Heart* Kate
Nelson/Talkingtree's journey to enlightenment culminates in her
taking on the mission of spreading the *yagé*, or Grandmother's
wisdom, in which she has been instructed by the guru/shaman
Armando:

> I think you have an idea of what you are here to do, he said.
> Oddly enough, she did.
> [...] I think I'm here to meet her; to understand where she's
> from. To see her living body before it is cut; to see her people
> whose health often depends on her. I am meant, I believe, to be
> her friend. And to be yours (219).[5]

Kate, by this time, can dream dreams that diagnose other people's
illnesses, and being sensitive to that gift she knows what to do to
heal them. A writer herself, Kate is thus endowed with the power,
and the responsibility, of a *curandera* (healer) in work and in life,
rather like her creator. For, by the time the twenty first century
comes around, Walker's work takes on an increasingly visionary
and spiritual quality, and the difference between the genres in
which she transmits that vision become more and more blurred to
the point where memoir, fiction, and essay form are almost indistin-
guishable from each other. Because of this confluence of ideas, this

penultimate chapter will discuss *By the Light of My Father's Smile* and *Now Is the Time to Open Your Heart* in the context of, and in dialogue with, the essay collection *We Are the Ones We Have Been Waiting For: Inner Light in a Time of Darkness* (2007), which is also a book of meditations, and *The Way Forward Is With a Broken Heart* (2000), part memoir and part short story collection. Their almost interchangeable titles bespeak their almost interchangeable contents, as we shall see.

BY THE LIGHT OF MY FATHER'S SMILE, OR FATHERS AND DAUGHTERS REVISITED

By the Light of My Father's Smile presents a tale of two sisters: Susannah, a novelist, and Magdalena/June, an academic, who as children migrate to Mexico and grow up there. They are the daughters of African American anthropologists who, although they are agnostics, have to masquerade as missionaries in order to secure the financial backing for their research. Their object of study is a mixed African American/Indian tribe called the Mundo, who believe in the continuity between life and death and in telling the truth, because 'it takes only one lie to unravel the world' (81).[6] The sisters' father, however, absorbs enough of the Christian teaching he is hired to transmit to begin to live such a lie, when he temporarily forgets his love for his daughter and punishes Magdalena for her sexual exploits with a Mexican Mundo boy, Manuelito. The beating Magdalena receives from her father – administered with Manuelito's silver-studded belt, to add insult to injury – is the cause of her and her sister Susannah's estrangement from him, and ultimately also from each other. Susannah sides with Magdalena against the father she loves and comes to resent her sister for it. In the end, however, both the father's trespass and Magdalena's envy of Susannah's happiness are forgiven, as each makes up with the others in the afterlife.

This plot of two sisters and a childhood trauma (another 'patriarchal wound') that ruins the life of one of them, is instantly recognisable as that of *The Color Purple* and *Possessing the Secret of Joy* rolled into one. As in the former, we encounter missionaries/anthropologists in a foreign land, who fail to convert or to fully understand an invented tribe (Olinka/Mundo). There is also again a lesbian relationship (between Susannah and her lover Pauline) in which both the closeness and the rift between sisters, caused by patriarchal intervention, is acted out. Most of all, the 'patriarchal wound' that is Magdalena's grief over the loss of her free sexuality, had its precursor in Tashi's mutilation in *Possessing the Secret of Joy*, while Susannah's pleasure in her bisexuality is an echo of Shug's in *The Color Purple*. Other familiar features of Walker's previous work are woven into this core narrative: the Greek dwarf Irene, who at first lives in a church like Miss Lissie in her temple, acts as a spirit guide to Susannah (who is an echo of Suwelo). Later, once she has inherited her father's fortune, Irene sails around the world like Mary Ann Haverstock did in *The Temple of My Familiar*, and lives for a while with the Pygmies in Africa – 'little people' like herself. Irene (whose name means 'peace') enlightens Susannah about the crimes of Europe, about the persecution of the gypsies and its similarity to the treatment of black people in America, and about worship of the Black Madonna in Greece, as in Africa. She also knows, as Miss Lissie did, of the witch hunts in Europe. These meant that in the Middle Ages 'Europe lost … its mother. Her strong mother', as a result of which it was made to 'shrink its spirit to half its size' (189). Another spirit guide is Manuelito, a Vietnam veteran who dies in a traffic accident shortly after his reunion with Magdalena. He is the one who instructs Señor Robinson, Magdalena's father, in the Mundo way of life and death. The Mundo believe in 'nonpossession of others' (96), and this lesson the father has yet to learn with regard to his daughters, even from beyond the grave. Manuelito tells him that

> The dead are required to finish two tasks before all is over with them: one is to guide back to the path someone you left behind who is lost, because of your folly; the other is to host a ceremony so that you and others you have hurt may face eternity reconciled and complete. (150)

For the father, this means that he has to make good with both Magdalena and Susannah, whereas Manuelito's task of reconciliation lies in Vietnam, where he has to face the people he murdered during the war. In a strange reversal of the usual relationship between the dead and the living, then, in this novel it is not the living who have to honour and remember their ancestors, but the other way around: the dead have a duty to help the living, and to atone for the wrongdoings they committed during their lifetime. Jana

Hecková, writing about *Now Is the Time to Open Your Heart* (but the idea works for *By the Light of My Father's Smile* too) puts it this way:

> ... the ancestors cease to be supreme beings advising and guiding the present mortals. Instead, they are perceived as human beings that once existed and, similarly to individuals in the present, had to face difficulties, some of which have remained unresolved.[7]

Walker's readers are used to having their credulity – and their patience – stretched, and *By the Light of My Father's Smile* offers no dispensation from that rule. As Gayle Pemberton aptly remarks, 'Fables demand a suspension of disbelief beyond the common or garden variety most fictions require. *By the Light of My Father's Smile* is so unreal, as if in translation from the Spanish, the Greek, the dead [*sic*]'.[8] And so, although the familiar contours of Walker's imaginative landscape are clearly visible here, we get to see them from a most unusual perspective: that of the recently dead, who still have unfinished business to clear up with the living. Set in Mexico and the United States, with a brief sojourn in Greece, the story is narrated by angels, that is, by all the main characters who successively 'cross over', bar the novelist Susannah who is the last to die and who, ironically, does not get to tell her own story.

This narration from beyond the grave may be interesting as an idea but, to quote one of the novel's own insights, 'ideas are made of blocks. Rigid and hard', whereas 'Stories are the way spirit is exercised' (195–6). In *By the Light of My Father's Smile*, ideas often have to stand in for narrative development; they are talked through by the characters, or literalised to comic effect in a sometimes discordant way. The rendering of Magdalena's death is an example. Although her love for Manuelito is in the end requited, her relationship with her father is not resolved and she dies, unfulfilled, from obesity. But rather than letting the grotesque image of a woman who eats herself to death resonate in its own right, Walker allows Magdalena to explain: 'It was as if my memories were lodged in my cells, and needed to be fed. If I lost weight perhaps my memories of Manuelito and my anger at my father would fade away. I felt so abandoned already, I did not want them to go' (125). This explanation is unnecessary; it will not let Magdalena and her story be. For the same reason, the dead narrators' all-too-human jokes (such as 'If I were not dead already, I would have killed myself') end up sounding lame and embarrassing (83). Walker's use of names, likewise, is at times crudely symbolic instead of subtly suggestive, and often their significance is explained by the characters themselves. Pauline, Susannah's lover, used to be Lily Paul, a name that combines the free sexuality of the biblical Lilith with the misogyny of St Paul, one of Christianity's church fathers. This is a rather dubious coupling for a woman whose sexuality is described as manly and aggressive – albeit, to be fair, from Señor Robinson's jealous narrative perspective – early on in the narrative. The Lilith part of her name aligns her with Magdalena: both are 'loose women', whose childhoods were ruined by violent men and whose relationship to Susannah is marked by the ambivalence of love and resentment. But then this ambivalence also is discussed at length by the women themselves, as if it weren't obvious enough already from the narrative development.

Walker makes it clear in her – now customary – acknowledgements that this novel is a tribute to Eros, because the ability to experience sexual pleasure is once again represented as the thing that makes, or breaks, a person's spirit. As noted above, Magdalena is an incarnation of Tashi in *Possessing the Secret of Joy*, but unlike Tashi Magdalena dies defeated, crushed as she is by the memory of her father's violence. In childhood, the unbroken 'wild' Magdalena was respected by the Mundo as a 'Changing Woman, a natural one, uninstructed and uninitiated, and therefore very rare'; they name her Mad Dog as an Indian honorific (93). Her father, however, sees her as true to her biblical name: a whore, and Manuelito's wife is – predictably – called Maria to highlight the madonna/whore dichotomy in Christian thinking.[9] After the beating with Manuelito's belt Magdalena herself chooses June as her name to signify the loss of her 'change purse' with the golden zipper, which symbolises – in heavily Freudian terms – her sexuality. Señor Robinson himself, however, is ultimately saved by Eros because, as Manuelito recognises, his sexual devotion to his wife Langley keeps the flame of erotic truth alive and wins him the protection of the Mundo elders, who guard him and watch over him from the other side.

There is a well-known essay by Audre Lorde titled 'Uses of the Erotic: The Erotic as Power' that has a lot in common with Walker's view of the spiritual and political importance of Eros. 'The erotic is a resource within each of us', Lorde writes,

> that lies in a deeply female and spiritual plane, firmly rooted in the power of our unexpressed or unrecognized feeling. In order to

perpetuate itself, every oppression must corrupt or distort those various sources of power within the culture of the oppressed that can provide energy for change. *For women, this has meant a suppression of the erotic as a considered source of power and information within our lives* (my emphasis).[10]

Like Walker's, Lorde's view of the erotic does not confine it to sexual pleasure alone but extends it to a realm of feeling that is an important source of knowledge, and in addition both connect the erotic to creativity and to spirituality. In the subtitle of *By the Light of My Father's Smile*, 'A Story of Requited Love, Crossing Over, and the Sexual Healing of the Soul' we find those elements combined, as they are also at the end of the novel, when Señor Robinson finally acknowledges what he has done to crush Magdalena's spirit. Manuelito explains that

> If you are in love, and going to meet your lover, to make love, you think of the moon as a father, happily looking down on you. For Mundo fathers are happy that their children, the girls as well as the boys, enjoy what your culture calls sex (212).

No wonder that Susannah, having lived a productive, creative, and fulfilling erotic life dies 'of old age, at home, in bed, in her sleep, and while dreaming', in sharp contrast to Magdalena who eats herself to death (216). The concept of 'father hunger', which is used in some psychological and psychiatric theories of anorexia, bulimia, and compulsive eating, recognises the connection between eating disorders and a disturbed relationship between fathers and daughters, especially around sexuality. As Margo Maine explains, 'Some women with eating problems report having been close to their fathers during childhood, but having felt abandoned or rejected by them as they matured. Most likely these men retreated or withdrew because of discomfort with their daughter's sexuality'.[11] Magdalena's over-eating can thus be read as a response to the withdrawal of her father's love; she literally hungers for it and stuffs herself with food so as to anaesthetise the pain of having lost it.

By the Light of My Father's Smile is also an exploration of Thanatos, the other side of Eros' coin, and potentially the more interesting because more innovative side. Walker allows the dead not just to figure in, but to *tell* this story of 'Requited Love, Crossing Over, and the Sexual Healing of the Soul'. However, the angels' view of life is disconcertingly similar to that of the living. The first of the dead narrators is

Mr. Robinson, who in the early chapters reports on one sexual adventure after another, as he is both remembering his own relations with his wife and witnessing Susannah's lovemaking with her husband, the Greek Petros, or with her lover Pauline. As Rudolph P. Byrd remarks,

'That Robinson is not an angel with the conventional trappings of wings and a halo is beside the point, inconsequential. What is of consequence, however, is that men, black men, black fathers possess the potentiality, as Walker intimates, to achieve that state of grace we associate with angels'.[12]

This is undoubtedly true, but for those of Walker's critics who have taken her to task for her purportedly negative representation of African American men, it may be cold comfort that their 'potentiality' to achieve a state of grace can only occur after death. Señor Robinson's witnessing of Susannah's sexual exploits with Pauline makes for particularly uncomfortable reading, because the father's perspective is, by implication, that of a voyeur who clearly resents his daughter's sexuality, and the more so when it is expressed and enjoyed with a female lover. Victoria Kingston registers her unease with this narrative perspective: '[the father] hovers constantly, with his nose, as it were, pressed against the window, voyeuristically relating to us details of Susannah's life that are entirely personal and would be denied to him as a living man'.[13] As a dead narrator/observer of Susannah's sexual pleasure, the father learns however to repent for his sins through the intervention of Manuelito, who joins him in the realm of the recently deceased. Magdalena, finally, is the third dead narrator; it is her task to reconcile herself with her sister, and she achieves this as she watches Susannah's 'crossing over' in the closing pages of the novel.

Possessing the Secret of Joy already prepared us for the spectre of a dead storyteller; Tashi, after all, begins her tale with the words 'I did not realize for a long time that I was dead. And that reminds me of a story'.[14] But Tashi, as we later find out, is only spiritually, metaphorically dead at this time; her physical death at the end of the novel coincides with a spiritual rebirth, as we saw in Chapter 6. In *By the Light of My Father's Smile* this order is reversed and the dead narrators speak, from the beginning, truly 'from the other side' of the crossing place in the river, the Vado, which signifies death and is reminiscent of the river Styx that the ancient Greeks believed they had to cross before arriving in the under- or afterworld. This is one of several cross-cultural parallels between the beliefs of the

Mundo (meaning 'world') and those of the ancient Greeks. When Lily Paul tells Susannah that she was raped at fifteen, the latter likens her to Persephone, who was raped by the god of the underworld and forced to spend half of each year there, during which time her mother, Demeter, 'turned the earth to winter' because she missed her daughter (105). The *motif* of betrayal, or not, by the mother – which Susannah and Lily Paul are discussing at this point – both echoes and redresses the betrayal of daughters by mothers in *Possessing the Secret of Joy*. For, as if to make up for her indictment of mothers in the practice of FGM, this novel is predominantly about fathers, as its title announces. Langley, the mother, is again a flamboyant Zora Neale Hurston-type of figure, but she remains largely in the background and disappears, as Gayle Pemberton remarks, all too quickly from the novel, as if Walker did not quite know what to do with her.[15]

FICTION OR AUTOBIOGRAPHY? THE DEATH OF AN AUTHOR

'By the light of my father's smile' is taken from the Mundo initiation song that Manuelito teaches Señor Robinson, *'por la luz de la sonrisa de mi padre'* (196). This is also the song that Magdalena sings, compulsively, as a child – for she is the one who has 'naturally' absorbed the Mundo world-view, in a way that her father could not. Significantly his voyeuristic preoccupation with surveillance of his daughters' sexuality leads him to mislearn the refrain of the song as *'por la luz de los ojos de mi padre'*, meaning 'by the light of my father's *eyes'*, and Manuelito has to put him straight about that as well: daughters don't need their fathers to watch over them, but to give them the light of his smiling approval of whatever it is in their nature to do and to be. Since father is the first model of masculinity that daughters come across in their lives, the theme of what that relationship between fathers and daughters ideally should be like is an important one. Much has been written, and filmed, about fathers and sons, usually in a recognisably oedipal frame, but – aside from incest – the question of father–daughter relations has received much less attention from writers and scholars. In Walker's work, the relationship between Ruth and Grange Copeland resembles that of father and daughter, but of course it isn't: the very fact that Grange is Ruth's grandfather, and one who has had the time and opportunity to reflect on his role as a *failed* father to Brownfield, makes it possible for that bond to work in a caring and nurturing way. Walker's essays and memoirs give some sources for the way Señor Robinson's relationship with his two daughters is represented in *By the Light of My Father's Smile*; after all, she has repeatedly written about her parents and siblings over the years, and how her relationships with them have changed over time. The first such foreshadowing of the dysfunctional nexus between Señor Robinson and Magdalena and Susannah can be glimpsed in an early autobiographical essay, 'Brothers and Sisters'. Here Walker describes how the girls and boys in her family were raised with the sexual double standard that meant boys would be allowed to go into town at night chasing girls, whereas girls had to stay home, because father 'thought all young women perverse'.[16] The father's punitive attitude towards his daughters' sexuality was, Walker notes, particularly marked in relation to her older sister, and the bond between Alice and this sister is rather similar to that between Magdalena and Susannah:

> I was spared the humiliation she was subjected to, though at the same time, I felt every bit of it. It was as if she suffered for my benefit, and I vowed early in my life that none of the things that made existence so miserable for her would happen to me.[17]

There was, then, a kind of solidarity of the younger sister with the older, but even this fellow feeling could not prevent that the older sister, as Walker chillingly adds, 'fell for the first man who loved her enough to beat her for looking at someone else, and when I was still in high school, she married him'.[18] The father's early example of a violent masculinity was thus reproduced in the husband, and so the cycle of domestic abuse perpetuated itself. But this is not the end of the story. Interestingly, Walker ends 'Brothers and Sisters' with a conciliatory note about her father, and her ability to forgive him, if only in death. This change in attitude she attributes to feminism: 'I was relieved to know his sexist behavior was not something uniquely his own, but, rather, an imitation of the behavior around us'.[19] In a later essay she goes so far as to call her father 'a victim of sexist ideology', and recalls that she 'battled with him throughout childhood' until leaving home at seventeen.[20] In between these two autobiographical pieces is an essay titled 'Father', in *Living by the Word*, that throws yet another light on the relationship between fathers and daughters. Walker describes here how she could not be content to be her father's favourite 'because a sister whom I loved was clearly not favorite material', and how her father over the years 'tended to become more and more like my worst characters the older he got', even administering a brutal beating to Alice and her brother Bobby, with a belt, for a misdemeanour.[21] The conciliatory tone is still there, but for different reasons: 'These days I feel we are on good terms, spiritually (my dreams of him are deeply loving and comforting ones), and that we both understand our relationship was a casualty of exhaustion and circumstances', the latter being the condition of poverty and the demands of raising a large family in the South. Walker here fills in more of her father's background, and it is very significant with regard to how he later raises his daughters:

> His mother had been murdered, by a man who claimed to love her, when he was eleven. His father, to put it very politely, drank, and terrorized his children.
>
> My father was so confused that when my sister Ruth appeared in the world and physically resembled his mother, and sounded like his mother, and had similar expressions, he rejected her and missed no opportunity that I ever saw to put her down. I, of course, took the side of my sister.[22]

Can it be any surprise, the reasoning in this essay goes, that father took it upon himself to police his daughters' virtue, if his own mother's sexual waywardness – *as he saw it* – had led to her murder, and his abandonment? Sexist behaviour is thus not all there is to forgive; there is also a familial history of loss and violence that does not need forgiving so much, as understanding in all its pernicious ramifications.[23]

A further and even more recent parallel with the father/daughter relationship in *By the Light of My Father's Smile* is offered in 'Kindred Spirits', a short story that is part memoir, in *The Way Forward Is With a Broken Heart*. Here two sisters, Rosa and Barbara, try to re-negotiate their relationship after years of estrangement. Rosa, like Susannah, is the youngest and she is a writer. Like Susannah also Rosa gets drawn into her sister's victimhood at the hands of a violent father:

> But *crack*, he had slapped her across the face. She was sixteen, plump and lovely. Rosa adored her. She ran immediately to get the knife, but she was so small no one seemed to notice her, wedging herself between them. But had she been larger and stronger

she might have killed him; for even as a child she was serious in all she did – and then what would her life, the life of a murderer, have been like?[24]

This passage leads us back to *By the Light of My Father's Smile* and the relationship between live daughters and dead fathers, and that between two sisters, shaped as their sense of sisterhood is by the violence of the father towards one of them. Here, as in the earlier representations of Walker's own childhood, we find avowed solidarity of the younger sibling with the older, abused one, with both making common cause against the father. Walker herself sees what goes on between Magdalena and Susannah in a different light. As if to furnish a perfect example of where comment on her own work is not helpful, in 'When Life Descends into the Pit', a commentary on *By the Light of My Father's Smile*, Walker describes Magdalena as having done 'a terrible wrong' to Susannah in childhood by drawing her sister into her resentment of their father, Señor Robinson. This is odd, because it reverses the guilt-and-atonement narrative of the novel, in which it is the father who needs to come to terms with his crime against Magdalena, rather than Magdalena having to make amends to Susannah for having demanded her sisterly solidarity. This then is one instance where the author's perception of her own work, or her intention, does not square with how the novel reads. To the reader, as Walker notes (strangely in the same essay) the novel

> is calling fathers in particular to come and witness the catastrophe into which [sexuality], this most basic expression of self-love and love-of-other has fallen. It maintains that female children are dying from the abandonment they suffer from their fathers the moment they become recognizable as sexual beings.[25]

This is an important theme and a crucial insight into the pathology of 'father hunger', here literalised in Magdalena's eating disorder, which leads her to fill the emotional emptiness inside her with food. Against this pathological model of fathering Walker sets the Mundo philosophy 'that sexuality is ... a mystery, a blessing and a wise teacher of the Self'.[26]

The Mundo are an invented tribe, like the Olinka in *Possessing the Secret of Joy* and *The Color Purple*, and they are 'marked for extinction' because of their holistic beliefs and way of life.[27] As Jack Forbes' *Africans and Native Americans* testifies, there is a long history of mixed-race black and Native American presence in Mexico, and the Mundo represent it here; when the Spanish conquered Middle and South America, they brought free Africans with them, whom they then enslaved, and that slave population subsequently mixed with the Spanish and indigenous populations.[28] Apart from this recognised minority history, however, Walker's conception of death is perhaps the only other feature of *By the Light of My Father's Smile* that warrants its Mexican references. As Octavio Paz observes:

> The opposition between life and death was not so absolute to the ancient Mexicans as it is to us. [...] Life had no higher purpose than to flow into death, its opposite and complement; and death, in turn, was not an end in itself: man fed the insatiable hunger of life with his death. Sacrifices had a double purpose: on the one hand man participated in the creative process, at the same time paying back to the gods the debts contracted by his species; on the other hand he nourished cosmic life and also social life, which was nurtured by the former.[29]

Paz's words have a peculiar resonance not only because this idea of continuity obviously informs Walker's text, but more eerily because *By the Light of My Father's Smile* ends, in effect, with a human sacrifice when Susannah, the novelist, dies along with her books. As the poem that Magdalena quotes during her vigil puts it: Susannah has become her own candle, willingly burning herself 'to light up the darkness around her' (221).

This final scene is as anachronistic a representation of a writer's aspiration to martyrdom as one could expect to find near the end of the twentieth century. As we shall see in the next chapter, Walker's increasingly visionary inclinations, evident in the essays as in the fiction, align her more with mediaeval mystics or black women preachers of a century ago, than with other contemporary writers. Though obviously – and ironically – Susannah's demise is a literal enactment of 'the death of the author' referred to at the beginning of this book, Walker's representation of this writer's self-immolation is no postmodern device to signal her lack of control of, or her abdication of responsibility for, the process of signification. If anything, it is the reverse: Susannah dies, contentedly, of old age – the only character in the novel to do so because she has lived a good life. Her refusal to be remembered is a protest against the long tradition in Western culture that holds the author to be immortal *because of* his (and I do mean 'his') writing: 'It is the need to be remembered that has caused most of the trouble in the world, [Susannah] said. Most of the conquering. Destruction of what is natural. War' (220). Walker thus borrows Susannah's voice to speak for herself: Susannah's final act is in keeping with the revision of Western thought that runs through all of Walker's writing, and here she articulates her author's views.

At century's end, and on the final page of *By the Light of My Father's Smile*, the question then arises what Susannah's act signifies in relation to Walker's anxiety about the survival of her person and her work that she has expressed elsewhere (see Chapter 4). Two answers present themselves: either *By the Light of My Father's Smile* articulates a superior wisdom, a spiritual growth in which that anxiety has finally been transcended, *or* it bespeaks a more desperate fear that the light of Alice Walker's imagination would indeed, with this novel, have burnt itself out. Each of these two readings, in its way, is as disturbing as the other, just as each, in its way, also fits the paradoxical persona that is Alice Walker: author and medium, writer and activist, woman and visionary 'mother of all that is here'. Yet somehow the idea of continuity between life and death is not enough to reconcile these contradictory readings and identities; somehow this novel does not provide an answer but a further question: having killed off the novelist, what would, or what *could* Alice Walker do next?

NOW IS THE TIME TO OPEN YOUR HEART: GRANDMOTHER STORIES

For those who know Walker's previous work well, *Now Is the Time to Open Your Heart* is a novel we have, in a sense, already read. At times it even looks like a (self-)parodic condensation of the themes and styles of that previous work, and in particular the theme and style of *The Temple of My Familiar*. There, as we saw in Chapter 5, the various characters' quest for enlightenment was charted less in narrative development or plot than in direct or reported dialogue, found documents, and in Miss Lissie's storytelling. Significantly the novel opens with one of the two main characters, Kate Talkingtree, meditating at a Buddhist retreat. Like Susannah in *By the Light of My Father's Smile*, Kate is a writer. During a slow, conscious-of-every-step walk 'she enjoyed the feeling of a heel touching the earth before the toe followed it. Meditating this way made her feel almost as slow as vegetation; it went well with her new name, a name she'd taken earlier, in the spring' (1). Kate's former surname, Nelson, is that of Walker's own grandmother on her father's side, who was murdered by one of her admirers when Willie Lee Walker was still a boy. This biographical fact introduces an important theme of the novel for, as Walker has explained in interview, it led her to explore in fiction what had been missing in life: 'This revelation, that I missed my grandmother terribly, and felt lost as I entered the latter part of my life, helped me to understand how human beings are collectively missing the presence in the culture of The Grandmother'.[30] Kate's inner peace is disturbed while listening to a talk about revolution by one of the Buddhist teachers at the retreat. To her surprise, the (white, European) teacher does not seem to know that the 'hot', because armed, revolutions in Africa, Cuba, and the Caribbean 'had been undermined not only by their own shortcomings but also by military interference from the United States' (2). Second, Kate notes that his audience is composed almost exclusively of white middle class people, who 'had the money and leisure time to be at a retreat' (3). Her dissatisfaction with the privilege and the unworldliness of the retreat then leads her to go on a journey, first down the Colorado river and then to the Amazon, to replenish her creativity and to be with kindred spirits, both of the human kind and those of the mind. Meanwhile Kate's partner Yolo, forced by Kate's departure to take a vacation in Hawai'i, finds himself experiencing a similar spiritual journey. In Hawai'i he is re-united with a former lover, Alma (meaning 'soul' in Spanish), and inducted in the ways of the Mahu by Aunty Perlua, a wise woman and storyteller, akin to Miss Lissie and to the African *griot*. Yolo has also chosen his own name, which is of Poewin Indian origin and means 'a place in the river where wild rushes grow' to replace the 'Henry' of his birth – not coincidentally the name of Walker's paternal grandfather (78). As in all of Walker's work, names are important here again as indicators of their owners' spiritual state. Autobiography and fiction frequently merge in *Now Is the Time To Open Your Heart*, and particularly so when it comes to naming and identity. According to biographer Evelyn White, Walker herself also changed her name: after the death of her mother Minnie Tallulah Grant Walker in 1993, Alice Malsenior Walker became Alice Tallulah-Kate Walker, thus absorbing both mother and paternal grandmother into her own proper name and identity.

The plot of *Now Is the Time to Open Your Heart*, such as it is, revolves around Kate and Yolo's two journeys, taken separately but leading to the same end: a literal homecoming to California, but also a homecoming to a more authentic or natural sense of self for both of them, and wedding plans to seal their re-discovered bond of love. The wedding guests will include all the participants in Kate's Amazonian adventure, black and white, her fellow travelers down the Colorado river, and Yolo's Hawai'ian friends. These multicultural and multiracial groups, as well as their spiritual leaders Anunu, Enoba, and Armando, have enabled Kate and Yolo to be spiritually reborn, and have thus made their reunion possible.

The narrative is symbolically bookended by the act of dismantling and rebuilding Kate's home altar, consisting of images of a range of deities and political and cultural icons like Che Guevara and Bessie Smith, with the usual accoutrements of candles, herbs, and a purple cloth. Yet we see Kate's progress in the additional placing, at the end, of a bottle of the 'grandmother medicine' and a clock with a decorative anaconda wound around it on the altar, for these objects have a particular spiritual significance. The *yagé* or grandmother medicine is, in more ways than one, the third central character of *Now Is the Time to Open Your Heart*. As the 'Afterword' explains, *yagé* or Ayahuasca is a potion used by South American Indians to free the soul from bodily confinement, so that it 'liberates its owner from the realities of everyday life and introduces him to wondrous realms of what he considers reality and permits him to communicate with his ancestors' (224). In line with Walker's personal theology of an immanent God or Goddess, first espoused by Shug in *The Color Purple*, the *yagé* works as an entheogen, meaning that it reveals the Goddess or God within the self (225). A bitter, foul-tasting potion, the *yagé* induces violent vomiting and vivid visions, which in indigenous cultures are interpreted to have healing and telepathic powers. But 'Grandmother' as a third main character in the novel does not just refer to the psychedelic drug used traditionally by the Amazonian Indians of Peru and by latter-day explorers of the mind, such as Allen Ginsberg and William Burroughs (who 'discovered' it on their psychedelic journeys in the 1960s).[31] 'Grandmother' in the novel is something more akin to a concept, a principle, a particular kind of spiritual wisdom that has the *yagé* as its means of transmission, but is personified in grandmotherly figures like the transgendered Aunty Perlua in Hawai'i, or the Grandmother-goddess figure of Amazonian cosmology. Most of all, as Kate and Yolo discover at the end of their quests, Grandmother is an aspect of the self. As such, she is akin to a Jungian archetype and hence part of the collective unconscious, which can be called forth through use of the *yagé* and with the help of an indigenous spiritual teacher like Armando, who administers and oversees Kate's *yagé* experience. For the *yagé* is not for the fainthearted. Kate describes to Yolo her fear in the Amazonian jungle when, under the influence of the *yagé*, she goes searching for the Grandmother, but feels completely lost. In the midst of such crisis, all the pieces of the puzzle that had forced her and Yolo to take to the road in the first place come together: 'And then, just as I was on the point of dying of loneliness and lack of direction, I wailed: *Oh, Grandmother, you are not here!* And she said: But *you* are' (210). This insight echoes the title of *Now Is the Time to Open Your Heart*'s twin volume, Walker's book of meditations, *We Are the Ones We Have Been Waiting For: Inner Light in a Time of Darkness*. The message of both is that the true revolution, the 'cool' and non-violent revolution of consciousness and enlightenment, comes from within and does not depend on political leadership or uncritical and unthinking devotion to some guru or godhead. Walker has emphasised this in interview too:

> The whole point of anything that is really, truly valuable to your soul, and to your own growth, is not to attach to a teacher, but rather to find out what the real deal is in the world itself. The teachings can help you, but really, we're all here with the opportunity to experience the reality of hereness. We all have that. I trust that.[32]

The twin dissatisfactions of Buddhist unwordliness and the class and race-privilege of New Age truth-seekers that launched Kate Talkingtree on her journey are therefore not so much resolved by the close of the novel as accepted, or made peace with. As a result, when Yolo and Kate are reunited, they exhibit every trait of the smug middle class-ness by the novel's end that Kate had found so problematic at its beginning:

> Later, in bed, he said to her: I loved eating supper with you (they had stopped to pick up the yummy Chinese vegetarian take-out they both craved); I loved being in the bath with you (she had emptied half a bottle of L'Occitane Ambre bubble bath into the tub); loved smelling and stroking you.
> She grinned. It *is* good, isn't it? She said.
> Amazingly, *yes*, he said, feeling her head settle on his chest. The world has never been in worse shape: global warming, animal extinctions, people fucked up and crazy, war. And then there are

us, harmless little humans who somehow get to nibble at the root of things ... (194)

It is tempting to attribute this passage's poor writing (a 'he said/she said' style that mars the novel throughout) to its autobiographical overtones. The bubble bath brandname and the 'yummy' that emanate from a supposedly omniscient narrator's keyboard, give away Walker's self-avowed pleasure in reliving 'some of my own discoveries about life in the person/character of Kate'.[33] Kate and Yolo's insights are Walker's own, mirrored – at times almost verbatim – in interviews and in *We Are the Ones We Have Been Waiting For*, where Walker's own house altar is described for example, and it is very similar to Kate's.[34] Be that as it may, if we read the passage as fiction, then Yolo and Kate's pillow talk shows that the 'cool revolution' in consciousness that the Buddhist teacher had spoken about in the first chapter, has now taken place for them despite Kate's initial misgivings. Gone is the guilt of middle class privilege and the dissatisfaction with an apolitical Buddhism; both now realise that world(ly) politics is not separate from, but integral to the revolution in consciousness, and both now recognise that class privilege is something to be enjoyed *and used* to gain insight into how the world's desperate plight has come into being and how it must be changed. Enlightenment thus begins at home, in the mind, even though they have had to travel far and wide to gain that insight. The title *Now Is the Time to Open Your Heart*, Walker explains in interview, comes from 'an icaro, a shamanic healing song that is sung during ayahuasca ceremonies'.[35] *An Open Heart* is also the title of a book by the Dalai Lama, and the injunction to 'open your heart' is to be taken quite literally, as an admonishment to all readers to follow in Walker's slow footsteps on the path to enlightenment and inner peace.

Like Grandmother *yagé*, the anaconda that is wound around Kate's clock and is added to her altar at the end of the novel also fulfils several symbolic functions at once in the narrative. Most obviously, the snake figures itself, a treacherous yet seductive creature that offers the choice between right and wrong, knowledge and virtue, in the Biblical story of Adam and Eve. It also refers to the various rivers that are an integral part of Kate's quest. A recurrent dream of a dry riverbed, and a daytime act of ceremonially burning 'not only some of her writing but several hundred dollar bills, just to demonstrate to herself that these items were not the God/Goddess of her life' force her to seek replenishment by an actual river, the Colorado (12).

Dreams, like the *yagé*, are means to enlightenment; Freud's 'royal road to the unconscious' is re-trodden in this novel as every stage of Kate's development is illustrated with dream sequences that bear encoded messages for her next course of action. One such, at the very beginning of the narrative, is a dream about a frozen anaconda that in turn brings with it a memory of a story about a snake told to Kate by an old woman 'from her days in the Black Freedom Movement' in the South (6). The woman's story ends in a series of questions focusing on the treacherous nature of a poisonous snake, unfrozen by human contact: 'Do we kill it or let it live? Do we ever believe its true nature and does that true nature ever change? And does ours?' (8) The first question is, of course, reminiscent of Meridian's dilemma, discussed in Chapter 3, whether or not to kill for the revolution. But the third question posed by the old woman – another wise Grandmother figure, obviously – adds an extra layer of complexity: '*And does ours?*' asks about the potential for evil in ourselves, it addresses what in Jungian terms is called the Shadow, the dark side in all of us that is at its most dangerous and destructive when unacknowledged. And it is no coincidence that the dry riverbed of Kate's first dream images another Jungian concept: that of the archetype, which Jung compared to a dry riverbed to which only the river can give content.[36] Because the Shadow needs to be acknowledged and made peace with, Kate has encounters with snakes during her *yagé*-induced visions in the Amazon jungle. Describing and analysing them with her teacher Armando, she learns first that for the indigenous people of this region the snake is Grandfather, who complements Grandmother *yagé*. A little later she is visited by a real, material snake, 'a serpent whose coloring blended perfectly with the damp umber of her dirt yard' (214). She is assured the creature is perfectly harmless, but it scares her all the same, and this then becomes the occasion for her to confront her Shadow, and to meditate on the true nature of the snake:

> Because of religious indoctrination, almost everyone feared and loathed the serpent. What damage had such hatred done to it; [...] what did the serpent think of humanity? [...] Black people had been cast outside the circle of goodwill for hundreds of years. This was perhaps the root of her feeling of kinship with the visitor (214).

The Biblical connection between black people who were said to have received the curse of Ham, and the serpent, which was made responsible for the original evil that drove humanity out of the Garden of Eden, is thus reinterpreted here as a fellow feeling of victimisation at the hands of Christianity and racism. As we would expect, Kate does not fail to note that there is a long-standing affinity between women and snakes as well, from Eve to Cleopatra, who had 'asps as pets' (214). And so the circle is completed: the Shadow is nothing to be afraid of; the Shadow, in fact, is deeply familiar and its demonisation is due to a racist, woman-hating, and religiously misguided dominant culture – which unsurprisingly is also a culture of domination.

This culture of domination is persistently critiqued in *Now Is the Time to Open Your Heart* by means of various subnarratives that illustrate the ubiquitous destructive presence of Europeans in the Americas, spreading across the continent from the Amazon to Hawai'i. The form this critique takes, however, with regard to US imperialism as a descendant of European rapaciousness, is quite surprising. Unusually, Walker's habitual acknowledgements appear at the beginning of the novel, and they are – as ever – instructive as to her sources and motivation for writing. Dedicated to 'Anunu and Enoba', both spiritual leaders in the narrative, the acknowledgements express gratitude to 'all the devas, angels, and bodhisattvas who accompany, watch over, and protect explorers, pioneers, and artists'. This motley crew is composed of holy figures from Hinduism, Christianity, and Buddhism, and the dedication equates the figure of the artist with that of the explorer and the pioneer. Compared to Walker's usual conception of the artist as visionary or medium, this is an unexpected conjunction. 'Explorer' and 'pioneer' are, after all, hardly innocent terms in American literature and history; from Columbus onwards, explorers and pioneers supposedly 'discovered' and 'settled' the Americas, but in doing so they plundered and stole Indian lands and worked those lands with African slaves. Why would Walker or her protagonists, artists all, want to ally themselves with this history of exploitation, rape, and pillage? We will come to answer that question in a roundabout way, by first looking in more depth at the novel's central issues.

DETOXING THE SOUL, CLEANSING THE NATION

As Gerri Bates writes, cleansing is 'a central theme in the novel. By means of nausea, regurgitation, and diarrhea Kate alters her state of consciousness to understand past lives and past experiences'.[37] As well as the indigenous medicine of *yagé* that induces Kate's bodily cleansing, the imagery of rivers also runs through the narrative as a cleansing and creative force, as we have seen. For it is not just bodies that need to be cleansed of toxins; minds are also to be cleansed of the flotsam and jetsam of personal and national histories, and to undergo a literal brainwash that reveals the light of truth underneath the false consciousness induced by consumerism and mass media. Armando, Kate's spirit guide in the Amazon, explains, for example, why watching TV and movies is dangerous:

> When you are caught up in the world that you did not design as support for your life and the life of people, it is like being caught in someone else's dream or nightmare. Many people exist in their lives in this way. I say exist because it is not really living. [...] You are going here and there, seeing this and that person; you do not know or care about them usually, they are just there, on your *interior screen*. Humankind will not survive if we continue in this way, most of us living lives in which our own life is not the center. (150; my emphasis)

Yolo has the same revelation after listening to Aunty Pearlua, who relates how women used to rule in Hawai'i, how the island until recently had a queen, Lili'uokalani, and that the indigenous Mahus like herself are born as males, but enjoined to live out their lives as women and as protectors of children. 'Wow, thought Yolo. All this going on in the world and some folks are just kicking back watching television' (130). Yolo's insight that cross-cultural reality is much more interesting and rich than the wildest mass-produced fiction in turn echoes Walker's sentiments in *We Are the Ones We Have Been Waiting For*: 'This is a time when teachings of all traditions are available to us [...] If we are lucky, we will have close friends of other cultures who will tell us, in phone call, letter, or e-mail, of a wise understanding of life passed on by earlier generations'.[38] A cynic might take Walker at her – rather postmodern – word and see all these teachings and cultures as a smorgasbord of spiritual options from which the Western consumer may choose to taste, and to consume whatever takes his or her fancy. But this would be facile, and deliberately misunderstand Walker's encouragement for us to replace the passive consumerism of mass culture with an active engagement with and understanding of other cultures, other parts of the world, and other times. What is more, she sees Americans as particularly well placed to fulfill such a mission, both in order to right wrongs of the past and because Americans, as a mixed people whose motto it is to forge unity from diversity (*e Pluribus Unum*), are unique in the world. It is not for nothing that *The Way Forward Is With a Broken Heart*, Walker's volume of memoirs and stories published in 2000, is dedicated 'To the American race', echoing Jean Toomer's view of a near-century before that an 'American race', which was neither black nor white but blended, was in the making. Kate registers the thought of a unique American race consciously even as she is purging her body under the influence of the *yagé*:

> I am an American ... Indigenous to the Americas. Nowhere else could I, this so-called Black person – African, European, Indio- exist. Only here. In Africa there would have been no Europeans, no Native Americans. In Europe, no Africans and no Indians. Only here; *only here*, she said, as the waves of vomiting continued (54).

Purging the body thus goes along with purging the mind of fixed or preconceived ideas about 'race': the Black American is a product of Africa *and* the Americas, and to recognise this is to come to terms with, and not to abdicate responsibility for, America's crimes as well as its virtues. Again, Walker articulates these ideas at greater length in *We Are the Ones We Have Been Waiting For*, when she asks her readers to meditate on their view of Americans and 'what it means to be an American – a *North* American: a person from the US of A'.[39] She relates this question not just to her American readers' personal and national identity but extends it even to American foreign policy, and suggests that anyone who is afraid of political leaders or countries elsewhere in the world should 'Consider a visit':[40]

> How do you wish to meet new people? By sharing recipes, and cooking and eating dinners together; by learning their medicines and dances and gardening techniques, their wisdom and philoso- phy; by listening to the sound of their language and trying to learn it? [...] Or do you wish to meet them via television, as they mourn the children you have killed? The temples and tombs you have shattered? The sacred Mother or Fatherland you have trashed?[41]

Another way of wording this question is to ask where world peace is going to come from – surely not from armed conflict and 'hot' revolutions aided by US military intervention, but from mutual understanding and cross-cultural appreciation of the world's natural and human resources. Such understanding and appreciation is assumed, however, in Walker's scheme, to converge in some kind of consensus about what is universally desirable and Good. When Yolo and Kate playfully fantasise about 'What would happen if our foreign policy centered on the cultivation of joy rather than pain', Yolo reproaches Kate for 'dreaming' when she talks about 'dropping bicycles and short skirts and jeans to women in Muslim countries' (192). Playful or not, evidently cross-cultural understanding and appreciation do not extend to *these* cultures and parts of the world; as in *Warrior Marks*, the question of what women want has only a single answer, and it is to be found – surprisingly, given Walker's critique of it elsewhere – in Western values and American (consumer) culture.

We can now return to the question posed earlier in this chapter, why in *Now Is the Time to Open Your Heart* Walker would ally the artist with explorers and pioneers, given the charged history of conquest and settlement that these prototypical American figures represent. One of the members of Kate's group who take the *yagé* in the Amazonian rainforest is Hugh Brentforth V, who is a descendant of white settlers in the West, and tells stories of his encounters with Indians native to the region. 'In the early days of moving west, clearing and claiming it, said Hugh, you could settle as much land as you could control simply by taking it from the Indians – with the help of the US Cavalry – and keeping them off it' (131). This taking of Native lands, then, backed up by armed government forces, foreshadowed the US' military adventures abroad, from Korea and Vietnam to Afghanistan and Iraq, and it is this history of theft and violence that not only Hugh Brentforth, but all the Americans in the group have to come to terms with. Before they can cleanse their minds and their bodies with the help of the *yagé*, their history must first be shared and owned up to and *told*; in a way, the telling itself, like Walker's writing, is a means of expurgating their toxic American heritage, their poisoned past. African Indian Americans like Kate, and African and Anglo-Indian Americans like Yolo (who, Kate thinks, has 'Frederick Douglass hair') are not exempt from this exercise, for they too have an unpalatable history to face: that of slavery (58). Although with the help of African American leaders like Frederick Douglass slavery was abolished a century and a half ago, the end of physical bondage and the beginning of legal self-ownership did not automatically bring liberation from enslaved *consciousness*. Again, Armando's teaching that 'the inner spirit is never enslaved' (94) is mirrored in *We Are the Ones We Have Been Waiting For*:

> As an African-Amerindian, whose ancestors were enslaved physically for hundreds of years and many of whose people remain psychically enslaved to this day, I speak as someone returning from that condition who does not intend to experience it ever again.[42]

Psychological enslavement, whether by mass media or various drug and other dependencies, has not been eradicated and needs active attention and effort. Yolo learns this in Hawai'i too, especially from his old flame Alma, who seeks solace in alcohol and tobacco after the death of her son from a drugs overdose, and Yolo himself is also addicted to smoking. Aunty Pearlua makes him and the other men in his circle aware that, if men are to keep a vow in favour of the protection of children, they should give up all their addictions, from coffee to drinking and smoking to sex, because: 'over our bodies we can have some control. We can make of our bodies exactly what it is our young people need to see. Health and well-being. *Freedom*' (180). This particular health message, then, is one of those subnarratives critiquing contemporary culture and American politics. In its idea of what ordinary people can do for themselves and for the future of the planet – freeing themselves of addiction, eating healthy food, getting to know people and spiritual traditions from other cultures, and turning away from the pernicious toxic influence of popular culture and mass media – lies freedom, and the possibility of world peace.

Mindful of messages like this, Roland Walter argues that Walker's fiction is part of a new literary trend that is moving away from nation-identity and towards relational identity. He sees *Now Is the Time to Open Your Heart* as a novel of what he calls 'transculturation', meaning 'a critical paradigm enabling us to trace the ways transmission occurs within and between different cultures, regions, and nations, particularly those in unequal relations of power rooted and routed in slavery, (neo)colonialism, migration, and/or diasporization'.[43] Walter's concept of transculturation is a particular take on the idea of an emerging fiction of globalisation, and it displaces or absorbs the older paradigms of comparative literature or

post-colonial writing. Its strength is that, as in post-colonial studies, the *unequal* power relations between what has sometimes been
called 'the West and the rest' become visible, but other than in the
post-colonial paradigm the emphasis is less on the legacy of oppression and exploitation by one set of fixed (racial, national, cultural)
identities of another than on exchange and mutual permeability. For
Walker, Walter writes, 'the solution is to open our hearts to what is
"completely outside the circle of goodwill."' In order to overcome
the barriers that alienate us from others and ourselves, we should
'[m]ake friends with' our 'fear[s]'.[44] Another way of putting this
is that Walker's twenty-first century work 'queers' creative and
theoretical practices, in the sense that she transgresses the boundaries of a national American literature and identity by importing
or, rather, incorporating spiritual and anthropological discourses
into her fiction. The binaries of self/other and fiction/non-fiction
are thus dissolved, and it becomes impossible to tell whether – to
take one perfect example – the Kate Talkingtree of the beginning
of the novel, who is African Amerindian and feels alienated from
white Europeans and Americans, would still identify as any kind of
race or ethnicity at all when at the end she kisses the anaconda clock
and places it 'in Buddha's lap' (223). Having absorbed into her very
being all the teachings of the world she has use for, and having reconciled herself with the burdens of personal and national history,
she is transformed down to her very core of self and free to take up
her mission as a healer.

The same goes, of course, for whether Kate's insights are those of
a fictional protagonist or those of Walker herself; fictionalized autobiography is in many ways a quintessentially queer genre because it
makes a nonsense of the supposed distinction between self-writing
and other-invention. Musing on the nature of writing, Kate concludes that '[a]ll of it that had life was anchored in the dreamworld',
whereas Walker in *We Are the Ones We Have Been Waiting For* argues
that 'In this time of global upheaval and global suffering, it is to our
dreams that we must turn for guidance; it is to the art inside us that
hungers to be born' (188).[45] The latter statement reminds us, as do so
many others in the novel, that the Walker vision we are concerned
with here was forged under the George W. Bush presidency, post
9/11: dark times for the US and for the world. As such, it is a vision
that deliberately seeks to counter the political language and belliger-
ent foreign policy of the time, such as 'war on terror', 'axis of evil',
and 'clash of cultures', as well as the invasion of Afghanistan and

Iraq, global warming and pollution, and so on. Walker has said in interview that *We Are the Ones We Have Been Waiting For* was written as 'a companion for this specific time, which I consider probably ... the most dangerous, frightening, unstable time that the earth has known and that human beings have ever known'. She explained that her regular publisher, Random House, did not want to publish it because they did not know what to do with a political book 'infused with spirituality'.[46] Random House did publish *Now Is the Time to Open Your Heart* however; evidently, for commercial purposes Walker can get away with fiction 'infused with spirituality', but not with an argument that makes much the same political points.

As we have seen in previous chapters, queering and querying genres and knowledges and histories and cultures is a creative practice in which Walker has been engaged for some time, and it has been accompanied, on the level of content, with representations of bisexual or queer figures such as Shug in *The Color Purple*, Pierre in *Possessing the Secret of Joy*, Susannah in *By the Light of My Father's Smile*, and here Kate, who is bisexual, as well as Aunty Pearlua, born as a man but living as a woman. In *Now Is the Time to Open Your Heart*, the latter has multiple functions, representing an ancient Hawai'ian transgendered custom and history, a further instantiation of Grandmother wisdom, a cosmic and at the same time deeply human (because archetypal) principle, and most literally a character in the novel who is Yolo's spirit-guide.[47] As noted at the very beginning of this chapter, Aunty echoes the multiple roles of Miss Lissie from *The Temple of My Familiar*, and this is but the most obvious of many similarities between the two novels: the Hawai'ian Queen Lili'uokalani is another incarnation of Queen Nzingha; Yolo is reminiscent of Suwelo, histories of women's rule and persecution are recounted yet again, and what psychoanalysts would call the 'working through' of traumatic memories and histories occurs once more in groups of storytellers and interlocutors, and along Jungian lines. Formally this translates into multiple voices who relate their findings to each other, albeit from a shifting third-person narrative perspective that privileges Kate and Yolo's evolving spiritual enlightenment. Other familiar figures from Walker's earlier writing appear here too, such as Saartjie Baartman, the 'Hottentot Venus' whose body parts were displayed throughout Europe in the nineteenth century, and Uncle Remus, the fictional teller of 'Negro' tales invented by Joel Chandler Harris, who was a resident of Eatonton, Alice Walker's home town.[48] But although the figures are familiar, the way they are used in *Now Is the Time to Open Your Heart* is more akin to the father-function in *By the Light of My Father's Smile* than to the much more reverential role of ancestors in Walker's early essays. Jana Hezková notes that ancestors in the later work have become obstacles rather than helpers of the living; 'The hierarchical relationship between the past and the present is thus re-evaluated; the past does not assist the present, but quite on the contrary, the present supplies aid for its own past'.[49] This all-too-human representation of wounded and flawed ancestors sometimes leads, as in *By the Light of My Father's Smile*, to awkward jokes (as when Kate disagrees with Remus and he responds, petulantly, with *'Who's the ancestor here?'*) that may be meant to convey the humour and playfulness in Kate's perspective, but more often than not read like Walker's mishandling of – for want of a better word – the novel's 'tone' (101).

AUTOBIOGRAPHICAL IMPULSE AND EMPATHIC FALLACY

Such mishandling may, again, be attributed to an autobiographical impulse. Interviewing Walker in 2001, Duncan Campbell reported that she had 'recently been in the Amazon and is off to Oaxaca in Mexico next month to study Spanish and to explore caves and volcanic peaks in Hawaii in May'.[50] From another interview we learn that Walker owns houses in California, Mexico, and Hawai'i, and that she increasingly often writes in Mexico because

> [t]here is the deep freedom of creating a fictional world in a country where I am perpetually learning the language. Everything feels invented, created, fictional, even my own existence. I move in and out of the story as if I am a character.[51]

This may explain why both *By the Light of My Father's Smile* and *Now Is the Time to Open Your Heart* read like poorly disguised autobiography rather than fully conceived fictional worlds.

A more important question than that of autobiography, though related to it, is posed by Richard Delgado and Jean Stefancic in an article on minority cultural production and the marketplace of ideas. They use the concept of 'empathic fallacy' to 'describe the mistaken belief that we can quickly and endlessly reform each other and ourselves through verbal means – by presenting arguments, novels, texts and films that show another side of the story'.[52] Stefancic and

Delgado thus argue that writing and films by people of colour cannot be effective to bring about social and cultural and political change. Because the question of how effective activist writing can be is so pertinent to Walker's project of changing the hearts and minds of her readers, their reasoning is worth quoting at length:

> Notions that are deeply inscribed in consciousness, that form part of the narrative by which we understand the world – including the counternarrative the dissenting writer offers – are for all intents and purposes unchangeable. Deeply inscribed narratives do not seem like narratives or stories at all, but the truth.[...] Furthermore, it is difficult to have one's counterstory ... heard. [...] Those most likely to attempt to circulate those stories – creative people of color – face additional obstacles in being taken seriously. They strike us as partial or biased because of their very membership in the group whose status they are attempting to lift. Moreover, the storyteller of color confronts a host of cultural narratives and rules that reduce his or her credibility and impact. Dominant stereotypes of persons of color present them as shrill, unintelligent, lazy, affirmative-action babies, or – at best – soulful, poetic, deep, and in touch with their feelings. *Who would take seriously a lecturer or storyteller like that?* (my emphasis).[53]

A writer like Walker, and texts like *By the Light of My Father's Smile*, *Now Is the Time to Open Your Heart*, *We Are the Ones We Have Been Waiting For*, and *The Way Forward Is With a Broken Heart*, offer an alternative narrative by which to understand the world and a new kind of knowledge that many would not recognise as knowledge at all, but as wishful fantasy, mere exotic ethnography, or fanciful esotericism. Knowledge, after all, is supposed to be the result of tried and tested arguments, procedures, and empirical data subjected to the closest critical scrutiny. In Western culture 'truth' is usually equated with provability and scientific evidence; spiritual 'truths', by contrast, are held to be mere belief systems, and revelations are often explained away by biochemical processes in the brain that are supposed to have 'caused' such strong visions and other psychedelic effects. This mode of thinking, so much taken for granted that it has become invisible as *a* mode among many others, Delgado and Stefancic would say, is a considerable obstacle to overcome, the more so as Walker may be seen, as a 'race-d' and 'ethnic' writer, as preaching not just to the converted, but in her own interest as a 'minority' woman writer speaking on behalf of other minorities and women. Undoubtedly, among the stereotypes they outline, Walker's imago would be that of the soulful, poetic, in-touch-with-feelings writer, one who has superior wisdom and vision *because* of her non-dominant position in American life and culture. On the other hand, how 'non-dominant' or how 'minority' is it to be a best-selling author whose work is taught widely from high school upwards, and who is known even outside her reading public for the film *The Color Purple*? Delgado and Stefancic may well be right that, as far as the dominant literary and mass culture is concerned, there is a credibility gap for writers like Walker who are identified with minority causes, and are bound to be read as 'deep' or 'soulful' when they are being read at all. But their parting shot, 'who would take seriously a writer or storyteller like that?' cannot be merely rhetorical in Walker's case, and it is this question that will take us to the next and final chapter.

8

A Writer's Activism – and its Critics: An Epilogue

A footnote to 'Recording the Seasons', an essay about leaving Mississippi written in 1976, states that whenever Alice Walker was called an 'activist' or 'veteran' of the Civil Rights movement, she 'cringed' at the inappropriateness of these epithets. The true activists and veterans, she said, were the young people in SNCC or women like Fannie Lou Hamer and men like Dr Martin Luther King Jr, people who risked their lives for freedom.[1] Although Walker had been writing since the early 1960s, leaving Mississippi did mark the start of her professional writing career and her withdrawal from activism as defined by the Civil Rights movement: putting your body on the line, campaigning under dangerous conditions, living at the grassroots without the possibility of retreat. Activism and writing, both of which require one's full concentration and commitment, are usually seen as antithetical, and in practical terms they would appear to be incompatible.[2] Like the author and the medium, the activist and the writer seem mutually exclusive identities, temperamentally opposed to one another. And yet, as noted in Chapter 1, Walker has sought to maintain both throughout her career. More than twenty years after 'Recording the Seasons' was written, she subtitled *Anything We Love Can Be Saved*, a collection of articles, autobiographical writings and essays, 'A Writer's Activism', and explained what she means by that:

> My activism – cultural, political, spiritual – is rooted in my love of nature and my delight in human beings. [...] I have been an activist all my adult life, though I have sometimes felt embarrassed to call myself one. In the Sixties, many of us were plagued by the notion that, given the magnitude of the task before us – the dismantling of American apartheid – our individual acts were puny. [...] The most 'revolutionary' often ended up severely beaten, in prison, or dead.[3]

In recalling the previous sense of 'embarrassment', Walker here both reclaims the activist identity she had disavowed in the footnote to her earlier essay, but she redefines it too: activism can be 'cultural and spiritual' as well as political. It consists in rewritings of history and of the literary tradition, in passing on ancient and 'alien' spiritual teachings and showing their relevance to today's troubled world, as much as in campaigning for Native American land rights, or protesting outside the prison where Dessie Woods is held for shooting the man who tried to rape her. Neither form of activism can stand in for the other, but they are complementary: activists who put their bodies at risk often lack time for self-reflection, while the words of those who have that time will be hollow if they are not heard and acted upon as well.

In Walker's definition, sometimes merely staying alive can be a form of activist defiance of the powers that be. She acknowledges her great-great-great-great-grandmother May Poole, an American slave, for fostering her belief in activism because May Poole's 'attitude and courage ... made it possible for her to attend the funerals of almost everyone who'd ever owned her'.[4] In May Poole's well-nigh mythical case (reputedly she lived to be 125 years old) activism evidently consisted in surviving the ravages of Southern history. Marjorie Pryse gives an interesting intertextual dimension to May Poole's incredible age and the connection Walker feels she has with this ancestor, when she notes the similarity between Walker's reference to this same grandmother in *In Search of Our Mothers' Gardens* and Susie King Taylor's *Reminiscences* of 1902, which records Taylor's knowledge of a great-great grandmother of 120 years old who was from Virginia and half-Indian. Pryse notes that this knowledge, and conscious use of heritage, contradicts the standard account of African American *dis*continuities in family history, and that it might point to 'a women's tradition, handed down along female lines'.[5] Maybe so. We saw, however, in Chapter 1 that Walker's search for and claiming of Zora Neale Hurston as her foremother was not without anxiety. The fact that others recognise Walker in a photograph of May Poole, with the implication that this ancestor's survivor spirit and courage have been passed on to her, may similarly be indicative of a fear that the survival of Walker's work and of her person cannot be taken for granted. In both her introductions to the complete poems and the complete short stories, published in the 1990s, Walker expresses surprise that she is still alive: 'I assumed I would be a suicide by the age of thirty' and 'I have outlived the telling of these tales! I don't believe I ever thought I would'.[6] These sentiments suggest that she experienced the conditions of living as an aspiring black woman writer in the late twentieth century as precarious and potentially (self-)destructive, but also that the activism which led her into danger saved her from giving up and taking her own life.[6] As Walker conceives of it, then, her activism *as a writer* covers the full spectrum from putting herself in physical danger for a political cause through to campaigning for peace while exercising free speech and ensuring her own spiritual survival and that of others. Writing about these issues continually, in a career that by now spans forty years and more, has meant however that Walker's activism and the work that reports on it has drawn critical fire from all directions. Often that criticism makes no distinction between the writing and the person, an elision that is exacerbated by Walker's own tendency to personalise the political and to put herself in the frame of every traumatic experience she encounters in the world and represents in her work. As Libby Brooks writes in an interview with Walker, '[Her] particular activism reflects a lyrical worldview which relies on individual voices rather than intellectual rigour. Her belief in telling your own tale is firmly rooted in her own story'.[7]

In this chapter I want to explore this activism that is 'rooted in her own story' a little further, for several reasons. It illuminates Walker's significance as a political writer and her place in the African American tradition, it is the chief reason why critics take exception to Walker's work and to her writerly persona, and as a result it sheds light on the political and cultural forces she has been, and still is, up against. As we shall see, the controversy her work has evoked has often been personally painful, but culturally productive, especially so when the politics of representation have collided head-on with the politics of middle America, of (hetero)sexuality, and of international feminism. In what follows then we shall consider Walker's activism and its critics, and Walker's writing and its critics, in order to at the end come to a re-evaluation of her *oeuvre* that sees her activism and her writing as integral to each other. Doing so will place Walker's work unexpectedly in a much older tradition of African American women's public presence than that of black women's writing since the 1970s, and hopefully do it more justice in the process.

A WRITER'S ACTIVISM – AND ITS CRITICS

As we have seen in previous chapters, Walker's activism has sometimes very successfully been translated into fiction (the Civil

Rights Movement in *Meridian*; the campaign against female genital mutilation in *Possessing the Secret of Joy*), but it has in recent years principally been represented in essays, interviews, speeches, and open letters that are published at regular intervals as collections of non-fictional prose. As a writer and activist, Walker travels the world to visit its troublespots and is an inveterate and apparently indefatigable reporter on what she finds there. In *Overcoming Speechlessness* she writes, for example, about her visits to Gaza and Rwanda to witness the aftermath of the atrocities that have taken place there. She explains how, on her speaking tours, she frequently draws analogies between local people's experiences of violent conflict and her own in the American South.[8] Activism abroad does not entail complacency at home, however. In *Anything We Love Can Be Saved* and in *We Are the Ones We Have Been Waiting For*, as in preceding essay collections, Walker writes about the United States' boycott of Cuba, the Million Man March, the exclusion of women from certain Native American rituals, the mistreatment of animals, dreadlocks and racial pride, and many other issues with both public/political and spiritual and personal dimensions. She gives interviews to small journals and political organisations to further the causes she believes in, from feminism and democracy to vegetarianism and Buddhism, and writes forewords to campaigning texts such as Mumia Abu-Jamal's *All Things Censored*.[9] She also regularly lectures to a variety of large and small audiences and spiritual and activist groups, and when they concern a particularly pressing cause these speeches are published as separate pamphlets or short books.[10] Since 2008, Walker has had her own website, where she maintains a blog on her current activist concerns and where readers can witness the genesis of new work.[11] All in all it seems that in this 'elder' stage of her life, Walker is as prolific, if not more so, than she was in her younger years, and the connection between her writing and activism or, rather, her writing *as* activism, continues unabated.

As a campaigning writer, Walker is probably best known for her sustained and vociferous protest against female genital mutilation, or FGM. It is worth revisiting this campaign and the virulent debate it has generated briefly here, because it illustrates so well how Walker's literary work is at times fully integral to her political activism, and how this particular protest involved a call for cultural and spiritual change as much as legal or political intervention (see also Chapter 6). Most of all, the debate around Walker's take on FGM quite crucially centred on her insistence that 'her own story' fuelled and legitimised what some saw as her interference with internal African affairs. What Delgado and Stefancic called 'the empathic fallacy' – the in their view mistaken belief that we can change others and ourselves through empathy and by means of cultural production (see the previous chapter) – was counteracted by Walker and Pratibha Parmar in their campaigning documentary film *Warrior Marks*, and its accompanying volume of interviews and background documents of the same title. How effective was this campaign, and to what extent did its autobiographical foundation and womanist principles contribute to the forging of cross-cultural solidarity on the way to global sisterhood?

As we saw in Chapter 6, a key question in the critical debate around *Possessing the Secret of Joy* and *Warrior Marks* was whether there is such a thing as a collective female experience across cultures and continents, and whether a universal right to bodily integrity and female sexual pleasure can be derived from such an experience. Walker believes so, and certainly she put her own suffering of physical injury (or 'mutilation', depending how you look at it) in the frame to make that argument. Furthermore, she explained the connection between physical trauma and activism in *Warrior Marks*. Recounting once again the childhood memory of her brother shooting her in the eye with a BB gun (see Chapter 1) which left both physical and psychological scars, Walker observes:

> It is true that I am marked forever, like the woman who is robbed of her clitoris, but it is not, as it once was, the mark of a victim. What the woman warrior learns if she is injured as a child, before she can even comprehend that there is a war going on against her, is that you can fight back, even after you are injured. Your wound itself can be your guide.[12]

The autobiographical fact of having been shot in the eye, which she terms a 'patriarchal wound', thus motivates Walker's personal sense of sisterhood with women who have undergone genital operations. In addition, the practice of and the debate around such operations condenses into a single issue many of Walker's long-standing themes, such as patriarchal violence against women and children, black women's sexual pleasure, diasporic relations between Africa and America, and womanist activism. In *Warrior Marks* neither Walker nor Parmar is naive about the controversial nature of their work. Asked what kind of responses she has had to her writing about a 'taboo subject', Walker answers:

> There are people who think that to speak about this is to stick your nose in somebody else's affairs, somebody else's culture. But there is a difference between culture and torture. I maintain that culture is not child abuse, it is not battering. People customarily do these things just as they customarily enslaved people, but slavery is not culture, nor is mutilation.[13]

The rhetorical statement that torture is not culture serves to justify Walker's campaign against FGM on humanitarian grounds, and to forge bonds of female solidarity between women in the West and those in Africa. Difficult as it is to resist such an appeal – for who would want to defend 'torture'? – it is nevertheless easy enough to counter the logic that inflicted pain or surgery equals torture (we only have to think of amputation, for example, or body piercings, or tattoos). Even if pain is suffered under duress, to call it 'torture' is already to interpret the fact of pain as a bad experience; but pain can be experienced and interpreted in all kinds of ways, of which pleasure or endurance for the sake of some higher ideal (childbirth being a prime example) are but two. Anthropologist Christine Walley describes a case study of female genital operations in Kenya, where

> The cutting was public and demonstrated to the community the bravery of the initiated. [...] Remarkably enough ... the initiates remained utterly stoic and expressionless throughout. We were told it is this ability to withstand the ordeal that confers adulthood, that allows one to marry and have children, and that binds one to one's age-mates.[14]

'Female circumcision', in other words, is not *necessarily* experienced as a form of 'torture' or even 'mutilation'. In the film *Warrior Marks* the black woman dancer, who interprets the drama of the documentary for us in extra-diegetic intercalary scenes, is used to contrast her strong, expressive, and sensual body with the mutilated and diminished figures of the African women being interviewed about FGM. Beyond the materiality of the body, however, there are no universals that determine the meaning of bodily experience, but only value judgments and values – such as those that invoke 'nature' against 'torture', and they are always already culturally inscribed.[15]

Even more problematic than this was Walker's attitude to Africa in the campaign against FGM. As a descendant of slaves and as a woman marked by a 'patriarchal wound', Walker claimed the right to speak for, to, and about 'Africa', an Africa that had to be (re-)invented because the origins of these slave ancestors could not be traced, cut off as they were from their history, language, and culture in the Middle Passage. The hypothetical link Walker made between herself and 'African' culture was that of slave women's mutilated bodies. To her African critics in particular, Walker's passionate and influential indictment of an indigenous 'African' practice appeared meddlesome, ill-informed, and offensive. Pratibha Parmar, with whom Walker made *Warrior Marks*, seemed to have foreseen this danger, along with the likelihood that Walker would be accused of patronising African women by imposing her feminist discourse upon them. In an interview with *Black Film Bulletin* in 1994 Parmar said:

> I had seen quite a few documentary films on this subject in the past and some had sensationalised the issue and some had approached it as Western outsiders. I often asked where were the African women's voices. In my research I found that African women had been fighting against this traditional practice for many years so, I was very keen to ensure that a wide variety of African women's voices would be in there in the film.[16]

Now, while it is true that African women figure prominently in the film *Warrior Marks*, there is less of a 'variety' than Parmar would have us believe. This is understandable in a campaigning film; quite naturally most of the African women who speak in it are already involved in activism against FGM. Those who are not, or who approve of female genital operations (like the elderly 'circumciser'), respond to Walker's leading questions with hostility or silence. The voices that are heard are the voices Walker and Parmar wanted to be heard, whereas others who disagree are represented as misguided in the film. This is done primarily through the visual language of *Warrior Marks*. Chimalum Nkwankwo comments on the 'cinematic trickery' of close-ups and *mise-en-scène*, which 'reduces venerable African mothers and grandmothers to gnarled ghouls and ogres in white and red waiting to devour innocent little girls'.[17] Jude Akudinobi uses even stronger language and regards the close-ups of the 'circumciser's' hand and, in particular, of her rusty knife as a kind of 'visual terrorism, since the meaning of female circumcision lies beyond the reach of artifice, technique, and fetishization'.[18] For these critics of Walker's campaign, and for Christine Walley, the varied meanings of female genital operations lie in a complex web of cultural power relations that involves 'the gendered politics of family organization, ethnic identity, colonial, and postcolonial states' in diverse geographic locations, as Walley puts it.[19]

What can we conclude from this brief survey of critical responses to Walker's FGM activism? There is no doubt that *Warrior Marks* and *Possessing the Secret of Joy* have raised consciousness and continue to generate an important discussion, not just about FGM but also about readers' and viewers' cultural values and the possibility of global sisterhood across cultural difference. Whatever their criticism of Walker, the contributors to Obioma Nnaemeka's collection *Female Circumcision and the Politics of Knowledge* all condemn female genital operations, and have 'registered their opposition to the practice and worked vigorously to end it'.[20] Yet what becomes clear is that the underlying issue is not one of body, but of discursive politics. Walker's critics see *Warrior Marks* and *Possessing the Secret of Joy*'s campaign against FGM as in part self-serving – because '[it] enables the West to see itself in a positive light' – and as partaking of a long tradition of Western voyeurism as regards African sexuality. Most of all they see it as a failure to reflect on discursive power relations between 'the West and the rest'.[21] What would happen, Obioma Nnaemeka asks, if the gaze were reversed:

> Will the women in the villages [Walker and Parmar] visited be allowed to wander freely in urban and rural United States and Britain to document women's oppression in all its disguises? Of course not; they will most likely be denied visas![22]

Nnaemeka thus forces us to consider the a-symmetry between Western activism against FGM and the way female genital operations are practiced and thought about and – most of all – *also* campaigned against in Africa. This asymmetry does not necessarily invalidate Walker's critique completely. In spite of it, at the level of theory at least, the ostensibly absolute and immovable opposition between cultural relativism and cultural imperialism can be reconfigured into something else. Christine Walley makes this point by asking of cultural relativists whether 'In using an uncritical notion of "culture", do we in fact create the same sense of difference, of estrangement from each other's lives and worlds, that is also generated in the flagrantly ethnocentric literature that opposes female genital operations'?[23] Walley identifies here a flaw in the reasoning on *both* sides of the debate: cultural imperialists or universalists should realise that, when it comes to FGM, there is no such thing as culture-free rationality (or nature, for that matter), while cultural relativists should not assume that cultural difference is so absolute as not to allow for *any* common ground. An alliance between Western and African campaigners against, and theorists of, female genital operations therefore should be possible if it is recognised that FGM cannot be eradicated as long as it is regarded, through Western eyes, as a single issue abstracted from local contexts and cultural knowledges. And, of course, that possibility has come about in large part because of the debate *Warrior Marks* and *Possessing the Secret of Joy* have generated. For, as Walley again reminds us, 'Discourse is also practice; it is not simply a way of understanding or thinking about the world, it is also a way of acting in it'.[24] If this is so, and if Walker's work has generated a lot more thought and discussion around female genital operations between Western and African feminists, *all* of whom are opposed to the practice, then it would seem that the 'empathic fallacy' is not a fallacy after all, but an effective discursive and representational strategy. In her campaign against FGM, Walker has demonstrated how 'activism – political, cultural, spiritual' can be highly influential, not just in terms of policy making but also in heightening awareness of the pitfalls of *and* the possibilities for an international, cross-cultural womanist movement. As we have seen, her own avowed experience of physical trauma was mobilised in the terminology of the 'patriarchal wound' to enable such cross-cultural solidarity on the grounds of empathy and shared experience, this time telling *other* women's stories because she believes them to be rooted in her own.

AN ACTIVIST'S WRITING – AND ITS CRITICS

That Walker's cross-cultural solidarity is predicated upon her own experience does not mean, however, that the significance of her work depends on the credibility and validity – or not – of such autobiographical conceits as the 'patriarchal wound'. Ultimately, a writer's literary *oeuvre* should be judged on its textual merits, not its 'rootedness in her own experience'. In other words: a writer's activism can be judged one way, and an activist's writing another. Some of the most simplistic – and vicious – criticism Walker's work has attracted has come from people who read 'her own story' back into the fiction, and personal attacks have been leveled at Walker since virtually the beginning of her career. From the time of her interracial marriage to Mel Leventhal through to the controversy generated by Steven Spielberg's film of *The Color Purple* she has been the target of *ad feminam* hostile criticism. Philip M. Royster's 'In Search of Our Father's Arms: Alice Walker's Persona of the Alienated Darling' exemplifies this:

> Alice Walker cannot afford to allow her protagonists to enjoy male sexuality, not merely because those protagonists believe that males, by nature, are inadequate humans (e.g., Celie's ridiculing of male genitalia along with her image of men as frogs or losers) but also because all the males with the potential for sexual relations with Walker's protagonists may be masks for her father.[25]

Royster's approach is designed to demolish a reputation and discredit a body of work by reducing Walker's womanist politics to 'envy, resentment, or anger' on the grounds of her involvement with white feminism, her representation of lesbianism, and – of course – her criticism of black male violence and abuse; Walker, in short, is only interested in 'dividing the race'.[26] To be sure, Royster's example was rather extreme, but the charge of race-betrayal is a familiar one, and Walker was certainly not the only African American woman writer to have incurred the critical wrath of black men – Ntozake Shange's 1977 play *For Colored Girls Who Have Considered Suicide When the Rainbow Is Enuf* for example caused every bit as much of a storm as did *The Color Purple* five years later.[27] That said, there can be little doubt that Walker's reputation as a 'brave', or at the very least 'controversial' writer is well deserved, even if in part it comes from her own advertisement of the negative press she has had, notably from African American men.[28] When Walker writes about the many and various controversies her work has generated and the critical voices that have sought to silence her, she is less an advocate for than a defender of her own work and her creative freedom. She is, in an important sense, her own ideal reader, which is why her fictional work has increasingly been surrounded with the protective layers of commentary on and explication of it in afterwords and essays. That her creative freedom has been more threatened in the

United States than in other parts of the world is an irony of which Walker is well aware:

> The freedom to speak and to write about life as one knows or imagines it is a right most Americans take for granted. It is that basic, and that precious. Even after all these years, nearly thirty, of writing that has engendered controversy, I am still undaunted in the face of possible condemnation and censorship. My country's gift to me. I continue to write the stories I believe to be spiritually authentic, creatively true. Stories that are medicine – sometimes bitter, but also sweet – for myself and for the tribe.[29]

Still, a self-styled writer/activist like Walker will always run the risk of having her writing judged by her political (and cultural/ spiritual) convictions and by what she chooses to disclose about her life, rather than on its literary merits, as the case of Royster indicates. Perhaps that is why, by way of pre-emptive strikes, afterwords to *The Color Purple* and *Possessing the Secret of Joy*, essays about *The Temple of My Familiar* and *By the Light of My Father's Smile*, *Warrior Marks* the book, and the 'Meditation on Life, Spirit, Art, and the Making of the Film *The Color Purple* Ten Years Later' that is *The Same River Twice* all serve as, even if they were not intended to be, authorial interventions in the critical debate that Walker's work has generated. As well as sharing her sources of inspiration and her spiritual vision, it is as if, in offering these paratexts, Walker is trying to control the reception of her fiction, and to pre-empt her critics. This defensiveness can have the unwanted side-effect, however, of not letting that fiction live – as polysemic art and as creative work beyond the reach of authorial intention and explication. Like many creative writers, Walker dislikes literary criticism because she sees it not as a forum in which meanings are opened up, but as an exercise in closed-mindedness:

> Criticism is something that I don't fully approve of, because I think for the critic it must be very painful to always look at things in a critical way. I think you miss so much. And you have to sort of shape everything you see to the way you're prepared to see it.[30]

This is a little strange coming from the astute and at times acerbic cultural critic who Walker also is; it is as if her own essayistic achievement and influence on literary and cultural criticism are disavowed.

More than personal sensitivity may be at stake here, however. In 'Getting as Black as My Daddy: Thoughts on the Unhelpful Aspects of Destructive Criticism' Walker has written about criticism that is abusive and anonymous and comes with threats in the morning post; she calls this 'verbal battering'. When comment on her work is simply *literarily* critical of her autobiographical writing and appears in *The Village Voice*, she sees it as a form of censorship or a demand for self-censorship, something that stifles her creativity. In 'Getting as Black as My Daddy' Walker enacts what would happen if she gave in to this demand for self-censorship, real or imagined: the piece ends abruptly and unfinished 'as a demonstration of what, because of battering rather than constructive criticism, is some- times lost'.[31] What gets lost as well in this rhetorical ploy, however, is a sense of perspective and discursive difference: 'constructive criticism' presumably does not have to be fan mail, just as a critical review surely does not equal hate mail either.

A similar tendency to overstate the harm done by the public debate that her work has generated can be found in *Banned*, a small volume that discusses public protests against the adoption of Walker's short story 'Roselily', her memoir/essay 'Am I Blue?', and *The Color Purple* in teaching. *Banned* by its very title suggests that Walker's work has been subjected to censorship and removed from library shelves, educational tests, and syllabi, but as it turns out the volume gives almost no evidence of this actually happening. Most attempts at public censorship of Walker's work, such as the proposal to remove 'Roselily' and 'Am I Blue?' from the California Learning Assessment System (CLAS) test, have failed, and what *Banned* in fact documents is how much *discussion* Walker's work has provoked in education. As Patricia Holt makes clear in her introduction, the stakes in this discussion are political, and revolve around protests from the ultra conservative Traditional Values Coalition and the Eagle Forum. A spokesperson for the latter organization for exam- ple complained that students found the stories to be

> [...] racist, sexist, classist, anti-religious and anti-parent. Some of the stories touch on environmentalism, gun control and the tra- ditional institution of marriage. [...] children are characterized as fatherless, alone and unwanted. [...] Fathers are often stereotyped as abusive and insensitive. Some are uneducated, ignorant, gun- carrying clods. In not one of the stories that I've interviewed stu- dents on was there a positive model of health. Not one.[32]

The issue is thus ideological: for the parents' rights religious and right wing lobby, it is about what values American schoolchildren should be taught via literature, and what 'positive role models' they should encounter in it; for Walker and her supporters, such as the American Civil Liberties Union and the California Teachers' Association, it is about the multi-interpretability of literature, development of critical thinking, and free speech. What *Banned* then does, in crying 'Censorship!' is close down a very lively and important debate about what tenth graders should be reading and discussing, a debate that goes to the heart of what constitute 'American values' in a multiracial and multicultural society. Walker comes out of it both victim and victor. As Patricia Holt puts it in the opening lines of her introduction:

> Alice Walker has the honor of being one of the most censored writers in American literature. Like Mark Twain, John Steinbeck, Madeleine D'Engle and J. D. Salinger, Walker has been the subject of so much controversy that too often the artistry of her work has been lost in the politics of the moment.[33]

That the second line is all too true does not make the first true too; the 'honor' of being censored (like the honour of being declared a 'state treasure' by the governor of California in 1994, at the same time as the CLAS controversy) is really the honour of being widely read and thought and talked about, surely no mean thing in a society dominated by visual and celebrity culture. Walker does draw fire and habitually 'walks into peril', as Ikenna Dieke puts it, and popular criticism of her work is all too often based on poor reading, bigotry, and political disagreement.[34] But disagreement is also what her didactic autobiographical persona invites or even provokes, and it is difficult to imagine that Walker would prefer her work *not* to be widely read, *not* discussed, *not* thought about and taken issue with. Readers' needs of her visionary, 'elder' persona cannot always be predicted or fulfilled, and her own celebrity status has affected Walker's reputation too – as the publicity surrounding the rift with her daughter amply shows. All this – the public controversy around the educational value of her work, the self-representation as visionary, and the being-in-the-news as a celebrity quite apart from the work and the activism – makes for an overcrowded field of literary reception with little room for manoeuvre and nuance between the opposing camps of those who love her or hate her.

It is worth remembering here that the balance in Walker criticism leans heavily towards uncritical adulation rather than vitriol or dismissal. If anything this explains why, despite the sheer amount of commentary on her work, the quality of it is often disappointing. Many of the hundreds of articles produced by the Walker critical industry are merely descriptive or – indeed – biographical rather than offering any analytical insight into the work, whereas serious criticism ought to avoid the mistake of conflating these different dimensions. It should be possible to admire the activist and find the writer wanting. It should be equally possible to credit the writer and remain critical of her agenda, but such distinctions can only be made once the work of aesthetic analysis *and* political (cultural/spiritual) reflection has been done. When Walker is dismissed as an ideologue whose work is a mere vehicle for leftist, racially divisive, feminist, or wacky New Age ideas, the significance of that work as art and as political/ cultural/spiritual intervention is diminished or misrecognised, as happened in the controversy around *The Color Purple* and the short stories 'Roselily' and 'Am I Blue', as discussed above. But recognising this does not mean that her fiction does not misfire, at times, on one, the other, or both fronts. Walker's work, like Walker criticism, is uneven. Where the writing and the activism work together to the mutual enhancement of both, as in *Meridian, The Color Purple*, 'Advancing Luna – and Ida B. Wells', 'Nineteen Fifty-Five', 'Looking for Zora', and *In Search of Our Mothers' Gardens*, to name but a few favourites, there is nothing in the literary tradition, black and white, to match them as aesthetic and (surreptitiously) didactic achievements. In *Possessing the Secret of Joy* also, the formal precision of the writing as an activist argument against female genital mutilation has to be admired, even if one does not agree with that argument. And where activism and writing do not mesh so successfully – in some of the poetry and short stories, in *The Third Life of Grange Copeland*, and in sections of *The Temple of My Familiar, By the Light of My Father's Smile*, and *Now Is the Time to Open Your Heart* as well as some of the later autobiographical writings – then it is because the language is trite, narrative and stylistic economy are lost, or the reader is patronised or – worse – denied any room to move and make her own meanings.

Alice Petry's critical assessment of the short stories is a good example of discerning criticism that identifies unevenness in technique and shows how this can undermine the texts' political/cultural/ spiritual vision. Petry compares the stories of *In Love and Trouble* with those in *You Can't Keep a Good Woman Down* and attributes the unintentionally comic effect of several stories in the latter ('Fame', 'Porn', 'The Lover') to 'Alice Walker's preference for telling over showing [which] suggests a mistrust of her readers, or her texts, or both'.[35] In my view the same misapprehension on Walker's part of the comic effect, intentional or not, of poor writing mars *By the Light of My Father's Smile* and *Now Is the Time to Open Your Heart*, as noted in the previous chapter. Petry's comments on this phenomenon are more insightful than David Bradley's similar, but more judgemental appraisal of the same short stories, which he says are flawed by 'unassimilated rhetoric, simplistic politics and a total lack of plot and characterization'.[36] Petry closely analyses a number of textual examples to show where style and characterisation are off beam, whereas Bradley provides no support for his dismissive appraisal. And when Petry argues that Walker's propensity to hold forth rather than dramatise also applies to 'Advancing Luna – and Ida B. Wells' (where the narrator is indeed intrusive and argumentative), it is possible to disagree with her. In this story the narrator's inconsistent perspective and multiple changes of mind (the story has four different endings) can equally well be read as highly effective in their formal enactment of its theme, that is: the dilemma of a black woman positioning herself between her gender and racial allegiances on the issue of interracial rape. Criticism like Petry's, in short, explains *how* the work works without requiring agreement *that* it does, and in Walker criticism, positive and negative, that distinction is often hard to find.

Perhaps it is in any case more easily demonstrable on the literary/technical side of Walker's writing than it is on the political, but another example may clarify how Walker's brand of personal/spiritual writing can backfire politically, as it often does in *Anything We Love Can be Saved*. As we have seen in the preceding chapters, her current activism in an important sense carries on where the Civil Rights movement left off, and a brief comparison with a political commentator's view of such post-Civil Rights activism can put Walker's stance into perspective. In an article in *Race & Class*, the political historian Manning Marable evaluated African American activism in the 1990s in the aftermath of Civil Rights and of black nationalism of the 1960s. Marable did not mention the cultural arena in which many of those 1960s debates have continued (in African American critical theory, in the canon wars, in the Clarence Thomas/Anita Hill and O. J. Simpson cases, in rap music – in short, in the politics of representation generally), but it is clear that his agenda for the 1990s was informed by those debates and not least by African American women's writing.

Marable identified three sites of struggle for black liberation: community, class, and gender, in a hard-nosed materialist analysis that acknowledged diversity, refused essentialism, and recognised that 'the primary victims and scapegoats of the Right are women of color and their children'.[37] Class, Marable noted, has virtually disappeared from mainstream political discourse, but he argued for its continuing importance because history shows 'that the way things are produced and distributed within society, the patterns of ownership and divisions of property, prefigure or set in motion certain consequences which, in turn, impact on everything else'.[38] If we put Marable's analysis next to Walker's politics, their bottom lines would be much the same. The model of local struggle around gender, community, and distribution of wealth and resources (she tends not to use 'class') have been central to Walker's project as a writer/activist since the 1960s. The example of Cuba serves as a ground of comparison for the United States' treatment of its poor, and her gender activism involves Native American and African women as well as black women living on welfare in the richest country on earth. As we saw in the previous chapter, the meditation exercises that follow each political essay in *We Are the Ones We Have Been Waiting For* ask for reflection on American foreign policy post 9/11, Castro, Gandhi, Buddhism, ecology, yoga, Palestine, and a host of other issues ranging from the geopolitical to the very, very domestic and everyday. In other words, her writing-as-activism runs the gamut of Marable's concerns but also widens his agenda beyond that of African Americans per se and beyond the United States. By comparing the two we can, however, see how *Anything We Love Can Be Saved* comes up short as activist writing: where Walker writes that Louis Farrakhan 'needed to be forgiven' for his anti-Semitism, Marable does not mince his words and describes Farrakhan unabashedly as 'homophobic, anti-Semitic and sexist'. And where Walker writes in 'A Letter to President Clinton' that she 'cares for' him and his family, Marable reminds his readers of Clinton's record regarding approval of the death penalty, a repressive crime bill, and welfare cuts 'which will devastate the households of millions of poor women and children'.[39] Not only does Walker's writing sometimes lack the critical edge that its political critique (which is also present in the pieces on Farrakhan and Clinton) demands, but it falls victim to the empathic fallacy when the language of 'forgiveness' and 'caring' obscures the distinction between interpersonal and political relations altogether. In personalising the latter through her focus on individual leadership figures, Walker trivialises the forces of oppression and domination that those groups to whom she wants to lend her heartfelt support are up against. Because it is a good example of Walker's rhetorical style when engaging in political/cultural/spiritual activism, it is worth quoting the final paragraph of 'A Letter to President Clinton' in full:

> I often disagree with you – your treatment of black women, of Lani Guinier and the wonderful Joycelyn Elders in particular, has caused me to feel a regrettable distance. Still, I care about you, Hillary, and Chelsea and wish you only good. [...]
>
> Similarly, I will always love and respect the Cuban people, and help them whenever I can. Their way of caring for all humanity has made them my family. Whenever you hurt them, or help them, *please think of me.*
>
> Sincerely,
> Alice Walker (my emphasis).[40]

Like Walker herself in the opening lines of this chapter, the reader 'cringes at the inappropriateness' of Walker's empathic language and at the fact that we are invited to share in such a spirit of conciliation and concern for the nation's leaders' souls. On these occasions, Walker's autobiographical voice does not fit the ostensible didactic purposes of the political essay; it is intrusive to the point of being narcissistic and it is, well, overblown.

Laurie McMillan gives a deft analysis of the virtues and perils of so-called personal criticism, the kind that Walker practices so powerfully in her essays:

> [...] because personal writing by nature has an inward focus, it can end up being self-absorbed and limited in scope rather than ultimately moving towards social change. If a narrative is meaningful only to the person who wrote it or to a select group of listeners, its political power becomes moot.[41]

McMillan's point is well taken, and articulates what some readers and critics find irritating in Walker's later activist essays and memoirs. A review of *Overcoming Speechlessness* for example objects to Walker's 'fuzzy writing' and lack of nuance in her analysis of the plight of the Palestinians, and remarks that her style of personal reporting means that 'Walker's first person singular tower[s] over

Gaza's rubble'.[42] Although her autobiographical voice was always didactic, in this more recent non-fictional work the earnestness of conviction and loss of self-irony in that voice undermine its political edge. Perhaps these texts signal a lack of connection with a readership beyond the Bay area, or it may be that discursive and cultural distinctions between the privileged and the dispossessed become too blurred in Walker's ever-widening global consciousness to be useful. Either way, when Walker's stated (and, no doubt, felt) empathy with the poor and oppressed all over the world is predicated on her own experience of suffering, then such empathy runs the risk of subsuming the other into the self. Of her campaigning in Africa against FGM she has written that

> Presenting my own suffering and psychic healing has been a powerful encouragement [...] to victims of mutilation who are ashamed or reluctant to speak of their struggle. Telling my own story in this context has also strengthened me, an unanticipated gift.[43]

Walker's empathy may indeed – who knows – have inspired victims of FGM to speak out, but in the wider context of African women's economic and cultural position her 'encouragement' and the fact that she herself gained strength from being able to tell *her* story yet again, seem presumptuous and out of proportion with regard to the plight of women in Kenya or Sudan.

A more recent example of Walker's writing as political/cultural/ spiritual activism may illustrate this point further. In a beautifully written short essay for the journal *Meridians* in 2009, 'Lest We Forget: An Open Letter to My Sisters, Who Are Brave', Walker engages with the Obama/Clinton presidential election. Beginning, in her trademark autobiographical style, with a memory of voter registration work in the American South, where white women were just as racist as white men and 'the broken bottles thrown at my head were gender free', she explains why she supported Barack Obama and not Hillary Clinton for President. Remarking, with her usual incisiveness, on the fact that Obama is always referred to as a 'black man' whereas Clinton is simply thought of as 'a woman', Walker adds:

> She carries all the history of white womanhood in America in her person; it would be a miracle if we, and the world, did not react to this fact. How dishonest it is, to attempt to make her innocent of her racial inheritance.[44]

This is sharp, analytical, and critical writing, and Walker makes an insightful political point by contrasting not Clinton's personal racism, but the burden of her racial *legacy* as a white woman with Obama's advantage on the world stage as a black man, because 'no baggage of past servitude or race supremacy' will mar his talks 'with any leader, woman, man, child, or common person, in the world'.[45] This does not mean that Walker is automatically supportive or uncritical of everything Obama stands for. Cuba surfaces here again:

> I want a grown-up attitude toward Cuba ... a country and a people I love; I want an end to the embargo that has harmed my friends and their children, children who, when I visit Cuba, *trustingly turn their faces up for me to kiss* (my emphasis).[46]

While it is rhetorically quite effective to think of the Cuban embargo as harming people one knows, or might know, because it enhances a sense of the world's interconnectedness and, by projection, of the reader's desired solidarity with the people of Cuba, the final part of the sentence then undermines that effectiveness by appearing gratuitously narcissistic and vain. Speaking as 'a woman and a person of three colors (African, Native American, European)' and '[t]rue to my inner Goddess of the Three Directions' Walker here does not just use 'her own story' of Southern segregation in making her argument, but she throws everything she has at it: her whole being and identity, and the purported wisdom of age 'after sixty-four years of life'.[47] The persona created in this writing is that of Alice Walker: Wise Old Woman of the West, rather than Alice Walker, shrewd political commentator and seasoned activist.[48]

(GRAND-)MOTHERING: IN SEARCH OF AN ALTERNATIVE TRADITION

Then again, there is another side to all this, which will lead us – one last time – back into 'deep history'. When asked about her relationship with her daughter Rebecca in an interview in 1998, Walker answered:

> Because of her, I know again the daughter and the mother I was. I've also discovered the world is full of mothers who've done their best and still hurt their daughters; that we have daughters

everywhere. [...] I feel like I have tons of daughters, ... and they're in good hands.[49]

Even if Walker was merely referring to her large following of young female readers in this statement, there is nevertheless an audacity in it – especially in light of the very public rift between her and her daughter that opened up in 2004 – that few other widely read contemporary women writers would dare to match. Maya Angelou and Toni Morrison have a large female following too, and their fans may well construct them as role models or wise women, but they do not style *themselves* as guiding spirits in their readers' lives: they are artists, but they are not visionaries or metaphorical moth- ers. In the history of black women's public speaking however, such apparent self-aggrandisement is not unprecedented, for Walker echoes – unwittingly perhaps, but maybe not – Sojourner Truth's self-representation as 'mother of all that is here'. Of course, it is easier to accept a self-proclaimed 'elder' status from a venerable old ex-slave of over a century ago than it is from a gracefully ageing, bestselling, living writer. But the hubris contained in the idea that real mothers all over the world, who have done their best, still hurt their daughters, whereas Walker's global brood are 'in good hands' can only be understood – if it is not to be dismissed as mere megalo- mania – if we read this in the context of a tradition. This tradition, I suggest, is characterised by a way of speaking and a way of conceiv- ing of individual, spiritual responsibility that has little or nothing to do with Hurston's fiction or Woolf's essays or the history of black women's writing, but links Walker with nineteenth-century African American women who were visionaries, itinerant preachers, aboli- tionists, and feminists; women like Sojourner Truth, Rebecca Cox Jackson, Amanda Berry Smith, and Jarena Lee.[50] In the twentieth century Fannie Lou Hamer, Ella Baker, Ruby Doris Smith Robinson, and other Civil Rights 'community mothers' perhaps represent a more down-to-earth version of it, but the distinctive features Walker shares with her nineteenth-century foremothers are those of the visionary rhetorical style and sense of mission of the mystic or lay preacher. Truth, Jackson, and Lee were Christians who practised their mission outside the institution of the Church in which women at that time were not even allowed to speak; their preaching was in that sense an act of feminist defiance – a form of activism, indeed.

Walker writes about Rebecca Cox Jackson in 'Gifts of Power', an essay that is rarely cited but worth rereading for its resonances with her own work. She asks in that essay what we are to make of Jackson's gnostic beliefs, in which the spirit of Christ is experienced in dreams and visions, not in the institution of the Church, and the resurrection does not happen after death but in life. Jackson, furthermore, believed in a divine Mother as well as in God the Father, and Walker likens this to pre-Western Indian and African religious worship of the goddess.[51] What we are to make of this, it would seem, is that somewhere along the line this nonconformist and feminist Christianity is transmuted into Walker's paganism, via the intermediate stage of Shug's liberation theology in *The Color Purple* (which still has a god in it, albeit not in church). Henry Louis Gates Jr traces an unwitting connection between Jackson, Hurston, and Walker in 'Color Me Zora', and is aware of Walker's conscious revision of Jackson and especially of the scene in *Gifts of Power* where Jackson describes how she was taught to read by divine inspiration:

> Walker ... makes much of this scene ... underscoring the fact that 'Jackson *was* taught how to read and write by the spirit within her.' When Walker dedicates *The Color Purple* 'to the Spirit', it is to this spirit which taught Rebecca Jackson to read.[52]

Black women's claim on orality (public speaking) and literacy are thus inscribed in this tradition from the outset and both, of course, are central to the Walker paradigm of a womanist creative tradition that is distinct from, but intersects with, black male and white feminist traditions. In the spiritual development of Walker's work, God first gives way to the Spirit (in *The Color Purple*) and then merges with the Cosmic Mother, who is also Nature, or the goddess (in *The Temple of My Familiar* and onwards from there) and becomes the Grandmother Spirit in *Sent By Earth* and *Now Is the Time to Open Your Heart*. In *Sent by Earth*, Walker's response to 9/11, the Grandmother Spirit is explained as

> The spirit of impartiality, equality, equanimity. Of nurturing but also of fierceness. It has no use for hierarchy. Or patriarchy. It tolerates violence against itself for a while, but will sooner or later rise up to defend itself. This is the spirit of the earth itself.[53]

The Great Cosmic Mother, Monica Sjöö and Barbara Mor's massive study of goddess worship and 'the religion of the earth', is Walker's paganist bible and an important source for much of her cultural/spiritual activism in her later essays and novels. It presents a global survey of pagan and female-centred religions and draws cross-cultural parallels to support the argument that goddess worship was not only anterior but also superior to the current major world religions, and that the time is ripe for Her comeback if the planet is to survive. For the present purpose of outlining an alternative 'visionary' tradition for Walker's later work, their chapter on America is the most illuminating. Sjöö and Mor distinguish between three streams of spiritual thought in eighteenth-century America: colonial Puritanism, the rational-humanist Deism of the writers of the Constitution, and a secular stream, which, they say:

> has always been an underground stream: that of wildness, of sensual innocence, of paganism. [...] Not a few European men (this stream was mostly male) did return to wilderness in America: they joined Indian tribes, or became frontiersmen. [...] This underground stream emerges as the real 'American Dream' – a peculiar 'lust for innocence' which is always sought, never found.[54]

Mor and Sjöö construct paganism as an indigenous 'religion' drawing on America's utopian traditions; they note that various nonconformist groups (Bohemians, hippies, Beats) have sought to revive it – not coincidentally in California, where Walker has been living since the 1970s and where New Age thinking has flourished. Their analysis makes it possible for us to see how various strands of religious thought and various styles of spiritual discourse, which have informed Walker's work in the past, come together in a syncretic paganism that has belief in the Great Cosmic Mother at its heart. The trajectory being sketched out moves from the nineteenth-century women preachers through – perhaps – Hurston's interest in Hoodoo, to the Civil Rights movement's redemptive ethos and from there via feminism to Native American and African cosmologies, paganism, goddess worship, South American indigenous use of entheogens, Buddhist spiritual practice and meditation – and Jung (see Chapters 5, 6, and 7). This ragbag of cultural and religious traditions, in other words, has in recent years hybridised into an eclectic wholistic philosophy that enables us to 'locate' Walker's work and her activist persona as 'mother of all that is here'.

And so Walker's current (grand-)maternal activist persona has a sense of mission which is consonant with that of her nineteenth-century visionary foremothers, but also with the modern paganist's well-nigh cosmic responsibility: 'The paganistic return is like the Buddhistic salvation from the world wheel: nobody really does it unless, until, we all do it', write Sjöö and Mor.[55] That sentiment is echoed, of course, in *We Are the Ones We Have Been Waiting For*, a title derived from a poem by June Jordan and song by Sweet Honey in the Rock, and a line that Walker cites again at the end of her essay 'Lest We Forget', quoted earlier. With this articulation both of the cosmic consciousness-raising task in hand for the paganist and its anti-rationalist, anti-Puritan, and anti-patriarchal ethos, we arrive at a point where the 'inappropriate' language of Walker's letter to President Clinton, or her willingness to mother the world's daughters, come into perspective: maybe they are less an individual idiosyncrasy marked by hyperbole and narcissistic overreach than a rhetorical style and a spiritual conviction that have a history and a tradition worth excavating to get the measure of Walker's project as an activist writer.

This tradition is very different from the purely literary one in which Walker's work is usually read; it is older, more eclectic and speculative and possibly less conscious on her part. But traditions, as Hortense Spillers reminds us, are made rather than found; they 'survive as *created social events* only to the extent that an audience cares to intersect them'.[56] My suggestion, above, of a visionary tradition intersects, but is by no means incompatible with, the African American tradition of conscious revision that Henry Louis Gates Jr and others have set out.[57] Walker figures prominently in that tradition: besides the 'common bond' with Hurston, critics have also seen her work in dialogue with that of writers as diverse as Richard Wright (*Native Son*/*The Third Life of Grange Copeland*), Frances Ellen Watkins Harper (*Iola Leroy*/*The Color Purple*), and Ralph Ellison (the Trueblood episode in *Invisible Man*/*The Color Purple*).[58] Walker herself has, of course, in her essays created a tradition of her own that includes Jean Toomer, Flannery O'Connor, Langston Hughes, and Rebecca Cox Jackson. Notably absent in that self-defined literary lineage are some of the other women writers of the Harlem Renaissance (Jessie Fauset, Nella Larsen), those later in the century (Ann Petry, Margaret Walker, Gwendolyn Brooks, Lorraine Hansberry) and the African American novelists of the late nineteenth century (Frances Ellen Watkins Harper and Pauline Hopkins). These absences would be striking if they were not so familiar: apart from Larsen, Hopkins, and Harper, these writers tend to be much less discussed in African American criticism too, and it may well be that they are less discussed *because* of Walker's impact on the writing of African American women's literary history.

Marjorie Pryse hints at this phenomenon in her introduction to *Conjuring: Black Women, Fiction and Literary Tradition*, in which she writes that this collection of essays on black feminist criticism 'is intended to free writers like Walker from the necessity of writing critical and biographical work – or at least to encourage others in the task of doing so'.[59] *Conjuring* has articles on Petry, Fauset, and Margaret Walker too, but the crux of the problem in writing traditions is articulated at the end by Hortense Spillers, who exposes the fiction of a monolithic 'African American tradition', or even of a moderately cohesive and continuous tradition of African American women's writing. Noting the divergences between the writing of Hurston on one hand, and Fauset and Larsen on the other, or that between Hurston and Petry, or Paule Marshall and Margaret Walker, Spillers writes that '"tradition" for black women's writing community is a matrix of literary *discontinuities* that partially articulate various periods of consciousness in the history of an African-American people'.[60] Spillers' argument about discontinuity is helpful because it works against a critical tendency to homogenise the category of 'black women writers' and to take the notion of 'the' African American tradition – even when defined, as in Deborah McDowell's work, as a dynamic 'changing same' of revision and dialogue – too far.[61] Besides, but no less importantly, the discontinuity model can also throw some light on the differences between contemporary African American women writers: Alice Walker, Toni Morrison, Gloria Naylor, Audre Lorde, Gayl Jones, Terry McMillan, Toni Cade Bambara, Paule Marshall, Maya Angelou – to mention only a few of the best known – are often discussed comparatively (or even together, in one breath) despite the fact that they are really very different writers, even if many of them draw on common cultural sources like jazz and blues, Afrocentric thought, the black vernacular, or folklore. In the preceding chapters such comparative discussion has only rarely been engaged in, because I wanted to make a case for Walker's particularity within and outside this field of black women's writing. One, or possibly *the* major difference that emerges is Walker's self-inscription as a visionary and a writer/activist.

The contrast with Morrison is perhaps particularly instructive: her and Walker's shared institutional status as favoured black women novelists, prizewinners, and bestsellers has nevertheless produced a very different kind of reception, both in the critical industry and in educational practice. Judging by the volume of 'serious' criticism, Morrison's work seems to invite theoretically informed approaches (psychoanalytic, post-modernist, poststructuralist) in a way that Walker's writing does not, whereas in the classroom *The Color Purple* is regarded as 'easy' next to the 'complexity' of, say, *Beloved* or *Jazz*. There is little to be gained from such a comparison, of course, except in so far as it highlights the tokenism that is writ large in the canonical status of these texts and in the writers' very different critical appeal.

Hortense Spillers identifies a change in the American classroom from a pedagogic practice that valorises 'difficult' texts (credited with 'complexity' and 'ambiguity') to those that maintain 'not only an allegiance to "power to the people", but also "talking" to "the people" in the now familiar accents of representation and mimesis'.[62] In the classroom, as in critical practice, I think that the differential appeal of Morrison and Walker shadows this movement, quite possibly to the detriment of both. If I can roughly translate Spillers' shift as a movement from primarily aesthetic analysis to a more politicised reading, then neither Walker's nor Morrison's reception benefit from a contest between aesthetics and politics that, to quote Walker one last time, 'they did not design'. Comparisons of this kind are invidious, and it is a mark of the institutional power invested in criticism, a power of which this book partakes, that it seems necessary to engage with the Walker/Morrison nexus only to refuse and refute its validity at the end. Nevertheless, it seems imperative to do so. In making my case for Walker's distinctiveness in the preceding chapters, I hope to have shown that her work comes out of, and responds to, a cultural arena in which there is room for more than just two major black women writers, neither of whom represents 'the' race nor 'the' African American tradition, if the latter is conceived as a smooth narrative. Cheryl Wall, like Spillers, argues for a different approach when she writes that '[b]y worrying the line of literary traditions, contemporary black women writers tell the stories that their predecessors could not'.[63] If Toni Morrison and Alice Walker are among 'only a handful of writers of fiction' who, to cite Spillers once more, 'have posed a staging of the mental theater as an articulate structure of critical inquiries into "the souls of black folk"', then that is one identifiable arena in which they differ from their literary ancestors.[64]

But of course, any notion of tradition, discontinuous and with a worried line or not, does not just look back but projects something into the future as well. In her article 'Beyond Morrison and Walker: Looking Good and Looking Forward in Contemporary Black Women's Stories' E. Shelley Reid has begun the important task of tracing how the work of the major black women writers of the late twentieth century is being continued, or taken issue with, or diverged from, in that of younger writers like Terry McMillan, A. J. Verdelle, Tina McElroy Ansa, Sapphire, and Bebe Moore Campbell. She agrees with Spillers that 'the great theme of African American texts in the 1970s and 1980s was the internal search for a recognizable self', but she sees the next generation of women writers taking that self rather for granted and moving on to more urban and contemporary themes and issues, rather than the historical subjects and rural settings of much of Walker's and Morrison's work.[65] Reid also notes how there is evidence of continuity in the frequent employment of multivocal narratives to represent '[t]he need for the whole community to participate in the storytelling ... emphasizing both the connectedness and the diversity of voices and views'.[66] There is less overt social protest, but more engagement with the plight of young black men, with women who are single parents, and – particularly in McMillan's work – concern with the trappings of the black middle class and its denuded, degraded versions of 'community' through professional networking in the 1990s. Such post-Civil Rights loss of community may be a useful context for Walker's work to come into its own as a spiritual alternative to and critique of consumer culture and postmodern anomie. We then end up with an Alice Walker who *both* stands in a tradition of visionary black women of the nineteenth century *and* points forward to a twenty-first century sensibility that uses 'one's own story' of suffering and healing to create new narratives, essays, memoirs, poems, and visions, for troubled times. For now, however, the younger writer who best articulates that particular sensibility, albeit in memoirs only, is Rebecca Walker, author of *Black White and Jewish: Autobiography of a Shifting Self* (2001) and *Baby Love: Choosing Motherhood After a Lifetime of Ambivalence* (2009).[67] Like her mother, Rebecca Walker is bisexual, and like her mother's too her writing queers American conceptions of race and sexuality as much as it que*ries* received notions of motherhood and feminism.

Perhaps it is fitting, as a closing gesture, to sum up what Morrison and Walker and the new generation of black women writers share with their post-colonial or diasporic contemporaries. Despite discontinuous traditions and across cultural difference, they create what Françoise Lionnet terms a new universalism:

> They write in the interstices between domination and resistance. [...] They appropriate the concept of universality in order to give it a new valence and to define broader commonalities. [...] Their works de-exoticize the non-West, indicating the centrality of their concerns to the self-understanding of people everywhere.[68]

This new universalism is Alice Walker's contribution to the 'immense story' of a multi-racial, cross-cultural tradition. To write in a way that is 'spiritually authentic, creatively true', and to pay the price in condemnation and controversy: that is freedom, America's gift to Alice Walker, and hers to the world.[69]

Notes

1. ALICE WALKER'S LIFE AND WORK: AN INTRODUCTION

1. John O'Brien, 'Alice Walker: An Interview' [1973], in Henry Louis Gates Jr and K. A. Appiah (eds), *Alice Walker: Critical Perspectives Past and Present* (New York: Amistad, 1993), p. 331.
2. David Swick, 'We Live in the Best of All Times: A Conversation with Alice Walker', http://www.shambhalasun.com.
3. O'Brien, 'Alice Walker', p. 331.
4. Cheryl A. Wall, *Worrying the Line: Black Women Writers, Lineage, and Literary Tradition* (Chapel Hill and London: University of North Carolina Press, 2005), pp. 210–11.
5. See for example June Jordan, *Technical Difficulties: Political Essays* (London: Virago, 1992) or Audre Lorde, *Sister, Outsider* (Trumansburg: The Crossing Press, 1984) and *The Cancer Journals* (London: Sheba, 1985).
6. Ruth-Ellen Boetcher Joeres and Elizabeth Mittman, 'An Introductory Essay', in Ruth-Ellen Boetcher Joeres and Elizabeth Mittman (eds), *The Politics of the Essay: Feminist Perspectives* (Bloomington: Indiana University Press, 1993), p. 16.
7. Roland Barthes, 'The Death of the Author' [1968], in Philip Rice and Patricia Waugh (eds), *Modern Literary Theory: A Reader*, second edition (London: Edward Arnold, 1992), pp. 114–18.
8. Candice M. Jenkins, 'Queering Black Patriarchy: The Salvific Wish and Masculine Possibility in Alice Walker's *The Color Purple*', *MFS Modern Fiction Studies*, 48:4 (2002), pp. 969–1000, 971.
9. Laurie McMillan, 'Telling a Critical Story: Alice Walker's *In Search of Our Mothers' Gardens*', *Journal of Modern Literature*, 28:1 (2004), pp. 107–23, 107–8.
10. Evelyn C. White, *Alice Walker: A Life* (New York and London: W. W. Norton 2004) p. 15.
11. Alice Walker, 'Now That You Are With Me Like My People and The Dignity of the World', in *We Are the Ones We Have Been Waiting For*, p. 151.
12. Alice Walker, 'The Black Writer and the Southern Experience' [1970], in *In Search of Our Mothers' Gardens: Womanist Prose* (London: Women's Press, 1984), p. 17.
13. Ibid., p. 21.
14. Sharon Wilson, 'An Interview with Alice Walker' [1984], in Gates and Appiah (eds), *Alice Walker*, p. 319.
15. Alice Walker, 'Childhood', in *We Are the Ones We Have Been Waiting For: Inner Light in a Time of Darkness*, pp. 33–4.

16. Alice Walker, 'Saving the Life That Is Your Own: The Importance of Models in the Artist's Life', in *In Search of Our Mothers' Gardens*, pp. 3–14; 'The Old Artist: Notes on Mr Sweet', in *Living by the Word: Selected Writings 1973–1987* (London: Women's Press, 1988), p. 38. 'The Revenge of Hannah Kemhuff' and 'To Hell with Dying' are both published in Alice Walker, *In Love and Trouble: Stories of Black Women* [1973] (London: Women's Press, 1984) and evoke two of Walker's literary ancestors and mentors: Zora Neale Hurston, whose *Mules and Men* informed the voodoo that appears in the former, and Langston Hughes, reminiscent of the old man in 'To Hell with Dying'. The latter, like *Langston Hughes: American Poet* (1974) and *Finding the Green Stone* (1991) was also published as a children's book, with illustrations by Catherine Deeter, in 1988.

17. Alice Walker, 'Beauty: When the Other Dancer Is the Self' [1984], in *In Search of Our Mothers' Gardens*, p. 386.

18. Ibid., p. 393.

19. Alice Walker and Pratibha Parmar, *Warrior Marks: Female Genital Mutilation and the Sexual Blinding of Women* (London: Jonathan Cape, 1993) p. 18.

20. O'Brien, 'Alice Walker: An Interview', p. 327.

21. Alice Walker, 'The Unglamorous But Worthwhile Duties of the Black Revolutionary Artist, or of the Black Writer Who Simply Works and Writes' [1971], in *In Search of Our Mothers' Gardens*, p. 130.

22. O'Brien, 'Alice Walker: An Interview', p. 330.

23. Ibid., p. 329.

24. Alice Walker, 'The Civil Rights Movement: What Good Was It?' [1967], in *In Search of Our Mothers' Gardens*, p. 125.

25. Alice Walker, 'The Only Reason You Want to Go to Heaven Is That You Have Been Driven Out of Your Mind (Off Your Land and Out of Your Lover's Arms)', in *Anything We Love Can Be Saved: A Writer's Activism* (London: Women's Press, 1997), p. 4.

26. Alice Walker, '"But Yet and Still the Cotton Gin Kept on Working …"' [1970], in *In Search of Our Mothers' Gardens*, p. 28.

27. 'Black and white together' was one of the verses of the best known Civil Rights song, 'We Shall Overcome'.

28. Walker looks back on the marriage and its aftermath in 'To My Young Husband', in *The Way Forward Is With a Broken Heart* (London: Women's Press, 2000) pp. 1–63.

29. Alice Walker, 'Breaking Chains and Encouraging Life' [1980], in *In Search of Our Mothers' Gardens*, pp. 287–8.

30. Alice Walker, '*One* Child of One's Own' [1979], in *In Search of Our Mothers' Gardens*, p. 367.

31. O'Brien, 'Alice Walker: An Interview', p. 337.

32. Walker, '*One* Child of One's Own', p. 372.

33. White, *Alice Walker* pp. 298–9. Also in Amy Goodman, '"I Am a Renegade, an Outlaw, a Pagan" – Author, Poet and Activist Alice Walker in Her Own Words', http://democracynow.org/2006/2/13/i_am_a_renegade_an_outlaw. The Sisterhood must have been a prime example of womanism in action at a time when black feminism was still under development, and it is puzzling that the only sources we

have for its existence are biographical. Always generous in acknowl-
edging, sharing, and often celebrating her sources and influences,
Walker's own reflections on the experience of being in a black women
writers' group are curiously lacking.

34. Alice Walker, 'Writing *The Color Purple*' [1982], in *In Search of Our Mothers' Gardens*, p. 357.
35. Duncan Campbell, 'A Long Walk to Freedom', *The Observer*, 25 February 2001, http://www.guardian.co.uk/books/2001/feb/25/fiction.features1.
36. White, *Alice Walker* p. 296; Rebecca Walker, *Black White and Jewish: Autobiography of a Shifting Self* (New York: Riverhead, 2001) p. 231 and *passim*. *Our Daughters Have Mothers Inc.*, the name of Walker's production company for the making of the film *Warrior Marks*, comes to look increasingly ironic, and bitterly so, in light of the very public rift between Alice and Rebecca Walker that occurred in 2004 and was splashed all over the press and the Internet, with salacious headlines; see for example Bill Peschel, 'Alice Walker Dumps Daughter', http://www.planetpeschel.com/index?/site/comments/alice_walker_dumps_daughter_.
37. Alice Walker, 'Coming in from the Cold: Welcoming the Old, Funny-talking Ancient Ones into the Warm Room of Present Consciousness, or, Natty Dread Rides Again!' [1984], in *Living by the Word*, p. 55.
38. Alice Walker, 'In the Closet of the Soul' [1987], in *Living by the Word*, p. 79.
39. Rose Marie Berger, 'Interview with Alice Walker', http://thumper-scorner.com/cgi/discus/board-admin.cgi?action=quick&do=.
40. Walker, 'In the Closet of the Soul', p. 82.
41. O'Brien, 'Alice Walker: An Interview', p. 332.
42. Walker, 'The Only Reason You Want to Go to Heaven', p. 17.
43. Miller's whole oeuvre focuses on various forms of child abuse; see, for example, *The Untouched Key: Tracing Childhood Trauma in Creativity and Destructiveness* (London: Virago, 1990) and *Banished Knowledge: Facing Childhood Injuries* (London: Virago, 1991).
44. Alice Walker, 'This That I Offer You: People Get Tired; Sometimes They Have Other Things to Do', in *Anything We Love Can Be Saved*, p. 177.
45. Walker, 'Zora Neale Hurston: A Cautionary Tale and a Partisan View' [1979], in *In Search of Our Mothers' Gardens*, p. 92.
46. Alice Walker (ed.), *I Love Myself When I am Laughing ... and Then Again When I Am Looking Mean and Impressive: A Zora Neale Hurston Reader* (New York: The Feminist Press, 1979).
47. Diane Sadoff, 'Black Matrilineage: The Case of Walker and Hurston', in Harold Bloom (ed.), *Alice Walker*, Modern Critical Views (New York: Chelsea House, 1989), p. 118.
48. Felicia Pride, 'Alice & Zora: An Interview with Valerie Boyd and Evelyn C. White (Biographies of Alice Walker and Zora Neale Hurston)' http://www.inmotionmagazine.com/ac05/f_pride1.html.
49. Kadiatu Kanneh, 'Mixed Feelings: When My Mother's Garden is Unfamiliar', in Sally Ledger, Josephine McDonagh, and Jane Spencer (eds), *Political Gender: Texts and Contexts* (London: Harvester Wheatsheaf, 1994), p. 36.

50. Lillie P. Howard (ed.), *Alice Walker and Zora Neale Hurston: The Common Bond* (London: Greenwood Press, 1993); Molly Hite, 'Romance, Marginality and Matrilineage: *The Color Purple* and *Their Eyes Were Watching God*', in Henry Louis Gates Jr (ed.), *Reading Black, Reading Feminist: A Critical Anthology* (New York: Meridian, 1990), pp. 431–54; Henry-Louis Gates Jr, 'Color Me Zora', in Gates and Appiah (eds), *Alice Walker*, pp. 239–60.

51. Gates Jr, 'Color Me Zora', p. 244; Michael Cooke, *Afro-American Literature in the Twentieth Century: The Achievement of Intimacy* (London: Yale University Press, 1984), p. 34.

52. Wilson, 'An Interview with Alice Walker', p. 324.

53. Trudier Harris, 'Our People, Our People', in Lillie P. Howard (ed.), *Alice Walker and Zora Neale Hurston*, p. 32.

54. Alice Walker, 'Saving the Life That Is Your Own: The Importance of Models in the Artist's Life' [1976], in *In Search of Our Mothers' Gardens*, p. 11.

55. Alice Walker, 'Everyday Use', in *In Love and Trouble*, pp. 47–59.

56. Wilson, 'An Interview with Alice Walker', p. 320.

57. O'Brien, 'Alice Walker: An Interview', p. 338.

58. Alice Walker, *Meridian* [1976] (London: Women's Press, 1983) p. 105.

59. Walker, *In Search of Our Mothers' Gardens*, pp. xi–xii.

60. Tuzyline Jita Allan, *Womanist & Feminist Aesthetics: A Comparative Review* (Athens: Ohio University Press, 1995), p. 6.

61. Ibid., p. 93.

62. Walker, '*One* Child of One's Own', pp. 363, 368.

63. Walker, 'Saving the Life That is Your Own', p. 5.

64. Ibid., p. 14; Alice Walker, 'The River: Honoring the Difficult', in *The Same River Twice*, p. 41.

65. Virginia Woolf, *A Room of One's Own* (New York: Harcourt Brace Jovanovich, 1927), p. 79.

66. Ibid., p. 362.

67. Ibid., p. 383. Evidently, from Rebecca's point of view writing and motherhood were rather less compatible than her mother thought they were: '"My mother did a lot of leaving to go to her writing retreat, which was over 100 miles away – so she'd go there and leave me a little bit of money, leave me in the care of a neighbor", recalls Rebecca, now 38. "When I was pregnant at 14, I think it was because I was so lonely that I was reaching out through my sexuality. My Mother's a crusader for daughters around the world, but couldn't see that her daughter was having a difficult time. It was me having to psycho-emotionally tiptoe around her, rather than her taking care of me."' Margaret Driscoll, 'The Day Feminist Icon Alice Walker Resigned as My Mother', *The Sunday Times*, 4 May 2008, http://entertainment.timesonline.co.uk/arts/_and_entertainment/books/article38667.

68. Alice Walker, 'In Search of Our Mothers' Gardens' [1974], in *In Search of Our Mothers' Gardens*, p. 234.

69. Walker, 'Saving the Life That is Your Own', p. 5.

70. Alice Walker, 'Beyond the Peacock: the Reconstruction of Flannery O'Connor' [1975], in *In Search of Our Mothers' Gardens*, p. 43; Cheryl A. Wall, *Worrying the Line*, p. 223.

71. Alice Walker, 'Alice Walker on the Movie *The Color Purple*', in *The Same River Twice*, p. 203.
72. Virginia Woolf, *Three Guineas* [1938] (Harmondsworth: Penguin, 1977), p. 125.
73. See, for example, Patricia Hill Collins, *Black Feminist Thought: Knowledge, Consciousness, and the Politics of Empowerment* (London: Routledge, 1991); Carole Boyce Davies, *Black Women, Writing and Identity: Migrations of the Subject* (London: Routledge, 1994); and the two volumes of *Moving Beyond Boundaries*: vol. 1, Carole Boyce Davies and 'Molara Ogundipe Leslie (eds), *International Dimensions of Black Women's Writing* (London: Pluto Press, 1995), and vol. 2, Carole Boyce Davies (ed.), *Black Women's Diasporas* (London: Pluto Press, 1995).
74. Walker, '*One* Child of One's Own', p. 378.
75. Allan, 'A Voice of One's Own', p. 137.
76. Allan, 'A Voice of One's Own', p. 133.
77. Toni Morrison, 'Unspeakable Things Unspoken: The Afro-American Presence in American Literature', *Michigan Quarterly Review* (Winter, 1988), p. 9.

2. *THE THIRD LIFE OF GRANGE COPELAND* (1970)

1. Alice Walker, *The Third Life of Grange Copeland* [1970], with a new Afterword (London: Women's Press, 1991); all page references are given in the text.
2. See, for example, Josephine Hendin's review, originally published in *Saturday Review*, 22 August 1970, and Robert Coles' in *The New Yorker*, 27 February 1971, both reprinted in Henry Louis Gates Jr and K. A. Appiah (eds), *Alice Walker: Critical Perspectives Past and Present* (New York: Amistad Press, 1993), pp. 3–8.
3. Amanda Davis, 'To Build a Nation: Black Women Writers, Black Nationalism, and the Violent Reduction of Wholeness', *Frontiers: a Journal of Women's Studies*, 26:3 (2005), pp. 24–53, 30.
4. Ibid., p. 24.
5. Klaus Ensslen, 'Collective Experience and Individual Responsibility: Alice Walker's *The Third Life of Grange Copeland*', in Peter Bruck and Wolfgang Karrer (eds), *The Afro-American Novel since 1960* (Amsterdam: Gruner, 1982), p. 194.
6. Kate Cochran, '"When the Lessons Hurt": *The Third Life of Grange Copeland* as Joban Allegory', *Southern Literary Journal*, 34:1 (Fall 2001), pp. 79–91, 79.
7. Hortense Spillers, 'Afterword: Cross-Currents, Discontinuities: Black Women's Fiction', in Marjorie Pryse and Hortense Spillers (eds), *Conjuring: Black Women, Fiction, and Literary Tradition* (Bloomington: Indiana University Press, 1985), p. 255.
8. Elliott Butler-Evans, *Race, Gender and Desire: Narrative Strategies in the Fiction of Toni Cade Bambara, Toni Morrison and Alice Walker* (Philadelphia: Temple University Press, 1989), p. 133.

9. Alice Walker, 'Interview with John O'Brien', in Gates and Appiah (eds), *Alice Walker*, p. 332.

10. Ensslen, 'Collective Experience and Individual Responsibility', pp. 210, 212.

11. W. Lawrence Hogue, 'History, the Feminist Discourse, and Alice Walker's *The Third Life of Grange Copeland'*, *MELUS*, 12:2 (1985), pp. 45–62, 55.

12. Madhu Dubey, *Black Women Novelists and the Nationalist Aesthetic* (Bloomington: Indiana University Press, 1994), p. 112.

13. W. Lawrence Hogue, 'Discourse of the Other: *The Third Life of Grange Copeland'*, in Harold Bloom (ed.), *Alice Walker* (New York: Chelsea House, 1989), p. 113.

14. Alice Walker, 'From an Interview', in *In Search of Our Mothers' Gardens: Womanist Prose* [1983] (London: Women's Press, 1984), pp. 250–1.

15. Dubey, *Black Women Novelists and the Nationalist Aesthetic*, p. 115.

16. Marlon B. Ross, 'In Search of Black Men's Masculinities', *Feminist Studies*, 24:3 (Autumn, 1998) pp. 599–626, 607.

17. David Marriott, *On Black Men* (New York: Columbia University Press, 2000), p. 98.

18. Richard Delgado and Jean Stefancic, 'Minority Men, Misery, and the Marketplace of Ideas', in Maurice Berger, Brian Wallis, and Simon Watney (eds), *Constructing Masculinity* (London and New York: Routledge 1995), pp. 211–20, 211.

19. Paul Gilroy, *The Black Atlantic*, p. 85, quoted by Jonathan Rutherford, 'Mr. Nice (and Mr. Nasty)', in Anna Tripp (ed.), *Gender*, Readers in Cultural Criticism (Basingstoke and New York: Palgrave Macmillan 2000), pp. 87–101, 95.

20. John Edgar Wideman, quoted by David Marriott, *On Black Men*, p. 96.

21. Ibid.

22. Marcellus Blount and George P. Cunningham, 'Introduction', in Marcellus Blount and George P. Cunningham (eds), *Representing Black Men* (Routledge: New York and London 1996), pp. ix–xv, xii.

23. And, obviously, also from queer theory. See for the challenge that queer theory poses to black nationalism and its conception of African American masculinity for example Amy Abugo Ongiri, 'We Are Family: Black Nationalism, Black Masculinity, and the Black Gay Cultural Imagination' *College Literature* 24:1 (1 February 1997), pp. 280–94.

24. Marcellus Blount, 'Caged Birds: Race and Gender in the Sonnet', in Joseph A. Boone and Michael Cadden (eds) *Engendering Men: the Question of Male Feminist Criticism* (New York: Routledge 1990) pp. 225–38, 227.

25. Ross, 'In Search of Black Men's Masculinities', p. 603.

26. Joyce A. Ladner, *Tomorrow's Tomorrow: The Black Woman* [1971] (New York: Doubleday, 1972), pp. 40, 43.

27. Robert Staples, 'The Myth of the Black Matriarchy', in *The Black Scholar* (January–February 1970); Toni Cade (ed.), *The Black Woman: An Anthology* (New York: New American Library, 1970).

28. Walker, 'Interview with John O'Brien', p. 335.

29. The ghost of Freud may even make a fleeting appearance in *The Third Life of Grange Copeland* when Mem gets a lift from the husband of the woman she works for, who 'was from the north and was dying, it was said, from cancer of the mouth. Some said he was a Jew, but they did not quite know what it was that made him different – his eyes didn't make you look at your feet like the eyes of other men' (p. 121).

30. Sigmund Freud, 'Family Romances' [1909], in *On Sexuality: Three Essays on the Theory of Sexuality and Other Works*, The Pelican Freud Library, vol. 7 (Harmondsworth: Penguin, 1977), p. 221.

31. Ibid., p. 223.

32. Ibid., p. 224.

33. Ibid., p. 221.

34. For the Emmett Till story see, for example, Studs Terkel, *Race* (London: Minerva, 1992), pp. 19–26 and Cynthia Griggs Fleming, 'African-Americans', in John D. Buenker and Lorman A. Ratner (eds), *Multiculturalism in the United States: A Comparative Guide to Acculturation and Ethnicity* (New York: Greenwood Press, 1992), pp. 20–1.

35. Robert James Butler, 'Alice Walker's Vision of the South in *The Third Life of Grange Copeland*', *African American Review*, 27:2, Black South Issue, Part 2 of 2 (1993), pp. 195–204, 197.

36. Alice Miller, *Banished Knowledge: Facing Childhood Injuries* [1988: *Das Verbannte Wissen*] (London: Virago, 1991), pp. 1–2.

37. Brownfield's fantasy echoes Lorraine Hansberry's 1959 play *A Raisin in the Sun*, in which Walter, the beleaguered father of a black family in Chicago, struggles to live up to his ambition to be a breadwinner and patriarch. His daydream of a better life as a businessman who comes home in a fancy car to his doting wife and children, under the gaze of their (black) gardener, looks as ludicrously unrealistic as Brownfield's. Lorraine Hansberry, *A Raisin in the Sun* [1959] in Jordan Y. Miller (ed.) *The Heath Introduction to Drama*, fifth edition (Lexington: DC Heath, 1996), pp. 841–914, 890.

38. Freud describes the Oedipal complex most succinctly in 'The Psychology of Women', in *New Introductory Lectures on Psychoanalysis* [1932] (London: The Hogarth Press and the Institute of Psychoanalysis, 1962), p. 166.

39. Frantz Fanon, *Black Skin, White Masks* [1952] (London: Pluto Press, 1986), pp. 152–3.

40. Fanon explains it as an existential moment in a footnote with a quotation from Sartre's *Anti-Semite and Jew*: 'Suddenly they [children] perceive that others [white people] know something about them that they do not know, that people apply to them an ugly and upsetting term [Yid; nigger] that is not used in their own families'; ibid., p. 72.

41. Linda Ruth Williams, *Critical Desire: Psychoanalysis and the Literary Subject* (London: Edward Arnold, 1995), p. 17 (original emphasis)

42. Gloria Wade-Gayles, *No Crystal Stair: Visions of Race and Sex in Black Women's Fiction* (New York: Pilgrim Press, 1984), p. 102.

43. Richard Godden, *Fictions of Capital: The American Novel from James to Mailer* (Cambridge: Cambridge University Press, 1990), p. 140.

44. Alice Walker, 'Afterword' to 1991 edition of *The Third Life of Grange Copeland*, p. 251.

45. Davis, 'To Build a Nation', p. 39.
46. Many oral histories of the Great Migration describe such disillusionment. See, for example, Nicholas Leman, *The Promised Land: the Great Black Migration and How It Changed America* (London: MacMillan 1991), Studs Terkel, *Race* (London: Minerva 1993), and Bob Blauner, *Black Lives, White Lives: Three Decades of Race Relations in America* (Berkeley: University of California Press, 1989).
47. For Walker's use of folklore in *The Third Life of Grange Copeland* see Trudier Harris, 'Folklore in the Fiction of Alice Walker: A Perpetuation of Historical and Literary Traditions', *Black American Literature Forum*, 11:1 (Spring, 1977), pp. 3–8.
48. Cochran, '"When the Lessons Hurt"', p. 86.
49. Melissa Walker, *Down From the Mountaintop: Black Women's Novels in the Wake of the Civil Rights Movement 1966–1989* (New Haven: Yale University Press, 1991), p. 115.
50. Peter Erickson, '"Cast Out Alone/to Heal/and Recreate Ourselves": Family-based Identity in the Work of Alice Walker', in Bloom (ed.), *Alice Walker*, pp. 5–24.
51. Dubey, *Black Women Novelists and the Nationalist Aesthetic*, p. 112.
52. Sandi Russell, *Render Me My Song: African-American Women Writers from Slavery to the Present* (New York: St Martin's Press, 1990), pp. 127, 122.
53. Fanon, *Black Skin, White Masks*, p. 142.

3. *MERIDIAN* (1976)

1. Alice Walker, 'The Civil Rights Movement: What Good Was It?' [1967] in *In Search of Our Mothers' Gardens: Womanist Prose* [1983] (London: Women's Press, 1984), pp. 119–29; *Meridian* [1976] (London: Women's Press, 1983); all page references will be given in the text.
2. Alice Walker, *Meridian* [1976] (London: Women's Press, 1983). All page references will be given in the text.
3. For the connections between feminism and Civil Rights see, for example, Sara Evans, *Personal Politics: The Roots of Women's Liberation in the Civil Rights Movement and the New Left* (New York: Random House, 1979).
4. Leigh Anne Duck, 'Listening to Melancholia: Alice Walker's *Meridian*', *Patterns of Prejudice*, 42:4–5 (2008), pp. 439–64, 463.
5. David Bradley, 'Telling the Black Woman's Story', *New York Times Magazine* (January 1984), p. 31.
6. Bearden was involved in the early 1960s in the Spiral Group, which wanted to work in support of the Civil Rights movement. For Bearden, see Regenia A. Perry, *Free within Ourselves: African-American Artists in the Collection of the National Museum of American Art* (Washington, DC: National Museum of American Art, Smithsonian Institution, 1992), pp. 29–36; for *Cane*, see Rachel Farebrother, *The Collage Aesthetic in the Harlem Renaissance* (Farnham: Ashgate, 2009).
7. 'Alice Walker', in Claudia Tate (ed.), *Black Women Writers at Work* [1983] (Harpenden: Oldcastle Books, 1989), p. 176.

8. Christine Hall, 'Art, Action and the Ancestors: Alice Walker's *Meridian* in Its Context', in Gina Wisker (ed.), *Black Women's Writing* (London: Macmillan, 1993), p. 97.

9. For example, Gloria Wade-Gayles, *No Crystal Stair: Visions of Race and Sex in Black Women's Fiction* (New York: The Pilgrim Press, 1984), p. 211; John F. Callahan, 'The Hoop of Language: Politics and the Restoration of Voice in *Meridian*', in Harold Bloom (ed.), *Alice Walker, Modern Critical Views* (New York: Chelsea House, 1988), p. 157; and Leigh Anne Duck, 'Listening to Melancholia', p. 460.

10. bell hooks, 'Gangsta Culture – Sexism and Misogyny', in *Outlaw Culture: Resisting Representation* (London: Routledge, 1994), p. 116.

11. 'Maya Angelou Talking with Rosa Guy', in Mary Chamberlain (ed.), *Writing Lines: Conversations Between Women Writers* (London: Virago, 1988), p. 17.

12. Leigh Anne Duck uses the phrase '*held* by the past' as indicative of Meridian's melancholia in Freud's definition.

13. Callahan, 'The Hoop of Language', p. 160.

14. Joseph E. Lowery, Methodist minister in Mobile in the 1950s, in Howell Raines, *My Soul Is Rested: Movement Days in the Deep South Remembered* [1977] (New York: Bantam, 1978), p. 66.

15. Bernice Johnson Reagon, 'Women as Culture Carriers in the Civil Rights Movement: Fannie Lou Hamer', in Vicki L. Crawford, Jacqueline Anne Rouse, and Barbara Woods (eds), *Women in the Civil Rights Movement: Torchbearers and Trailblazers 1941–1965* [1990] (Bloomington: Indiana University Press, 1993), pp. 103–4.

16. James Farmer in Raines, *My Soul Is Rested*, p. 134.

17. Johnson Reagon, 'Women as Culture Carriers in the Civil Rights Movement', pp. 103–4.

18. Andrew Ross, 'The Gangsta and the Diva', *The Nation*, 22/29 August 1994, p. 192.

19. hooks, 'Gangsta Culture', p. 116.

20. bell hooks, 'Ice Cube Culture: A Shared Passion for Speaking Truth', in *Outlaw Culture*, pp. 125–43, 136.

21. Yet, as hooks never fails to point out, 'To the white-dominated mass media, the controversy over gangsta rap makes great spectacle. Besides the exploitation of these issues to attract audiences, a central motivation for highlighting gangsta rap continues to be the sensationalist drama of demonizing black youth culture in general and the contributions of young black men in particular'; hooks, 'Gangsta Culture', p. 115.

22. Alice Walker, *The Temple of My Familiar* [1989] (Harmondsworth: Penguin, 1990), p. 262.

23. Thulani Davis, *1959* [1992] (London: Penguin, 1993); Toni Cade Bambara, *The Salt Eaters* [1980], (London: Women's Press, 1982).

24. Roberta M. Hendrickson, 'Remembering the Dream: Alice Walker, *Meridian*, and the Civil Rights Movement', *MELUS*, 24:3 (Autumn 1999), pp. 111–28, 112, 120.

25. Alan Nadel, 'Reading the Body: *Meridian* and the Archeology of Self', in Henry Louis Gates Jr and K. A. Appiah (eds), *Alice Walker: Critical Perspectives Past and Present* (New York: Amistad, 1993), p. 156.

26. Greil Marcus, 'Review of *Meridian*' [1976], in Gates and Appiah (eds), *Alice Walker*, p. 12.
27. Duck, 'Listening to Melancholia', pp. 457–8.
28. Fannie Lou Hamer, cited in Kay Mills, *This Little Light of Mine: the Life of Fannie Lou Hamer* (New York: Penguin, 1994), p. 79.
29. Dave Dennis in Raines, *My Soul Is Rested*, p. 301.
30. This phrase is cited by Mills in *This Little Light of Mine*, p. 87.
31. Mary Aickin Rothschild, 'White Women Volunteers in the Freedom Summers: Their Life and Work in a Movement for Social Change', *Feminist Studies*, 5:3 (Fall 1979), p. 482.
32. SNCC Members of the Atlanta Project, 'A Position Paper on Race', in Joanne Grant (ed.), *Black Protest: History, Documents, Analyses 1619 to the Present*, second edition (New York: Random House, 1991), p. 453.
33. Pia Thielmann, 'Alice Walker and the "Man Question"', in Ikenna Dieke (ed.) *Critical Essays on Alice Walker* (Westport, CT and London: Greenwood Press, 1999), pp. 67–82, 73.
34. Howard Zinn, 'The Limits of Non-Violence', in Joanne Grant (ed.), *Black Protest*, pp. 312–17; James Forman, 'Black Manifesto' in the same collection, pp. 443–4. Interestingly, Walker knew Zinn at Spelman College, and admired him. He, in turn, encouraged her in her efforts to become a writer; see Evelyn C. White, *Alice Walker: A Life* (New York and London: W. W. Norton and Company, 2004), pp. 67–89 *passim*.
35. 'Alice Walker', in Tate (ed.), *Black Women Writers at Work*, pp. 179–80.
36. Anne Moody, *Coming of Age in Mississippi* (New York: Doubleday, 1968), p. 328.
37. Dave Dennis, cited by Raines in *My Soul Is Rested*, pp. 304, 302.
38. Lawrence Guyot in interview with Raines, *My Soul Is Rested*, p. 317.
39. Deborah E. McDowell, 'The Self in Bloom: Walker's *Meridian*', in Gates and Appiah (eds), *Alice Walker*, p. 173. See also my psychoanalytic reading of *Meridian*: 'Healing the Body Politic: Alice Walker's *Meridian*', in Maria Lauret, *Liberating Literature: Feminist Fiction in America* (London and New York: Routledge, 1994), pp. 124–43; and Duck, 'Listening to Melancholia', which presents a persuasive psychoanalytic reading of Meridian as a character, but is less convincing on the novel as a whole, largely because it ignores the ethos of the Civil Rights Movement.
40. Amy-Jacques Garvey, 'Women as Leaders' [1925], in Gerda Lerner (ed.), *Black Women in White America: A Documentary History* (New York: Panther, 1972), p. 578.
41. Moody, *Coming of Age in Mississippi*, pp. 370, 371.
42. Marcus, 'Review of *Meridian*', p. 11; Jean Toomer, 'The Blue Meridian' [1925], in Darwin T. Turner (ed.), *The Wayward and the Seeking: A Collection of Writings by Jean Toomer* (Washington, DC: Howard University Press, 1982), pp. 214–34. Felipe Smith even sees a Toomer-like figure in Truman, and notes 'Walker's strategy of intertextual reference' in the 'coincidence of Walker's heroine having the same name as a favourite retreat of Toomer's in Washington, DC – Meridian Hill'; Felipe Smith, 'Alice Walker's Redemptive Art', in Ikenna Dieke (ed.) *Critical Essays on Alice Walker* (Westport, CT and London: Greenwood Press, 1999), pp. 109–25, 118.

43. Sojourner Truth, cited by Lerner in *Black Women in White America*, p. 371.
44. Alice Walker, 'A Name Is Sometimes an Ancestor Saying Hi, I'm With You', in *Living by the Word: Selected Writings 1973–1987* [1986] (London: Women's Press, 1986), p. 97.
45. Jack Forbes, *Africans and Native Americans: The Language of Race and the Evolution of Red-Black Peoples*, second edition (Urbana: University of Illinois Press, 1993), pp. 62, 189.
46. Sojourner Truth, 'Convention of the American Equal Rights Association, New York City 1867', in Lerner (ed.), *Black Women in White America*, p. 569.
47. Ibid., p. 370.
48. Hall, 'Art, Action and the Ancestors', pp. 98–9.
49. Martha J. McGowan, 'Atonement and Release in Alice Walker's *Meridian*', *Studies in Modern Fiction*, 23:1 (1981), pp. 25–36; Barbara Christian, 'The Black Woman Artist as Wayward', in *Black Feminist Criticism: Perspectives on Black Women Writers* (New York: Pergamon, 1985), p. 89, rpt. in Bloom (ed.), *Alice Walker*, p. 47.
50. Susan Willis, *Specifying: Black Women Writing the American Experience* (Madison: University of Illinois Press, 1987), p. 124.
51. For this kind of critique of women's liberation, see Patricia Hill Collins, *Black Feminist Thought: Knowledge, Consciousness, and the Politics of Empowerment*, Perspectives on Gender, vol. 2 (London: Routledge, 1991); Angela Davis, *Women, Race and Class* (London: Women's Press, 1982); bell hooks, *Ain't I a Woman: Black Women and Feminism* (London: Pluto Press, 1982); and my own *Liberating Literature*, which draws on these sources.
52. Toni Morrison, *Beloved* (New York: Signet, 1987).
53. Rhetaugh Graves Dumas, 'Dilemmas of Black Females in Leadership', in LaFrances Rodgers-Rose (ed.), *The Black Woman* (London: Sage, 1980), p. 210.
54. Kathleen Cleaver, for example, believed that the premature death of Ruby Doris Smith Robinson was due to the combined demands of marriage, motherhood, political organising and particularly the many conflicts within and between those areas of work, and Fannie Lou Hamer's health was never the same after she was beaten in jail and could not take the time out for – nor could she afford – the medical treatment that was necessary for a full recovery. See Ann Standley, 'The Role of Black Women in the Civil Rights Movement', in Crawford et al. (eds), *Women in the Civil Rights Movement*, p. 197.
55. Ella Baker, 'Developing Community Leadership', in Lerner (ed.), *Black Women in White America*, pp. 345–52.
56. Lawrence Guyot, interviewed in Raines, *My Soul Is Rested*, p. 261.
57. Ibid.
58. Alice Walker, 'The Right to Life: What Can the White Man ... Say to the Black Woman?' *The Nation*, 22 May 1989, in Katrina Vanden Heuvel (ed.), *The Nation: Selections from the Independent Magazine of Politics and Culture 1865/1990* (London: Pluto Press, 1991), pp. 462–3.
59. I have written elsewhere of the way in which interracial rape is treated contextually in *Meridian* and in the short story 'Advancing Luna – and

Ida B. Wells', which is usefully read as its companion piece; Lauret, *Liberating Literature*, pp. 131–3.

60. Gloria T. Hull, Patricia Bell Scott, and Barbara Smith (eds), *All the Women Are White, All the Men Are Black, But Some of Us Are Brave: Black Women's Studies* (Old Westbury: The Feminist Press, 1982).

61. Hall, 'Art, Action and the Ancestors', p. 105.

62. Walker, 'The Civil Rights Movement: What Good Was It?' p. 120.

63. Ibid.

64. Franklin McCain, interviewed by Raines in *My Soul Is Rested*, p. 79.

65. Fannie Lou Hamer, cited by Bernice Johnson Reagon, 'Women as Culture Carriers: Fannie Lou Hamer', in Crawford el al. (eds), *Women in the Civil Rights Movement*, p. 216.

4. *THE COLOR PURPLE* (1982)

1. Sally Placksin, *Jazzwomen 1900 to the Present: Their Lives and Music* [1982] (London: Pluto Press, 1985), p. 20.

2. Alice Walker, 'Looking for Zora' [1975], in *In Search of Our Mothers' Gardens: Womanist Prose* [1983] (London: Women's Press, 1984), pp. 93–116.

3. Alice Walker, *The Color Purple* [1982] (London: Women's Press, 1983); all page references are given in the text.

4. Felipe Smith, 'Alice Walker's Redemptive Art', in Ikenna Dieke (ed.), *Critical Essays on Alice Walker* (Westport, CT and London: Greenwood Press, 1999), pp. 109–25, 119.

5. Candice M. Jenkins, 'Queering Black Patriarchy: The Salvific Wish and Masculine Possibility in Alice Walker's *The Color Purple*', *MFS Modern Fiction Studies*, 48:4 (2002), pp. 969–1000, 970.

6. Some of this debate is documented in Walker's collection *The Same River Twice: Honoring the Difficult. A Meditation on Life, Spirit, Art and the Making of the Film* The Color Purple *Ten Years Later* (London: Women's Press, 1996). For reception of the film, see also Jacqueline Bobo, '*The Color Purple*: Black Women as Cultural Readers', in E. Deirdre Pribram (ed.), *Female Spectators: Looking at Film and Television* (London: Verso, 1988), pp. 90–109.

7. From Tony Brown, 'Blacks Need to Love One Another', quoted in Alice Walker, *Banned* (San Francisco: Aunt Lute Books, 1996), p. 104.

8. Ibid., p. 103.

9. Alan Sinfield, contribution to Brighton LTP (Literature Teaching Politics) Group, *Problems of the Progressive Text: The Color Purple by Alice Walker* (Brighton: LTP, 1985), p. 117.

10. The literature on the culture wars is extensive, but see for example Paul Berman (ed.), *Debating P.C.: The Controversy over Political Correctness on College Campuses* (New York: Bantam Doubleday Dell, 1992) and Ronald Takaki (ed.), *From Different Shores: Perspectives on Race and Ethnicity in America* (Oxford: Oxford University Press 1995), Chapter VI 'Prospects', pp. 277–99.

11. bell hooks, 'Writing the Subject: Reading *The Color Purple*', in Harold Bloom (ed.), *Alice Walker, Modern Critical Views* (New York: Chelsea House, 1988), p. 215. Also published as 'Reading and Resistance: *The Color Purple*', in Henry Louis Gates Jr (ed.), *Reading Black, Reading Feminist: A Critical Anthology* (New York: Penguin, 1990), pp. 454–71; and in Henry Louis Gates Jr and K. A. Appiah (eds), *Alice Walker: Critical Perspectives Past and Present* (New York: Amistad, 1993), pp. 284–95.

12. Robyn Warhol, 'How Narration Produces Gender: Femininity as Affect and Effect in Alice Walker's *The Color Purple*', *Narrative*, 9:2 (May 2001), pp. 182–7, 182.

13. See for example Priscilla L. Walton, '"What She Got To Sing About?": Comedy and *The Color Purple*'; and Dror Abend-David, 'The Occupational Hazard: The Loss of Historical Context in Twentieth Century Feminist Readings, and a New Reading of the Heroine's Story in Alice Walker's *The Color Purple*', both in Dieke (ed.), *Critical Essays on Alice Walker*, pp. 185–96 and pp. 13–20 respectively; and Linda Abbandonato, 'Rewriting the Heroine's Story in *The Color Purple*', in Henry Louis Gates, Jr and K. A. Appiah (eds), *Alice Walker: Critical Perspectives Past and Present* (New York: Amistad 1993), pp. 296–308.

14. Lauren Berlant, 'Race, Gender and Nation in *The Color Purple*', in Gates and Appiah (eds), *Alice Walker*, p. 212.

15. Darryl Pinckney, 'Black Victims, Black Villains', *The New York Review of Books*, 29 January 1987, p. 17.

16. bell hooks, 'Writing the Subject: Reading *The Color Purple*', in Bloom (ed.), *Alice Walker*, p. 217.

17. Melissa Walker, *Down from the Mountaintop: Black Women's Writing in the Wake of the Civil Rights Movement, 1966–1989* (New Haven and London: Yale University Press, 1991), pp. 63, 71.

18. Leder asserts that *The Color Purple* is 'set in rural Georgia in the twenties, thirties, and forties', but there is no way of being certain about that time frame. Priscilla Leder, 'Alice Walker's American Quilt: *The Color Purple* and American Literary Tradition', in Dieke (ed.), *Critical Essays on Alice Walker*, pp. 141–51, 143.

19. See, for example, Charles Proudfit, 'Celie's Search for Identity: A Psychoanalytic Developmental Reading of Alice Walker's *The Color Purple*', *Contemporary Literature*, 32:1 (Spring, 1991), pp. 12–37; Daniel W. Ross, 'Celie in the Looking Glass: The Desire for Selfhood in *The Color Purple*', *Modern Fiction Studies*, 34:1 (1988), pp. 69–84; John J. Hiers, 'Creation Theology in Alice Walker's *The Color Purple*', *Notes on Contemporary Literature*, 14:4 (September 1984), pp. 2–3; Delores S. Williams, 'Black Women's Literature and the Task of Feminist Theology', in Clarissa W. Atkinson, Constance H. Buchanan, and Margaret R. Miles (eds), *Immaculate & Powerful: The Female in Sacred Image and Social Reality* (Boston: Beacon Press, 1985), pp. 88–110.

20. Wendy Wall, 'Lettered Bodies and Corporeal Texts', in Appiah and Gates (eds), *Alice Walker*, p. 271.

21. See for example Michael Awkward, *Inspiriting Influences: Tradition, Revision and Afro-American Women's Novels* (New York: Columbia

University Press, 1989), p. 139; Valerie Babb, '*The Color Purple*: Writing to Undo What Writing Has Done', *Phylon*, 47:2 (June 1986), pp. 107–16; Berlant, 'Race, Gender, and Nation in *The Color Purple*', p. 228; King-Kok Cheung, "'Don't Tell": Imposed Silences in *The Color Purple* and *The Woman Warrior*', *PMLA*, 103:2 (March 1988), pp. 162–74; Karla F. C. Holloway, *Moorings and Metaphors: Figures of Culture and Gender in Black Women's Literature* (New Brunswick: Rutgers University Press, 1992), p. 28.

22. See for example Awkward, *Inspiriting Influences*, p. 138; Marjorie Pryse, 'Introduction: Zora Neale Hurston, Alice Walker, and the Ancient Power of Black Women', in Marjorie Pryse and Hortense J. Spillers (eds), *Conjuring: Black Women, Fiction, and Literary Tradition* (Bloomington: Indiana University Press, 1985), p. 15.

23. Maya Angelou, *I Know Why the Caged Bird Sings* [1969] (London: Virago, 1984).

24. Christine Froula, 'The Daughter's Seduction: Sexual Violence and Literary History', *Signs*, 11:4 (Summer, 1986), pp. 621–44; Martha Cutter, 'Philomela Speaks: Alice Walker's Revisioning of Rape Archetypes in *The Color Purple*', *MELUS*, 25:3–4 (Autumn–Winter, 2000), pp. 161–80, 163.

25. Molly Hite, *The Other Side of the Story: Structures and Strategies of Contemporary Feminist Narrative* (London: Cornell University Press, 1989), p. 110.

26. Walton, '"What She Got To Sing About?"' p. 186.

27. Elizabeth Fifer, 'Alice Walker: The Dialect and Letters of *The Color Purple*', in Catherine Rainwater and William J. Schweick (eds), *Contemporary American Women Writers: Narrative Strategies* (Lexington: University Press of Kentucky, 1985), p. 163.

28. Linda Abbandonato, 'Rewriting the Heroine's Story in *The Color Purple*', in Gates and Appiah (eds), *Alice Walker*, pp. 296–308.

29. Walton, '"What She Got To Sing About?"', p. 188.

30. Henry Louis Gates Jr, *The Signifying Monkey: A Theory of African-American Literary Criticism* (Oxford: Oxford University Press, 1989), p. xvi; Wall, 'Lettered Bodies and Corporeal Texts', p. 272.

31. See for example Anonymous, 'The Signifying Monkey' [1964], in Paul Lauter et al. (eds), *The Heath Anthology of American Literature*, vol. 2 (Lexington: D. C. Heath, 1990), pp. 202–3.

32. See Gates, *The Signifying Monkey*, pp. 51–5 and passim.

33. For these functions see, for example, Geneva Smitherman, *Talkin' and Testifying': the Language of Black America* (Boston: Houghton Mifflin, 1977), pp. 119–20.

34. Marjorie Pryse, 'Introduction: Zora Neale Hurston, Alice Walker and the Ancient Power of Black Women', in Pryse and Spillers (eds), *Conjuring*, p. 19.

35. Philip Brian Harper, Anne McClintock, José Esteban Muñoz, and Trish Rosen, 'Queer Transexions of Race, Nation, and Gender', *Social Text*, 52:3 (Autumn–Winter, 1997), pp. 1–4, 1; E. Patrick Johnson, '"Quare" Studies, or (Almost) Everything I Know about Queer Studies I Learned from My Grandmother', in E. Patrick Johnson and

Mae G. Henderson (eds), *Black Queer Studies: A Critical Anthology* (Durham: Duke University Press, 2005), pp. 124–57, 125.

36. Jenkins, 'Queering Black Patriarchy', pp. 973–4.

37. Ibid., pp. 975, 994.

38. Linda Selzer, 'Race and Domesticity in *The Color Purple*', *African American Review* 29:1 (Spring, 1995), pp. 67–83, 80.

39. Siobhan Somerville, *Queering the Color Line: Race and the Invention of Homosexuality in American Culture* (Durham and London: Duke University Press, 2000), p. 137.

40. Selzer, 'Race and Domesticity in *The Color Purple*', p. 68.

41. Ibid., p. 80.

42. Calvin C. Hernton, *The Sexual Mountain and Black Women Writers: Adventures in Sex, Literature, and Real Life* (New York: Doubleday, 1987), p. 6.

43. Houston A. Baker Jr, *Workings of the Spirit: The Poetics of Afro-American Women's Writing* (London: University of Chicago Press, 1991), p. 42.

44. Harriet Jacobs, *Incidents in the Life of a Slave Girl, Written by Herself*, ed. Lydia Maria Child [1861], edited and introduction by Jean Fagan Yellin (London: Harvard University Press, 1987).

45. Gates, *The Signifying Monkey*, p. 52.

46. See for these points Walter J. Ong, *Orality and Literacy: The Technologizing of the Word*, New Accents Series [1982] (London: Routledge, 1989).

47. Christine Hall, 'Art, Action and the Ancestors: Alice Walker's *Meridian* in Context', in Gina Wisker (ed.), *Black Women's Writing* (London: Macmillan, 1993), pp. 102, 104.

48. In Anne Bradstreet's famous poem 'The Prologue' of 1650, for example, the oft-quoted lines are: 'I am obnoxious to each carping tongue/who says my hand a needle better fits' [than a pen] – Celie, obviously, has no such disdain for the needle. Indeed, as Martha Cutter observes, 'Sewing is … a key way individuals communicate with each other, signifying their friendship and interconnectedness'. Anne Bradstreet, 'The Prologue', in Nina Baym et al. (eds), *The Norton Anthology of American Literature vol. A, Literature to 1820*, sixth edition (New York: W. W. Norton, 2003), pp. 239–40, 239; Cutter, 'Philomela Speaks', p. 172.

49. Tamar Katz, '"Show Me How to Do Like You": Didacticism and Epistolary Form in *The Color Purple*', in Bloom (ed.), *Alice Walker*, pp. 185–93.

50. Graham Connah, *African Civilizations, Precolonial Cities and States in Tropical Africa: An Archaeological Perspective* (Cambridge: Cambridge University Press, 1987), p. 101; and map of precolonial trade routes and commodities in West Africa, p. 118.

51. Frances D. Gage/Sojourner Truth, '"Reminiscences of Frances D. Gage of Sojourner Truth", for May 28–29, 1851', in Paul Lauter et al. (eds), *The Heath Anthology of American Literature*, vol. 1, p. 1912; Frederick Douglass, 'What to the Slave is the Fourth of July?' [1852], in the same volume, pp. 1704–23.

52. Billie Holiday, 'My Man' (Yvain/Charles/Willemetz/Pollock) and 'Good Morning Heartache' (Higginbotham/Drake/Fisher), both MCA Ltd and recorded on Decca between 1944 and 1950, on *Billie Holiday: the Essential Recordings* (MCA Records: 1993); 'I've Got a Right to Sing

the Blues' (Harold Arlen/Ted Koehler), recorded 25 August 1955 in Los Angeles, on *The Essential Billie Holiday* (Polygram: 1992).

53. Warhol, 'How Narration Produces Gender', p. 2.
54. Cora Kaplan, 'Keeping the Color in *The Color Purple*', in *Sea Changes: Essays in Culture and Feminism* (London: Verso, 1986), pp. 177–87.
55. For a thoughtful account of problems in teaching *The Color Purple*, see also Alison Light, 'Fear of the Happy Ending: *The Color Purple*, Reading, and Racism', in Linda Anderson (ed.), *Plotting Change: Contemporary Women's Fiction* (London: Edward Arnold, 1990), pp. 85–98; and June Jordan, 'Nobody Mean More to Me Than You and the Future Life of Willie Jordan', in *Moving Towards Home: Political Essays* (London: Virago, 1989), pp. 175–89.
56. Ray Pratt, *Rhythm and Resistance: Explorations in the Political Uses of Popular Music* (New York: Praeger, 1990), p. 83.
57. Alice Walker, 'Nineteen Fifty-Five', in *You Can't Keep a Good Woman Down* (London: Women's Press, 1982), pp. 3–20. Maria V. Johnson has researched the many parallels between 'Nineteen Fifty-Five' and Elvis in great depth in '"You Just Can't Keep a Good Woman Down": Alice Walker Sings the Blues', *African American Review*, 30:2 (Summer, 1996), pp. 221–36. For a reading of this short story as a signifying practice see David J. Mickelsen, '"You Ain't Never Caught a Rabbit": Covering and Signifyin' in Alice Walker's "Nineteen Fifty-Five"', *Southern Quarterly*, 42: 3 (Spring, 2004), pp. 5–21.
58. Alice Walker, 'Everyday Use', in *In Love and Trouble* [1973] (London: Women's Press, 1984), pp. 47–59. For an interesting take on this story see Sam Whitsitt, 'In Spite of It All: A Reading of Alice Walker's "Everyday Use"', *African American Review*, 34:3 (2000), pp. 443–59.
59. LeRoi Jones, *Blues People: Negro Music in White America* (New York: Morrow Quill, 1963), p. 93.
60. Hortense J. Spillers, 'Interstices: A Small Drama of Words', in Carole S. Vance (ed.), *Pleasure and Danger: Exploring Female Sexuality*, second edition (London: Pandora, 1992), p. 87.
61. Bessie Smith, 'I'm Wild at That Thing' (Williams) and 'You've Got to Give Me Some' (Williams) (n.d.) on *Blue Spirit Blues* (Tring International plc: n.d.)
62. Shanyn Fiske, 'Piecing the Patchwork Self: A Reading of Walker's *The Color Purple*', *The Explicator*, 66:3 (Spring, 2008), pp. 150–3, 153.
63. Michele Russell, 'Black-Eyed Blues Connections: Teaching Black Women', in Gloria T. Hull et al. (eds), *All the Women Are White, All the Men Are Black, But Some of Us Are Brave: Black Women's Studies* (Old Westbury: The Feminist Press, 1982), p. 202.
64. Michele Russell, 'Slave Codes and Liner Notes', in Hull et al. (eds), *But Some of Us Are Brave*, p. 131.
65. Tricia Bent-Goodley, a scholar of domestic violence, cites the work of Angela Y. Davis on the blues in the 1920s to illustrate its role 'as an outlet for poor and working class African American women to express how they felt about the violence they experienced in their intimate relationships'; Tricia B. Bent-Goodley, 'Eradicating Domestic Violence

in the African American Community: A Literature Review and Action Agenda', *Trauma, Violence, and Abuse*, 2:4 (2001), pp. 316–30, 319.

66. Pratt, *Rhythm and Resistance*, p. 85.
67. Jordan, 'Nobody Mean More to Me Than You', p. 176.
68. Ibid., p. 177.
69. Ethel Waters, 'My Man' (Yvain/Charles/Willernetz/Pollock). In her introduction, Waters says she sings it as she did in 1924, but the actual recording date is unknown. On *Who Said Blackbirds Are Blue?* (Sandy Hook Records: 1981).
70. Deanna Campbell Robinson et al. (eds), *Music at the Margins: Popular Music and Global Cultural Diversity* (London: Sage, 1991), p. 44.
71. I thank John Moore for alerting me to the French origin of this song.
72. Patricia Hill Collins, *Black Feminist Thought: Knowledge, Consciousness and the Politics of Empowerment* (New York and London: Routledge, 1991), p. 102.
73. Paul Gilroy, *The Black Atlantic: Modernity and Double Consciousness* (London: Verso, 1993), p. 99.
74. See for a detailed theoretical exploration of this issue Elizabeth Abel, 'Black Writing, White Reading: Race and the Politics of Feminist Interpretation', *Critical Inquiry*, 19:3 (Spring, 1993), pp. 470–98. Abel concludes: 'If we produce our readings cautiously and locate them in a self-conscious and self-critical relation to black feminist criticism, these risks … would be counterbalanced by the benefits of broadening the spectrum of interpretation, illuminating the social determinants of reading, and deepening our recognition of our racial selves and the "others" we fantasmatically construct – and thereby expanding the possibilities of dialogue across as well as about racial boundaries', p. 498.
75. Alice Walker, 'Saving the Life That Is Your Own: The Importance of Models in the Artist's Life' [1976], in *In Search of Our Mothers' Gardens: Womanist Prose* [1983] (London: Women's Press, 1984), p. 5.
76. Gilroy, *The Black Atlantic*, p. 106.
77. Missy Dehn Kubitschek, 'Subjugated Knowledge: Towards a Feminist Exploration of Rape in Afro-American Fiction', in Joel Weixlmann and Houston A. Baker Jr (eds), *Black Feminist Criticism and Critical Theory* (Greenwood: Penkevill, 1988), pp. 45, 48.
78. Jordan, 'Nobody Means More to Me Than You', p. 175.
79. Babb, '*The Color Purple*: Writing to Undo What Writing Has Done', p. 107.

5. *THE TEMPLE OF MY FAMILIAR* (1989)

1. Alice Walker, *The Temple of My Familiar* [1989] (Harmondsworth: Penguin, 1990); all page references will be given in the text.
2. Bonnie Braendlin, 'Alice Walker's *The Temple of My Familiar* as Pastiche', *American Literature*, 68:1 (March 1996), pp. 47–67, 50.
3. Quoted on the book jacket, and cited by Evelyn C. White, *Alice Walker: A Life* (New York: W. W. Norton, 2004), p. 445.

4. Lillie P. Howard, 'Benediction: A Few Words About *The Temple of My Familiar*, Variously Interpreted, and *Possessing the Secret of Joy*', in Howard (ed.), *Alice Walker and Zora Neale Hurston: The Common Bond* (London: Greenwood Press, 1993), p. 141, 142.

5. Alice Walker, 'Writing *The Color Purple*' [1982], in *In Search of Our Mothers' Gardens: Womanist Prose* [1983] (London: Women's Press, 1984), pp. 355–60.

6. Gloria Anzaldúa, *Borderlands/La Frontera: The New Mestiza* (San Francisco: Aunt Lute Books, 1987), pp. 69–70.

7. C. G. Jung, 'Approaching the Unconscious', in C. G. Jung et al. (eds), *Man and His Symbols* [1964] (London: Picador, 1978), p. 6.

8. Anthony Storr, *Jung* (London: Fontana, 1986), p. 13.

9. Jung, 'Approaching the Unconscious', p. 81.

10. For Jung's approach to the unconscious via a dialogue with one's 'inner cast of characters' see also Demaris S. Wehr, *Jung & Feminism: Liberating Archetypes* (London: Routledge, 1990), p. 58.

11. Ngũgĩ wa Thiong'O, *Decolonising the Mind: The Politics of Language in African Literature* (London: James Currey, 1986), pp. 56–7.

12. Carol Iannone, 'A Turning of the Critical Tide?' *Commentary*, 88:5 (November 1989), pp. 57–9.

13. Larry J. Zimmerman, *Native North America*, Living Wisdom Series (London: Macmillan, 1996), p. 7.

14. I take this formulation from J. Laplanche's *New Foundations for Psychoanalysis*, trans. David Macey (Oxford: Basil Blackwell, 1989), p. 118, but unfortunately he gives no reference to Jung for this concept.

15. C. G. Jung, 'Some Aspects of Modern Psychotherapy', in *The Practice of Psychotherapy: Essays on the Psychology of the Transference and Other Subjects*, second edition, trans. R. F. C. Hull (London: Routledge, 1993), p. 35.

16. C. G. Jung, 'The Aims of Psychotherapy', in *The Practice of Psychotherapy*, p. 52.

17. Alice Walker, *The Color Purple* [1982] (London: Women's Press, 1983), pp. 243, 244.

18. J. M. Coetzee, [Review of *The Temple of My Familiar*] [1989 *New York Times Book Review*] in Henry Louis Gates Jr and K. A. Appiah (eds), *Alice Walker: Critical Perspectives Past and Present* (New York: Amistad, 1993), p. 26.

19. Ursula K. LeGuin, [review of *The Temple of My Familiar*] [1989 *San Francisco Review of Books*] in Gates and Appiah (eds), *Alice Walker*, p. 23.

20. Robert O. Stephens, *The Family Saga in the South: Generations and Destinies* (London: Louisiana State University Press, 1995), p. 6.

21. See Maria V. Johnson, '"You Just Can't Keep a Good Woman Down": Alice Walker Sings the Blues', *African American Review*, 30:2 (Summer, 1996) pp. 221–36, 234 on Elvis, particularly in relation to Walker's short story 'Nineteen Fifty-Five', in *You Can't Keep a Good Woman Down* (London: Women's Press, 1982), pp. 3–20.

22. Hazel Carby, 'The Politics of Fiction, Anthropology, and the Folk: Zora Neale Hurston', in Géneviève Fabre and Robert O'Meally (eds), *History & Memory in African-American Culture* (New York: Oxford University Press, 1994), p. 38.

23. Madelyn Jablon, *Black Metafiction: Self-Consciousness in African American Literature* (Iowa City: University of Iowa Press 1997), p. 53.
24. Adam Sol, 'Questions of Mastery in Alice Walker's *The Temple of My Familiar*', *Critique: Studies in Contemporary Fiction*, 43:4 (Summer, 2002), pp. 393–404, 394.
25. Eudora Welty, cited by Stephens in *The Family Saga in the South*, p. 7.
26. Ikenna Dieke, 'Walker's *The Temple of My* Familiar: Womanist as Monistic Idealist', in Ikenna Dieke (ed.), *Critical Essays on Alice Walker* (Westport, CT and London: Greenwood Press, 1999), pp. 127–39, 136.
27. Terry Dehay, 'Narrating Memory', in Amritjit Singh, Joseph T. Skerrett Jr, and Robert E. Hogan (eds), *Memory, Narrative and Identity: New Essays in Ethnic American Literatures* (London: Northeastern University Press, 1996), p. 33.
28. Ibid., p. 31.
29. Eva Lennox Birch, *Black American Women's Writing: A Quilt of Many Colours* (London: Harvester Wheatsheaf, 1994), p. 236.
30. Toni Morrison, 'Unspeakable Things Unspoken: The Afro-American Presence in American Literature', *Michigan Quarterly Review* (Winter, 1988), p. 32.
31. Paul Gilroy, *The Black Atlantic: Modernity and Double Consciousness* (London: Verso, 1993) p. 2.
32. Kwame Anthony Appiah, *In My Father's House: Africa in the Philosophy of Culture* (Oxford: Oxford University Press, 1992), p. viii.
33. Wolfgang Karrer, 'Nostalgia, Amnesia, and Grandmothers: The Uses of Memory in Albert Murray, Sabine Ulibarri, Paula Gunn Allen, and Alice Walker', in Singh et al. (eds), *Memory, Narrative and Identity*, p. 142.
34. Alice Walker, 'Saving the Life That Is Your Own', in *In Search of Our Mothers' Gardens* (London: Women's Press, 1984), p. 5.
35. Jung, 'The Aims of Psychotherapy', p. 50.
36. Susan Willis, 'Memory and Mass Culture', in Fabre and O'Meally (eds), *History & Memory in African-American Culture*, p. 179.
37. Braendlin, 'Alice Walker's *The Temple of My Familiar* as Pastiche', p. 49.
38. Bessie Head, 'Notes on Novels' [1978], in *A Woman Alone: Autobiographical Writings* (London: Heinemann, 1990), p. 64.
39. Ngũgĩ, 'The Language of African Literature', in *Decolonising the Mind*, p. 64.
40. Birch, *Black American Women's Writing*, p. 230.
41. Merlin Stone, *When God Was a Woman* (London: Harcourt Brace Jovanovich, 1976), p. 33. For a critique of feminist understandings and uses of the witch figure see Justyna Sempruch, 'Feminist Constructions of the "Witch" as a Fantasmatic Other', *Body & Society*, 10:4 (2004), pp. 113–33.
42. LeGuin [review of *The Temple of My Familiar*], p. 22.
43. Stone, *When God Was a Woman*, p. 20.
44. Martin Bernal, *Black Athena: The Afro-Asiatic Roots of Classical Civilization. Volume I. The Fabrication of Ancient Greece 1785–1985* [1987] (London: Vintage, 1991), pp. 51–2, 2.
45. Spelling of her name varies; see Sander Gilman, 'Black Bodies, White Bodies: Toward an Iconography of Female Sexuality in Late Nineteenth

Century Art, Medicine and Literature', in Henry Louis Gates Jr (ed.), *'Race', Writing and Difference* (London: University of Chicago Press, 1986), p. 257.

46. Interestingly, this Kroeber was Ursula LeGuin's grandfather, which might explain some of the reason why LeGuin was sympathetic to Walker's vision in *The Temple of My Familiar*.

47. The best-known source on Ishi's life is Theodora Kroeber, *Ishi in Two Worlds: A Biography of the Last Wild Indian in North America* (Berkeley: University of California Press, 1961).

48. In an essay on the genesis of *The Temple of My Familiar*, Walker does not mention any of the parallels I am tracing here; 'Turquoise and Coral: The Writing of *The Temple of My Familiar*', in *Anything We Love Can Be Saved: A Writer's Activism* (London: Women's Press, 1997), pp. 111–17.

49. Hearst adopted the *nom de guerre* 'Tania' while with the S. L. A., and a 'Tanya' appears in *The Temple of My Familiar*, as Fanny's white child-hood friend. Patricia Hearst told her own story in *Every Secret Thing* (Garden City, NY: Doubleday, 1982).

50. It is discussed as a captivity narrative in Christopher Castiglia, *Bound and Determined: Captivity, Culture-Crossing, and White Womanhood from Mary Rowlandson to Patty Hearst* (London: University of Chicago Press, 1996), pp. 87–105; and in Joan Didion, 'Girl of the Golden West', in *After Henry* (London: Simon & Schuster, 1992), pp. 95–109.

51. For extracts from the diaries and notes of these women travellers see, for example, Mary Morris (ed.), *The Virago Book of Women Travellers* (London: Virago, 1994); Rebecca Stefoff, *Women of the World: Women Travellers and Explorers* (Oxford: Oxford University Press, 1992); and Jane Robinson (ed.), *Unsuitable for Ladies: An Anthology of Women Travellers* (Oxford: Oxford University Press, 1994).

52. Deborah Anne Hooker observes the same 'disconnect from an animate landscape' in the acquisition of literacy by former slaves like Olaudah Equiano; see Deborah Anne Hooker, 'Reanimating the Trope of the Talking Book in Alice Walker's "Strong Horse Tea"', *The Southern Literary Journal*, 37:2 (2005), pp. 81–102, 88.

53. A reference to *Maru* and *A Question of Power* by Bessie Head is par-ticularly interesting, for *A Question of Power* is just as visionary a novel as *The Temple of My Familiar* wants to be, and has as its protagonist a woman who, like Miss Lissie, has two lovers and an extraordinarily rich psychic life. It is tempting, even, to see Head's character as the model for Miss Lissie, and to interpret the latter's name as an amalgam of Alice and Bessie.

54. Howard Zinn, *A People's History of the United States* [1980] (New York; Harper Collins, 1990), p. 9.

6. *POSSESSING THE SECRET OF JOY* (1992)

1. Alice Walker, *Possessing the Secret of Joy* (London: Women's Press, 1992); all page references will be given in the text.

2. Lynn Pifer and Tricia Slusser make a similar point in '"Looking at the Back of Your Head": Mirroring Scenes in Alice Walker's *The Color Purple* and *Possessing the Secret of Joy*', *MELUS*, 23:4 (Winter, 1998), pp. 47–57, 47.

3. Gay Wilentz, '"What Is Africa to Me?": Reading the African Cultural Base of (African) American Literary History', *American Literary History*, 15:3 (2003), pp. 639–53, 639.

4. Kadiatu Kanneh, *African Identities: Race, Nation and Culture in Ethnography, Pan-Africanism and Black Literatures* (London: Routledge, 1998), p. 110.

5. Eva Lennox Birch, *Black American Women's Writing: A Quilt of Many Colours* (London: Harvester Wheatsheaf, 1994), p. 238.

6. Other critics have noted this precedent in Walker's *oeuvre* too, for example Omofolabo Ajayi-Soyinka, 'Transcending the Boundaries of Power and Imperialism: Writing Gender, Constructing Knowledge', in Obioma Nnaemeka (ed.), *Female Circumcision and the Politics of Knowledge: African Women in Imperialist Discourses* (Westport, CT and London: Praeger 2005), pp. 47–77, 70; and Eloise Brière, 'Confronting the Western Gaze' in the same volume, pp. 165–80, 169.

7. Alice Walker, '*One* Child of One's Own: A Meaningful Transgression within the Work(s)' [1979], in *In Search of Our Mothers' Gardens: Womanist Prose* [1983] (London: Women's Press, 1984), p. 373.

8. Ibid., p. 361.

9. Ibid., p. 362.

10. In contrast to Walker's reading of white feminism's fear of black women's sexuality, Oyeronke Oyewumi reminds us that, on the contrary, Westerners have always had 'voyeuristic and groin-centered preoccupations with Africa', and she cites the exhibition of Saartjie Baartman in the nineteenth century (as discussed in Chapter 5) as a typical example of the West's sexualising gaze on Africa. Oyeronke Oyewumi, 'Alice in Motherland: Reading Alice Walker on Africa and Screening the Color "Black"', *Jenda: A Journal of Culture and African Women Studies*, 1:2 (2001), http://jendajournal.com/vol1.2/oyewumi.html.

11. Obioma Nnaemeka, 'African Women, Colonialist Discourses, and Imperialist Interventions', in Nnaemeka (ed.), *Female Circumcision and the Politics of Knowledge: African Women in Imperialist Discourses* (Westport, CT and London: Praeger, 2005), pp. 27–46, 34–5.

12. Whether one calls what Tashi or the women Walker and Parmar interview in *Warrior Marks* have suffered 'female genital mutilation', 'initiation', 'female circumcision', 'excision', 'infibulation', or 'clitoridectomy' makes a difference, both clinically and ideologically. Under the general heading of 'female genital mutilation', the World Health Organization distinguishes four major types, with differing consequences as regards women's sexual pleasure and childbearing: 'Clitoridectomy: partial or total removal of the clitoris (a small, sensitive and erectile part of the female genitals) and, rarely, the prepuce (the fold of skin surrounding the clitoris) as well. Excision: partial or total removal of the clitoris and the labia minora, with or without excision of the labia majora (the labia are "the lips" that surround the vagina). Infibulation: narrowing of the

vaginal opening through the creation of a covering seal. The seal is
formed by cutting and repositioning the inner, and sometimes outer,
labia, with or without removal of the clitoris. Other: all other harmful
procedures to the female genitalia for non-medical purposes, e.g. prick-
ing, piercing, incising, scraping and cauterizing the genital area'; World
Health Organization, 'Factsheet 241: Female Genital Mutilation' (May
2008) http://www.who.int/mediacentre/factsheets/fs241/en/index.
html.

13. See, for example, contributors to Obiomo Nnaemeka's collection, *Female Circumcision and the Politics of Knowledge.*
14. Christine J. Walley, 'Searching for "Voices": Feminism, Anthropology, and the Global Debate over Female Genital Operations', *Cultural Anthropology*, 12:3 (August 1997), pp. 405–38, 408.
15. Alice Walker and Pratibha Parmar, *Warrior Marks: Female Genital Mutilation and the Sexual Blinding of Women* (London: Jonathan Cape, 1993), p. 307.
16. Nontsasa Nako, 'Possessing the Voice of the Other: African Women and the "Crisis of Representation" in Alice Walker's *Possessing the Secret of Joy', Jenda: A Journal of Culture and African Women Studies*, 1:2 (2001), http://www.jendajournal.com/vol1.2/nako.html.
17. Walker, '*One* Child of One's Own', p. 379.
18. Ibid., p. 377.
19. Ibid., p. 379.
20. Ibid., p. 365.
21. See, for example, Patricia Hill Collins, *Black Feminist Thought: Knowledge, Consciousness and the Politics of Empowerment* (London: Routledge, 1991).
22. Walter J. Ong, *Orality and Literacy: The Technologizing of the Word*, New Accents Series [1982] (London: Routledge, 1988), p. 41.
23. Nawal El Saadawi, *The Hidden Face of Eve: Women in the Arab World* (London: Zed Books, 1980), p. 8.
24. Asma El Dareer, *Woman, Why Do You Weep? Circumcision and Its Consequences* (London: Zed Press, 1982); Awa Thiam, *Black Sisters, Speak Out: Feminism and Oppression in Black Africa* [1978, *La Parole aux Négresses*] (London: Pluto Press, 1986); and Efua Dorkenoo and Scilla Elworthy, *Female Genital Mutilation: Proposals for Change* (London: Minority Rights Group 1991) all appeared before *Possessing the Secret of Joy* and *Warrior Marks*; the bestsellers Waris Dirie, *Desert Flower* (London: Virago 2001) and Fauziya Kassindja et al. *Do They Hear You When You Cry?* (New York: Bantam 1999) after.
25. Ama Ata Aidoo, 'Ghana: To Be a Woman', in Robin Morgan (ed.), *Sisterhood Is Global: The International Women's Movement Anthology* (New York: Doubleday, 1984), p. 258.
26. Ibid., p. 262.
27. Olakunle George, 'Alice Walker's Africa: Globalization and the Province of Fiction', *Comparative Literature*, 53:4 (Autumn, 2001), pp. 354–72, 370.
28. Ibid.
29. I owe this reference to Gina Dent, 'Black Pleasure, Black Joy: An Introduction', in Gina Dent (ed.), *Black Popular Culture* (Seattle: Bay

Press, 1992), p. 19 and to Angeletta K. M. Gourdine, 'Postmodern Ethnography and the Womanist Mission: Postcolonial Sensibilities in *Possessing the Secret of Joy'*, *African American Review*, 30:2 (1996), p. 238.

30. Margaret Kent Bass, 'Alice's Secret', *CLA Journal*, 38:1 (September 1994), p. 5.
31. W. E. B. DuBois, *The Souls of Black Folk* [1903], rpt. in *Three Negro Classics* (New York: Avon, 1965), p. 215.
32. James Clifford, *The Predicament of Culture: Twentieth Century Ethnography, Literature and Art* (London: Harvard University Press, 1988), pp. 10, 11.
33. See for example Thiam, *Black Sisters, Speak Out* and El Saadawi, *The Hidden Face of Eve*; these are discussed further in Chapter 8.
34. Jomo Kenyatta, *Facing Mount Kenya: The Tribal Life of the Gikuyu* [1938] (London: Seeker & Warburg, 1961), p. 162. Margaret Kent Bass also rereads this text in 'Alice's Secret'.
35. Ibid., p. 133.
36. Ibid., p. 146.
37. Ibid., p. xix.
38. John Mbiti, *African Religions & Philosophy* (London: Heinemann, 1969), p. 123.
39. Ibid, p. 57.
40. L. Amede Obiora, 'The Anti-Female Circumcision Campaign Deficit', in Nnaemeka (ed.), *Female Circumcision and the Politics of Knowledge*, pp. 183–208, 189.
41. Oyeronke Oyewumi criticises Walker's representational strategy for the way it imbues anthropology with authority: 'she follows the traditional Western cultural imperialist patterns of objectifying, demonizing, and homogenizing Africa, and her debt in this regard [is to] the racism of nineteenth century French *"anthropologie"'*; Oyewumi, 'Alice in Motherland', http://www.jendajournal.com/vol.1.2/oyewumi.html.
42. For a related discussion of Clifford and Walker, see Gourdine, 'Postmodern Ethnography and the Womanist Mission'.
43. Clifford, *The Predicament of Culture*, pp. 46, 40.
44. Ibid., pp. 60, 89.
45. Ibid., p. 60.
46. For a critical examination of *animus* and *anima* see Anthony Storr, 'Archetypes and the Collective Unconscious', in *Jung*, Fontana Modern Masters (London: Fontana Press, 1986), pp. 39–61.
47. C. G. Jung, *Analytical Psychology: Its Theory and Practice (The Tavistock Lectures)* [1935] (London: Routledge, 1986), p. 155.
48. Ibid., p. 165.
49. Ibid., p. 166.
50. See for example Sander L. Gilman, 'Black Bodies, White Bodies: Toward an Iconography of Female Sexuality in Late Nineteenth Century Art, Medicine and Literature', in Henry Louis Gates Jr (ed.), *'Race', Writing and Difference* (London: University of Chicago Press, 1986), p. 257.
51. Jung, *Analytical Psychology*, p. 166.
52. Ibid., p. 181.
53. Ibid., p. 183.
54. Ibid., p. 172.

55. Ibid., p. 186.
56. Geneva Cobb Moore makes the same point in observing that 'Walker strips Africa of the romantic image bestowed upon it by black writers in the 1960s and the Harlem Renaissance of the 1920s'. Geneva Cobb Moore, 'Archetypal Symbolism in Alice Walker's *Possessing the Secret of Joy*', *Southern Literary Journal*, 33:1 (2000), pp. 111–22, 112.
57. Charles R. Larson, [review of] *'Possessing the Secret of Joy'* [5 July 1992, *The Washington Post Book World*] in Henry Louis Gates Jr and K. A. Appiah (eds), *Alice Walker: Critical Perspectives Past and Present* (New York: Amistad, 1993), pp. 27–9; Birch, *Black American Women's Writing*, p. 237.
58. Kimberley Joyce Pollock, 'A Continuum of Pain: A Woman's Legacy in Alice Walker's *Possessing the Secret of Joy*', in Elizabeth Brown-Guillory (ed.), *Women of Color: Mother–Daughter Relationships in 20th Century Literature* (Austin: University of Texas Press, 1996), pp. 38, 50; and Tina McElroy Ansa, [review of *Possessing the Secret of Joy*] [5 July 1992, *The Los Angeles Times Book Review*] in Gates and Appiah (eds), *Alice Walker*, p. 34.
59. Bass, 'Alice's Secret', pp. 10, 9. Similarly scathing responses to Walker's FGM campaign can be found in Michael C. Mbabuike, 'African Feminists and Feminisms', *African Studies Review*, 45:3 (December 2002), pp. 63–6 and a number of contributions to Obioma Nnaemeka's *Female Circumcision*, such as those from Chimalum Nkwankwo, Jude Akudinobi, and L.Amede Obiora.
60. Kadiatu Kanneh, 'Feminism and the Colonial Body', in Bill Ashcroft, Gareth Griffiths, and Helen Tiffin (eds), *The Post-Colonial Studies Reader* (London: Routledge, 1995), p. 347.
61. For a similar analysis of 'the' Third World woman in Western feminist scholarly discourse, see Chandra Talpade Mohanty's seminal essay 'Under Western Eyes: Feminist Scholarship and Colonial Discourses', in Patrick Williams and Laura Chrisman (eds), *Colonial Discourse and Post-colonial Theory: A Reader* (London: Harvester Wheatsheaf, 1993), pp. 196–220.
62. Gay Wilentz, 'Healing the Wounds of Time', *Women's Review of Books*, 10:5 (1993), pp. 16–17, 16.
63. Gourdine, 'Postmodern Ethnography and the Womanist Mission', p. 242.
64. Asma El Dareer, *Woman, Why Do You Weep? Circumcision and Its Consequences* (London: Zed Press, 1982). The copy whose marginal notes I quote is in the library at the University of Sussex, Great Britain.
65. Walker and Parmar, *Warrior Marks*, p. 270.
66. Dent, 'Black Pleasure, Black Joy', p. 4.

7. *BY THE LIGHT OF MY FATHER'S SMILE* (1998) AND *NOW IS THE TIME TO OPEN YOUR HEART* (2004)

1. Lovalerie King, 'African American Womanism: From Zora Neale Hurston to Alice Walker', in Maryemma Graham (ed.), *The Cambridge*

Companion to the African American Novel (Cambridge: Cambridge University Press, 2004), pp. 233–52, 239.

2. Alice Walker, *We Are the Ones We Have Been Waiting For: Inner Light in a Time of Darkness* (London: Weidenfeld and Nicholson, 2007), p. 133.

3. Ibid., p. 186.

4. In an interview with *Guardian* journalist Duncan Campbell, Walker said that *The Way Forward Is With a Broken Heart* may have been 'the conclusion of a 30 year writing cycle. "At the moment, I'm thinking that I may write more or I may not because I may want to do something else with the rest of my life"', http://www.guardian.co.uk/books/2001/feb/25/fiction.features1.

5. Alice Walker, *Now Is the Time to Open Your Heart: A Novel* (London: Weidenfeld and Nicholson, 2004); all page references will be given in the text.

6. Alice Walker, *By the Light of My Father's Smile: A Story of Requited Love, Crossing Over, and the Sexual Healing of the Soul* (London: Women's Press, 1998); all page references will be given in the text.

7. Jana Hecková, '"Timeless People": The Development of the Ancestral Figure in Three Novels By Alice Walker', http://www-cpopas.uni-regensburg.de/articles/issue_09/09_03_text_heckova.php.

8. Gayle Pemberton, 'Fantasy Lives', *The Women's Review of Books*, 16:3 (December 1998), pp. 20–1, 21.

9. Although again, to be fair, the predictability of this pairing is acknowledged in the text: 'Maria? I said. Her name's Maria? Goddess, I thought, how predictable' (86).

10. Audre Lorde, 'Uses of the Erotic: The Erotic as Power' [1978] in *Sister/Outsider: Essays and Speeches* (Freedom, CA: The Crossing Press, 1984), pp. 53–9.

11. Margo Maine, *Father Hunger: Fathers, Daughters & Food* (Carlsbad, CA: Gürze Books, 1991), p. 95.

12. Rudolph P. Byrd [Review of Alice Walker, *By the Light of My Father's Smile*] *African American Review*, 33:4 (Winter, 1999), pp. 719–22, 720.

13. Victoria Kingston, [Review of Alice Walker, *By the Light of My Father's Smile*], *The English Review*, 10:3 (1 February 2000), p. 9. This living man's desire to police Magdalena and Susannah's sexual lives is in many ways reminiscent of 'The Child Who Favoured Daughter', in *In Love and Trouble: Stories of Black Women* [1973] (London: Women's Press, 1984), pp. 35–46.

14. Alice Walker, *Possessing the Secret of Joy* (London: Women's Press, 1992), p. 3.

15. Pemberton, 'Fantasy Lives', p. 21.

16. Alice Walker, 'Brothers and Sisters' [1975], in *In Search of Our Mothers' Gardens* (London: Women's Press, 1984), pp. 326–31, 327.

17. Ibid., p. 327.

18. Ibid., p. 329.

19. Ibid., p. 330.

20. Alice Walker, 'The Only Reason You Go to Heaven Is That You Have Been Driven Out of Your Mind (Off Your Land and Out of Your Lover's Arms): Clear Seeing, Inherited Religion, and the Pagan Self', in

Anything We Love Can Be Saved: A Writer's Activism (London: Women's Press, 1997) pp. 3–26, 19.

21. Alice Walker, 'Father' [1984], in *Living By the Word: Selected Writings 1973–1987* (London: Women's Press, 1988), pp. 9–17, 11.

22. Ibid., p. 14.

23. The story is told once more in Evelyn White's biography: *Alice Walker: A Life* (London and New York: W. W. Norton, 2004), pp. 240–1.

24. Alice Walker, 'Kindred Spirits' in Walker, *The Way Forward Is With a Broken Heart* (London: Women's Press, 2000), pp. 64–83, 77.

25. Walker, 'When Life Descends Into the Pit', in *We Are the Ones*, pp. 38–46, 39.

26. Ibid., p. 41.

27. Ibid., p. 41.

28. Jack D. Forbes, *Africans and Native Americans: The Language of Race and the Evolution of Red-Black Peoples*, second edition (Urbana and Chicago: University of Illinois Press, 1993), p. 165; see also Chapter 5. The African presence in Mexico, however, is often ignored, which is why recently the so-called Third Root Program has been initiated to counteract discrimination through scholarship and awareness raising of Mexico's African heritage; 'Afro-Mexicans' in *World Directory of Minorities*, http://www.minorityrights.org/?lid=4455&templ=.

29. Octavio Paz, *The Labyrinth of Solitude: Life and Thought in Mexico*, trans. Lysander Kemp [1959 *El Laberinto de la Soledad*] (Harmondsworth: Penguin, 1983), p. 46.

30. Anonymous, 'Author Interview: An Interview with the Author: Alice Walker', http://www.randomhouse.com/catalog/display.pperl?isbn=97808129713928&view=auqa.

31. Peter Stafford, in an online article on *yagé*, observes that Ginsberg and Burroughs' *The Yagé Letters*, published in 1963, 'undoubtedly increased interest in this brew made from a "vine of the soul"'; Peter Stafford, 'Ayahuasca, Yagé and Harmaline', Chapter 7 of the Third Edition of the *Psychedelics Encyclopedia*, http://www.biopark.org/peru/Ayaharmaline.html.

32. David Swick, 'We Live in the Best of Times: An Interview with Alice Walker', *Shambala Sun* (May 2007), http://www.shambhalasun.com/index.php?option=com_content&task=view&id=3091&Itemid=244.

33. Anonymous, 'Author Interview', loc. cit.

34. Walker, *We Are the Ones*, p. 216.

35. Although there it is the Spanish 'Ya Es el Tiempo Para Abrir Tu Corazón', 'though originally it would have been in a language indigenous to the Americas'; ibid.

36. Anonymous, 'Archetypes', http://www.geocities.com/mindstuff/jung1.html.

37. Gerri Bates, *Alice Walker: A Critical Companion*, Critical Companions to Popular Contemporary Writers Series (Westport, CT and London: Greenwood Press, 2005), p. 169.

38. Walker, *We Are the Ones*, p. 42.

39. Ibid., p. 140.

40. Ibid., p. 139.

41. Ibid., p. 141.
42. Ibid., p. 116.
43. Roland Walter (citing an earlier article by himself), 'The Americas Between Nation-Identity and Relation-Identity: Literary Dialogues', *Interfaces Brasil/Canada, Rio Grande*, 6 (2006), pp. 233–48, 238. http://revistabecan.com.br/arquivos/1157682777.pdf.
44. Ibid., p. 241.
45. Walker, *We Are the Ones*, p. 188.
46. David Swick, 'We Live in the Best of Times', http://www.shambhalasun.com/index.php?option=com_content&task=view&id=3091&Itemid=244.
47. Although, quite rightly, the online *Encyclopedia of Gay, Lesbian, Bisexual, Transgender, and Queer Culture* warns that 'it is problematic … to use western terms such as *gay, lesbian, transgender,* or even *homosexuality* to refer to indigenous categories, as each of these English words have culturally specific meanings'. Anonymous, 'Pacific Islands', http://www.glbtq.com/social-sciences/pacific_islands.html.
48. See 'The Dummy in the Window: Joel Chandler Harris and the Invention of Uncle Remus', in Alice Walker, *Living by the Word: Selected Writings 1973–1987* (London: Women's Press, 1988), pp. 25–32.
49. Hecková, 'Timeless People', http://www-cpopas.uni-regensburg.de/articles/issue_09/09_03_text_heckova.php.
50. Campbell, 'A Long Walk to Freedom', http://www.guardian.co.uk/books/2001/feb/25/fiction.features1.
51. Anonymous, 'Author Interview' http//www.randomhouse.com/catalog/display.pperl?isbn=9780812971392&view=auqa.
52. Richard Delgado and Jean Stefancic, 'Minority Men, Misery, and the Marketplace of Ideas', in Maurice Berger, Brian Wallis, and Simon Watson (eds), *Constructing Masculinity* (London and New York: Routledge, 1995), pp. 211–20, 218.
53. Ibid., p. 219.

8. A WRITER'S ACTIVISM – AND ITS CRITICS: AN EPILOGUE

1. Alice Walker, 'Recording the Seasons' [1976], in *In Search of Our Mothers' Gardens: Womanist Prose* [1983] (London: Women's Press, 1984), p. 225.
2. See on this point also Tillie Olsen, 'The Strike', in Charlotte Nekola and Paula Rabinowitz (eds), *Writing Red: An Anthology of American Women Writers, 1930–1940* (New York: The Feminist Press, 1987), pp. 245–51; also 'Political Silences', in *Silences* (London: Virago, 1980), pp. 143–4.
3. Alice Walker, 'Introduction', to *Anything We Love Can Be Saved: A Writer's Activism* (London: Women's Press, 1997), p. xx.
4. Alice Walker, 'Acknowledgements', in *Anything We Love Can Be Saved*, p. ix.
5. Marjorie Pryse, 'Introduction: Zora Neale Hurston, Alice Walker, and the "Ancient Power" of Black Women', in Marjorie Pryse and Hortense J. Spillers (eds), *Conjuring: Black Women, Fiction, and Literary Tradition* (Bloomington: Indiana University Press, 1985), pp. 3–4.

6. Alice Walker, 'Preface' to *Her Blue Body Everything We Know: Earthling Poems 1965–1990 Complete* (London: Women's Press, 1991), p. xv; 'Author's Preface' to *The Complete Stories* (London: Women's Press, 1994), p. ix.
7. Libby Brooks, 'Nobody's Darling', *Guardian*, 29 April 1998, p. 7.
8. Alice Walker, *Overcoming Speechlessness* (New York: Seven Stories Press, 2010).
9. Many of the interviews are available on the World Wide Web, for example through organisations like feminist.com, democracynow.org, and shambalasun.com, and some have been collected in Alice Walker and Rudolph P. Byrd, *The World Has Changed: Conversations with Alice Walker* (New York: The New Press, 2010); Alice Walker, 'Foreword: We Are in This Place for a Reason' in Mumia Abu-Jamal, *All Things Censored*, edited by Noelle Hanrahan (New York: Seven Stories Press, 2001), pp. 15–19.
10. For example, *Sent by Earth: A Message from the Grandmother Spirit After the Attacks on the World Trade Center and Pentagon*, Open Media Pamphlet Series (New York: Seven Stories Press, 2001), and *Overcoming Speechlessness*.
11. Walker's website is http://www.alicewalker.info; the blog can be found at http://www.alicewalkerblog.com.
12. Alice Walker and Pratibha Parmar, *Warrior Marks: Female Genital Mutilation and the Sexual Blinding of Women* (London: Jonathan Cape, 1993), p. 18.
13. Walker and Parmar, *Warrior Marks*, p. 270.
14. Walley, 'Searching for "Voices"', p. 410.
15. This is not to deny that the *material* reality of having parts of your body removed transcends cultural difference, and therefore may seem to lend itself to transcultural empathy. But it is to say that such empathy is an act of interpretation; as a practice and as an experience female genital operations are meaningless outside the context of culture, since it is culture that constitutes them as a meaningful experience at all, whether positive or negative.
16. Victoria Moyston, 'Women Warriors' [an interview with Pratibha Parmar], *Black Film Bulletin*, 1:3–4 (Autumn–Winter, 1993–4), p. 12.
17. Chimalum Nwankwo, 'Parallax Sightlines: Alice Walker's Sisterhood and the Key to Dreams', in Nnaemeka (ed.), *Female Circumcision and the Politics of Knowledge*, pp. 219–43, 229.
18. Jude Akudinobi, 'Libidinal Quicksand: Imperial Fictions, African Femininity, and Representation', in Nnaemeka (ed.), *Female Circumcision and the Politics of Knowledge*, pp. 135–64, 150.
19. Walley, 'Searching for "Voices"', p. 429.
20. Obiomo Nnaemeka, 'The Challenges of Border-Crossing: African Women and Transnational Feminisms', in Nnaemeka (ed.), *Female Circumcision and the Politics of Knowledge*, pp. 3–18, 3.
21. Nnaemeka, 'The Challenges of Border-Crossing', p. 9.
22. Ibid., p. 14.
23. Walley, 'Searching for "Voices"', p. 427.
24. Ibid., p. 430.
25. Philip M. Royster, 'In Search of Our Father's Arms: Alice Walker's Persona of the Alienated Darling', *Black American Literature Forum*, 20:4 (Winter, 1986), p. 367.

26. Ibid., pp. 357, 361.
27. See, for example, Robert Staples on Shange and Michelle Wallace in 'The Myth of Black Macho: A Response to Angry Black Feminists', *The Black Scholar* (March–April 1979), pp. 24–33; Mel Watkins, 'Sexism, Racism and Black Women Writers', *New York Times Book Review*, 15 June 1986, pp. 1–3; and Darryl Pinckney, 'Black Victims, Black Villains', *The New York Review of Books*, 29 January 1987, pp. 17–20.
28. Some of the best Walker criticism has been written by African American men such as Henry Louis Gates Jr, Houston Baker, and Calvin Hernton, as well as black and white feminist critics, and some white men.
29. Walker, *We Are the Ones*, p. 186.
30. Sharon Wilson, 'An Interview with Alice Walker' [1984], in Gates and Appiah (eds), *Alice Walker*, p. 320.
31. Alice Walker, 'Getting as Black as My Daddy: Thoughts on the Unhelpful Aspects of Destructive Criticism', in *Anything We Love Can Be Saved*, p. 151.
32. Alice Walker, *Banned* (San Francisco: Aunt Lute Books, 1996), p. 87.
33. Patricia Holt, 'Introduction', in Alice Walker, *Banned*, p. 1.
34. Ikenna Dieke, 'Introduction: Alice Walker, a Woman Walking into Peril', in Ikenna Dieke (ed.), *Critical Essays on Alice Walker*, pp. 1–12.
35. Alice Hall Petry, 'Walker: The Achievement of the Short Fiction', in Henry Louis Gates Jr and K. A. Appiah (eds), *Alice Walker: Critical Perspectives Past and Present* (New York: Amistad, 1993), p. 204.
36. David Bradley, in an otherwise thoughtful article, 'Telling the Black Woman's Story', *New York Times Magazine* (January 1984), p. 32.
37. Manning Marable, 'Rethinking Black Liberation: Towards a New Protest Paradigm', *Race & Class*, 38:4 (April–June 1997), p. 10.
38. Ibid., p. 9.
39. Alice Walker, 'What That Day Was Like For Me: The Million Man March' and 'A Letter to President Clinton', both in *Anything We Love Can Be Saved*, pp. 106, 209. Marable, 'Rethinking Black Liberation', pp. 7, 5.
40. Walker, 'A Letter to President Clinton', p. 209.
41. Laurie McMillan, 'Telling a Critical Story: Alice Walker's *In Search of Our Mothers' Gardens*', *Journal of Modern Literature*, 28:1 (2004), pp. 107–23, 110.
42. Pierre Tristam, 'Overcoming Speechlessness: Alice Walker in Gaza', http://middleeast.about.com/b/2009/07/28/overcoming-speechless ness-alice-walker-in-gaza/.
43. Alice Walker, '"You All Have Seen": If the Women of the World Were Comfortable, This Would be a Comfortable World', in *Anything We Love Can Be Saved*, p. 31.
44. Alice Walker, 'Lest We Forget: An Open Letter to My Sisters, Who Are Brave', *Meridians: Feminism, Race, Transnationalism*, 9:1 (2009), pp. 183–8, 184, 186.
45. Ibid., p. 186.
46. Ibid., p. 185.
47. Ibid., p. 185.
48. Evelyn C. White's biography, *Alice Walker: A Life* (New York and London: W. W. Norton, 2004) refers to some of Walker's activist travels.

More recent coverage can be found on the World Wide Web, including a video of Walker taken in her kitchen in support of the Obama campaign in 2007, http://www.youtube.com/watch?v=W3-9gq_htUo; and getting herself arrested on International Women's Day, 2003. Amy Goodman, '"I Am a Renegade, an Outlaw, a Pagan" – Author, Poet and Activist Alice Walker in her own Words', http://www.democracynow.org/2006/2/13/i_am_a_renegade_an_outlaw.

49. Brooks, 'Nobody's Darling', p. 7.
50. Sojourner Truth was illiterate and did not write, but her *Narrative of Sojourner Truth* was recorded by Olive Gilbert; *The Life and Religious Experiences of Jarena Lee, a Colored Lady* and *An Autobiography: The Story of the Lord's Dealings with Mrs Amanda Smith, the Colored Evangelist* have both been published in the Schomburg Library of Nineteenth Century Black Women Writers, and Rebecca Cox Jackson's writings have been collected and edited by Jean McMahon Humez as *Gifts of Power: the Writings of Rebecca Jackson, Black Visionary, Shaker Eldress* (Amherst: University of Massachusetts Press, 1981).
51. Alice Walker, 'Gifts of Power: the Writings of Rebecca Jackson' [1981], in *In Search of Our Mother's Gardens*, pp. 78–9.
52. Henry Louis Gates Jr, 'Color Me Zora', in Gates and Appiah (eds), *Alice Walker*, p. 243.
53. Alice Walker, *Sent by Earth: A Message from the Grandmother Spirit After the Attacks on the World Trade Center and Pentagon*, Open Media Pamphlet Series (New York: Seven Stories Press, 2001), p. 47.
54. Monica Sjöö and Barbara Mor, *The Great Cosmic Mother: Rediscovering the Religion of the Earth*, second edition (San Francisco: Harper, 1991), p. 335.
55. Ibid., p. 336.
56. Hortense J. Spillers, 'Afterword: Cross-Currents, Discontinuities: Black Women's Fiction', in Pryse and Spillers (eds), *Conjuring*, pp. 249–61, 250.
57. Henry Louis Gates Jr, 'Introduction', to Henry Louis Gates Jr (ed.), *Reading Black, Reading Feminist: A Critical Anthology* (New York: Meridian, 1990), p. 7.
58. See, for example, Lillie P. Howard (ed.), *Alice Walker and Zora Neale Hurston: The Common Bond* (London: Greenwood Press, 1993); on Walker and Wright, Spillers, 'Afterword: Cross-Currents, Discontinuities', pp. 254–6; on Walker and Harper, Deborah E. McDowell, '"The Changing Same": Generational Connections and Black Women Novelists', in Gates (ed.), *Reading Black, Reading Feminist*, pp. 91–115 and McDowell, *"The Changing Same": Black Women's Writing, Criticism, and Theory* (Bloomington: Indiana University Press 1995); on Walker and Ellison David Wyatt, 'Alice Walker', in *Out of the Sixties: Storytelling and the Vietnam Generation* (Cambridge: Cambridge University Press, 1993), pp. 122–37.
59. Pryse and Spillers (eds), *Conjuring*, p. 21.
60. Spillers, 'Afterword', p. 251.
61. See for example Mc Dowell's reading of Frances Ellen Watkins Harper in dialogue with Alice Walker, particularly on the representation of

sexuality in '"The Changing Same": Generational Connections and Black Women Novelists – *Iola Leroy* and *The Color Purple*', in Deborah E. McDowell, *"The Changing Same": Black Women's Literature, Criticism, and Theory* (Bloomington: Indiana University Press 1995), pp. 34–57.

62. Spillers, 'Afterword', p. 259.

63. Cheryl A. Wall, *Worrying the Line: Black Women Writers, Lineage, and Literary Tradition* (Chapel Hill and London: University of North Carolina Press, 2005), p. 245.

64. Hortense Spillers, '"All the Things You Could Be by Now, If Sigmund Freud's Wife Was Your Mother": Psychoanalysis and Race', *boundary 2*, 23:2 (1996), pp. 76–141, 100.

65. E. Shelley Reid, 'Beyond Morrison and Walker: Looking Good and Looking Forward in Contemporary Black Women's Stories', *African American Review*, 34: 2 (Summer, 2000), pp. 313–28, 314.

66. Ibid., p. 321.

67. A sentence such as 'This image of white boys out of control, drunk and hurling the word *nigger* around, frightens me, reminds me of lynching photographs I've seen', has the same chilling quality that her mother's prose often has. Jumping from the postmodern present into the violent, segregated Southern past within the space of a few words, this line could have come from Alice Walker's pen just as easily; Rebecca Walker, *Black, White, and Jewish: Autobiography of a Shifting Self* (New York: Riverhead, 2001), p. 288.

68. Françoise Lionnet, *Postcolonial Representations: Women, Literature, Identity* (London: Cornell University Press, 1995), p. 5.

69. Alice Walker, *We Are the Ones We Have Been Waiting For: Inner Light in a Time of Darkness* (London: Weidenfeld and Nicholson, 2007), p. 186.

Select Bibliography

WORKS BY ALICE WALKER

The Third Life of Grange Copeland [1970] rpt. with a new Afterword (London: Women's Press, 1991).

In Love and Trouble: Stories of Black Women [1973] (London: Women's Press, 1984).

Meridian [1976] (London: Women's Press, 1983).

(ed.), *I Love Myself When I Am Laughing ... And Then Again When I Am Looking Mean and Impressive: A Zora Neale Hurston Reader* (New York: The Feminist Press, 1979).

The Color Purple [1982] (London: Women's Press, 1983).

You Can't Keep a Good Woman Down (London: Women's Press, 1982).

In Search of Our Mothers' Gardens: Womanist Prose [1983] (London: Women's Press, 1984).

Living by the Word: Selected Writings 1973–1987 [1986] (London: Women's Press, 1986).

To Hell with Dying (London: Harcourt Brace, 1988).

'The Right to Life: What Can the White Man ... Say to the Black Woman?' *The Nation*, 22 May 1989, rpt. in Katrina Vanden Heuvel (ed.), *The Nation: Selections from the Independent Magazine of Politics and Culture 1865/1990* (London: Pluto Press, 1991), pp. 460–3.

The Temple of My Familiar [1989] (Harmondsworth: Penguin, 1990).

Finding the Green Stone (London: Hodder & Stoughton, 1991).

Her Blue Body Everything We Know: Earthling Poems 1965–1990 Complete (London: Women's Press, 1991).

Possessing the Secret of Joy (London: Women's Press, 1992).

with Pratibha Parmar, *Warrior Marks: Female Genital Mutilation and the Sexual Blinding of Women* (London: Jonathan Cape, 1993).

The Complete Stories (London: Women's Press, 1994).

The Same River Twice: Honoring the Difficult. A Meditation on Life, Spirit, Art and the Making of the Film The Color Purple *Ten Years Later* (London: Women's Press, 1996).

Banned, with an introduction by Patricia Holt (San Francisco: Aunt Lute Books, 1996).

Anything We Love Can Be Saved: A Writer's Activism (London: Women's Press, 1997).

By the Light of My Father's Smile (London: Women's Press, 1998).

The Way Forward Is With a Broken Heart (London: Women's Press, 2000).

'Foreword: We Are in This Place for a Reason', in Mumia Abu-Jamal, *All Things Censored*, edited by Noelle Hanrahan (New York: Seven Stories Press, 2001), pp. 15–19.

269

Sent by Earth: A Message from the Grandmother Spirit After the Attacks on the World Trade Center and Pentagon, Open Media Pamphlet Series (New York: Seven Stories Press, 2001).

A Poem Traveled Down My Arm: Poems and Drawings (New York: Random House, 2003).

Absolute Trust in the Goodness of the Earth: New Poems (New York: Random House, 2003).

Now Is the Time to Open Your Heart: A Novel (London: Weidenfeld and Nicholson, 2004).

We Are the Ones We Have Been Waiting For: Inner Light in a Time of Darkness (London: Weidenfeld and Nicholson, 2007).

Overcoming Speechlessness (New York: Seven Stories Press, 2010).

INTERVIEWS

Anonymous, 'Author Interview: An Interview with the Author: Alice Walker', http://www.randomhouse.com/catalog/display.pperl?isbn=97808129713928&view=auqa.

Berger, Rose Marie, 'Interview with Alice Walker', http://thumperscorner.com/cgi/discus/board-admin.cgi?action=quick&do=.

Campbell, Duncan, 'A Long Walk to Freedom', *The Observer*, 25 February 2001, http://www.guardian.co.uk/books/2001/feb/25/fiction.features1.

Goodman, Amy, '"I Am a Renegade, an Outlaw, a Pagan" – Author, Poet and Activist Alice Walker in Her Own Words', http://democracynow.org/2006/2/13/i_am_a_renegade_an_outlaw.

O'Brien, John, 'Alice Walker: An Interview' [1973], in Gates and Appiah (eds), *Alice Walker*, pp. 326–46.

Swick, David, 'We Live in the Best of All Times: A Conversation with Alice Walker', http://www.shambhalasun.com.

Walker, Alice and Rudolph P. Byrd, *The World Has Changed: Conversations with Alice Walker* (New York: The New Press, 2010).

Wilson, Sharon, 'An Interview with Alice Walker' [*Kalliope*, 6:2 (1984)], rpt. in Gates and Appiah (eds), *Alice Walker*, pp. 319–25.

CRITICISM AND CONTEXT

Abbandonato, Linda, 'Rewriting the Heroine's Story in *The Color Purple*', in Gates and Appiah (eds), *Alice Walker*, pp. 296–308.

Abend-David, Dror, 'The Occupational Hazard: The Loss of Historical Context in Twentieth Century Feminist Readings, and a New Reading of the Heroine's Story in Alice Walker's *The Color Purple*', in I. Dieke (ed.), *Critical Essays on Alice Walker*, pp. 13–20.

Aidoo, Ama Ata, 'Ghana: To Be a Woman', in Robin Morgan (ed.), *Sisterhood Is Global: The International Women's Movement Anthology* (New York: Doubleday, 1984), pp. 258–65.

Allan, Tuzyline Jita, *Womanist & Feminist Aesthetics: A Comparative Review* (Athens: Ohio University Press, 1995).

Appiah, Kwame Anthony, *In My Father's House: Africa in the Philosophy of Culture* (Oxford: Oxford University Press, 1992).

Awkward, Michael, *Inspiriting Influences: Tradition, Revision and Afro-American Women's Novels* (New York: Columbia University Press, 1989).

Babb, Valerie 'The Color Purple: Writing to Undo What Writing Has Done', *Phylon*, 47:2 (June 1986), pp. 107–16.

——, *Workings of the Spirit: The Poetics of Afro-American Women's Writing* (London: University of Chicago Press, 1991).

Banks, Emma Davis and Keith Byerman, *Alice Walker: An Annotated Bibliography, 1968–1986* (New York: Garland, 1989).

Bass, Margaret Kent, 'Alice's Secret', *CLA Journal*, 38:1 (September 1994), pp. 1–10.

Bates, Gerri, *Alice Walker: A Critical Companion*, Critical Companions to Popular Contemporary Writers Series (Westport, CT and London: Greenwood Press, 2005).

Berlant, Lauren, 'Race, Gender and Nation in *The Color Purple*', in Gates and Appiah (eds), *Alice Walker*, pp. 211–39.

Birch, Eva Lennox, *Black American Women's Writing: A Quilt of Many Colours* (London: Harvester Wheatsheaf, 1994).

Blauner, Bob, *Black Lives, White Lives: Three Decades of Race Relations in America* (Berkeley: University of California Press, 1989).

Bloom, Harold (ed.), *Alice Walker: Modern Critical Views* (New York: Chelsea House, 1988).

Blount, Marcellus, and George P. Cunningham (eds), *Representing Black Men* (Routledge: New York and London 1996).

Bobo, Jacqueline, 'The Color Purple: Black Women as Cultural Readers', in E. Deirdre Pribram (ed.), *Female Spectators: Looking at Film and Television* (London: Verso, 1988), pp. 90–109.

Boetcher Joeres, Ruth-Ellen and Elizabeth Mittman (eds), *The Politics of the Essay: Feminist Perspectives* (Bloomington: Indiana University Press, 1993).

Bradley, David, 'Telling the Black Woman's Story', *New York Times Magazine* (January 1984), pp. 24–37.

Braendlin, Bonnie, 'Alice Walker's *The Temple of My Familiar* as Pastiche', *American Literature*, 68:1 (March, 1996), pp. 47–67.

Brooks, Libby, 'Nobody's Darling', *Guardian*, 29 April 1998, pp. 6–7.

Butler-Evans, Elliott, *Race, Gender and Desire: Narrative Strategies in the Fiction of Toni Cade Bambara, Toni Morrison and Alice Walker* (Philadelphia: Temple University Press, 1989).

Butler, Robert James, 'Alice Walker's Vision of the South in *The Third Life of Grange Copeland*', *African American Review*, 27:2, Black South Issue, Part 2 of 2 (1993), pp. 195–204.

Cade, Toni (ed.), *The Black Woman: An Anthology* (New York: New American Library, 1970).

Callahan, John F., 'The Hoop of Language: Politics and the Restoration of Voice in *Meridian*', in H. Bloom (ed.), *Alice Walker*, pp. 153–84.

Carby, Hazel, 'The Politics of Fiction, Anthropology, and the Folk: Zora Neale Hurston', in Fabre and O'Meally (eds), *History & Memory in African-American Culture*, pp. 28–44.

Cheung, King-Kok, '"Don't Tell": Imposed Silences in *The Color Purple* and *The Woman Warrior'*, *PMLA*, 103:2 (March 1988), pp. 162–74.

Christian, Barbara, *Black Feminist Criticism: Perspectives on Black Women Writers* (New York: Pergamon, 1985).

Clifford, James, *The Predicament of Culture: Twentieth Century Ethnography, Literature and Art* (London: Harvard University Press, 1988).

Cochran, Kate, '"When the Lessons Hurt": *The Third Life of Grange Copeland* as Joban Allegory', *Southern Literary Journal*, 34:1 (Fall 2001) pp. 79–91.

Collins, Patricia Hill, *Black Feminist Thought: Knowledge, Consciousness, and the Politics of Empowerment*, Perspectives on Gender, vol. 2 (London: Routledge, 1991).

Cooke, Michael, *Afro-American Literature in the Twentieth Century: The Achievement of Intimacy* (London: Yale University Press, 1984).

Crawford, Vicki L., Jacqueline Anne Rouse, and Barbara Woods (eds), *Women in the Civil Rights Movement: Torchbearers and Trailblazers 1941–1965* [1990] (Bloomington: Indiana University Press, 1993).

Cutter, Martha, 'Philomela Speaks: Alice Walker's Revisioning of Rape Archetypes in *The Color Purple'*, *MELUS*, 25:3–4 (Autumn–Winter, 2000), pp. 161–80.

Davies, Carole Boyce, *Black Women, Writing and Identity: Migrations of the Subject* (London: Routledge, 1994).

—— (ed.), *Moving Beyond Boundaries: Vol. 2, Black Women's Diasporas* (London: Pluto Press, 1995).

—— and 'Molara Ogundipe-Leslie (eds), *Moving Beyond Boundaries: Vol. 1, International Dimensions of Black Women's Writing* (London: Pluto Press, 1995).

Davis, Amanda, 'To Build a Nation: Black Women Writers, Black Nationalism, and the Violent Reduction of Wholeness', *Frontiers: A Journal of Women's Studies*, 26:3 (2005), pp. 24–53.

Davis, Angela, *Women, Race and Class* (London: Women's Press, 1982).

Dehay, Terry, 'Narrating Memory', in Singh et al. (eds), *Memory, Narrative and Identity*, pp. 26–44.

Delgado, Richard, and Jean Stefancic, 'Minority Men, Misery, and the Marketplace of Ideas', in Maurice Berger, Brian Wallis, and Simon Watney (eds), *Constructing Masculinity* (London and New York: Routledge, 1995), pp. 211–20.

Dent, Gina (ed.), *Black Popular Culture* (Seattle: Bay Press, 1992).

Dieke, Ikenna (ed.), *Critical Essays on Alice Walker* (Westport, CT and London: Greenwood Press, 1999).

——, 'Introduction: Alice Walker, a Woman Walking into Peril', in I. Dieke (ed.), *Critical Essays on Alice Walker*, pp. 1–12.

——, 'Walker's *The Temple of My Familiar*: Womanist as Monistic Idealist', in I. Dieke (ed.) *Critical Essays on Alice Walker*, pp. 127–39.

Dubey, Madhu, *Black Women Novelists and the Nationalist Aesthetic* (Bloomington: Indiana University Press, 1994).

Duck, Leigh Anne, 'Listening to Melancholia: Alice Walker's *Meridian*', *Patterns of Prejudice*, 42:4–5 (2008), pp. 439–64.

El Dareer, Asma, *Woman, Why Do You Weep? Circumcision and Its Consequences* (London: Zed Press, 1982).

El Saadawi, Nawal, *The Hidden Face of Eve: Women in the Arab World* (London: Zed Books, 1980).

Ensslen, Klaus, 'Collective Experience and Individual Responsibility: Alice Walker's *The Third Life of Grange Copeland*', in Peter Bruck and Wolfgang Karrer (eds), *The Afro-American Novel since 1960* (Amsterdam: Gruner, 1982), pp. 189–218.

Erickson, Peter, '"Cast Out Alone/to Heal/and Recreate Ourselves": Family-Based Identity in the Work of Alice Walker', in H. Bloom (ed.), *Alice Walker*, pp. 5–24.

Evans, Sara, *Personal Politics: The Roots of Women's Liberation in the Civil Rights Movement and the New Left* (New York: Random House, 1979).

Fabre, Géneviève and Robert O'Meally (eds), *History & Memory in African-American Culture* (New York: Oxford University Press, 1994).

Fanon, Frantz, *Black Skin, While Masks* [1952] (London: Pluto Press, 1986).

Fifer, Elizabeth, 'Alice Walker: The Dialect and Letters of *The Color Purple*', in Catherine Rainwater and William J. Schweick (eds), *Contemporary American Women Writers: Narrative Strategies* (Lexington: University Press of Kentucky, 1985), pp. 155–71.

Fiske, Shanyn, 'Piecing the Patchwork Self: A Reading of Walker's *The Color Purple*', *The Explicator*, 66:3 (Spring, 2008), pp. 150–3.

Forbes, Jack D., *Africans and Native Americans: the Language of Race and the Evolution of Red-Black Peoples*, second edition (Urbana and Chicago: University of Illinois Press, 1993).

Freud, Sigmund, 'Family Romances' [1909], in Sigmund Freud, *On Sexuality: Three Essays on the Theory of Sexuality and Other Works*, The Pelican Freud Library, vol. 7 (Harmondsworth: Penguin, 1977).

Froula, Christine, 'The Daughter's Seduction: Sexual Violence and Literary History', *Signs*, 11:4 (Summer, 1986), pp. 621–44.

Gates, Henry Louis Jr, *The Signifying Monkey: A Theory of African-American Literary Criticism* (Oxford: Oxford University Press, 1989).

—— (ed.), *Reading Black, Reading Feminist: A Critical Anthology* (New York: Meridian, 1990).

——, 'Color Me Zora', in Gates and Appiah (eds), *Alice Walker*, pp. 239–60.

—— and K. A. Appiah (eds), *Alice Walker: Critical Perspectives Past and Present* (New York: Amistad, 1993).

George, Olakunle, 'Alice Walker's Africa: Globalization and the Province of Fiction', *Comparative Literature* 53:4 (Autumn, 2001), pp. 354–72.

Gilroy, Paul, *The Black Atlantic: Modernity and Double Consciousness* (London: Verso, 1993).

Gourdine, Angeletta K. M., 'Postmodern Ethnography and the Womanist Mission: Postcolonial Sensibilities in *Possessing the Secret of Joy*', *African American Review*, 30:2 (1996), pp. 237–44.

Hall, Christine, 'Art, Action and the Ancestors: Alice Walker's *Meridian* in Its Context', in Gina Wisker (ed.), *Black Women's Writing* (London: Macmillan, 1993), pp. 96–110.

274 *Select Bibliography*

Harper, Philip Brian, Anne McClintock, José Esteban Muñoz, and Trish Rosen, 'Queer Transexions of Race, Nation, and Gender', *Social Text*, 52:3 (Autumn–Winter, 1997), pp. 1–4.

Harris, Trudier, 'Folklore in the Fiction of Alice Walker: A Perpetuation of Historical and Literary Traditions', *Black American Literature Forum*, 11:1 (Spring, 1977), pp. 3–8.

Hecková, Jana, '"Timeless People": The Development of the Ancestral Figure in Three Novels By Alice Walker', http://www-cpopas.uni-regensburg.de/articles/issue_09/09_03_text_heckova.php.

Hendrickson, Roberta M., 'Remembering the Dream: Alice Walker, *Meridian*, and the Civil Rights Movement', *MELUS*, 24:3 (Autumn, 1999), pp. 111–28.

Hernton, Calvin C., *The Sexual Mountain and Black Women Writers: Adventures in Sex, Literature, and Real Life* (New York: Doubleday, 1987).

Hite, Molly, *The Other Side of the Story: Structures and Strategies of Contemporary Feminist Narrative* (London: Cornell University Press, 1989).

——, 'Romance, Marginality and Matrilineage: *The Color Purple* and *Their Eyes Were Watching God*', in Gates (ed.), *Reading Black, Reading Feminist*, pp. 431–54.

Hogue, W. Lawrence, 'Discourse of the Other: *The Third Life of Grange Copeland*', in H. Bloom (ed.), *Alice Walker*, pp. 97–114.

——, 'History, the Feminist Discourse, and Alice Walker's *The Third Life of Grange Copeland*', *MELUS*, 12:2 (1985), pp. 45–62.

Holloway, Karla F. C., *Moorings and Metaphors: Figures of Culture and Gender in Black Women's Literature* (New Brunswick: Rutgers University Press, 1992).

Hooker, Deborah Anne, 'Reanimating the Trope of the Talking Book in Alice Walker's "Strong Horse Tea"', *The Southern Literary Journal*, 37:2 (2005), pp. 81–102.

hooks, bell, *Ain't I a Woman: Black Women and Feminism* (London: Pluto Press, 1982).

——, *Outlaw Culture: Resisting Representation* (London: Routledge, 1994).

Howard, Lillie P. (ed.), *Alice Walker and Zora Neale Hurston: The Common Bond* (London: Greenwood Press, 1993).

Hull, Gloria T., Patricia Bell Scott, and Barbara Smith (eds), *All the Women Are White, All the Men Are Black, But Some of Us Are Brave: Black Women's Studies* (Old Westbury: The Feminist Press, 1982).

Iannone, Carol, 'A Turning of the Critical Tide?' *Commentary*, 88:5 (November, 1989), pp. 57–9.

Jablon, Madelyn, *Black Metafiction: Self-Consciousness in African American Literature* (Iowa City: University of Iowa Press, 1997).

Jenkins, Candice M. 'Queering Black Patriarchy: The Salvific Wish and Masculine Possibility in Alice Walker's *The Color Purple*', *MFS Modern Fiction Studies*, 48:4 (2002), pp. 969–1000.

Johnson, E. Patrick and Mae G. Henderson (eds), *Black Queer Studies: A Critical Anthology* (Durham: Duke University Press, 2005).

Johnson, Maria V., '"You Just Can't Keep a Good Woman Down": Alice Walker Sings the Blues', *African American Review*, 30:2 (Summer, 1996), pp. 221–36.

Jones, LeRoi, *Blues People: Negro Music in White America* (New York: Morrow Quill, 1963).

Jordan, June, *Moving Towards Home: Political Essays* (London: Virago, 1989).

——, *Technical Difficulties: Selected Political Essays* (London: Virago, 1992).

Jung, Carl G., *Analytical Psychology: Its Theory and Practice* (*The Tavistock Lectures*) [1935] (London: Routledge, 1986).

——, *The Practice of Psychotherapy: Essays on the Psychology of the Transference and Other Subjects*, second edition, trans. R. F. C. Hull (London: Routledge, 1993).

——, M. L. von Franz, Joseph L. Henderson, Jolande Jacobi, and Aniela Jaffé (eds), *Man and His Symbols* [1964] (London: Picador, 1978).

Kanneh, Kadiatu, 'Mixed Feelings: When My Mother's Garden is Unfamiliar', in Sally Ledger, Josephine McDonagh, and Jane Spencer (eds), *Political Gender: Texts and Contexts* (London: Harvester Wheatsheaf, 1994), pp. 28–36.

——, 'Feminism and the Colonial Body', in Bill Ashcroft, Gareth Griffiths, and Helen Tiffin (eds), *The Post-Colonial Studies Reader* (London: Routledge, 1995), pp. 346–8.

——, *African Identities: Race, Nation and Culture in Ethnography, Pan-Africanism and Black Literatures* (London: Routledge, 1998).

Kaplan, Cora, 'Keeping the Color in *The Color Purple*', in *Sea Changes: Essays in Culture and Feminism* (London: Verso, 1986), pp. 177–87.

Karrer, Wolfgang, 'Nostalgia, Amnesia, and Grandmothers: the Uses of Memory in Albert Murray, Sabine Ulibarri, Paula Gunn Allen, and Alice Walker', in Singh et al. (eds), *Memory, Narrative and Identity*, pp. 128–44.

Katz, Tamar, '"Show Me How to *Do* Like You": Didacticism and Epistolary Form in *The Color Purple*', in H. Bloom (ed.), *Alice Walker*, pp. 185–93.

King, Lovalerie, 'African American Womanism: From Zora Neale Hurston to Alice Walker', in Maryemma Graham (ed.), *The Cambridge Companion to the African American Novel* (Cambridge: Cambridge University Press, 2004), pp. 233–52.

Kubitschek, Missy Dehn, 'Subjugated Knowledge: Towards a Feminist Exploration of Rape in Afro-American Fiction', in Joel Weixlmann and Houston A. Baker Jr (eds), *Black Feminist Criticism and Critical Theory* (Greenwood: Penkevill, 1988), pp. 43–56.

Lauret, Maria, *Liberating Literature: Feminist Fiction in America* (London: Routledge, 1994).

——, 'Alice Walker', in Henry Louis Gates Jr. and Evelyn Brooks Higginbotham (eds), *African American Lives* (New York and Oxford: Oxford University Press, 2004), pp. 840–2.

——, 'Alice Walker', in David Seed (ed.), *A Companion to Twentieth Century United States Fiction* (Oxford: Wiley-Blackwell, 2009), pp. 489–96.

Leder, Priscilla, 'Alice Walker's American Quilt: *The Color Purple* and American Literary Tradition', in Dieke (ed.), *Critical Essays on Alice Walker*, pp. 141–51.

Lerner, Gerda (ed.), *Black Women in White America: A Documentary History* (New York: Panther, 1972).

Light, Alison, 'Fear of the Happy Ending: *The Color Purple*, Reading, and Racism', in Linda Anderson (ed.), *Plotting Change: Contemporary Women's Fiction* (London: Edward Arnold, 1990), pp. 85–98.

Lorde, Audre, 'Uses of the Erotic: the Erotic as Power', in *Sister/Outsider: Essays and Speeches*, The Crossing Press Feminist Series (Freedom, CA: The Crossing Press, 1984).

Mbiti, John, *African Religions & Philosophy* (London: Heinemann, 1969).

McDowell, Deborah E., *"The Changing Same": Black Women's Literature, Criticism, and Theory* (Bloomington: Indiana University Press, 1995).

——, 'The Self in Bloom: Walker's *Meridian*', in Gates and Appiah (eds), *Alice Walker*, pp. 168–78.

McGowan, Martha J., 'Atonement and Release in Alice Walker's *Meridian*', *Studies in Modern Fiction*, 23:1 (1981), pp. 25–36.

McMillan, Laurie, 'Telling a Critical Story: Alice Walker's *In Search of Our Mothers' Gardens*', *Journal of Modern Literature*, 28:1 (2004), pp. 107–23.

Marriott, David, *On Black Men* (New York: Columbia University Press, 2000).

Mickelsen, David J., '"You Ain't Never Caught a Rabbit": Covering and Signifyin' in Alice Walker's "Nineteen Fifty-Five"', *Southern Quarterly*, 42:3 (Spring, 2004), pp. 5–21.

Miller, Alice, *Banished Knowledge: Facing Childhood Injuries* [1988: *Das Verbannte Wissen*] (London: Virago, 1991).

Mohanty, Chandra Talpade, 'Under Western Eyes: Feminist Scholarship and Colonial Discourses', in Patrick Williams and Laura Chrisman (eds), *Colonial Discourse and Post-Colonial Theory: A Reader* (London: Harvester Wheatsheaf, 1993), pp. 196–220.

Moody, Ann, *Coming of Age in Mississippi* (New York: Doubleday, 1968).

Moore, Geneva Cobb, 'Archetypal Symbolism in Alice Walker's *Possessing the Secret of Joy*', *Southern Literary Journal*, 33:1 (2000), pp. 111–22.

Morrison, Toni, Unspeakable Things Unspoken: The Afro-American Presence in American Literature', *Michigan Quarterly Review* (Winter, 1988), pp. 1–34.

Moyston, Victoria, 'Women Warriors' [an interview with Pratibha Parmar], *Black Film Bulletin*, 1:3–4 (Autumn–Winter, 1993–4), pp. 12–13.

Nadel, Alan, 'Reading the Body: *Meridian* and the Archeology of Self', in Gates and Appiah (eds), *Alice Walker*, pp. 155–67.

Nako, Nontsasa, 'Possessing the Voice of the Other: African Women and the "Crisis of Representation" in Alice Walker's *Possessing the Secret of Joy*', *Jenda: A Journal of Culture and African Women Studies*, 1:2 (2001) http://www.jendajournal.com/vol1.2/nako.html.

Nnaemeka, Obioma, (ed.), *Female Circumcision and the Politics of Knowledge: African Women in Imperialist Discourses* (Westport, CT and London: Praeger, 2005).

Nora, Pierre, 'Between Memory and History: *Les Lieux de Mémoire*', in Fabre and O'Meally (eds), *History and Memory in African-American Culture*, pp. 284–300.

Ong, Walter J., *Orality and Literacy: The Technologizing of the Word*, New Accents Series [1982] (London: Routledge, 1989).

Oyewumi, Oyeronke, 'Alice in Motherland: Reading Alice Walker on Africa and Screening the Color "Black"', *Jenda: A Journal of Culture and African Women Studies*, 1:2 (2001) http://www.iiav.nl/ezines/web/JENda/Vol1(2001)Nr2/jendajournal/oyewumi.pdf.

Pemberton, Gayle, 'Fantasy Lives', *The Women's Review of Books*, 16:3 (December 1998), pp. 20–1.

Petry, Alice Hall, 'Walker: The Achievement of the Short Fiction', in Gates and Appiah (eds), *Alice Walker*, pp. 193–210.

Pifer, Lynn, and Tricia Slusser, '"Looking at the Back of Your Head": Mirroring Scenes in Alice Walker's *The Color Purple* and *Possessing the Secret of Joy*', *MELUS*, 23:4 (Winter, 1998), pp. 47–57.

Pinckney, Darryl, 'Black Victims, Black Villains', *The New York Review of Books*, 29 January 1987, pp. 17–20.

Placksin, Sally, *Jazzwomen 1900 to the Present: Their Lives and Music* [1982] (London: Pluto Press, 1985).

Pollock, Kimberley Joyce, 'A Continuum of Pain: A Woman's Legacy in Alice Walker's *Possessing the Secret of Joy*', in Elizabeth Brown-Guillory (ed.), *Women of Color: Mother–Daughter Relationships in 20th Century Literature* (Austin: University of Texas Press, 1996), pp. 38–56.

Pratt, Ray, *Rhythm and Resistance: Explorations in the Political Uses of Popular Music* (New York: Praeger, 1990).

Proudfit, Charles, 'Celie's Search for Identity: A Psychoanalytic Developmental Reading of Alice Walker's *The Color Purple*', *Contemporary Literature*, 32:1 (Spring, 1991), pp. 12–37.

Pryse, Marjorie and Hortense J. Spillers (eds), *Conjuring: Black Women, Fiction, and Literary Tradition* (Bloomington: Indiana University Press, 1985).

Raines, Howell, *My Soul Is Rested: Movement Days in the Deep South Remembered* [1977] (New York: Bantam, 1978).

Reid, E. Shelley, 'Beyond Morrison and Walker: Looking Good and Looking Forward in Contemporary Black Women's Stories', *African American Review*, 34:2 (Summer, 2000), pp. 313–28.

Ross, Daniel W., 'Celie in the Looking Glass: The Desire for Selfhood in *The Color Purple*', *Modern Fiction Studies*, 34:1 (1988), pp. 69–84.

Ross, Marlon B., 'In Search of Black Men's Masculinities', *Feminist Studies*, 24:3 (Autumn, 1998), pp. 599–626.

Royster, Philip M., 'In Search of Our Father's Arms: Alice Walker's Persona of the Alienated Darling', *Black American Literature Forum*, 20:4 (Winter, 1986), pp. 347–70.

Sadoff, Diane F., 'Black Matrilineage: The Case of Walker and Hurston', in H. Bloom (ed.), *Alice Walker*, pp. 115–34.

Singh, Amritjit, Joseph T. Skerrett Jr, and Robert E. Hogan (eds), *Memory, Narrative and Identity: New Essays in Ethnic American Literatures* (London: Northeastern University Press, 1996).

Smith, Felipe, 'Alice Walker's Redemptive Art', in Dieke (ed.), *Critical Essays on Alice Walker*, pp. 109–25.

Sjöö, Monica and Barbara Mor, *The Great Cosmic Mother: Rediscovering the Religion of the Earth*, second edition (San Francisco: Harper, 1991).

Smitherman, Geneva, *Talkin' and Testifyin': The Language of Black America* (Boston: Houghton Mifflin, 1977).

Sol, Adam, 'Questions of Mastery in Alice Walker's *The Temple of My Familiar*', *Critique: Studies in Contemporary Fiction*, 43:4 (Summer, 2002) pp. 393–404.

Somerville, Siobhan, *Queering the Color Line: Race and the Invention of Homosexuality in American Culture* (Durham and London: Duke University Press, 2000).

Spillers, Hortense, 'Afterword: Cross-Currents, Discontinuities: Black Women's Fiction', in Pryse and Spillers (eds), *Conjuring*, pp. 249–61.

——, '"All the Things You Could Be by Now, If Sigmund Freud's Wife Was Your Mother": Psychoanalysis and Race', *boundary 2*, 23:2 (1996) pp. 76–141.

Staples, Robert, 'The Myth of Black Macho: A Response to Angry Black Feminists', *The Black Scholar* (March–April, 1979), pp. 24–33.

——, 'The Myth of the Black Matriarchy', in *The Black Scholar*, 12:6 (1981), pp. 26–34.

Stephens, Robert O., *The Family Saga in the South: Generations and Destinies* (London: Louisiana State University Press, 1995).

Stone, Merlin, *When God Was a Woman* (London: Harcourt Brace Jovanovich, 1976).

Storr, Anthony, *Jung*, Fontana Modern Masters (London: Fontana Press, 1986).

Tate, Claudia (ed.), *Black Women Writers at Work* [1983] (Harpenden: Old Castle Books, 1989).

Thiam, Awa, *Black Sisters, Speak Out: Feminism and Oppression in Black Africa* [1978, *La Parole aux Négresses*] (London: Pluto Press, 1986).

Thielmann, Pia 'Alice Walker and the "Man Question"', in Dieke (ed.), *Critical Essays on Alice Walker*, pp. 67–82.

Thiong'O, Ngũgĩ wa, *Decolonising the Mind: The Politics of Language in African Literature* (London: James Currey, 1986).

Walker, Rebecca, *Black White and Jewish: Autobiography of a Shifting Self* (New York: Riverhead, 2001).

Wade-Gayles, Gloria, *No Crystal Stair: Visions of Race and Sex in Black Women's Fiction* (New York: Pilgrim Press, 1984).

Walker, Melissa, *Down From the Mountaintop: Black Women's Novels in the Wake of the Civil Rights Movement, 1966–1989* (New Haven: Yale University Press, 1991).

Wall, Cheryl A., *Worrying the Line: Black Women Writers, Lineage, and Literary Tradition* (Chapel Hill and London: University of North Carolina Press, 2005).

Wall, Wendy, 'Lettered Bodies and Corporeal Texts', in Gates and Appiah (eds), *Alice Walker*, pp. 261–74.

Walley, Christine J., 'Searching for "Voices": Feminism, Anthropology, and the Global Debate over Female Genital Operations', *Cultural Anthropology*, 12:3 (August, 1997), pp. 405–38.

Walton, Priscilla L., '"What She Got To Sing About?": Comedy and *The Color Purple*', in Dieke (ed.), *Critical Essays on Alice Walker*, pp. 185–96.

Warhol, Robyn, 'How Narration Produces Gender: Femininity as Affect and Effect in Alice Walker's *The Color Purple*', *Narrative*, 9:2 (May, 2001), pp. 182–7.

Watkins, Mel, 'Sexism, Racism and Black Women Writers', *New York Times Book Review*, 15 June 1986, pp. 1; 35–7.

White, Evelyn C., *Alice Walker: A Life* (New York and London: W. W. Norton, 2004).

Whitsitt, Sam, 'In Spite of It All: A Reading of Alice Walker's "Everyday Use"', *African American Review*, 34:3 (2000), pp. 443–59.

Wilentz, Gay, 'Healing the Wounds of Time', *Women's Review of Books*, 10:5 (1993), pp. 16–17.

——, '"What Is Africa to Me?": Reading the African Cultural Base of (African) American Literary History', *American Literary History*, 15:3 (2003), pp. 639–53.

Williams, Delores S., 'Black Women's Literature and the Task of Feminist Theology', in Clarissa W. Atkinson, Constance H. Buchanan, and Margaret. R. Miles (eds), *Immaculate & Powerful: The Female in Sacred Image and Social Reality* (Boston: Beacon Press, 1985), pp. 88–110.

Willis, Susan, *Specifying: Black Women Writing the American Experience* (Madison: University of Illinois Press, 1987).

——, 'Memory and Mass Culture', in Fabre and O'Meally (eds), *History & Memory in African-American Culture*, pp. 178–87.

Winchell, Donna Haisty, *Alice Walker* (New York: Twayne, 1992).

Wisker, Gina (ed.), *Black Women's Writing* (London: Macmillan, 1993).

World Health Organization, 'Factsheet 241: Female Genital Mutilation' (May 2008) http://www.who.int/mediacentre/factsheets/fs241/en/index.html.

Wyatt, David, 'Alice Walker', in *Out of the Sixties: Storytelling and the Vietnam Generation* (Cambridge: Cambridge University Press, 1993), pp. 122–37.

Zinn, Howard, *A People's History of the United States* [1980] (New York: Harper Collins, 1990).

WEB RESOURCES

Alice Walker's blog: http://www.alicewalkerblog.com.
Alice Walker's website: http://www.alicewalker.info.

Index